X WINDOW

APPLICATIONS PROGRAMMING

ERIC F. JOHNSON
KEVIN REICHARD

ADVANCED
COMPUTER
BOOKS

MANAGEMENT INFORMATION SOURCE, INC.

COPYRIGHT

P.O. Box 5277
Portland, Oregon 97208-5277
(503) 282-5215

Fourth Printing

ISBN 1-55828-016-2

Library of Congress Catalog Card Number: 89-31752

ACKNOWLEDGMENTS

The programs in this book were written under Apple's A/UX 1.0 on a Mac IIx and under SunOS 4.0 and 3.5 on Sun 386i and 3/260 workstations, using X version 11 releases 2 and 3, in both monochrome and color.

We'd like to thank Bob Williams, our supportive publisher at MIS:Press, who gave us the opportunity to break into the book-publishing field. We'd also like to thank Kristi Canelo, Doedy Hunter, Keri Walker, and Ric Jones of Apple Computer, who came through with our every request and consistently went above and beyond the realm of duty. Kudos also go to Jim Boulware and Peter Hill—Jim for providing toys and Peter for helping us make better use of them—as well as Brian Anderson and Julie Swanson of Adams Publishing of Minneapolis/St. Paul.

Robert Scheifler and Jim Gettys, creators of X and responsible for the famous paper on the X Window System, certainly have made our lives more interesting and fun. The unnamed creator of the X Gumby cursor will live long in our hearts and proves that at least someone at the X Consortium has fun, too. And we wouldn't have been able to present all the pictures in this book if not for Jef Poskanzer's portable bitmap library.

Finally, we'd like to thank Penny Johnson Reichard for her patience and understanding after too many evenings and weekends spent in front of a computer.

TABLE OF CONTENTS

DISK ORDER FORM
ON LAST PAGE
OF BOOK

This is a book about learning the X Window System. It is the type of book we wanted, but couldn't find, when we needed to learn how to write applications for the X Window System: a book that shows how to easily and painlessly start programming in X. This book grew out of our early experiences with porting software to run under the X Window System. When that project began, every available book or article on X was eagerly grabbed and read. Most of the material provided a reference to the X library, or Xlib, calls—and not much else. While those books are extremely valuable for advanced X programming, they didn't provide a suitable introduction to X, nor did they provide real-life examples of X programming.

This introduction will outline some basic X concepts and structures, as well as the X Window System's history. Don't worry if you aren't ready to jump into X programming right after reading this introduction; it's merely meant to get you acquainted with the X terminology and environment. Everything mentioned in this introduction will be explained in more detail in later chapters.

This book is not a reference manual covering every aspect of X. Instead, it aims at providing you with a running start at creating application programs under X. What we found missing in other books was how to put the various X function calls together: how, for example, to draw rubber-band lines (covered in Chapter 7) or how, even, to draw a line in red on the display (covered in Chapter 3). In short, it was hard for us to divine the simple things on which you can build more detailed applications.

The X Window System is a large and complex system. Much of that complexity comes from the fact that X attempts to deal with virtually every type of computer graphics display available. X also attempts to provide a complete graphics system—complete enough to create windowing interfaces a la Macintosh and complete enough to handle graphics-intensive page-design or computer-aided design (CAD) packages.

This book concentrates on showing you how to get things done and get them done right now. The X Window System is far too large and complex to deal with completely in one book. This is not a pure reference work, but a tutorial describing the key features you will need to get started writing X Window System applications. The key features introduced in a given chapter are listed in the summary at the end of that chapter so can you go back and review them if needed.

The X Window System shows great promise toward solving a seemingly intractable problem: how to provide a common interface across many different computers that are running a number of operating systems with a number of different displays. X provides a graphical interface that runs on everything from IBM PCs to large mainframes and supercomputers. Cray supercomputers can display their output on DEC or Apollo workstation displays. Almost every major computer vendor, from Apple Computer to Xerox, from Hewlett-Packard to Sun Microsystems, is committed to the X Window System.

This book is intended for X beginners, in business and academia, who have a working knowledge of the C programming language and are attempting to do any of the following:

- determine the feasibility of committing to the X Window System
- port company software to run under X
- provide a multivendor common look and feel for applications

- learn about the latest networked graphical windowing system
- begin applications development under X

THE HISTORY OF X

To gain a conceptual understanding of the X Window System, you might find it helpful to look at X's history and note the initial goals of the X Window System designers.

In 1984, Massachusetts Institute of Technology (MIT) officials were faced with a problem common to the business and academic computing worlds: They were the owners of a motley set of incompatible workstations acquired through donation and purchase. The goal was to build a network of graphical workstations that could be used as teaching aids. Faced with a crazy quilt of operating systems and hardware vendors, MIT officials decided to form Project Athena, an MIT development team working in association with DEC and IBM.

Project Athena's solution was to design a network that would run local applications while being able to call on remote sources. This network was roughly based on a Stanford University software environment called W. By linking together IBMs, DECs, and other disparate workstations through a graphical networking environment, the designers created the first operating environment that was truly hardware and vendor independent, the X Window System.

As Jim Gettys, Bob Schieffler, and Ron Newman wrote in their book *X Window System: C Library and Protocol Reference* (DEC Press, 1988), the development team had the following goals when designing X:

- Do not add new functionality unless an implementation cannot complete a real application without it.
- It is as important to decide what a system is not as to decide what it is. Do not serve all the world's needs, but make the system extensible so that additional needs can be met in an upwardly compatible fashion.
- The only thing worse than generalizing from one example is generalizing from no examples at all.

- If a problem is not completely understood, it is probably best to provide no solution at all.
- If you get 90 percent of the desired effect for 10 percent of the work required to get 100 percent, use the simpler solution.
- Isolate complexity as much as possible.
- Provide mechanism rather than policy. In particular, place user interface policy in the client's hands.

Note that of these guidelines the final one is the most applicable to the needs addressed in this book; it will be discussed further when X Window System philosophies are addressed.

The X Window System was a success. By 1986, news of X had spread to the point where the outside world was asking for access. In response, X10.4 was released on tape for a nominal fee (in much the same fashion as early implementations of UNIX). Outside development on X10 slowed down, however, when it became apparent that version 11 would be incompatible with version 10.

In March 1988, MIT officially released version 11, release 2 even though an incomplete release numbered 1 appeared earlier in September 1987. Current X Window System development is now overseen by the X Consortium, formed in January 1988 (see Appendix E for more information).

The X Window System has been prominent in computer news, as the X Consortium members have been quick to introduce several products based on X. In addition, X got a boost in January 1989 when the Open Software Foundation endorsed proposals from Digital Equipment, Hewlett-Packard, and Microsoft to incorporate X as a major component in its graphical user interface—a graphical interface designed to make UNIX easier to use.

WHY X NOW?

To a large extent, X Window is the right windowing system at the right time. In the past, hardware on the minicomputer level and down didn't have the horsepower to support such a powerful graphics networking system at an affordable price. With the rise of powerful workstations and microcomputers, the X Window System thus becomes a most viable product.

In addition, there are several other reasons why X is a desirable development tool.

A Flexible Windowing System

The X Window System supplies a smooth and flexible user interface at a time when users are growing increasingly accustomed to window-style interfaces. Witness the enormous success of the Apple Macintosh and the increasing acceptance for Microsoft Windows on the microcomputer level, coupled with the popularity enjoyed by Sun Microsystems' NeWS and Digital Equipment Corporation's DECWindows. Over the years, research has shown that windowing interfaces are easier to learn and use than character-based interfaces. While X is merely part of the trend toward windowing systems, it has more flexibility and greater potential than any of the aforementioned systems.

To a large extent, those systems are tied to a single hardware environment and a single vendor. As we kick off an era where linking computers of all sorts is a paramount concern for software designers and developers anywhere, such limitations hinder efforts at cross-vendor development. That's not true with the X Window System. X is operating-system independent and network transparent. By separating the window manager and the window server, it's possible to link together disparate makes of hardware without costly emulation cards and exotic networking schemes. Because the user interface is only making X calls, there is no reliance on any operating system.

That's because of the designers' original credo of providing mechanism, not policy. The software designer—and, to an extent, the user—has the final say on how exactly how the interface will look. Through programming, the application itself defines the window interface and the "look and feel" of the application. Lawsuits aside, you could set up any kind of interface you want. Looking for icons and windows a la Macintosh? No problem. Looking for something that looks more like NeWS? Again, no problem. As far as X is concerned, the look and feel of the interface is relatively unimportant. X provides the mechanism upon which you can build many different user-interface styles.

This especially becomes important when discussing the X Window System and the UNIX operating system. In the past, UNIX has been accused—and rightfully so—of having a terribly unfriendly and cryptic user interface. With the X Window System as an interface, UNIX applications can be made easier to use. In fact, the same argument can be applied to other operating systems that have been accused of being unfriendly, such as MS-DOS and VMS.

X, by being operating-system independent, encourages the portability of software. The standard X C library routines, called Xlib, are the same on every machine running X, which means your interface code ports directly from one machine to another because all the X calls are the same. Because the user interface typically takes up 30 to 60 percent of the code, your applications are a lot more portable.

Shared Resources

The X Window System allows devices such as mice, keyboards, and graphics displays to be shared by several programs at the same time. Actually, as far as X is concerned, your entire workstation is a display—a display consists of a keyboard, a pointing device (usually a mouse), and one or more monitor screens. Multiple screens can work together, linked by the keyboard and the pointing device.

Uniformity across Product Lines

As mentioned, the X Window System has been adapted to several different operating systems, including UNIX, MS-DOS, A/UX, and VMS. The X Window System is a standard application execution environment. Applications written for one machine don't need to be rewritten for other machines.

The X Window System has been endorsed as a graphic windowing environment by several large computer corporations that formed the X Consortium. The consortium's membership includes as full members Apollo Computer, Apple Computer, AT&T, Bull, Digital Equipment Corp., Fujitsu, Hewlett-Packard, IBM, NCR, Sony, Sun Microsystems, Wang, and Xerox; and as associate members Adobe Systems, Carnegie-Mellon University, and the Software Productivity Consortium. (A full list of consortium members can be found in Appendix E.) In essence, X has been adopted by the major hardware manufacturers as a windowing system of choice.

WHAT IS X?

Now that you know why the X Window System is such a fabulous operating environment, we'll give you the conceptual nuts and bolts of the X Window System.

A Client/Server Axis

The X Window System architecture is based on a simple client/server relationship in which the **display server** is the program that controls and draws all output to the display monitors, tracks client input, and updates your windows accordingly, while **clients** are application programs that perform specific tasks. Because X is a networked environment, the client and server don't necessarily compute on the same system (although they certainly can and do in a number of situations). Instead, the X Window System allows **distributed processing**. For example, an Apollo workstation can run an X server and call upon the processing power of a Cray supercomputer within the network, displaying the results of the Cray's computations on the Apollo's monitor.

This is the first time—but not the last—where you will find X terminology differing slightly from accepted computer science terminology. In the microcomputer and minicomputer network worlds, a server is the hardware device running at the center of the network, distributing data and processing power to networked workstations and terminals. That's not 100-percent true in the X world, however. For our purposes, a server is a local software program that controls a display. Because other systems on the network have access to your display, the X server cannot be thought of the same way file servers are thought of in a local-area network (LAN).

In X, a display is a keyboard, pointing device (usually a mouse), and one or more screens, usually associated with a computer workstation. As you can see in Figure I.1, the display server keeps track of multiple input, allowing users to run several different clients (such as a database manager, word processor, and a graphics application). A display can be running multiple screens linked together by the keyboard and mouse. But as long as a single user is limited to a single workstation, the multiple screens constitute a single display.

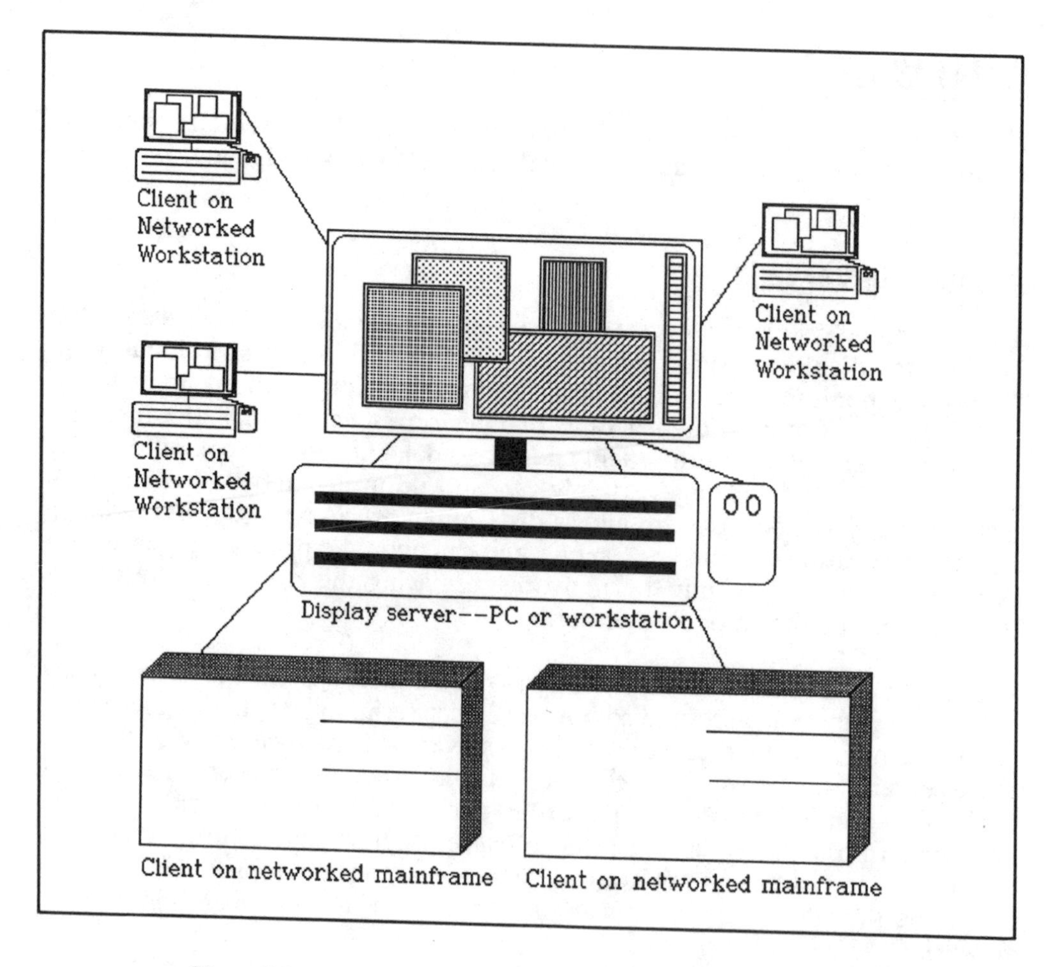

Figure I.1 *The display server in a networked environment.*

The server acts as the traffic cop between programs (called either clients or applications) running on local or remote systems and the power of the local system. The server does the following:

- allows access to a display by other clients
- sends network messages
- intercepts other network messages from other clients
- performs two-dimensional drawing, freeing up the client from processing-intensive graphics
- keeps track of resources (such as windows, cursors, fonts, and graphics contexts) that are shared between clients
- allows distributed processing, as mentioned above
- allows multitasking, if X is used in conjunction with a multitasking operating system. (When used with UNIX, for example, X allows you to call on UNIX's multitasking capabilities.)

And, perhaps most importantly, the server tracks input from the display and informs the clients. In X, such inputs are called **events**. When you press down a key, that's an event; when you let it back up, that's another event. Similarly, when you manipulate your cursor with a mouse, that's still another event. These events are delivered to the applications through an event queue. Events are discussed in greater detail in Chapters 5 and 6.

As mentioned previously, clients are applications programs that can be run simultaneously. The terms "application" and "client" are used interchangeably throughout the book. A client can use several servers simultaneously, depending on the network configuration. There are several kinds of clients; two will be covered in this introduction, and several more will be covered in Appendix D.

Unlike many systems, such as the Macintosh OS, the window manager is the client that oversees the sizing and placing of windows on your display. All X Window System installations should come equipped with **uwm**, which stands for Universal or Ultrix Window Manager; uwm allows you to resize windows, arrange your window order, create more windows, and perform several other functions. In Chapter 8, window managers are explained in more depth.

Because the X Window System produces bit-mapped graphics, it is possible to install terminal emulators on a multi-user system without the added expense of a workstation or personal computer. `xterm`, for example, emulates a DEC VT102 or Tektronix 4014 terminal and allows you to run multiple applications, using "dumb" terminals. This is mainly to provide compatibility with the huge array of software written for ASCII terminals.

THE SUM OF ITS PARTS

In many ways X is the sum of its parts. By first seeing X split up into its components, you can later see how the components work together.

The generic X Window System as shipped by MIT consists of the Xlib graphics subroutine library, the X network protocol, an X toolkit, and several window managers (described earlier). The application programmer links the client program through Xlib, a library of graphics and window functions.

Xlib

Xlib contains about 300 routines that map to X Protocol requests or provide utility functions. What Xlib actually does is covert the C language function calls to the X protocol request that implements the given function, such as `XDrawLine` to draw a line. These functions include creating, destroying, moving, and sizing windows; drawing lines and polygons (which will be explained in Chapter 2); setting background patterns; and tracking the mouse. Xlib also allows you to access windows in a variety of ways, including overlapping and simultaneous output to multiple windows. It supports multiple fonts, common raster operations, line drawing, and both color and monochrome applications.

X Toolkits

X toolkits are program subroutine libraries that can make programming easier. These toolkits, from such vendors as Hewlett-Packard, AT&T/Sun, IBM/Project Athena, DEC, and Sony, vary slightly and are under constant revision, but there are a number of similarities between the different implementations. Most toolboxes, for example, include scroll bars, buttons, pop-up menus, window borders, and dialog boxes. Toolkits are covered in greater detail in Chapter 15.

The X Network Protocol

The X network protocol defines data structures used to transmit requests between clients and servers. Technically speaking, the X network protocol is an asynchronous stream-based interprocess communication instead of being based on procedure calls or a kernal-call interface. The applications don't do the work here; the protocol is a function of Xlib. This structure speeds up information exchange.

If you are interested (and, quite frankly, there's no reason to be interested under most circumstances), the protocol specification is supplied by the MIT X Consortium on tape (see Appendix E) and defined in "X Window System Protocol, Version 11," by Robert Scheifler, which is contained as part of the distribution tape. You may already have the document on-line if you are working on a UNIX system; it can be found on the directory tree under `doc/Protocol/spec`.

Currently, the X network protocol is implemented only on DECnet and TCP/IP, although future implementations with other networking schemes are planned.

WHAT YOU NEED TO RUN X

Virtually any computer in any class—micro, mini, mainframe—can run X. When you start researching, you'll find that there are very few machines that don't already have X products on the market.

This is one big advantage to a vendor-independent system. If you are not able to shell out the big bucks for a Sun workstation or DEC VAX, there are versions of X Window that run over MS-DOS. Typically, at the microcomputer level, you need at least an AT-level machine with graphics boards and enhancements to run X well. In addition, White Pine Systems has released an X implementation for the Macintosh operating system. To keep on top of X at the microcomputer level, you need to put some work into the project—new announcements are arriving almost daily, and the field is constantly changing.

Also hitting the market are dedicated X Window terminals. Several vendors, such as Acer, Visual Technologies, Tektronix, NCD, and Graphon, have released X terminals. These terminals are usually built around a Motorola 680X0 and come equipped with between one and two megabytes of memory. Because X is graphics-intensive, you'll need all the power you can get, especially when you stray below the workstation levels. These terminals are not cheap either, usually priced between $2,000 and $4,000.

THIS BOOK'S APPROACH TO X

This book is organized into 15 chapters that introduce you to key concepts of X Window System programming. Because the best way to learn how to program something is to do it, each chapter will include source code examples. In Section I, each chapter will describe a stand-alone program that implements the concepts described in the chapter. In Section II, each chapter will build on one program, a full-fledged X Window System application. (No, you won't have to program using the ubiquitous "Hello World" example—if you're really interested in a "Hello World" X programming example we'll tell you where to find it in Appendix F, which lists some additional X Window System resources.) Section III introduces the X toolkit sets. These toolkits are under constant revision, so Section III will introduce basic toolkit concepts and identify the major suppliers—after that, you're on your own. The other five appendices deal with color, event types, the graphics context, sample X clients, and ordering the X Window System.

Be warned, however, the assumption is that you have a working knowledge of the C programming language. Although there are X Window System implementations in other programming languages, all examples given herein are in C.

Following is a breakdown of the chapters:

- Section I—Learning X Programming
  - Chapter 1—Building A First X Program
  - Chapter 2—Drawing with X
  - Chapter 3—Using Color
  - Chapter 4—Using Text
  - Chapter 5—Events
  - Chapter 6—Keyboard Events
  - Chapter 7—Rubber-Band Lines
  - Chapter 8—X Standards and Interacting with Window Managers

- Section II—Building an X Window System Application
  - Chapter 9—Introducing the Draw Application
  - Chapter 10—Multiple-Window Applications
  - Chapter 11—Event Processing in the Draw Application
  - Chapter 12—Pop-Up Windows and Dialog Boxes
  - Chapter 13—The Draw Application Source Code
  - Chapter 14—Enhancing the Draw Application

- Section III—X Toolkits
  - Chapter 15—Introduction to X Toolkits

- Appendices
  - A—The X Color Data Base
  - B—X Event Types and Structures
  - C—The Graphics Context
  - D—Some Sample X Client Programs
  - E—How to Order X Window
  - F—For More Information on X Window

TYPOGRAPHICAL CONVENTIONS

In this book, the following typographical conventions have been used:

C program code references (such as function names and file names) within a text paragraph will appear in a Courier 12-point typeface, as in the following example:

> The function `XDisplayName` will translate the NULL into the actual name used by X.

Actual program examples and listings will appear in the following line printer typeface:

```
/*
**      eventx.c
**
**      Contains the event loop (where the major action of most
**      X-based programs occurs).
**
*/
```

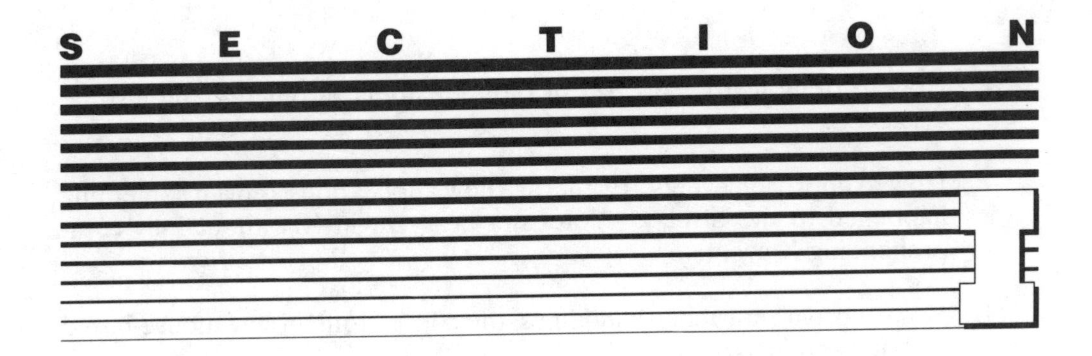

LEARNING X PROGRAMMING

This section begins with an explanation of the X Window System, followed by the very basics of what you'll need to know to create your own X Window applications. You'll learn the following:

- How to establish a connection to the server, followed by a sample X program that introduces you to X theories and procedures.
- How to draw using X. After all, X is a graphical interface, and most important graphical applications involve some kind of drawing.
- How to incorporate color into your X applications. This includes a description of the X color data base, which simplifies matters for the programmer.

- How to draw text. How to call different fonts through X will also be discussed.
- How to approach events. Events are how applications know if something happened to the display. You can't program in X without fully comprehending X events.
- How to program rubber-band lines, the cornerstone of any mouse-based drawing application.
- How to interact with X window managers. The extended topics you need to make sure this interraction occurs are covered.

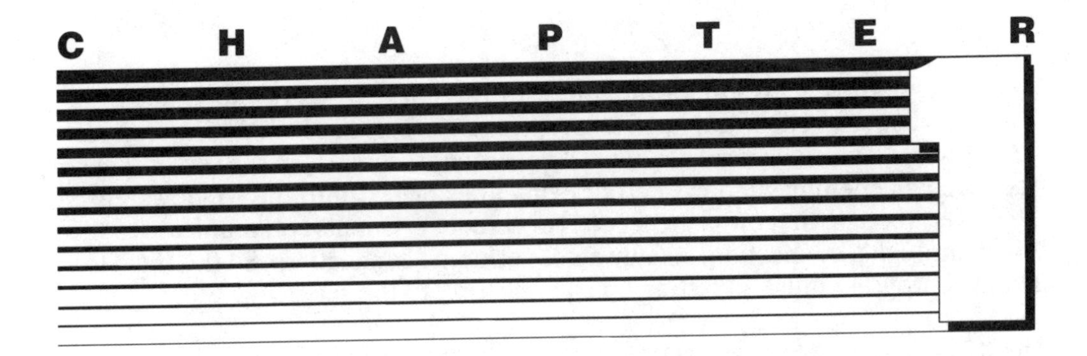

BUILDING A FIRST X PROGRAM

This chapter discusses how to construct your first X program, which opens a connection to the X server and then reports some information about the server. The code for this first program is built in three C program files: `initx.c`, `quitx.c`, and `test1.c`. Two more example programs are then built from the first program. The second example program opens a minimalist window, and the third example program fleshes out the `openWindow` function and adds an icon bitmap.

Throughout this book, a similar structure is followed. The various parts of any program will be separated into modules, with the full intent of reusing the modules later (or enhancing and then reusing them). In each chapter, only those source files that have changed since previous chapters will be presented. Some chapters may add more code to these files as more concepts are introduced, but the idea is to reuse as much code as possible (and save typing chores for the reader).

X is a network-oriented window system with two parts: a **server** that controls a display screen and **client** application programs—programs such as text editors, spreadsheets, and clock displays. The clients request services of the server—services such as opening windows and drawing lines or text into the windows. It is the server, though, that owns the screen (or screens). Clients communicate to the server through a connection, usually a network-type connection. So the first step in any X program must be setting up a connection to the server.

The `XOpenDisplay` call sets up a network connection to the server. Depending on which machine you use to run the X server, this connection could be a TCP/IP socket, a DECnet connection, or perhaps a shared memory link on a local machine. Not to worry, though—`XOpenDisplay` will set up the proper connection. `XOpenDisplay` takes one parameter, the name of the display (server) you want to talk to (this name is a character string). A typical default display is the local machine and screen (e.g., if you are using a Sun 386i workstation with one monitor, the typical default display will be the console screen with the Sun's keyboard and mouse). Following is the sample code for opening a connection with the default display server.

```
#include    <stdio.h>
#include    <X11/Xlib.h>
.
.
.
Display    *theDisplay;    /* -- A pointer to a display structure */

theDisplay = XOpenDisplay( NULL );
```

Every C source file that calls the X library (or Xlib) routines should include the header file `Xlib.h`. By convention, this file will be located in a subdirectory `X11` (usually in `/usr/include/X11` or `/usr/local/include/X11` on machines running the UNIX operating system). Some of the other header files in the X11 directory will be introduced later, as needed.

Almost all Xlib routines start with a capital X. The `XOpenDisplay` function takes a display name as a parameter and returns a pointer to a `Display` structure. This `Display` pointer will be used in almost every X function call thereafter (it specifies which display the X output should go to).

The NULL parameter to XOpenDisplay specifies the default display (actually, it tells XOpenDisplay to use the DISPLAY environment variable, and the DISPLAY environment variable should be set to the default display name). Because X is a network-oriented windowing system, you could specify that you want your windows to appear on another display on another machine. For example, you may want to run a numerically intensive client program on a Cray-2 and display the output on an Apollo workstation display.

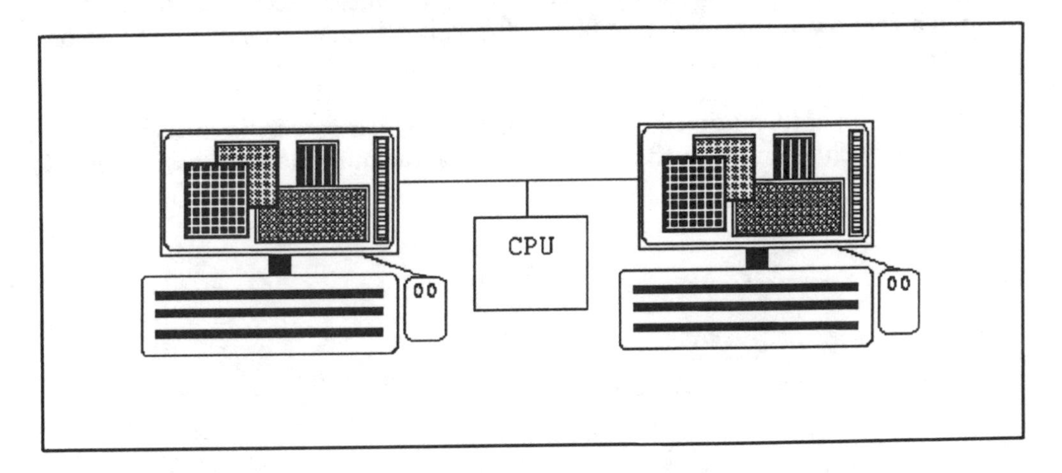

Figure 1.1 *Two computers connected over a network, running X.*

For now, though, the default display will be fine. If XOpenDisplay returns NULL, no connection was made. The program is essentially over for all intents and purposes, as no windows will appear without first establishing a connection.

```
if ( theDisplay == NULL )
        {
        fprintf( stderr,
          "ERROR: Could not open a connection to X on display %s\n",
          XDisplayName( NULL ) );
        exit( 1 );
        }
```

The function XDisplayName will translate the NULL into the actual name used by X (based on the value of the DISPLAY environment variable). For the default display, this is usually "unix:0.0".

EXAMPLE 1: A MINIMALIST X PROGRAM

The previous code listing is about the smallest functioning X program possible. Of course, it doesn't really do anything except establish a connection to X.

Once you have a connection to X, it is a good idea to ask the X server if it supplies color planes (or is monochrome) and how big the display screen is. If the display screen is 640 by 480 pixels (such as on an Apple Macintosh IIx), you do not want to open a window at pixel location 800, 800 because that location wouldn't be on the screen.

The first bit of information needed establishes which screen is in use. Some computers, such as those in the Sun 3 family, allow multiple screens for one X server.

```
int             theScreen;
.
.
.
theScreen = DefaultScreen( theDisplay );
```

Note that before you call the macro `DefaultScreen`, you need to have successfully established a connection to the X server.

The number of bit planes (for color or gray-scale monitors) is returned by the macro `DefaultDepth`.

```
int             theDepth;
.
.
.
theDepth = DefaultDepth( theDisplay, theScreen );
```

If `theDepth` is 1, then you have a monochrome system.

The size of the screen is returned from two macros: `DisplayWidth` and `DisplayHeight`.

```
int             theWidth, theHeight;
.
.
.
theWidth    = DisplayWidth( theDisplay, theScreen );
theHeight   = DisplayHeight( theDisplay, theScreen );
```

These two macros return the size of the display in pixels (or picture elements), which is the number of dots on the screen in the vertical (`DisplayHeight`) and horizontal (`DisplayWidth`) directions.

Other useful information includes the vendor who wrote the X server and the server-code version. As of this writing, the most recent version of X is X version 11, release 3. Many commercial servers are still using release 2. (All of the code in this book was tested on both releases 2 and 3.)

```
printf( "%s version %d of the X Window System X%d R%d\n",
        ServerVendor( theDisplay ),
        VendorRelease( theDisplay ),
        ProtocolVersion( theDisplay ),
        ProtocolRevision( theDisplay ) );
```

The `ServerVendor` macro returns a string that usually contains a vendor name, such as "MIT X Consortium" or "Apple Computer, Inc." The `VendorRelease` macro is a number for the vendor's version of the server. This number is mainly useful when providing bug reports to the vendor.

`ProtocolVersion` should return the version (or major) number—in this case, 11. `ProtocolRevision` is less clear; it seems that it should return the release number, but instead it usually returns a 0. For the generic MIT X Consortium release, `ProtocolVersion` returns 11, `ProtocolRevision` returns 0, and `VendorRelease` returns 3, for X11 R3. Thus, if you are using an X server from another vendor (such as Hewlett-Packard), you might have difficulty figuring out if you are running X11 R3 or R2 (or perhaps R4).

Finally, when you are done with the connection to the X server (usually at the end of your program), it is a nice practice to close the connection gracefully, as in the following example:

```
XCloseDisplay( theDisplay );
```

Under the UNIX operating system, when your program terminates, UNIX usually breaks all connections, making the call to `XCloseDisplay` technically unnecessary. But X runs on more than one operating system, and it is a good idea to be nice to the X server by calling `XCloseDisplay` before your program terminates.

Example 1 Source Code

As outlined in the previous section, the first X program presented here will open a connection to the X server and then report some information about the server. The code is built up in three C program files: `initx.c`, `quitx.c`, and `test1.c`.

The file `initx.c` sets up the connection to the X server. The file `quitx.c` closes the connection. The test file `test1.c` provides the main function and calls the various routines.

The file `initx.c` contains the meat of the first program. It contains two functions, `initX` and `getXInfo`.

The `initX` function sets up the connection to the X server. `getXInfo` gets some information about the server and prints that information. It is assumed here that the program will be called from an `xterm` window so that `printf` will work properly. `xterm` is another client application program running under X. It provides a shell terminal into the UNIX operating system (or whatever operating system your machine runs) to run standard terminal-oriented programs such as the vi editor or the C compiler.

The contents of file `initx.c` are as follows:

```
/*
**      initx.c
**
**      Initialization code to talk to the X server
**
*/

#include  <X11/Xlib.h>
#include  <X11/Xutil.h>
#include  <stdio.h>
```

continued...

...from previous page

```
/*
**      Program-wide Globals.
**
*/

Display         *theDisplay;    /* -- Which display                  */
int             theScreen;      /* -- Which screen on the display    */
int             theDepth;       /* -- Number of color planes         */

/*
**      initX()
**      Sets up the connection to the X server and stores information
**      about the environment.
**
*/

initX()

{       /* -- function initX  */

        /*
        **      1) Establish a connection to the X Server.  The connection
        **      is asked for on the local server for the local display.
        **
        */

        theDisplay = XOpenDisplay( NULL );

        /* -- Check if the connection was made */
        if ( theDisplay == NULL )
                {
                fprintf( stderr,
                   "ERROR: Cannot establish a connection to the X Server %s\n",
                   XDisplayName( NULL ) );
                exit( 1 );
                }

        /*
        **      2) Check for the default screen and color plane depth.
        **      If theDepth == 1, then we have a monochrome system.
        **
        */


        theScreen = DefaultScreen( theDisplay );
        theDepth  = DefaultDepth( theDisplay, theScreen );
```

continued...

...from previous page

```
}       /* -- function initX  */




/*
**      getXInfo prints information to the starting terminal
**      (usually an xterm) about the current X Window display
**      and screen.
*/

getXInfo()

{       /* -- function getXInfo */

        /*
        **      You will find many funny values when you check the X
        **      information below.  It should be something to the tune of:
        **      MIT X Consortium (vendor)
        **      3 (vendor release)
        **      X11 R3 (or R2, the Version and Revision numbers).
        **      But, on most implementations, this information
        **      does not seem to jibe.
        **      On the generic MIT X Consortium release for
        **      X11R3, you might see X11R0, with a vendor release # of 3
        **
        */

        printf( "%s version %d of the X Window System, X%d R%d\n",
                ServerVendor( theDisplay ),
                VendorRelease( theDisplay ),
                ProtocolVersion( theDisplay ),
                ProtocolRevision( theDisplay ) );

        /*
        **      Now, print some more detailed information about the
        **      display.
        **
        */
        if ( theDepth == 1 )
                {
                printf( "Color plane depth.............%d (monochrome)\n",
                        theDepth );
                }
        else
                {
                printf( "Color plane depth.............%d\n",
                        theDepth );
                }
```

continued...

...from previous page

```
        printf( "Display Width.................%d\n",
                DisplayWidth( theDisplay, theScreen ) );
        printf( "Display Height................%d\n",
                DisplayHeight( theDisplay, theScreen ) );
        printf( "The display %s\n", XDisplayName( theDisplay ) );

}       /* -- function getXInfo */


/*
**      end of file initx.c
**
*/
```

The file `quitx.c` is very simple, and in this program it merely closes the connection to X. In later chapters, it will be expanded to free up other X resources before the program quits.

The contents of file `quitx.c` are as follows:

```
/*
**      quitx.c
**
**      routines to close down X
**
*/

#include  <X11/Xlib.h>
#include  <X11/Xutil.h>

extern  Display         *theDisplay;


/*
**      quitX()
**
**      closes the connection to the X server
**
*/

quitX()
```

continued...

...from previous page

```
{       /* -- function quitX  */

        XCloseDisplay( theDisplay );

}       /* -- function quitX  */

/*
**      end of file quitx.c
**
*/
```

The file `test1.c` handles the main function. The contents of file `test1.c` are as follows:

```
/*
**      A minimalist X program.
**
**      All this program does is establish a connection to the
**      X server.  If this connection cannot be made, you will not
**      make a lot of progress.  Some of the things this program
**      tests are hidden, i.e., it tests whether you have the X11
**      library installed in a readable directory, as well as
**      the X Window header (include) files.
**
*/

main()

{
        /*
        **      Set up our connection to X
        */

        initX();

        /*
        **      Get some info on the display and print it
        */

        getXInfo();

        quitX();

}


/*
**      end of file.
*/
```

Finally, you need a Makefile to put it all together. Part of the purpose of having such a simple first program is to test out the X setup on your machine. If the compiler cannot find the X include files, for example, this problem must be dealt with before you can go on. The other area of concern is finding the X library (X11) for the link phase. If you do have problems in these areas, check with your system administrator (each machine may have a different setup). In most cases, the include files are in /usr/include/X11, and the library is in /usr/lib or /usr/lib/X11—if you are running X under the UNIX operating system.

The format of this Makefile will be reused in each chapter:

```
##      X Project Makefile for Chapter 1, example 1
##
##
EXEC=   test1
##
##      -g = Debugging info
##      -O = Optimize (cannot have -g then)
CFLAGS= -O
##
##      Libraries
##      X11     X11 graphics library
##
LIBS=   -lX11
##
##
OBJECTS=        initx.o         \
                quitx.o         \
                test1.o
##
##      Command to compile and link objects together
##
$(EXEC):        $(OBJECTS)
                cc -o $(EXEC) $(OBJECTS) $(LIBS)
##
##
##      end of make file
##
```

Try out this first program to be sure everything on your machine is set up correctly to compile and link X programs. Trying out this program will also show you whether the X server is up and running. Unfortunately, this program is not very interesting to run. A more interesting program would at least open up a window (after all, "Window" is the X Window System's middle name).

EXAMPLE 2: OPENING A MINIMALIST WINDOW

The X Window System primarily handles **windows** – rectangles on the screen that can be drawn, can overlap, and can be stacked on top of one another. Your next step, then, is to open up a window on the display. Unfortunately, opening a window under X is rather complicated. The reason for the complexity here is X's stated goal of providing a *mechanism*, not a *policy*, for user-interface design. This usually means that each X library function must include numerous options and parameters. This section will go through the process of opening a window on the display step by step. Another later example will add more features.

To open up a window under X, you must make a number of choices, from the simple – where it should go – to the more complex, such as attributes of the window's border (thick, thin, or nonexistent; red, blue, or black colored; and so on). Under X, each window has an identifier of the `Window` type (which is usually an unsigned, long, 32-bit integer). Once this window identifier is returned from X, it is used to specify which window you want to draw to in later drawing calls.

In this example, you will create a function, `openWindow`, to handle all the details of creating a window and then placing it on the screen. In later examples, you will add to `openWindow` as more options are covered in the text. By placing the details within the `openWindow` function, you are isolating the specifics of window creation from the other code.

Creating a Window

The first step in creating an X window is to set up a few **attributes**. In this first example, you will concentrate on just a few – more will come later. The attributes are placed in an `XSetWindowAttributes` structure. A **mask** is also set up that tells X which parts of the structure are used and which are unused, so you do not need values for all the structure's fields.

```
#include <X11/Xlib.h>
.
.
.
XSetWindowAttributes                theWindowAttributes;
unsigned long                       theWindowMask;
.
.
.
theWindowAttributes.border_pixel      =
                BlackPixel( theDisplay, theScreen );

theWindowAttributes.background_pixel  =
                WhitePixel( theDisplay, theScreen );
theWindowAttributes.override_redirect = True;

/*
**      Set the Mask for which fields we are actually using.
*/

theWindowMask = (CWBackPixel | CWBorderPixel | CWOverrideRedirect );
```

Setting the `border_pixel` field tells X you want a "black" border for the window. All X servers have at least two colors defined by macros: `BlackPixel` and `WhitePixel`. These colors do not actually need to be black and white but should at least be distinguishable from one another. The advantage of using the `BlackPixel` and `WhitePixel` macros is that they should have values on all X displays—monochrome, gray-scale, or color—making the code portable between monochrome and color displays. In the previous code section, the window border is set to `BlackPixel`, and the inside background of the window is set to `WhitePixel`. The `override_redirect` field tells any window manager in use to leave this request alone. Leaving a window alone usually means not putting a title bar around the window and essentially not messing with the window in any way. This overriding is normally considered unfriendly (to say the least) to the window manager. The `override_redirect` field is typically set to `True` for transient pop-up menus and other windows that will only appear on the screen for a short time.

As stated earlier, X defines procedures (the "mechanism") for how to implement many different types of user interfaces, but it does not explicitly define the policy of how those interfaces will look. Much of this policy is implemented in a **window manager**. Users are free to run any window manager they choose (or none at all). X11 itself comes with two window managers, `uwm` and `wm`. The `uwm` window manager is sort of a minimalist window manager that generally stays out of the way of your windows. The `wm` window manager, on the other hand, puts separate title bars on windows (sometimes called **decorations**). Much of the latest work using X has been in the area of standardizing interfaces and window managers. Digital Equipment Corp. has developed the DECwindows window manager. AT&T and Sun Microsystems are working on Open Look, and the Open Software Foundation calls their interface Motif (made up of parts of the DECwindows and the Hewlett-Packard/Microsoft Presentation Manager interface). All X programs should be set up to interact to some degree with any window manager.

The `override_redirect` field, if set to `True`, tells the window manager to please leave the window alone. If it is set to `False`, the window manager can do what it wants to the window. Try the example program with the `override_redirect` field set to both `True` and `False`. When it is set to `False`, the window manager (if one is in use) may prompt the user to locate and size the window, using a mouse or other pointing device.

The mask then tells X which of the fields in the `XSetWindowAttributes` structure are actually used for the current request. For each field, there is a symbol defined that specifies that the field is set. In this case, the symbols are `CWBackPixel`, `CWBorderPixel`, and `CWOverrideRedirect`. By `or`ing these values together, you set the correct bit pattern in `theWindowMask`.

The `XSetWindowAttributes` structure is then passed to X as part of the `XCreateWindow` call.

```
.
.
.
int             border_width = 3;
Window          theNewWindow;

theNewWindow = XCreateWindow( theDisplay,
                RootWindow( theDisplay, theScreen ),      /* -- parent */
                x, y,
                width, height,
                border_width,
                theDepth,
                InputOutput,
                CopyFromParent,
                theWindowMask,
                &theWindowAttributes );
```

`XCreateWindow` will return the window identifier (of `Window` type) or 0 if the call was not successful (which may occur if the X server is out of memory). The first parameter to `XCreateWindow` is the display to place the window on (remember, X can run multiple displays on multiple machines all at once). The next parameter is the parent window for the new window.

If you are creating a subwindow for an application, then the parent is obvious. The first window your program creates, however, appears to have no parent (it is a top-level window). X solves this problem by making a special window called the `RootWindow`. The `RootWindow` is essentially the background of the display screen. It is as large as the screen and is the parent (or farthest ancestor) of all windows on a given screen. The macro `RootWindow` returns the `Window` ID for this window.

Next, `XCreateWindow` asks for the window's location. All locations in X are given in pixels. For any rectangular shape (such as a window or box), this pixel location is the upper left corner. X also gives sizes in pixels, and most routines call for a width and height (in pixels) to specify a size. The screen may not be big enough for your request, so X may change the location. In addition, the window manager has the option of arbitrarily changing where your window will go. So it is best to view all parameters sent to an X server as requests, requests which may or may not be honored.

The border width specifies how wide a window's border should be. Some windows may want to have a width of 0 for no border (although a window manager can force a border or something that looks like a border).

The depth parameter specifies the number of color planes. It is a good idea to use the system default depth (accessed in the previous code).

`InputOutput` specifies the window class. Virtually all windows are `InputOutput` class (or type). Transparent windows (often used for drawing rubber-band lines) are called `InputOnly` windows.

`CopyFromParent` specifies that the window's visual should be copied from the parent window (in this case, the `RootWindow`). Altering the visual is a rather advanced topic and is beyond the scope of this book. In most cases, a `Copy-FromParent` will suffice.

The next value is a mask value that specifies which values from `theWindowAttributes` are actually being used (the rest will be assumed to take on default values). The Xlib frequently uses the concept of masks to specify which values in a complex structure are actually filled in. Unfortunately, sometimes the mask is part of the structure, and sometimes, as in the `XSetWindowAttributes` structure, the mask is not part of the structure. The final parameter is then a pointer to the `XSetWindowAttributes` structure set up in the previous code.

In more generic terms, the Xlib call `XCreateWindow` has the following parameters:

```
XCreateWindow(  theDisplay,
                theParentWindow,
                x, y,
                width, height,
                theBorderWidth,
                theDepth,
                theClass,
                theVisual,
                theAttributeMask,
                theAttributes );


Display                 *theDisplay;
Window                  theParentWindow;
int                     x, y,;
unsigned int            width, height;
unsigned int            theBorderWidth;
int                     theDepth;
unsigned int            theClass;
Visual                  *theVisual;
unsigned long           theAttributeMask;
XSetWindowAttributes    *theAttributes;
```

theClass can be InputOutput, InputOnly, or CopyFromParent.

The simple call to open up a window is rather long, but X is a complex system. There is another call to open a window—XCreateSimpleWindow—but for most application programs, it will be easier to use XCreateWindow because you will need to make more calls to fill in other values that are not passed to XCreateSimpleWindow. XCreateSimpleWindow resembles the following:

```
XCreateSimpleWindow( theDisplay,
                theParentWindow,
                x, y,
                width, height,
                theBorderWidth,
                theBorder,
                theBackground );
```

```
Display                 *theDisplay;
Window                  theParentWindow;
int                     x, y,;
unsigned int            width, height;
unsigned int            theBorderWidth;
unsigned long           theBorder;
unsigned long           theBackground;
```

As in this example, theBorder is typically set to the value of BlackPixel, and theBackground is typically set to the value of WhitePixel. When you use XCreateSimpleWindow, the new window will inherit the depth, visual, and class from its parent. The remaining parameters will take default values.

Sending "Hints" to the Window Manager

After creating a window, you should send **hints** to the window manager (if a window manager is running). The basic set of hints described here consists of simply the position and size of the new window. Window managers can choose a different position and size for you, so you are hinting that this is really the position and size you want. (Ideally, the window manager would not need these particular hints, as it should be able to pick up these values from the X server. Unfortunately, that's the way life under X is.) In later chapters, more of the XSizeHints structure will be explained. Here, you will just set the position and size. As in previous examples, there is a mask to set, showing which values of the structure are being used (filled in).

```
XSizeHints              theSizeHints;

theSizeHints.flags      = PPosition | PSize;
theSizeHints.x          = x;
theSizeHints.y          = y;
theSizeHints.width      = width;
theSizeHints.height     = height;
```

In this case, the flags field is special. The value `PPosition` means that the *program* chooses the position (and that the x and y fields are filled in). The value `USPosition` means that the *user* chooses the position. Some window managers provide more regard to the user's position than the program's position. Depending on the style of interface you want, it may be tempting to lie to the window manager here and always state that the user chooses the position. (X, again, provides the mechanism and not the policy for designing user interfaces.)

Usually, though, the `USPosition` flag is set if the user passed a command-line parameter for the position, and the `PPosition` flag is set if the program is using a default value in lieu of a user-requested position. The `PSize` value provides the same type of information about the window's size. It means that the width and height fields are filled in, and that these values were set by the program. `USSize` states the same, but that the user specified the size. Once the `XSizeHints` structure has some values, it is passed on to the window manager with the `XSetNormalHints` call.

```
XSetNormalHints( theDisplay,
        theNewWindow,
        theSizeHints );

Display         *theDisplay;
Window          theNewWindow;
XSizeHints      *theSizeHints;
```

Note that unlike the `XCreateWindow` call, the mask is part of the `XSize-Hints` structure.

After all this hinting, it is time to actually put the window on the screen. `XCreateWindow` just "created" a window. Actually having a window appear is a different matter with X. The `XMapWindow` call "maps" the window to the screen. (At this point, the window manager may intervene and change the placement of your window.)

```
XMapWindow( theDisplay,
        theNewWindow );

Display          *theDisplay;
Window           theNewWindow;
```

XMapRaised behaves the same as XMapWindow, but it also raises the new window to the top (causing it to appear over other windows that may be in the way). In most cases, XMapWindow will appear to act the same way as XMap-Raised, but XMapRaised is explicit about raising the new window to the top. XMapRaised takes the same parameters as XMapWindow.

```
XMapRaised( theDisplay, theNewWindow );
```

You can later unmap a window with the XUnmapWindow call, using the same parameters: XUnmapWindow(theDisplay, theNewWindow).

Flushing the Display

To aid performance, the Xlib keeps a queue of your output calls to the X server. Certain Xlib calls flush out this queue by sending all the requests to the X server as part of one communication. Because all communication with the X server is over a network connection (and network connections place an overhead on each message passed), it is a good idea to queue up messages to send a number of requests with one communication packet.

There are times, though, when you want the X server to display all the output queued up so far. Use the XFlush function at these times. XFlush takes one parameter, the display pointer. (This display pointer is used in almost every Xlib call.)

```
XFlush( theDisplay );

Display          *theDisplay;
```

Judicious use of the XFlush call can improve the appearance of applications and user perceptions of speed. For example, if you are drawing out a whole windowful of spreadsheet cells, call the Xlib drawing functions for the whole window, and then call XFlush to send out all the output at once. This technique generally looks better than drawing each cell one at a time—even if the total time for the drawing is the same—because of the user's perception of the speed. If all the items appear to be drawn at the same time, the perception of speed is enhanced. This method also means there is less network traffic, which may be an issue in some systems.

Note: If you are used to version 10 of the X Window System (such as X10 R4), remember that XFlush now takes a display parameter. In X10, XFlush did not take any parameters.

Destroying the Window

Before exiting a program, it is a good idea to destroy all the windows used—that is, to be frugal with the resources the X server is required to maintain. The XCloseDisplay call will normally destroy all windows you have set up, but it is a good idea to destroy any windows, as soon as you are done with them. To do this, use the XDestroyWindow function,

```
.
.
.
XDestroyWindow( theDisplay,
        theWindow );
```

where

```
Display *theDisplay;
Window  theWindow;
```

Example 2 Source Code

So, putting it all together, the second example program adds one new file to the library of routines being built in this book—windowx.c—used to open windows on a display screen. A new file, testlb.c, shows how to call the new functions. Two files from the previous example—initx.c and quitx.c—are reused here (reusing is much easier than rebuilding).

This program will simply place a window on the screen and then wait 10 seconds to give you time to view the window. Windows are one of the most complex areas of the X Window System.

The contents of file `windowx.c` are as follows:

```
/*
**      windowx.c
**
**      Window opening routine
**
*/

#include  <X11/Xlib.h>
#include  <X11/Xutil.h>
#include  <stdio.h>

/*
**      Program-wide Globals.
**
*/

extern  Display         *theDisplay;     /* -- Which display                        */
extern  int             theScreen;       /* -- Which screen on the display          */
extern  int             theDepth;        /* -- Number of color planes               */

#define         BORDER_WIDTH      2

/*
**      openWindow
**
**      This function takes a x, y pixel location for the upper
**      left corner of the window, as well as a width and height
**      for the size of the window.
**      It opens a window on the X display, and returns the window
**      id. It is also passed a flag that specifies whether the
**      window is to be a pop-up window (such as a menu) or
**      not.  This initial version does not implement that feature.
**
**      1) Set up the attributes desired for the window.
**      2) Open a window on the display.
**      3) Now tell the window manager about the size and location.
**      4) Ask X to place the window visibly on the screen.
**      5) Flush out all the queued up X requests to the X server
**
**      Note: with this program, you can either be friendly or
**      unfriendly to the window manager, if one is running.
```

continued...

...from previous page

```
**      See the section on override_redirect below. If you
**      set override_redirect to True, you are being unfriendly
**      to the window manager.
**
*/


Window
openWindow( x, y, width, height, flag )


int     x, y;            /* -- Where the window should go        */
int     width, height;   /* -- Size of the window                */
int     flag;            /* -- if > 0 then the window is a pop-up */

{       /* -- function openWindow */
        XSetWindowAttributes      theWindowAttributes;
        XSizeHints                theSizeHints;
        unsigned            long  theWindowMask;
        Window                    theNewWindow;

        /*
        **      1) Set up the attributes desired for the window.
        **      Note that window managers may deny us some of
        **      these resources. Note also that setting override_redirect
        **      to True will tell the window manager to leave our
        **      window alone. Try this program by setting
        **      override_redirect to False.
        */

        theWindowAttributes.border_pixel      =
                    BlackPixel( theDisplay, theScreen );
        theWindowAttributes.background_pixel  =
                    WhitePixel( theDisplay, theScreen );
        theWindowAttributes.override_redirect = True;

        theWindowMask = CWBackPixel | CWBorderPixel | CWOverrideRedirect;


        /*
        **      2) Open a window on the display.
        **
        */

        theNewWindow = XCreateWindow( theDisplay,
                    RootWindow( theDisplay , theScreen ),
                    x, y,
                    width, height,
                    BORDER_WIDTH,
                    theDepth,
```

continued...

...from previous page

```
                        InputOutput,
                        CopyFromParent,
                        theWindowMask,
                        &theWindowAttributes );

        /*
        **      3) Now tell the window manager about the size and location.
        **      we want for our windows.
        **
        */

        theSizeHints.flags      = PPosition | PSize;        /* -- what we want */
        theSizeHints.x          = x;
        theSizeHints.y          = y;
        theSizeHints.width      = width;
        theSizeHints.height     = height;

        XSetNormalHints( theDisplay, theNewWindow, &theSizeHints );


        /*
        **      4) Ask X to place the window visibly on the screen.
        **      Up to now, the window has been created but has not
        **      appeared on the screen. Mapping the window places it
        **      visibly on the screen.
        **
        */

        XMapWindow( theDisplay, theNewWindow );

        /*
        **      5) Flush out all the queued up X requests to the X server
        **
        */

        XFlush( theDisplay );

        /*
        **      6) Return the window ID, which is needed to specify
        **      which window to draw to.
        **
        */

        return( theNewWindow );

}       /* -- function openWindow */


/*
**      end of file windowx.c
**
*/
```

The new test file that calls the openWindow function is test1b.c. The changes are relatively minor, so you might want to edit test1.c from earlier in this chapter to just add the new features. A new function, openWindow, is created that takes the window's location and size as parameters (as well as a flag for a pop-up window—to be detailed later). openWindow returns the Window ID of the new window.

When the program is done, test1b.c calls XDestroyWindow to free up the window's data in the X server.

The contents of file test1b.c are as follows:

```
/*
**      The test program. All this program does is pop up a window,
**      wait 10 seconds, and quit -- very simple, but it demonstrates
**      the initial concepts for using X.
**
*/

/*
**      Most every program that uses X will need to include
**      Xlib.h -- which contains many definitions for X types
**      and symbols.
**
*/

#include   <X11/Xlib.h>

extern  Display *theDisplay;


main()

{
        Window  theWindow, openWindow();

        /*
        **      Set up our connection to X
        */

        initX();

        /*
        **      Get some info on the display and print it
        */

        getXInfo();
```

continued...

...from previous page

```
        /*
        **      Open a window
        */

        theWindow = openWindow( 100, 100,         /* -- x, y location        */
                                200, 200,         /* -- width, height        */
                                0 );              /* -- This is NOT a pop-up */

        /*
        **      Wait awhile
        */

        sleep( 10 );

        /*
        **      Close the connection.
        */
        XDestroyWindow( theDisplay, theWindow );
        quitX();

}


/*
**      end of file.
*/
```

The modified Makefile simply adds `windowx.c` and `test1b.c` (removing the old `test1.c`).

The contents of the Makefile for Example 2 are as follows:

```
##      X Project Makefile for Chapter 1, example 2
##
EXEC=   test1b
##
## DEFINES
##
##
##      -g = Debugging info
##      -O = Optimize (cannot have -g then)
CFLAGS= -O
##
##
```

continued...

...from previous page

```
##      Libraries
##      X11     X11 graphics library
##
LIBS=   -lX11
##
##
OBJECTS=        initx.o         \
                quitx.o         \
                windowx.o       \
                test1b.o
##
##      Command to compile and link objects together
##
$(EXEC):        $(OBJECTS)
                cc -o $(EXEC) $(OBJECTS) $(LIBS)
##
##
##      end of make file
##
```

EXAMPLE 3: FLESHING OUT THE openWindow FUNCTION

This next and final example for Chapter 1 further fleshes out the `openWindow` function created earlier.

Icons

Some window managers support **icons** for application windows. Icons especially help for smaller monitor screens. These icons can be drawn with the `bitmap` program and converted to an X data type called a `Pixmap` with the `XCreateBitmapFromData` Xlib call. The name is sort of a misnomer, as it creates a Pixmap and not a Bitmap data type.

The first step is to create a bitmap file for the icon, called "`theIcon`" here. This file is included into the file `windowx.c`.

```
.
.
.
#include "theIcon"
        .
        .
        .
        Pixmap                  theIconPixmap;
        .
        .
        .
        theIconPixmap = XCreateBitmapFromData( theDisplay,
                                theNewWindow,
                                theIcon_bits,
                                theIcon_width,
                                theIcon_height );
```

The format of the XCreateBitmapFromData call is as follows:

```
Display         *theDisplay;
Window          theNewWindow;
char            *theIcon_bits;
unsigned int    theIcon_width, theIcon_height;
```

Actually, the Window parameter is technically a Drawable and not just a Window. A Drawable can be either a Window or a Pixmap, and both can be used as the destination for most graphics Xlib calls. For these purposes, only windows will be used.

Because icons are the domain of the window manager, the manager may require icons to be a certain size and shape. Instead of having your programs keep a range of icons in various sizes and shapes—hoping one will be accepted by the window manager—it is simpler to just try out one icon that seems to work under a variety of window managers. If the window manager doesn't accept the icon, you lose. If your program keeps a range of icons in various shapes and sizes, you still lose if you don't have the correct size, and you will have gone to considerably more effort. Anyway, window managers are not always in use, and window managers are not required to accept any icons from your program. So there is no real reason to worry unduly about the icon sizes and shapes; it really isn't worth the effort or added complexity for your programs, unless you really like icons.

A sample icon bitmap file follows, but you can certainly create your own. In the sample icon that follows, a 64-by-64 pixel size is used. It appears to work on a number of workstations running different window managers.

Once the icon is created as a `Pixmap`, it is passed to the window manager through the `XSetWMHints` (for "X Set Window Manager Hints") Xlib call, as in the following example,

```
.
.
.
XWMHints        theWMHints;
.
.
.
theWMHints.icon_pixmap   = theIconPixmap;
theWMHints.initial_state = NormalState;
theWMHints.flags         = IconPixmapHint | StateHint;

XSetWMHints( theDisplay,
        theNewWindow,
        &theWMHints );
```

where the parameters are

```
Display         *theDisplay;
Window          theNewWindow;
XWMHints        *theWMHints;
```

Again, there is a flag field that tells the X server which of the `XWMHints` structure's fields are filled in by your program. In this case, there are two fields set: `icon_pixmap` (created in the previous code fragment) and `initial_state`.

The `initial_state` field can have a number of values:

```
DontCareState
NormalState
ZoomState
IconicState
InactiveState
```

Most applications will use NormalState. ZoomState asks that the window manager "zoom" the window (to something like full-screen size). Many window managers do not support this request. IconicState is supported more often. If the program asks for an initial_state of IconicState, it is asking that the window start as an icon. Icons are good ways to free up precious screen space. InactiveState tells the window manager that normally the application is seldom used. Some window managers may use an inactive menu or other way to show this.

Example 3 Source Code

The third example fleshes out the function openWindow in the file windowx.c (later examples will add still more to the basic process of opening a window). This example also adds an icon bitmap file. The same test file (test1b.c) can be reused, as well as the same Makefile.

The revised contents of file windowx.c are as follows:

```
/*
**      windowx.c
**
**      Window opening routine
**      Modified for example 3 of Chapter 1
**
*/

#include  <X11/Xlib.h>
#include  <X11/Xutil.h>
#include  <stdio.h>

/*
**      The bitmap file "theIcon" is a file made from the
**      X11 program bitmap, which is a general-purpose bitmap
**      editor. You can use the bitmap file as presented, or
**      create your own.
**
*/

#include  "theIcon"

/*
**      Program-wide Globals.
**
*/
```

continued...

...from previous page

```
extern  Display        *theDisplay;    /* -- Which display             */
extern  int            theScreen;      /* -- Which screen on the display */
extern  int            theDepth;       /* -- Number of color planes    */

#define         BORDER_WIDTH    2

/*
**      openWindow
**
**      This function takes a x, y pixel location for the upper
**      left corner of the window, as well as a width and height
**      for the size of the window.
**      It opens a window on the X display, and returns the window
**      id. It is also passed a flag that specifies whether the
**      window is to be a pop-up window (such as a menu) or
**      not. This initial version does not implement that feature.
**
**      1) Set up the attributes desired for the window.
**      2) Open a window on the display.
**      ** 3) Set up an icon for the window.
**      ** 4) Send "Hints" to the Window Manager.
**      5) Now tell the window manager about the size and location.
**      6) Ask X to place the window visibly on the screen.
**      7) Flush out all the queued up X requests to the X server
**
**      Note: with this program, you can either be friendly or
**      unfriendly to the window manager, if one is running.
**      See the section on override_redirect below. If you
**      set override_redirect to True, you are being unfriendly
**      to the window manager.
**
*/


Window
openWindow( x, y, width, height, flag )


int     x, y;           /* -- Where the window should go        */
int     width, height;  /* -- Size of the window                */
int     flag;           /* -- if > 0 then the window is a pop-up */

{       /* -- function openWindow */
        XSetWindowAttributes    theWindowAttributes;
        XSizeHints              theSizeHints;
        unsigned        long    theWindowMask;
        Window                  theNewWindow;
        Pixmap                  theIconPixmap;
        XWMHints                theWMHints;
```

continued...

...from previous page

```
/*
**      1) Set up the attributes desired for the window.
**      Note that window managers may deny us some of
**      these resources.  Note also that setting override_redirect
**      to True will tell the window manager to leave our
**      window alone. Try this program by setting
**      override_redirect to False.
*/
theWindowAttributes.border_pixel      =
                BlackPixel( theDisplay, theScreen );
theWindowAttributes.background_pixel  =
                WhitePixel( theDisplay, theScreen );
theWindowAttributes.override_redirect = True;

theWindowMask = CWBackPixel | CWBorderPixel | CWOverrideRedirect;


/*
**      2) Open a window on the display.
**
*/

theNewWindow = XCreateWindow( theDisplay,
                RootWindow( theDisplay , theScreen ),
                x, y,
                width, height,
                BORDER_WIDTH,
                theDepth,
                InputOutput,
                CopyFromParent,
                theWindowMask,
                &theWindowAttributes );

/*
**      3) Set up an icon for the window.
**      Each window should also register an Icon with the
**      window manager. This icon is used if the window
**      is shrunk down to an iconic form by the user
**      (through interaction with a window manager).
**
*/

theIconPixmap = XCreateBitmapFromData( theDisplay,
                        theNewWindow,
                        theIcon_bits,
                        theIcon_width,
                        theIcon_height );
```

continued...

...from previous page

```
/*
**      4) Send "Hints" to the Window Manager.
**      Before this window will appear on the display,
**      an X window manager may intercept the call and
**      place the window where it wants to. This next section
**      tells the window manager "hints" as to where the
**      window should go.
**
*/
theWMHints.icon_pixmap   = theIconPixmap;
theWMHints.initial_state = NormalState;
theWMHints.flags         = IconPixmapHint | StateHint;

XSetWMHints( theDisplay, theNewWindow, &theWMHints );

/*
**      5) Now tell the window manager about the size and location.
**      we want for our windows.
**
*/
theSizeHints.flags      = PPosition | PSize;        /* -- what we want */
theSizeHints.x          = x;
theSizeHints.y          = y;
theSizeHints.width      = width;
theSizeHints.height     = height;

XSetNormalHints( theDisplay, theNewWindow, &theSizeHints );


/*
**      6) Ask X to place the window visibly on the screen.
**      Up to now, the window has been created but has not
**      appeared on the screen. Mapping the window places it
**      visibly on the screen.
**
*/
XMapWindow( theDisplay, theNewWindow );

/*
**      7) Flush out all the queued up X requests to the X server
**
*/

XFlush( theDisplay );

/*
**      8) Return the window ID, which is needed to specify
**      which window to draw to.
**
*/
```

continued...

...from previous page

```
        return( theNewWindow );

}       /* -- function openWindow */



/*
**      end of file windowx.c
**
*/
```

Icon Bitmaps

The third example program creates an icon for the window from a bitmap file "theIcon". You can use the X standard client program called bitmap to create your own icon bitmap (as long as you name the file theIcon and use the bitmap program, the code that follows should accept it just fine). Note that in general you are not required to name icon bitmaps "theIcon"—that's just how the name is designated in the code that follows.

The contents of the file theIcon are as follows:

```
#define theIcon_width 64
#define theIcon_height 64
static char theIcon_bits[] = {
   0x00, 0x00, 0x00, 0x00, 0x00, 0x00, 0x00, 0x00, 0x00, 0x00, 0x00, 0x00,
   0x00, 0x00, 0x00, 0x00, 0xfc, 0xff, 0xff, 0xff, 0xff, 0xff, 0xff, 0x1f,
   0x04, 0x00, 0x00, 0x00, 0x00, 0x00, 0x00, 0x10, 0x04, 0x00, 0x00, 0x00,
   0x00, 0x00, 0x00, 0x30, 0xe4, 0x00, 0x00, 0x00, 0x00, 0x00, 0x80, 0x73,
   0xe4, 0x01, 0x00, 0x00, 0x00, 0x00, 0xc0, 0x73, 0xe4, 0x03, 0x00, 0x00,
   0x00, 0x00, 0xe0, 0x73, 0xc4, 0x07, 0x00, 0x00, 0x00, 0x00, 0xf0, 0x71,
   0x84, 0x0f, 0x00, 0x00, 0x00, 0x00, 0xf8, 0x70, 0x04, 0x1f, 0x00, 0x00,
   0x00, 0x00, 0x7c, 0x70, 0x04, 0x3e, 0x00, 0x00, 0x00, 0x00, 0x3e, 0x70,
   0x04, 0x7c, 0x00, 0x00, 0x00, 0x00, 0x1f, 0x70, 0x04, 0xf8, 0x00, 0x00,
   0x00, 0x80, 0x0f, 0x70, 0x04, 0xf0, 0x01, 0x00, 0x00, 0xc0, 0x07, 0x70,
   0x04, 0xe0, 0x03, 0x00, 0x00, 0xe0, 0x03, 0x70, 0x04, 0xc0, 0x07, 0x00,
   0x00, 0xf0, 0x01, 0x70, 0x04, 0x80, 0x0f, 0x00, 0x00, 0xf8, 0x00, 0x70,
   0x04, 0x00, 0x1f, 0x00, 0x00, 0x7c, 0x00, 0x70, 0x04, 0x00, 0x3e, 0x00,
   0x00, 0x3e, 0x00, 0x70, 0x04, 0x00, 0x7c, 0x00, 0x00, 0x1f, 0x00, 0x70,
   0x04, 0x00, 0xf8, 0x00, 0x80, 0x0f, 0x00, 0x70, 0x04, 0x00, 0xf0, 0x01,
   0xc0, 0x07, 0x00, 0x70, 0x04, 0x00, 0xe0, 0x03, 0xe0, 0x03, 0x00, 0x70,
   0x04, 0x00, 0xc0, 0x07, 0xf0, 0x01, 0x00, 0x70, 0x04, 0x00, 0x80, 0x0f,
   0xf8, 0x00, 0x00, 0x70, 0x04, 0x00, 0x00, 0x1f, 0x7c, 0x00, 0x00, 0x70,
   0x04, 0x00, 0x00, 0x3e, 0x3e, 0x00, 0x00, 0x70, 0x04, 0x00, 0x00, 0x7c,
```

continued...

...from previous page

```
0x1f, 0x00, 0x00, 0x70, 0x04, 0x00, 0x00, 0xf8, 0x0f, 0x00, 0x00, 0x70,
0x04, 0x00, 0x00, 0xf0, 0x07, 0x00, 0x00, 0x70, 0x04, 0x00, 0x00, 0xf0,
0x03, 0x00, 0x00, 0x70, 0x04, 0x00, 0x00, 0xf0, 0x07, 0x00, 0x00, 0x70,
0x04, 0x00, 0x00, 0xf8, 0x0f, 0x00, 0x00, 0x70, 0x04, 0x00, 0x00, 0x7c,
0x1f, 0x00, 0x00, 0x70, 0x04, 0x00, 0x00, 0x3e, 0x3e, 0x00, 0x00, 0x70,
0x04, 0x00, 0x00, 0x1f, 0x7c, 0x00, 0x00, 0x70, 0x04, 0x00, 0x80, 0x0f,
0xf8, 0x00, 0x00, 0x70, 0x04, 0x00, 0xc0, 0x07, 0xf0, 0x01, 0x00, 0x70,
0x04, 0x00, 0xe0, 0x03, 0xe0, 0x03, 0x00, 0x70, 0x04, 0x00, 0xf0, 0x01,
0xc0, 0x07, 0x00, 0x70, 0x04, 0x00, 0xf8, 0x00, 0x80, 0x0f, 0x00, 0x70,
0x04, 0x00, 0x7c, 0x00, 0x00, 0x1f, 0x00, 0x70, 0x04, 0x00, 0x3e, 0x00,
0x00, 0x3e, 0x00, 0x70, 0x04, 0x00, 0x1f, 0x00, 0x00, 0x7c, 0x00, 0x70,
0x04, 0x80, 0x0f, 0x00, 0x00, 0xf8, 0x00, 0x70, 0x04, 0xc0, 0x07, 0x00,
0x00, 0xf0, 0x01, 0x70, 0x04, 0xe0, 0x03, 0x00, 0x00, 0xe0, 0x03, 0x70,
0x04, 0xf0, 0x01, 0x00, 0x00, 0xc0, 0x07, 0x70, 0x04, 0xf8, 0x00, 0x00,
0x00, 0x80, 0x0f, 0x70, 0x04, 0x7c, 0x00, 0x00, 0x00, 0x00, 0x1f, 0x70,
0x04, 0x3e, 0x00, 0x00, 0x00, 0x00, 0x3e, 0x70, 0x04, 0x1f, 0x00, 0x00,
0x00, 0x00, 0x7c, 0x70, 0x84, 0x0f, 0x00, 0x00, 0x00, 0x00, 0xf8, 0x70,
0xc4, 0x07, 0x00, 0x00, 0x00, 0x00, 0xf0, 0x71, 0xe4, 0x03, 0x00, 0x00,
0x00, 0x00, 0xe0, 0x73, 0xe4, 0x01, 0x00, 0x00, 0x00, 0x00, 0xc0, 0x73,
0xe4, 0x00, 0x00, 0x00, 0x00, 0x00, 0x80, 0x73, 0x04, 0x00, 0x00, 0x00,
0x00, 0x00, 0x00, 0x70, 0x04, 0x00, 0x00, 0x00, 0x00, 0x00, 0x00, 0x70,
0xfc, 0xff, 0xff, 0xff, 0xff, 0xff, 0xff, 0x7f, 0xf0, 0xff, 0xff, 0xff,
0xff, 0xff, 0xff, 0x7f, 0xe0, 0xff, 0xff, 0xff, 0xff, 0xff, 0xff, 0x7f,
0x00, 0x00, 0x00, 0x00, 0x00, 0x00, 0x00, 0x00};
```

Use the same Makefile as well as the same `initx.c`, `quitx.c`, and `testlb.c` as in the last example.

SUMMARY

- To have your applications put windows on a display, you must first set up a connection to the X server.
- To open up a window, you must first **create** the window. After it is created, you should send some information about the window, called **hints**, to the **window manager** (which may or may not be running). Then, the window should be mapped to the screen, where it actually appears.
- Some window managers support **icons** for application windows. Icons especially help for smaller monitor screens. These icons can be drawn with the `bitmap` program, a standard X client, and converted to an X data type called a `Pixmap` with the `XCreateBitmapFromData` Xlib call.

Xlib Functions and Macros Introduced in This Chapter

BlackPixel
DefaultScreen
DefaultDepth
DisplayWidth
DisplayHeight
ProtocolVersion
ProtocolRevision
ServerVendor
VendorRelease
WhitePixel
XCloseDisplay
XCreateBitmapFromData
XCreateSimpleWindow
XCreateWindow
XDisplayName
XDestroyWindow
XFlush
XMapWindow
XMapRaised
XOpenDisplay
XSetNormalHints
XSetWMHints
XUnmapWindow

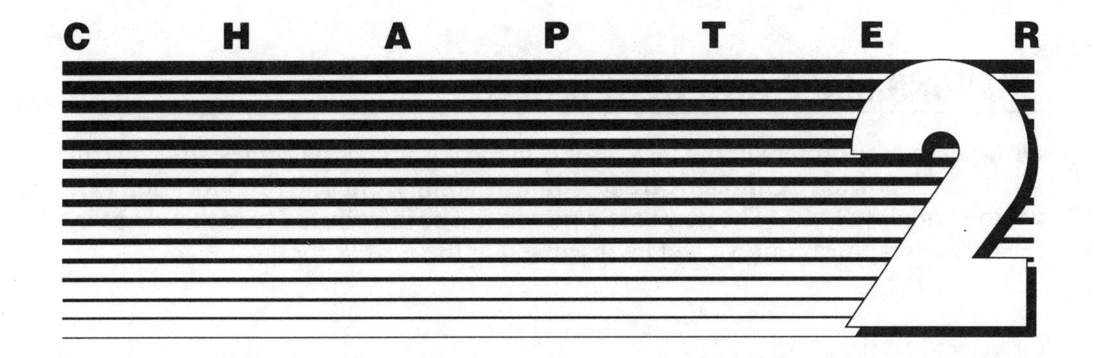

DRAWING WITH X

Once you have a window on the screen display, the next step is to put something into the window. This chapter discusses some of the commands frequently used for drawing items such as lines, rectangles, and ovals. A new data type is introduced in this chapter: the GC, or **graphics context**.

DRAWING LINES AND RECTANGLES

Drawing lines is rather simple in X, as it is in most graphics packages. As you can see in the following example, X treats a line as going from one pixel location (x1, y1) to another (x2, y2). The new data type you will be introduced to in this chapter, the `GC`, or graphics context, will be discussed in the next section.

```
XDrawLine( theDisplay,
        theWindow,
        theGC,
        x1, y1,
        x2, y2 );

Display         *theDisplay
Drawable        theWindow;
GC              theGC;
int             x1, y1;
int             x2, y2;
```

The `Drawable` can be a `Window` or a `Pixmap`, though in most cases it will be a `Window`.

In X, the coordinate origin is in the *upper* left corner of the window. The x-coordinate axis grows going to the right. The y coordinate grows going *down*.

Drawing rectangles is very similar to drawing lines, except that X treats all rectangular shapes as having a location (x, y) and a size (width, height), as in the following example:

```
XDrawRectangle( theDisplay,
        theWindow,
        theGC,
        x, y,
        width, height );

Display         *theDisplay
Drawable        theWindow;
GC              theGC;
int             x, y;
unsigned int    width, height;
```

All measurements are in **pixels** (short for "picture elements"), which are dots on the screen. The size of these dots and the number of pixels on a screen will vary greatly; for example, a graphic that is 1" high on one monitor will undoubtedly be a different height on another vendor's screen.

THE GRAPHICS CONTEXT

The **graphics context**, or `GC`, is a catch-all data structure that contains almost everything needed to specify parameters for drawing. It contains information about the foreground and background colors, the width of the pen for drawing lines, and whether the line should be dashed or solid (Appendix C contains a listing of the `GC`'s full contents). For now, the main thing you need to know about the graphics context is that one must be created for the window in order for you to begin drawing.

`GC`s are tied to `Windows` (or to `Pixmaps` as `Drawables`). When a graphics context is created, you must specify which `Window` (or `Drawable`) it is created for; however, you can have more than one `GC` for a given window (for more information, see Chapter 8).

Creating the Graphics Context for a Window

The function `XCreateGC` creates a new graphics context for a given window, as in the following example:

```
.
.
.
XGCValues       theGCValues;
GC              theNewGC;
unsigned long   theValueMask;
.
.
.
theValueMask  = 0L;
theNewGC      = XCreateGC( theDisplay,
                      theWindow,
                      theValueMask,
                      &theGCValues );
```

Officially, the parameters are as follows:

```
Display         *theDisplay;
Drawable        theWindow;
unsigned long   theValueMask;
XGCValues       *theGCValues;
```

The structure XGCValues can be filled in with values to change from the default. If so, the value mask needs to have certain bits set to tell the X server that the given values are being set. In this case (and in most cases), the GC can be created with just the straight defaults (see Appendix C for more information on the GC).

The most common use of a GC is to set colors for the foreground and background. The foreground color is the color that lines are drawn in. The background color is often used as the background for drawing text (as will be shown in Chapter 4). Thus far, the only colors in use are BlackPixel and WhitePixel, which work on any X workstation, color or monochrome. Chapter 3 will show you how to set other colors on color screens.

```
.
.
.
Display         *theDisplay;
GC              theGC;
unsigned long   theBlackPixel;
unsigned long   theWhitePixel;
.
.
.
XSetForeground( theDisplay,
                theGC,
                theBlackPixel );

XSetBackground( theDisplay,
                theGC,
                theWhitePixel );
```

EXAMPLE 1: DRAWING LINES AND RECTANGLES

In this chapter's first example program, the library of routines for use with X is extended with a new file, `drawx.c`. `drawx.c` contains basic drawing commands for creating primitive shapes, such as lines and rectangles, in a window. These initial functions are very short but can be later modified to draw items in different ways and form a consistent interface with ovals and circles (discussed later in this chapter).

For now, `drawx.c` contains the following two functions,

```
drawLine( theWindow, theGC, x1, y1, x2, y2 )
```

which draws a line from (x1, y1) to (x2, y2) in the given window, and

```
drawRectangle( theWindow, theGC, x, y, width, height )
```

which draws a rectangle located at (x, y) with size (width, height).

The file `windowx.c` is changed; it now creates a `GC` with each window that is created. Because windows are normally put on the screen to be drawn in, it makes sense to create the `GC` at the same time the window is created. Very few windows are created and are not drawn in by an application program. Therefore, the `openWindow` function now has an extra parameter,

```
openWindow( x, y, width, height, popUpFlag, theGC )
```

where the `GC` will contain a newly-made `GC` when the `Window` is returned.

```
int      x, y;
int      width, height, popUpFlag;
GC       *theGC;
```

A new function, createGC, is added to the file windowx.c to perform the actual work of creating a graphics context.

```
createGC( theWindow, theGC )
        Window  theWindow;
        GC      *theGC;
```

createGC returns a 0 if an error occurred in creating the GC and a 1 if the GC was created without an error. createGC also initializes the GC's foreground and background colors, with calls to XSetForeground and XSetBackground (mainly to provide examples of their use, certainly not for efficiency).

Because createGC is using pixel values for BlackPixel and WhitePixel, these values are now stored in global variables in the file initx.c. These values will be used again and again, so it is easier to store them in variables than to keep calling the macros BlackPixel and WhitePixel.

The test file test2.c is based on the old test1b.c from Chapter 1, but it now draws lines and rectangles. The file quitx.c is used unchanged.

Example 1 Source Code

The contents of the file drawx.c are as follows:

```
/*
**      drawx.c         X11 simple drawing functions; Chapter 2, Example 1.
**
*/

#include    <X11/Xlib.h>
#include    <X11/Xutil.h>

/* -- external globals, from initx.c */
extern  Display         *theDisplay;

/*
**      drawLine
**      Draws a line from (x1, y1) to (x2, y2) in the window
**      theWindow, using the graphics context theGC.
**
*/
```

continued...

...from previous page

```
drawLine( theWindow, theGC, x1, y1, x2, y2 )

Window  theWindow;                      /* -- the window to draw it in */
GC      theGC;                          /* -- Graphics Context       */
int     x1, y1;                         /* -- Starting location      */
int     x2, y2;                         /* -- Ending location        */

{       /* -- function drawLine */

        XDrawLine( theDisplay,
                theWindow,
                theGC,
                x1, y1,
                x2, y2 );

}       /* -- function drawLine */


/*
**      drawRectangle
**      Draws a rectangle (outlines or frames a rectangle) in the
**      given window and with the given graphics context.
**
*/

drawRectangle( theWindow, theGC, x, y, width, height )

Window  theWindow;              /* -- the window to draw it in                */
GC      theGC;                  /* -- Graphics Context                        */
int     x, y;                   /* -- Starting location, upper left corner    */
int     width, height;          /* -- Size of the rectangle                   */

{       /* -- function drawRectangle */

        XDrawRectangle( theDisplay,
                theWindow,
                theGC,
                x, y,
                width, height );

}       /* -- function drawRectangle */


/*
**      end of file drawx.c
**
*/
```

The contents of the file `windowx.c` are as follows:

```
/*
**      windowx.c
**
**      Window opening routine
**
*/

#include  <X11/Xlib.h>
#include  <X11/Xutil.h>
#include  <stdio.h>

/*
**      The bitmap file "theIcon" is a file made from the
**      X11 program bitmap, which is a general-purpose bitmap
**      editor. You can use the bitmap file as presented, or
**      create your own.
**
*/

#include  "theIcon"

/*
**      Program-wide Globals.
**
*/

extern  Display         *theDisplay;     /* -- Which display              */
extern  int             theScreen;       /* -- Which screen on the display */
extern  int             theDepth;        /* -- Number of color planes      */
extern  unsigned long   theBlackPixel;   /* -- System "Black" color  */
extern  unsigned long   theWhitePixel;   /* -- System "White" color        */

#define         BORDER_WIDTH    2

/*
**      openWindow
**
**      This function takes a x, y pixel location for the upper
**      left corner of the window, as well as a width and height
**      for the size of the window.
**      It opens a window on the X display and returns the window
**      id. It is also passed a flag that specifies whether the
**      window is to be a pop-up window (such as a menu) or
**      not. This initial version does not implement that feature.
**      The GC theNewGC is a graphics context that is created for the
**      window, and returned to the caller. The GC is necessary for
**      drawing into the window.
**
```

continued...

...from previous page

```
**      1) Set up the attributes desired for the window.
**      2) Open a window on the display.
**      3) Set up an icon for the window.
**      4) Send "Hints" to the Window Manager.
**      5) Now tell the window manager about the size and location.
**      6) Create a graphics context for the window.
**      7) Ask X to place the window visibly on the screen.
**      8) Flush out all the queued up X requests to the X server
**
**      Note: with this program, you can either be friendly or
**      unfriendly to the window manager, if one is running.
**      See the section on override_redirect below. If you
**      set override_redirect to True, you are being unfriendly
**      to the window manager.
**
**
*/


Window
openWindow( x, y, width, height, flag, theNewGC )


int     x, y;               /* -- Where the window should go        */
int     width, height;      /* -- Size of the window                */
int     flag;               /* -- if > 0 then the window is a pop-up */
GC      *theNewGC;          /* -- Returned Graphics Context         */


{       /* -- function openWindow */
        XSetWindowAttributes      theWindowAttributes;
        XSizeHints                theSizeHints;
        unsigned          long    theWindowMask;
        Window                    theNewWindow;
        Pixmap                    theIconPixmap;
        XWMHints                  theWMHints;

        /*
        **      1) Set up the attributes desired for the window.
        **      Note that window managers may deny us some of
        **      these resources. Note also that setting override_redirect
        **      to True will tell the window manager to leave our
        **      window alone. Try this program by setting
        **      override_redirect to False.
        */

        theWindowAttributes.border_pixel      = theBlackPixel;
        theWindowAttributes.background_pixel  = theWhitePixel;
        theWindowAttributes.override_redirect = True;

        theWindowMask = CWBackPixel | CWBorderPixel | CWOverrideRedirect;
```

continued...

...from previous page

```
/*
**      2) Open a window on the display.
**
*/

theNewWindow = XCreateWindow( theDisplay,
                RootWindow( theDisplay , theScreen ),
                x, y,
                width, height,
                BORDER_WIDTH,
                theDepth,
                InputOutput,
                CopyFromParent,
                theWindowMask,
                &theWindowAttributes );

/*
**      3) Set up an icon for the window.
**      Each window should also register an Icon with the
**      window manager. This icon is used if the window
**      is shrunk down to an iconic form by the user
**      (through interaction with a window manager).
**
*/

theIconPixmap = XCreateBitmapFromData( theDisplay,
                        theNewWindow,
                        theIcon_bits,
                        theIcon_width,
                        theIcon_height );

/*
**      4) Send "Hints" to the Window Manager.
**      Before this window will appear on the display,
**      an X window manager may intercept the call and
**      place the window where it wants to. This next section
**      tells the window manager "hints" as to where the
**      window should go.
**
*/
theWMHints.icon_pixmap   = theIconPixmap;
theWMHints.initial_state = NormalState;
theWMHints.flags         = IconPixmapHint | StateHint;

XSetWMHints( theDisplay, theNewWindow, &theWMHints );

/*
**      5) Now tell the window manager about the size and location
**      we want for our windows.
**
*/
```

continued...

...from previous page

```
        theSizeHints.flags    = PPosition | PSize;        /* -- what we want */
        theSizeHints.x        = x;
        theSizeHints.y        = y;
        theSizeHints.width    = width;
        theSizeHints.height   = height;

        XSetNormalHints( theDisplay, theNewWindow, &theSizeHints );


        /*
        **      6) Create a graphics context for the window.
        **
        */

        if ( createGC( theNewWindow, theNewGC ) == 0 )
                {
                XDestroyWindow( theDisplay, theNewWindow );
                return( (Window) 0 );
                }


        /*
        **      7) Ask X to place the window visibly on the screen.
        **      Up to now, the window has been created but has not
        **      appeared on the screen. Mapping the window places it
        **      visibly on the screen.
        **
        */

        XMapWindow( theDisplay, theNewWindow );

        /*
        **      8) Flush out all the queued up X requests to the X server
        **
        */

        XFlush( theDisplay );

        /*
        **      9) Return the window ID, which is needed to specify
        **      which window to draw to.
        **
        */

        return( theNewWindow );

}       /* -- function openWindow */
```

continued...

...from previous page

```
/*
**      createGC creates a graphics context for the given window.
**      A graphics context is necessary to draw into the window.
**
**      Returns 0 if there was an error, 1 if all is A-OK.
**
*/

createGC( theNewWindow, theNewGC )

Window  theNewWindow;
GC      *theNewGC;

{       /* -- function createGC */
        XGCValues       theGCValues;

        *theNewGC = XCreateGC( theDisplay,
                        theNewWindow,
                        (unsigned long) 0,
                        &theGCValues );

        if ( *theNewGC == 0 )    /* -- Unable to create a GC */
                {
                return( 0 );    /* -- Error                 */
                }
        else
                {
            /* --  Set Foreground and Background defaults for the new GC */
            XSetForeground( theDisplay,
                        *theNewGC,
                        theBlackPixel );

            XSetBackground( theDisplay,
                        *theNewGC,
                        theWhitePixel );

            return( 1 ); /* -- A-OK                         */
            }

}      /* -- function createGC */

/*
**     end of file windowx.c
**
*/
```

The contents of the file `initx.c` are as follows:

```
/*
**      initx.c
**
**      Initialization code to talk to the X server
**
*/

#include  <X11/Xlib.h>
#include  <X11/Xutil.h>
#include  <stdio.h>

/*
**      Program-wide Globals.
**
*/

Display             *theDisplay;        /* -- Which display                */
int                 theScreen;          /* -- Which screen on the display  */
int                 theDepth;           /* -- Number of color planes       */
unsigned long       theBlackPixel;      /* -- System "Black" color         */
unsigned long       theWhitePixel;      /* -- System "White" color         */

/*
**      initX()
**      Sets up the connection to the X server and stores information
**      about the environment.
**
*/

initX()

{       /* -- function initX  */

        /*
        **      1) Establish a connection to the X Server. The connection
        **      is asked for on the local server for the local display.
        **
        */

        theDisplay = XOpenDisplay( NULL );

        /* -- Check if the connection was made */
        if ( theDisplay == NULL )
                {
                fprintf( stderr,
                   "ERROR: Cannot establish a connection to the X Server  %s\n",
                   XDisplayName( NULL ) );
                exit( 1 );
                }
```

continued...

...from previous page

```
        /*
        **      2) Check for the default screen and color plane depth.
        **      If theDepth == 1, then we have a monochrome system.
        **
        */

        theScreen     = DefaultScreen( theDisplay );
        theDepth      = DefaultDepth( theDisplay, theScreen );
        theBlackPixel = BlackPixel( theDisplay, theScreen );
        theWhitePixel = WhitePixel( theDisplay, theScreen );

}       /* -- function initX  */


/*
**      getXInfo prints information to the starting terminal
**      (usually an xterm) about the current X Window display
**      and screen.
*/

getXInfo()

{       /* -- function getXInfo */

        /*
        **      You will find many funny values when you check the X
        **      information below. It should be something to the tune of:
        **      MIT X Consortium (vendor)
        **      3 (vendor release)
        **      X11 R3 (or R2, the Version and Revision numbers).
        **      But, on most implementations, this information
        **      does not seem to jibe.
        **      On the generic MIT X Consortium release for
        **      X11R3, you might see X11R0, with a vendor release # of 3
        **
        */

        printf( "%s version %d of the X Window System, X%d R%d\n",
                ServerVendor( theDisplay ),
                VendorRelease( theDisplay ),
                ProtocolVersion( theDisplay ),
                ProtocolRevision( theDisplay ) );

        /*
        **      Now, print some more detailed information about the
        **      display.
        **
        */
```

continued...

...from previous page

```
        if ( theDepth == 1 )
              {
              printf( "Color plane depth.............%d (monochrome)\n",
                    theDepth );
              }
        else
              {
              printf( "Color plane depth.............%d\n",
                    theDepth );
              }

        printf( "Display Width.................%d\n",
               DisplayWidth( theDisplay, theScreen ) );
        printf( "Display Height................%d\n",
               DisplayHeight( theDisplay, theScreen ) );

        printf( "The display %s\n", XDisplayName( theDisplay ) );

}       /* -- function getXInfo */


/*
**      end of file initx.c
**
*/
```

The contents of the test file `test2.c` are as follows:

```
/*
**      Chapter 2, Example 1
**
**      This program pops up a window and then draws into it.
**
*/

#include    <X11/Xlib.h>

/*
**      external GLOBALS from initx.c
*/

extern Display              *theDisplay;
```

continued...

...from previous page

```
main()

{
        Window theWindow, openWindow();
        GC     theGC;

        /*
        **      Set up our connection to X
        */

        initX();

        /*
        **      Get some info on the display and print it
        */

        getXInfo();

        /*
        **      Open a window
        */

        theWindow = openWindow( 100, 100,   /* -- x, y location        */
                                300, 300,   /* -- width, height        */
                                0,          /* -- This is NOT a pop-up */
                                &theGC );   /* -- Graphics Context     */

        /*
        **      Draw into the Window
        */

        drawLine( theWindow, theGC,
                10, 10,             /* -- Starting location in x, y */
                100, 100 );         /* -- Ending location in x, y   */

        drawRectangle( theWindow, theGC,
                100, 100,           /* -- Starting location in x, y */
                100, 100 );         /* -- width and height          */

        /*
        **      Send all output to the screen
        */

        XFlush( theDisplay );

        /*
        **      Wait awhile
        */

        sleep( 10 );
```

continued...

...from previous page

```
        /*
        **      Close the connection to the X server.
        */
        XDestroyWindow( theDisplay, theWindow );

        quitX();

}


/*
**      end of file.
*/
```

The Makefile for Chapter 2 is as follows:

```
##      X Project Makefile for Chapter 2
##
EXEC=  test2
##
## DEFINES
##
##
##      -g = Debugging info
##      -O = optimize (cannot use -g then)
CFLAGS=         -O
##
##
##      Libraries
##      X11     X11 graphics library
##
LIBS=  -lX11
##
##
OBJECTS=        initx.o         \
                drawx.o         \
                quitx.o         \
                windowx.o       \
                test2.o
##
##      Command to compile and link objects together
##
$(EXEC):        $(OBJECTS)
                cc -o $(EXEC) $(OBJECTS) $(LIBS)
##
##
##      end of make file
##
```

DRAWING OVALS FROM ARCS

Lines and rectangles are easy to draw in X; ovals, though, are a bit harder. X has no base calls for drawing circles, ellipses, or ovals. The only way to draw this kind of output is to invent your own strategy. Probably the simplest way is to draw an arc that goes all the way around a circular path, generating an oval shape. In X, an arc is bounded by a rectangle, and the sweep of the arc is limited to the box formed by the rectangle. The arc begins at a start angle and draws an arc for a distance specified by a path angle. If that isn't confusing enough, the angle values are given in 64ths of a degree—meaning a full circular path is 360 degrees times 64—or 23040. To make an arc go all the way around to form an oval, the start angle should be 0, and the path angle should be 360*64. In the code that follows, these two constants are defined as `START_CIRCLE` (0) and `FULL_CIRCLE` (360× 64) because it is much easier to deal with named constants than to try to figure out what the heck 23040 means.

```
XDrawArc( theDisplay,
          theWindow,
          theGC,
          x, y,
          width, height,
          start_angle,
          path_angle );

Display           *theDisplay
Drawable          theWindow;
GC                theGC;
int               x, y;
unsigned int      width, height;
int               start_angle;      /* -- should = 0 for an oval      */
int               path_angle;       /* -- should = 360*64 for an oval */
```

In the next code example, a created `drawOval` routine takes care of the start and path angles and follows the consistent interface introduced so far in this book. By hiding the internal details, you can now forget all about 64ths of a degree.

```
drawOval( theWindow, theGC, x, y, width, height )

Window            theWindow;
GC                theGC;
int               x, y;
int               width, height;
```

FILLING OVALS AND RECTANGLES

All of the drawing commands discussed so far simply draw the outline of an object. Many times, though, you want to fill an object in. X calls the operation of drawing the outline **drawing** and the operation of filling in an object **filling**. This may seem overly simple, but it is a way of keeping the Xlib function calls apart. An XDrawSomething routine draws an outline of a Something shape, while an XFillSomething fills in the object.

Thus, the calls to fill rectangles and ovals simply look like the routines already discussed in this chapter, but the "Draw" part is replaced by a "Fill" part.

```
XFillArc( theDisplay,
        theWindow,
        theGC,
        x, y,
        width, height,
        startAngle,
        pathAngle );

Display         *theDisplay
Drawable        theWindow;
GC              theGC;
int             x, y;
unsigned int    width, height;
int             startAngle;     /* -- should = 0 for an oval      */
int             pathAngle;      /* -- should = 360*64 for an oval */
```

```
XFillRectangle( theDisplay,
        theWindow,
        theGC,
        x, y,
        width, height );

Display         *theDisplay
Drawable        theWindow;
GC              theGC;
int             x, y;
unsigned int    width, height;
```

EXAMPLE 2: DRAWING AND FILLING OVALS AND RECTANGLES

In this second example program, the drawing commands `drawLine` and `drawRectangle` are enhanced with `drawOval`, `fillOval`, and `fillRectangle`. For now, all drawing is in the system default `BlackPixel`. In Chapter 3, this same program will be extended to draw lines and shapes in color. The file `drawx.c` has the routines just discussed added to it, and the file `test2b.c` has a set of drawing test calls in it. The files `initx.c`, `quitx.c`, and `windowx.c` are reused from the previous example, and so is the Makefile.

Example 2 Source Code

The contents of the file `drawx.c` are as follows:

```
/*
**      drawx.c         X11 simple drawing functions
**
*/

#include    <X11/Xlib.h>
#include    <X11/Xutil.h>

/*
**      X11 draws ovals as Arcs, Arcs which start at angle 0
**      and traverse the full circle. X11 measures angles in
**      terms of 1/64 degrees. Thus, traversing the full circle
**      means going around an angle 360*64.
**
*/

#define     FULL_CIRCLE         (360*64)
#define     START_CIRCLE        0


/* -- external globals, from initx.c */
extern  Display         *theDisplay;

/*
**      drawLine
**      Draws a line from (x1, y1) to (x2, y2) in the window
**      theWindow, using the graphics context theGC.
**
*/
```

continued...

...from previous page

```
drawLine( theWindow, theGC, x1, y1, x2, y2 )

Window  theWindow;          /* -- the window to draw it in */
GC      theGC;              /* -- Graphics Context         */
int     x1, y1;             /* -- Starting location        */
int     x2, y2;             /* -- Ending location          */

{       /* -- function drawLine */

        XDrawLine( theDisplay,
                theWindow,
                theGC,
                x1, y1,
                x2, y2 );

}       /* -- function drawLine */


/*
**      drawRectangle
**      Draws a rectangle (outlines or frames a rectangle) in the
**      given window and with the given graphics context.
**
*/

drawRectangle( theWindow, theGC, x, y, width, height )

Window  theWindow;      /* -- the window to draw it in                  */
GC      theGC;          /* -- Graphics Context                          */
int     x, y;           /* -- Starting location, upper left corner      */
int     width, height;  /* -- Size of the rectangle                     */

{       /* -- function drawRectangle */

        XDrawRectangle( theDisplay,
                theWindow,
                theGC,
                x, y,
                width, height );

}       /* -- function drawRectangle */



/*
**      fillRectangle
**      Fills a rectangle (outlines or frames a rectangle) in the
**      given window and with the given graphics context.
**
*/
```

continued...

...from previous page

```
fillRectangle( theWindow, theGC, x, y, width, height )

Window  theWindow;       /* -- the window to fill it in          */
GC      theGC;           /* -- Graphics Context                  */
int     x, y;            /* -- Starting location, upper left corner */
int     width, height;   /* -- Size of the rectangle             */

{       /* -- function fillRectangle */

        XFillRectangle( theDisplay,
                theWindow,
                theGC,
                x, y,
                width, height );

}       /* -- function fillRectangle */


/*
**      drawOval
**      Draws the framed outline of an oval. This oval is bounded
**      by a rectangle from x, y (upper left corner) of size
**      width, height.
**
*/

drawOval( theWindow, theGC, x, y, width, height )

Window  theWindow;       /* -- the window to draw it in          */
GC      theGC;           /* -- Graphics Context                  */
                         /* -- For the bounding rectangle:       */
int     x, y;            /* -- Starting location, upper left corner */
int     width, height;   /* -- Size of the rectangle             */

{       /* -- drawOval */

        XDrawArc( theDisplay,
                theWindow,
                theGC,
                x, y,
                width, height,
                START_CIRCLE,
                FULL_CIRCLE );

}       /* -- drawOval */
```

continued...

...from previous page

```
/*
**      fillOval
**      Fills the framed outline of an oval. This oval is bounded
**      by a rectangle from x, y (upper left corner) of size
**      width, height.
**
*/

fillOval( theWindow, theGC, x, y, width, height )

Window  theWindow;       /* -- the window to fill it in          */
GC      theGC;           /* -- Graphics Context                  */
                         /* -- For the bounding rectangle:       */
int     x, y;            /* -- Starting location, upper left corner */
int     width, height;   /* -- Size of the rectangle             */

{       /* -- fillOval */

        XFillArc( theDisplay,
                theWindow,
                theGC,
                x, y,
                width, height,
                START_CIRCLE,
                FULL_CIRCLE );

}       /* -- fillOval */

/*
**      end of file drawx.c
**
*/
```

The contents of the new test file `test2.c` are as follows:

```
/*
**      Chapter 2, Example 2
**
**      This program pops up a window and then draws into it.
**
*/

#include   <X11/Xlib.h>

/*
**      external GLOBALS from initx.c
*/
```

continued...

...from previous page

```
extern  Display         *theDisplay;


main()

{
        Window  theWindow, openWindow();
        GC      theGC;

        /*
        **      Set up our connection to X
        */

        initX();

        /*
        **      Get some info on the display and print it
        */

        getXInfo();

        /*
        **      Open a window
        */

        theWindow = openWindow( 100, 100,           /* -- x, y location        */
                                300, 300,           /* -- width, height        */
                                0,                  /* -- This is NOT a pop-up */
                                &theGC );           /* -- Graphics Context     */

        /*
        **      Draw into the Window
        */

        drawOval( theWindow, theGC,
                10, 10,         /* -- Starting location in x, y */
                100, 100 );     /* -- width and height          */

        fillRectangle( theWindow, theGC,
                100, 100,       /* -- Starting location in x, y */
                100, 100 );     /* -- width and height          */

        /*
        **      Send all output to the screen
        */

        XFlush( theDisplay );

        /*
        **      Wait awhile
        */
```

continued...

...from previous page

```
        sleep( 10 );

        /*
        **      Close the connection to the X server.
        */
        XDestroyWindow( theDisplay, theWindow );

        quitX();

}
/*
**      end of file.
*/
```

DRAWING MULTIPLE LINES, RECTANGLES, AND ARCS

Each drawing routine previously shown requires at least one interaction with the X server, including clipping the output and setting up the graphics context values. If you want to draw many lines, rectangles, or arcs (that is, lines, rectangles, or arcs with the same graphics context – meaning the same color and same size), there are a number of X routines to draw multiple objects. All the items, though, must share the same `Drawable` (usually a `Window`) and the same graphics context, as in the following example:

```
XDrawArcs( theDisplay,
        theWindow,
        theGC,
        theArcs,
        theNumberOfArcs );

XFillArcs( theDisplay,
        theWindow,
        theGC,
        theArcs,
        theNumberOfArcs );

Display         *theDisplay;
Drawable        theWindow;
XArc            *theArcs;
int             theNumberOfArcs;
```

For XDrawArcs and XFillArcs, each arc is described in an array element in an array of XArc structures (or structs). The XArc structure is as follows:

```
typedef struct
        {
        short           x, y;
        unsigned short  width, height;
        short           angle1, angle2;
        } XArc;
```

When drawing multiple arcs, you must allocate an array of XArc structs, with as many elements as you plan on drawing. For example, the following code draws two arcs on the screen:

```
.
.
.
XArc     theArcs[ 42 ];
.
.
.

theArcs[ 0 ].x      = 100;
theArcs[ 0 ].y      = 100;
theArcs[ 0 ].width  = 50;
theArcs[ 0 ].height = 50;
theArcs[ 0 ].angle1 = 0;
theArcs[ 0 ].angle2 = 360*64;

theArcs[ 1 ].x      = 200;
theArcs[ 1 ].y      = 200;
theArcs[ 1 ].width  = 50;
theArcs[ 1 ].height = 50;
theArcs[ 1 ].angle1 = 0;
theArcs[ 1 ].angle2 = 360*64;

theNumberOfArcs     = 2;

XDrawArcs( theDisplay,
        theWindow,
        theGC,
        theArcs,
        theNumberOfArcs );
```

Like the multiple arc routines, the multiple rectangle routines also define a structure, this time called `XRectangle`:

```
typedef struct
        {
        short           x, y;
        unsigned short  width, height;
        } XRectangle;

XDrawRectangles( theDisplay,
        theWindow,
        theGC,
        theRects,
        theNumberOfRects );

XFillRectangles( theDisplay,
        theWindow,
        theGC,
        theRects,
        theNumberOfRects );

Display         *theDisplay;
Drawable        theWindow;
XRectangle      *theRects;
int             theNumberOfRects;
```

Lines, too, have their own structure, called `XPoint`, for a multiple-line drawing function, `XDrawLines`:

```
typedef struct
        {
        short x, y;
        } XPoint;
```

In the case of `XDrawLines`, instead of specifying the number of lines, you specify the number of points. All points are drawn connected, which is different from the `XRectangle` example,

```
XDrawLines( theDisplay,
        theWindow,
        theGC,
        thePoints,
        theNumberOfPoints,
        theMode );

Display         *theDisplay;
Drawable        theWindow;
XPoint          *thePoints;
int             theNumberOfPoints;
int             theMode;
```

where `theMode` can have one of two values:

```
CoordModeOrigin
CoordModePrevious
```

`CoordModeOrigin` means that each point is specified relative to the `Drawable`'s origin (usually the `window`'s origin). This is the way most would expect `XDrawLines` to act. `CoordModePrevious` specifies that each point's x and y coordinates are relative to the last point in the `XPoint` array. The first point is relative to the origin of the `Drawable`. This mode can be good for drawing lines in what is called "turtle" geometry, in which the ending point of one line is the starting location for the next, and all movements are described as the motion from the last point (i.e., relative to the last point).

These points can also be drawn as unconnected points, using the `XDrawPoints` function:

```
XDrawPoints( theDisplay,
        theWindow,
        theGC,
        thePoints,
        theNumberOfPoints,
        theMode );

Display         *theDisplay;
Drawable        theWindow;
XPoint          *thePoints;
int             theNumberOfPoints;
int             theMode;
```

You can also draw just one point, of course, with XDrawPoint, as in the following example:

```
XDrawPoint( theDisplay,
        theWindow,
        theGC,
        x, y );

Display         *theDisplay;
Drawable        theWindow;
int             x, y;
```

SUMMARY

- X has a number of routines for drawing into a window. In fact, most window-drawing functions can also draw into an arbitrary pixel area called a Pixmap (such as an icon).
- Lines and rectangles seem to be the basic X drawing functions. Ovals and circles have no basic routines in X, so you must come up with a means to draw them on your own, such as by drawing the arc of an entire circle.
- For performance reasons, X has multiple-drawing functions, such as XDrawLines, to cut down the network traffic and speed drawing when you want to draw a number of lines or other graphic objects (with the same color, same pen size, and same GC).

Xlib Functions and Macros Introduced in This Chapter

XCreateGC
XDrawArc
XDrawArcs
XDrawLine
XDrawLines
XDrawPoint
XDrawPoints
XDrawRectangle
XDrawRectangles
XFillArc
XFillArcs
XFillRectangle
XFillRectangles
XSetBackground
XSetForeground

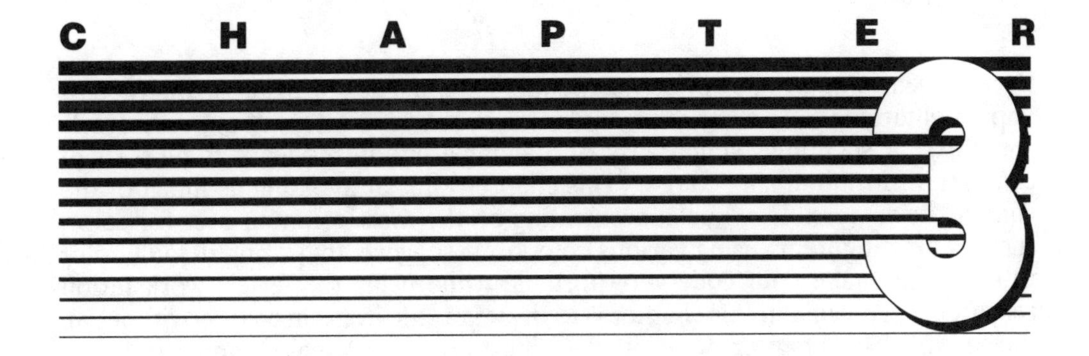

USING COLOR

Drawing in color is fun. It can make selections clearer and highlight key areas of an interface. Unfortunately, color also is one of the most nonstandard aspects of graphic workstations. It seems that each graphic workstation uses a different means for specifying color. Some have color tables, some have color planes, and all seem to be different.

Color is probably the hardest area to grasp when trying to understand X. This chapter concentrates on the basic skills of drawing lines in red, green, or medium slate blue. After finishing this chapter, you may want to look up the X reference material from the X server vendor for your workstation if you really want more complexity than is presented here.

Because X attempts to be device-independent, it must deal with all the many color implementations. As a consequence, color is one area where X appears overly complex. A seemingly simple task of drawing a line in red leads to all sorts of contortions in initializing colors. This chapter aims at avoiding as much of the complexity as possible, while concentrating on the most common uses for color, such as drawing items using various colors. It suggests that using default color values helps make your code very portable while using the fewest workstation resources. The goal in this chapter is to draw graphic items in color—without all the mess. This chapter does not describe the entire X color model in depth because it just isn't needed for most applications, quite frankly, and it is far too easy for the programmer to get bogged down in excruciating detail work that doesn't yield tangible improvements.

THE PORTABILITY AND USEFULNESS OF COLOR APPLICATIONS

As stated previously, color is fun. But it is not fun for those who only own monochrome systems. Before requiring color for your application, think carefully about whether the color is actually needed. Adding even low-end color to a workstation typically adds $2,000 to $5,000 to the cost of the hardware, and much, much more if you want the ultimate in color workstations. Therefore, many installations have only monochrome or gray-scale systems. By requiring color, you will be precluding many potential users from ever using your software.

In addition, a significant number of people are partially or fully color blind. Others have a hard time differentiating between various hues—especially variations on blue. When designing a user interface, you must keep all these factors in mind.

Color, of course, can certainly add meaning to displays of data. Color, for example, can highlight dangerous areas in red on an industrial factory application. When all is said and done, color interfaces usually look better than monochrome. So using color is a trade-off: your interfaces look better in color, but the potential audience for an application may not be able to appreciate a color interface or may not have the computer hardware to do so.

When you design the interface, following a few guidelines will certainly help in this trade-off:

- Design the original interface in monochrome (black-and-white). That way, you can still produce a monochrome version. One worthwhile piece of advice (from Apple Computer's *Inside Macintosh* series) is to color the black bits only. That way the interface will still work in black-and-white. In the previous examples, checking the macro `DefaultDepth` for a value of one means the program is running on a monochrome screen.

- Avoid going hog-wild with colors. Unless you are attempting realistic image visualization, stick to a maximum of about eight colors. Again, too many colors will confuse the user. (However, if you are ray-tracing 3D views, you will want to use all the colors available on your screen.)

- Design your code to be as portable as possible. Stick to the most common areas of color handling in X. This means you won't take full advantage of everyone's display (especially if they use Silicon Graphics workstations). But your applications will be more likely to work, and work well, on different hardware. One of the prime advantages of the X Window System is that it runs on many different workstations by many different vendors.

Most of the different workstations that the X Window System can run on are built on an RGB color model, which means that red, green, and blue phosphors within each pixel are combined to form the different hues on the screen. Electron beams excite the phosphors, which in turn provide the color. Simultaneously exciting all phosphors produces a white pixel; when all are unexcited, you're left with a black pixel.

Color displays use multiple bits within a pixel to further specify colors. These bits are also known as **planes**, and the most common color display contains between four and eight planes. You have access to many colors, even though a limited number of them are actually on the display at a time.

In contrast, monochrome displays only have one plane, and the phosphor is either on or off. Gray scales are simulated by making the red, green, and blue values equal, as shown in Appendix A.

At the other end of the spectrum, there are more and more workstations with up to 24 planes. These are high-performance systems; you can see many more colors at a time at a greater resolution, but the trade-off is the overwhelming complexity of administering these screens. And, of course, these monitors are rather costly.

Obviously, there must be a way for the base system to tell X its type. This is done through the **visual class.** There are six visual classes in X: `GrayScale`, `PseudoColor`, `DirectColor`, `StaticGray`, `StaticColor`, and `TrueColor`. The static visual classes are read-only, while the others are read/write. Having read/write classes normally means that you can manipulate aspects of the visual class through your application programs.

If you want to get technical, you could write sections of your code that would handle each visual class differently to get the most performance out of each system. This means, however that you would essentially be duplicating your graphics code six times over with a very limited payback.

Instead, it would be much easier to follow certain conventions and try to use the system defaults wherever possible, thereby making your applications work on any display monitor running X.

COLORMAPS IN X

The X Window System uses the concept of a `Colormap` to define the colors available to an application program. You need a `Colormap` to specify the colors you want to appear. In most cases, the standard `Colormap` for a given workstation screen should be used. The easiest way to get a `Colormap` of your own is to use the default `Colormap`, as in the following:

```
#include <X11/Xlib.h>

        .
        .
        .
        Display         *theDisplay;
        int             theScreen;
        Colormap        theColormap;    /* -- default System color map */
        .
        .
        .
        theDepth        = DefaultDepth( theDisplay, theScreen );
        theColormap     = DefaultColormap( theDisplay, theScreen );
```

In the previous example, note that if theDepth is 1, then you have a monochrome system, which makes the Colormap pretty useless. It is a good idea, and a most portable idea, to use the default Colormap. Some workstations have a hardware read-only Colormap, one that you cannot modify. Other workstations have limited memory resources; don't forget that color normally takes up a lot of RAM. If at all possible, try to use the default system Colormap.

EXAMPLE 1: DRAWING A LINE IN RED

Once you have a Colormap, you must accomplish three things to set up a user drawing a line in red (or any other color). First, you need to find a match in the X server's color data base for the name of your color. Second, you must allocate (or find) a color cell in your Colormap for the color. Third, you need to set the foreground color in a graphics context to the color you want to draw in. Note the following example:

```
.
.
.

GC      theGC;
char    *theName = "red";

XColor          theRGBColor, theHardwareColor;
int             theStatus;

if ( theDepth > 1 )
        {
        theStatus = XLookupColor( theDisplay,
                        theColormap,
                        theName,
                        &theRGBColor,
                        &theHardwareColor );
```

First, find a match in the X server's system-wide color data base for the name of your color, using the function XLookupColor. XLookupColor tries to find a match between the text name of the color, stored in theName, and an entry in the system color data base (usually stored in a file /usr/lib/X11/rgb, with /usr/lib/X11/rgb.txt being an ASCII version that humans can read). If there is a match, XLookupColor will return a nonzero value. Appendix A contains a list of the color names supported by the default color data base. This color data base may seem strange, as its values were originally based on a particular graphics display in use at MIT and used by the makers of X.

Also, 66 is a strange number of colors because you usually see 64 or 256 or 16 colors or some other power of two. In addition, the 66 different colors include many variations of blue. But, strange as it may seem, these colors are replicated on most X color systems, and from the list of 66 colors, you should be able to choose seven or so for your interface.

When using these colors, do not enter any spaces in the names. Also, case does not matter, as MediumSlateBlue and MEDIUMSLATEBLUE should resolve to the same color. Most people find MediumSlateBlue easier to read, though.

`theRGBColor` returns the RGB (or Red-Green-Blue) components from the color data base. `theRGBColor` is of the `XColor` structure type, which is defined as follows:

```
typedef struct
        {
        unsigned long    pixel;
        unsigned short   red;
        unsigned short   green;
        unsigned short   blue;
        char             flags;
        char             pad;
        } XColor;
```

In this example, the red, green, and blue fields are the most important.

`theHardwareColor` returns the RGB components of the closest hardware match for the asked-for color. Sometimes this match may not be the best (especially with a pink that doesn't seem too pink); however, it is the default, and it is widely available on most X servers. The MIT X Consortium has asked that aesthetic-minded users come up with better color matches for various color systems—but with few people volunteering for the work. You get what you pay for, or in this case probably much more than you paid for, as the X Window System is normally available free of charge or for the cost of a tape.

After a color name has been looked up in the system color data base, a particular color cell must be found in the application's `Colormap`. In the following example, `theHardwareColor` is used, with the function `XAllocColor`, to either find an existing color cell in `theColormap` or to allocate a new cell for that color.

```
.
.
.
theStatus = XAllocColor( theDisplay,
                theColormap,
                &theHardwareColor );
```

If `XAllocColor` returns a nonzero value, then the call was successful. Once the call is successful, you have a pixel value that is an entry into `theColormap` where the new color is located. Previously, two standard pixel values, `White-Pixel` and `BlackPixel`, were used. Now the colored pixel value can be used in the same way. The function `XSetForeground`, as in Chapter 2, will set a graphics context to use the given foreground color pixel value—in this case, the result of the `XAllocColor` call. Now, the drawing calls introduced in Chapter 2 can be used to draw lines in red, green, or NavyBlue.

```
GC              theGC;
.
.
.
/*
**      Set the foreground color
*/
XSetForeground( theDisplay,
        theGC,
        theHardwareColor.pixel );
```

And that is all there is to starting out with color in X, which may be all you need for your applications.

Example 1 Source Code

The first example introduces a new source file, `colorx.c`, which will contain all color-specific functions for the programs to be developed in this book. Example 1 begins with a new function, `setColorWithName`, that takes a given graphics context and tries to set the GC's color to the color name passed to the function. The `setColorWithName` function uses the method previously outlined to set up the colors, as in the following example:

```
setColorWithName( theGC, theName )

GC      theGC;
char    *theName;
```

The file `initx.c` is modified to include an initialization to set up the default `Colormap` into a globally accessed variable, `theColormap`. The file `test3.c` draws the same items drawn in Chapter 2 but sets each one in a different color. If your X server is running color, you should see a reasonable approximation of red, green, and blue. The files `quitx.c` and `drawx.c` remain the same as they were in Chapter 2.

The contents of the file `colorx.c` are as follows:

```
/*
**      colorx.c
**      Sets up colors
**
*/

#include   <X11/Xlib.h>
#include   <X11/Xutil.h>

/*
**      test program external GLOBALS
*/

extern  Display        *theDisplay;
extern  Colormap       theColormap;
extern  int            theDepth;       /* -- How many color planes, if any? */
extern  unsigned long  theBlackPixel;  /* -- System drawing color           */
extern  unsigned long  theWhitePixel;  /* -- System background color        */


/*
**      setColorWithName sets the given graphics context GC with the foreground
**      color named by the English text name.
**
**      It is not very efficient.  Ideally, all colors would be
**      allocated at the beginning of a program.
**
*/

setColorWithName( theGC, theName )
```

continued...

...from previous page

```
GC      theGC;
char    theName[];

{       /* -- function setColorWithName */
        XColor  theRGBColor, theHardwareColor;
        int     theStatus;


        if ( theDepth > 1 )
                {
                theStatus = XLookupColor( theDisplay,
                                theColormap,
                                theName,
                                &theRGBColor,
                                &theHardwareColor );

                if ( theStatus != 0 )
                        {
                        theStatus = XAllocColor( theDisplay,
                                        theColormap,
                                        &theHardwareColor );

                        if ( theStatus != 0 )
                                {
                                /*
                                **      Set the foreground color
                                */
                                XSetForeground( theDisplay,
                                        theGC,
                                        theHardwareColor.pixel );
                                XFlush( theDisplay );
                                }

                        }

                }

}       /* -- function setColorWithName */



/*
**      end of file colorx.c
**
*/
```

The contents of the file `initx.c` are as follows:

```
/*
**      initx.c
**
**      Initialization code to talk to the X server
**
*/

#include  <X11/Xlib.h>
#include  <X11/Xutil.h>
#include  <stdio.h>

/*
**      Program-wide Globals.
**
*/

Display         *theDisplay;     /* -- Which display                   */
int             theScreen;       /* -- Which screen on the display     */
int             theDepth;        /* -- Number of color planes          */
unsigned long   theBlackPixel;   /* -- System "Black" color            */
unsigned long   theWhitePixel;   /* -- System "White" color            */
Colormap        theColormap;     /* -- default System color map        */

/*
**      initX()
**      Sets up the connection to the X server and stores information
**      about the environment.
**
*/

initX()

{       /* -- function initX  */

        /*
        **      1) Establish a connection to the X Server.  The connection
        **      is asked for on the local server for the local display.
        **
        */

        theDisplay = XOpenDisplay( NULL );

        /* -- Check if the connection was made */
        if ( theDisplay == NULL )
                {
                fprintf( stderr,
                   "ERROR: Cannot establish a connection to the X Server %s\n",
                   XDisplayName( NULL ) );
                exit( 1 );
                }
```

continued...

...from previous page

```
        /*
        **      2) Check for the default screen and color plane depth.
        **      If theDepth == 1, then we have a monochrome system.

        **
        */

        theScreen     = DefaultScreen( theDisplay );
        theDepth      = DefaultDepth( theDisplay, theScreen );
        theBlackPixel = BlackPixel( theDisplay, theScreen );
        theWhitePixel = WhitePixel( theDisplay, theScreen );
        theColormap   = DefaultColormap( theDisplay, theScreen );

}       /* -- function initX  */



/*
**      getXInfo prints information to the starting terminal
**      (usually an xterm) about the current X Window display
**      and screen.
*/

getXInfo()

{       /* -- function getXInfo */

        /*
        **      You will find many funny values when you check the X
        **      information below.  It should be something to the tune of:
        **      MIT X Consortium (vendor)
        **      3 (vendor release)
        **      X11 R3 (or R2, the Version and Revision numbers).
        **      But, on most implementations, this information
        **      does not seem to jibe.
        **      On the generic MIT X Consortium release for
        **      X11R3, you might see X11R0, with a vendor release # of 3
        **
        */

        printf( "%s version %d of the X Window System, X%d R%d\n",
                ServerVendor( theDisplay ),
                VendorRelease( theDisplay ),
                ProtocolVersion( theDisplay ),
                ProtocolRevision( theDisplay ) );

        /*
        **      Now, print some more detailed information about the
        **      display.
        **
        */
```

continued...

...from previous page

```
        if ( theDepth == 1 )
                {
                printf( "Color plane depth.............%d (monochrome)\n",
                        theDepth );
                }
        else
                {
                printf( "Color plane depth.............%d\n",
                        theDepth );
                }

        printf( "Display Width................%d\n",
                 DisplayWidth( theDisplay, theScreen ) );
        printf( "Display Height...............%d\n",
                 DisplayHeight( theDisplay, theScreen ) );


        printf( "The display %s\n", XDisplayName( theDisplay ) );

}       /* -- function getXInfo */


/*
**      end of file initx.c
**
*/
```

The contents of the test file `test3.c` are as follows:

```
/*
**      test3.c
**
**      Chapter 3, Example 1
**
*/

#include   <X11/Xlib.h>

/*
**      external GLOBALS for the test program
*/

extern  Display         *theDisplay;


main()
```

continued...

...from previous page

```
{
        Window          theWindow, openWindow;
        GC              theGC;

        /*
        **      Set up our connection to X
        */
        initX();


        /*
        **      Get some info on the display and print it out
        */

        getXInfo();


        /*
        **      Open a window
        */

        theWindow = openWindow( 100, 100,       /* -- x, y, location   */
                                300, 300,       /* -- width, height    */
                                0,              /* -- NOT a pop-up     */
                                &theGC );       /* -- Graphics Context */


        /*
        ** Try out the drawing commands, in this example,
        ** we draw and fill ovals, instead of rectangles.
        **
        */

        setColorWithName( theGC, "red" );
        drawLine( theWindow, theGC,
                10, 10, 100, 100 );

        setColorWithName( theGC, "green" );
        drawOval( theWindow, theGC,
                100, 100, 100, 100 );

        setColorWithName( theGC, "blue" );
        fillOval( theWindow, theGC,
                200, 200, 100, 100 );

        XFlush( theDisplay );


        sleep( 10 );
```

continued...

...from previous page

```
        /*
        **      Close the connection to the X Server
        */
        XDestroyWindow( theDisplay, theWindow );
        quitX();

}


/*
**      end of file test3.c
*/
```

EXAMPLE 2: USING MORE COLORS, AGAIN AND AGAIN

If you intend to create an efficient, speedy application (and who doesn't?), the time it takes to convert an English color name like "LimeGreen" into a color representation may simply be too long should you plan on using multiple colors, such as in a drawing program (and especially for a color like LimeGreen). Constantly looking up the various color names in the color data base will slow your system down, as will constantly trying to reallocate color cells. Instead, the second example initializes the default color data base at the beginning of the program and places the results into an array of pixel values, one for each of the 66 default colors. This means that the index into the array can specify any color for use later on.

In this chapter's second example, the Xlib functions previously introduced are reused, this time to set up a color array from the default `Colormap`. The function `initDefaultColors` is placed in the file `colorx.c`. This function should be called near the beginning of a program to set up a color array for later use. It goes through an initialized array of character strings containing the color names from Appendix A. You may want to order these colors in a special manner, or, to save typing, only include the color names you want. (Note that gray can be spelled "gray" or "grey.") Once this color array is set up, colors can be referred to by their position within this color array. This position is an integer value. To help the readability of your programs, you may want to create a C header file and define symbol names for the color text names, as in the following example:

```
#define    RED        49
```

Defining symbol names for the color text names will make your code much easier to read and to program. For this example, however, no header file was created, to save on the already prodigious typing chores.

`initDefaultColors` takes no parameters. It has special code to check for a monochrome system (if `theDepth` equals 1) and then sets all colors except white to be black. This strategy follows from the advice mentioned earlier in this chapter: Color the black pixels only. This program should work just fine on either a monochrome or color system.

Anytime after `initDefaultColors` is called, you can use the new function `setColor` to set a graphics context to a given color. Instead of `setColorWithName`, which takes an English name for the color, you pass `setColor` a number that is an index into the color array `thePixels` (an array of 66 unsigned long integers). For example, the number 28 is the index into the color LimeGreen (or the closest approximation to LimeGreen supported by your system). LimeGreen has a wonderfully tacky look reminiscent of the 1970s, which is why that color is brought out for special notice.

`setColor` takes the following parameters:

```
setColor( theGC, colorNumber )

GC      theGC;
int     colorNumber;
```

`setColorWithName`, introduced previously in Example 1, is modified to look into the new array set up in the current example instead of allocating a color cell each time.

The second example program modifies the `test3.c` file to display all the default colors in a window, which gives you a good feel for the available default choices.

Example 2 Source Code

The files `colorx.c` and `test3.c` are changed in the second example. The files `initx.c`, `quitx.c`, and `drawx.c` remain the same.

The contents of file `colorx.c` are as follows:

```
/*
**      colorx.c
**      Sets up colors
**
*/

#include    <X11/Xlib.h>
#include    <X11/Xutil.h>

/*
**      test program external GLOBALS
*/

extern  Display         *theDisplay;
extern  Colormap        theColormap;
extern  int             theDepth;       /* -- How many color planes, if any? */
extern  unsigned long   theBlackPixel;  /* -- System drawing color           */
extern  unsigned long   theWhitePixel;  /* -- System background color        */


/*
**      Set up English text for colors
**
*/

#define                 maxPixels       66

unsigned long           thePixels[ maxPixels ];
char                    *theColorNames[ maxPixels ] =
                        {       "Aquamarine",           /* -- 0  */
                                "Black",                /* -- 1  */
                                "Blue",                 /* -- 2  */
                                "BlueViolet",           /* -- 3  */
                                "Brown",                /* -- 4  */
                                "CadetBlue",            /* -- 5  */
                                "Coral",                /* -- 6  */
                                "CornflowerBlue",       /* -- 7  */
                                "Cyan",                 /* -- 8  */
                                "DarkGreen",            /* -- 9  */
                                "DarkOliveGreen",       /* -- 10 */
                                "DarkOrchid",           /* -- 11 */
                                "DarkSlateBlue",        /* -- 12 */
                                "DarkSlateGrey",        /* -- 13 */
                                "DarkTurquoise",        /* -- 14 */
                                "DimGrey",              /* -- 15 */
                                "Firebrick",            /* -- 16 */
                                "ForestGreen",          /* -- 17 */
                                "Gold",                 /* -- 18 */
```

continued...

...from previous page

```
                "Goldenrod",            /* -- 19  */
                "Grey",                 /* -- 20  */
                "Green",                /* -- 21  */
                "GreenYellow",          /* -- 22  */
                "IndianRed",            /* -- 23  */
                "Khaki",                /* -- 24  */
                "LightBlue",            /* -- 25  */
                "LightGrey",            /* -- 26  */
                "LightSteelBlue",       /* -- 27  */
                "LimeGreen",            /* -- 28  */
                "Magenta",              /* -- 29  */
                "Maroon",               /* -- 30  */
                "MediumAquamarine",     /* -- 31  */
                "MediumBlue",           /* -- 32  */
                "MediumForestGreen",    /* -- 33  */
                "MediumGoldenrod",      /* -- 34  */
                "MediumOrchid",         /* -- 35  */
                "MediumSeaGreen",       /* -- 36  */
                "MediumSlateBlue",      /* -- 37  */
                "MediumSpringGreen",    /* -- 38  */
                "MediumTurquoise",      /* -- 39  */
                "MediumVioletRed",      /* -- 40  */
                "MidnightBlue",         /* -- 41  */
                "Navy",                 /* -- 42  */
                "Orange",               /* -- 43  */
                "OrangeRed",            /* -- 44  */
                "Orchid",               /* -- 45  */
                "PaleGreen",            /* -- 46  */
                "Pink",                 /* -- 47  */
                "Plum",                 /* -- 48  */
                "Red",                  /* -- 49  */
                "Salmon",               /* -- 50  */
                "SeaGreen",             /* -- 51  */
                "Sienna",               /* -- 52  */
                "SkyBlue",              /* -- 53  */
                "SlateBlue",            /* -- 54  */
                "SpringGreen",          /* -- 55  */
                "SteelBlue",            /* -- 56  */
                "Tan",                  /* -- 57  */
                "Thistle",              /* -- 58  */
                "Turquoise",            /* -- 59  */
                "Violet",               /* -- 60  */
                "VioletRed",            /* -- 61  */
                "Wheat",                /* -- 62  */
                "White",                /* -- 63  */
                "Yellow",               /* -- 64  */
                "YellowGreen"           /* -- 65  */
        };
```

continued...

...from previous page

```
/*
**      setColorWithName sets the given graphics context GC with the foreground
**      color named by the English text name.
**
**      It is not very efficient.  Ideally, all colors would be
**      allocated at the beginning of a program.
**
*/


setColorWithName( theGC, theName )

GC      theGC;
char    theName[];

{       /* -- function setColorWithName */
        int             i;

        i = 0;
        while( ( strcmp( theName, theColorNames[ i ] ) != 0 ) &&
             ( i < maxPixels ) )
                {
                i++;
                }

        if ( i < maxPixels )
                {
                /* -- Set the foreground color */
                XSetForeground( theDisplay,
                                theGC,
                                thePixels[ i ] );

                }

}       /* -- function setColorWithName */


/*
**      initDefaultColors Attempts to set up a local color table with
**      the default X11 colors.  After this, colors can be accessed
**      by a color number, rather than an English name.
**      Note that this function tries to use the default
**      color table.  On a monochrome system, all colors
**      will turn into BlackPixel.  The background white
**      color will turn into WhitePixel.
**
*/
```

continued...

...from previous page

```
initDefaultColors()

{       /* -- function initDefaultColors */
        XColor              theRGBColor, theHardwareColor;
        int                 theStatus;
        int                 i;


        if ( theDepth > 1 )
                {
                for( i = 0; i < maxPixels; i++ )
                        {
                        theStatus = XLookupColor( theDisplay,
                                            theColormap,
                                            theColorNames[ i ],
                                            &theRGBColor,
                                            &theHardwareColor );

                        if ( theStatus != 0 )
                                {
                                theStatus = XAllocColor( theDisplay,
                                                theColormap,
                                                &theHardwareColor );

                                if ( theStatus != 0 )
                                        {
                                        thePixels[ i ] = theHardwareColor.pixel;
                                        }
                                else
                                        {
                                        thePixels[ i ] =  theBlackPixel;
                                        }
                                }
                        }
                }
        else
                {
                /*
                **      Monochrome system
                */

                for( i = 0; i < maxPixels; i++ )
                        {
                        if ( strcmp( "white", theColorNames[ i ] ) == 0 )
                                {
                                thePixels[ i ] = theWhitePixel;
                                }
```

continued...

...from previous page

```
                        else
                                {
                                thePixels[ i ] = theBlackPixel;
                                }
                        }
                }

}       /* -- function initDefaultColors */


/*
**      setColor sets the GC theGC to have a foreground color of colorNumber.
**
*/


setColor( theGC, colorNumber )

GC      theGC;
int     colorNumber;

{       /* -- function setColor */

        if ( ( colorNumber < maxPixels ) && ( colorNumber >= 0 ) )
                {
                /* -- Set the foreground color */
                XSetForeground( theDisplay,
                        theGC,
                        thePixels[ colorNumber ] );

                }

}       /* -- function setColor */

/* ________________________________________________________________ */


/*
**      end of file colorx.c
**
*/
```

The contents of file `test3.c` are as follows:

```
/*
**      test3.c
**
**      Chapter 3, Example 2
**
*/

#include    <X11/Xlib.h>

/*
**      external GLOBALS for the test program
*/

extern  Display         *theDisplay;


main()

{
        Window  theWindow, openWindow;
        GC      theGC;
        int     counter;
        int     x, y;


        /*
        **      Set up our connection to X
        */
        initX();


        /*
        **      Get some info on the display and print it out
        */

        getXInfo();


        /*
        **      Set up the default colors
        */

        initDefaultColors();

        /*
        **      Open a window
        */
```

continued...

...from previous page

```
        theWindow = openWindow( 100, 100,           /* -- x, y, location   */
                                400, 400,           /* -- width, height    */
                                0,                  /* -- NOT a pop-up     */
                                &theGC );           /* -- Graphics Context */


        sleep( 4 );     /* -- wait to get window on screen */

        /*
        ** Try out the drawing commands, in color.
        **
        */

        x = 1;
        y = 1;

        for( counter = 0; counter < 66; counter++ )
                {
                setColor( theGC, counter );
                fillOval( theWindow,
                        theGC,
                        x, y,
                        20, 20 );

                x += 30;
                if ( x > 270 )
                        {
                        x  = 1;
                        y += 40;
                        }
                }

        XFlush( theDisplay );



        sleep( 10 );

        /*
        **      Close the connection to the X Server
        */
        XDetroyWindow( theDisplay, theWindow ):
        quitX();


}
/*
**      end of file test3.c
*/
```

SUMMARY

This introduction to X color is purposely brief, concentrating on the essential details. This topic becomes extremely complex if you choose to delve farther into color with X and is beyond the scope of this book.

- If at all possible, try to use the default `Colormap` and design your applications to work in monochrome or color.
- If you use the default `Colormap`, the first step for drawing in color is to find a match for the color name in the system-wide color data base with `XLookupColor`.
- Then, allocate a color cell (or find a matching cell) with the function `XAllocColor`.
- Finally, set a graphics context so that its foreground color is the color you want. Draw using this graphics context.

Xlib Functions and Macros Introduced in This Chapter

```
DefaultColormap
XAllocColor
XLookupColor
```

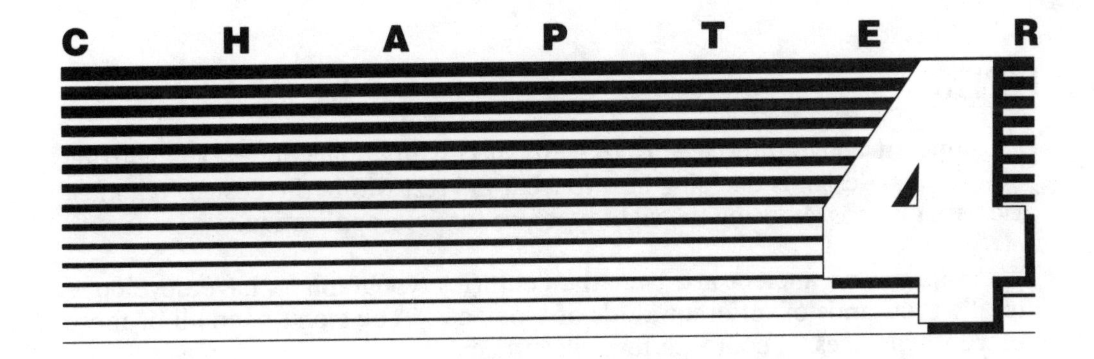

USING TEXT

The most common operation in a windowing system is drawing text. Nearly every application program, large or small, relies on text in one way or another. This chapter discusses how X treats text and how to use attractive text displays to your advantage.

FONTS

Designing attractive interfaces is a key to successful applications. The starting point for any design is deciding how to treat the text within the design. In most cases, that means choosing the right typeface for your application.

Typography is an ancient art; over the centuries typographers have developed literally thousands of different kinds of typefaces. You won't need all of these different typefaces, of course; a few will suffice.

You gain access to these different typefaces by loading fonts. A complete set of characters of one size of one typeface—including upper- and lowercase letters, punctuation marks, and numerals—is called a **font**. All fonts in X are **bitmaps**; each character has a specific bit pattern within the font. Each face, style, and size corresponds to at least one font—e.g., Times at 25 pixels high and Times at 12 pixels high are two different fonts. This is different from Adobe's PostScript-defined fonts. Adobe fonts are described by an outline, which can be resized, depending on the dimensions defined by the application, and later filled in. Different fonts and typefaces have different characteristics:

- Fonts are either **serif** or **sans serif**. Serif characters have a smaller line that finishes off a large stroke, such as the strokes at the top and bottom of the letter "I"; sans serif fonts do not have these finishing strokes. This text, for instance, is set in a serif face, while the headlines are set in a sans serif face.

- A font can have **proportional** or **fixed** character widths. A fixed-width font allows the same width for each character: for example, in a fixed-width font, an "i" takes up as much space as an "m" does. A fixed-width font emulates a typewriter. A proportional-width font emulates typeset material, such as the letters on this page. It allows a greater amount of space for wide characters (such as the letter "w") than it does for narrow characters (such as the letter "l").

- Some fonts are better suited to particular tasks than others. For example, the serif font used in this text is easier to read than many sans serif faces. But more elaborate serif fonts are more suited to special effects or headlines, as are all bold faces. You want to make your text as easy to read as possible; you must know which fonts to use for emphasis and know which fonts to use for readability.

- Additionally, in X, there are **single-byte** (8-bit) fonts and **two-byte** (16-bit) fonts. The single-byte fonts can handle up to 256 characters, while the two-byte fonts can handle up to 65,536 characters. Only one two-byte font (the Kanji font used for a Japanese terminal emulator) is included in X.

Loading Fonts

Before a font can be used by your program, it must be loaded into the X server. The X server then shares the font among all programs that want to use it. When all references to a font are over, the X server can free up the memory and data structures associated with the font. Thus, loading a font does not load the font into your application program; the font is loaded into the server. To load a font, use `XLoadQueryFont`.

```
Display         *theDisplay;
XFontStruct     *fontStruct;
char            *fontName;
.
.
.
fontStruct      = XLoadQueryFont( theDisplay, fontName );

if ( fontStruct != 0 )
        {
        /*
        **      Use the font...
        */
        }
else
        {
        /*
        **      The program could NOT load the font;
        **      an error has occurred.
        */
        }
```

`XLoadQueryFont` returns a pointer to an `XFontStruct` structure. This structure contains a host of information about the font. The most useful information tells how large the font is; however, if you don't care about the size of the font, you can use the function `XLoadFont` to just determine a font ID. (With `XLoadQueryFont`, the font ID is stored in the `fid` field of the `XFontStruct` struct, or `fontStruct->fid`.) Note that the font ID allows you to draw text but does not have enough information to get the font's size.

```
Display         *theDisplay;
char            *fontName;
Font            theFont;
.
.
.
theFont = XLoadFont( theDisplay, theName );
```

Normally, you will want to use the function XLoadQueryFont rather than just use XLoadFont to get the font ID.

Setting Up the Graphics Context

To draw with a newly loaded font, you must set a graphics context in which to use that font when drawing. To do this, use the function XSetFont:

```
Display         *theDisplay;
XFontStruct     *fontStruct;
GC              theGC;
.
.
.
XSetFont( theDisplay, theGC, fontStruct->fid );
```

Drawing Text

Once you have set up a graphics context with a font, you can start to draw text. X has two main functions for drawing text: XDrawString and XDrawImageString. The main difference between these two functions is that XDrawString only draws the foreground bits of a character, while XDrawImageString draws both the foreground and the background (the foreground in the GC's foreground color and the background in the GC's background color). In Figure 4.1, XDrawImageString displays all the letters of the string. XDrawString, however, does not overwrite the background bits of the string.

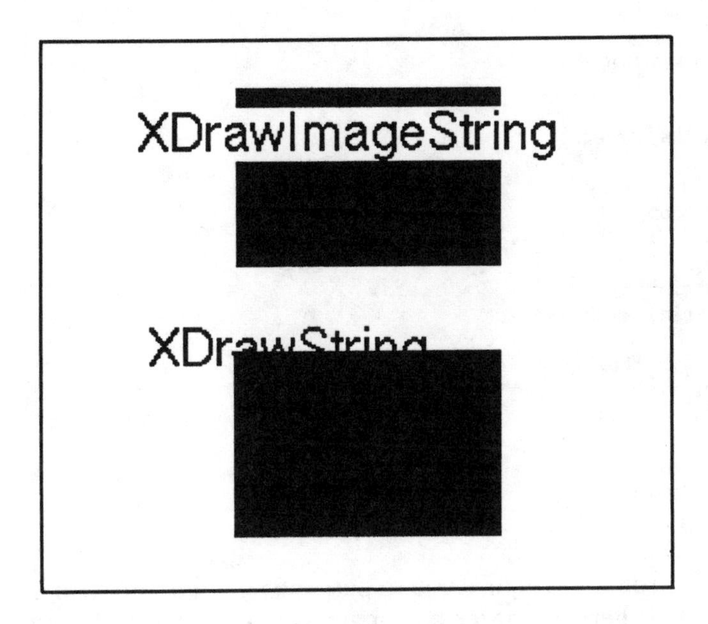

Figure 4.1 *XDrawImageString and XDrawString*

```
Display         *theDisplay;
Drawable        theWindow;
GC              theGC;
int             x, y;
char            *theString;
int             theStringLength;
.
.
.
/*
**      Assuming theString points to a character string,
**      get the length of the string it points to.
*/
theStringLength = strlen( theString );
```

continued...

...from previous page

```
/*
**      Draw the string.
*/
XDrawString( theDisplay,
        theWindow,
        theGC,
        x, y,
        theString,
        theStringLength );

XDrawImageString( theDisplay,
        theWindow,
        theGC,
        x, y,
        theString,
        theStringLength );
```

All draw string routines require you to pass the length of the string. The Xlib call will assume that there are at least as many characters in the string as you tell it. In other words, don't lie to the server.

Where the Text Is Drawn

X draws text starting at an x, y pixel location. The x coordinate location is at the beginning (far left) of the text string. The y coordinate location starts at the text baseline (see Figure 4.2). Letters that drop below the baseline, such as "p," "q," and "j," drop below the y coordinate location given to `XDrawString`. Thus, letters can and will go both above and below the y position.

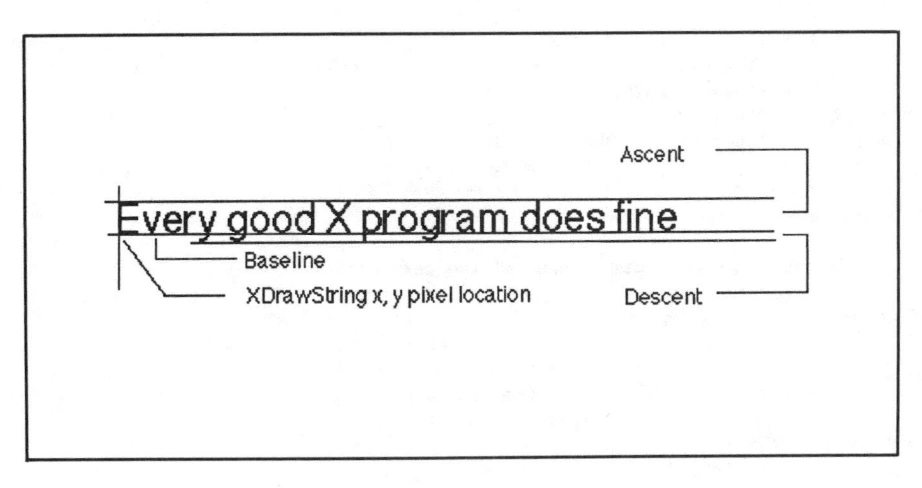

Figure 4.2 *X text baseline*

Finding Out How Large a Font Is

To help position a text string, it is a good idea to figure out how large the string will appear in a given font. For a fixed-width font, such as 9x15 in X, the width of any text string will be the number of characters times the width of one character:

```
theWidth = strlen( theString) * oneCharWidth;
```

For proportional-width fonts, such as variable in X, though, this is not the case. As mentioned earlier in this chapter, in a proportional-width font, letters such as "W" and "M" are far wider than letters such as "i," "l," and "t."

In all cases, to find out the width of a text string in a given font, use the `XTextWidth` function.

```
int             theWidth;
int             theCharLength;
XFontStruct     *fontStruct;
char            *theString = "How wide am I?";
.
.
.
/*
**      Get the length, in characters, of the text string.
*/
theCharLength = strlen( theString );

/*
**      Get the width, in pixels, of the text string.
*/
theWidth= XTextWidth( fontStruct,
                theString,
                theCharLength );
```

Finding the height of a character string is a bit different from finding the width. In most cases, what you want is the possible height of the font, rather than just the height of the particular string because most checks on a font height are to determine the vertical spacing of lines of text (e.g., line 1 should not write over line 2).

To find the possible height of a font, you can access elements of the `XFontStruct`.

```
int             theFontHeight;
XFontStruct     *fontStruct;
.
.
.
theFontHeight = fontStruct->ascent + fontStruct->descent;
```

The `XFontStruct` in its entirety (from the include file `X11/Xlib.h`), resembles the following:

```
typedef struct {
    XExtData     *ext_data;       /* -- Place for X extension data */
    Font         fid;             /* -- Font ID for the font */
    unsigned     direction;       /* -- "hint" for direction the font is drawn */
    unsigned     min_char_or_byte2;      /* -- first character */
    unsigned     max_char_or_byte2;      /* -- last character  */
    unsigned     min_byte1;       /* -- first row of chars that exists */
    unsigned     max_byte1;       /* -- last row of chars that exists  */
    Bool         all_chars_exist; /* -- flag if all chars have non-zero size */
    unsigned     default_char;    /* -- char to print for an undefined char */
    int          n_properties;    /* -- how many properties there are */
    XFontProp    *properties;     /* -- pointer to array of additional props */
    XCharStruct  min_bounds;      /* -- minimum bounds over all existing char  */
    XCharStruct  max_bounds;      /* -- minimum bounds over all existing char  */
    XCharStruct  *per_char;       /* -- first_char to last_char information */
    int          ascent;          /* -- extent above baseline for spacing */
    int          descent;         /* -- descent below baseline for spacing */
} XFontStruct;
```

Freeing Up Fonts

When you are done using a font, tell the X server. This way, the X server can make the most efficient use of the limited resources (such as memory) available in the workstation. Two functions free up the font, `XFreeFont` and `XUnloadFont`. Use `XFreeFont` if you originally loaded the font into an `XFontStruct` structure (with `XLoadQueryFont`). Use `XUnloadFont` if you originally loaded the font and just used the font ID (with `XLoadFont`).

```
Display         *theDisplay;
XFontStruct     *fontStruct;
.
.
.
XFreeFont( theDisplay, fontStruct );

Display         *theDisplay;
Font            theFont;
.
.
.
XUnloadFont( theDisplay, theFont );
```

As a general rule, always try to free up resources in the X server when you are done using them.

Tips on Using Fonts

When people inexperienced with design principles suddenly have access to many different fonts, they usually go wild in their use of different typefaces. The end result, unfortunately, is usually a very unattractive design, resembling a ransom note made up of disparate letter clips from different newspapers and magazines. Aesthetically speaking, therefore, it is a good idea to avoid using very many fonts. If the output looks like a ransom note, it probably won't look professional unless you are aiming for a certain effect, such as laughter from your users. For best results, generally stick to one font per window and two fonts maximum. Aim for an integrated look and feel to your software. Try to stick to standard fonts, the most likely fonts to be available on the greatest number of systems. Use a special larger font for emphasis.

Finding the Available Fonts

A standard X application program called `xlsfonts` will list the available fonts on a workstation. Using this program will tell you which fonts are available to the system. For example, the following command,

```
% xlsfonts -l
```

might list the following fonts:

```
DIR  MIN  MAX EXIST DFLT PROP ASC DESC NAME
-->    0  127   all    0    7   8    2 6x10
-->    1  127   all   32    7   8    4 6x12
-->    0  127   all    0    6  10    3 6x13
-->    0  127   all    0    7  10    3 8x13
-->    0  127   all    0    7  10    3 8x13bold
-->    0  127   all    0    7  12    3 9x15
-->    1  126  some   32    7  12    2 a14
-->    1  127  some    0    7  20    5 apl-s25
-->    0  108  some    0    7   8   18 arrow3
-->   66   82  some    0    7  23    2 chp-s25
-->   32  107  some    0    7  40   10 chs-s50
-->   65   65   all    0    7   0  155 crturz
-->    0  153   all    0    7  16   17 cursor
-->    1  122  some    0    7  24    5 cyr-s25
-->    1  122  some    0    7  30    8 cyr-s30
-->    1  124  some    0    7  30    8 cyr-s38
```

continued...

...from previous page

```
-->   32  124  some    0   7  36    10 dancer
-->   69   70   all    0   7   0   170 ent
-->   11  126  some    0   7  16     4 fcor-20
-->    1  126  some    0   7  11     2 fg-13
-->   11  126  some    0   7  11     5 fg-16
-->   11  126  some    0   7  13     5 fg-18
-->    1  126  some    0   7  15     5 fg-20
-->   11  127  some    0   7  17     5 fg-22
-->    0  127   all    0   7  20     5 fg-25
-->    1  127   all    0   7  25     5 fg-30
-->    1  127   all    0   7  33     7 fg-40
-->   32  127   all    0   7  20     5 fg1-25
-->    1  126  some    0   7  11     2 fgb-13
-->    1  127   all    0   7  20     5 fgb-25
-->   11  126  some    0   7  20     5 fgb1-25
-->   11  126  some    0   7  20    10 fgb1-30
-->    5  126  some    0   7  15     5 fgi-20
-->   11  126  some    0   7  20     5 fgi1-25
-->    0  127   all    0   7  17     5 fgs-22
-->    0  127   all    0   6  10     3 fixed
-->    1  127   all    0   7  20     5 fqxb-25
-->    1  127  some    0   7  20     5 fr-25
-->    1  127  some    0   7  23    10 fr-33
-->   11  126  some    0   7  20     5 fr1-25
-->    0  127   all    0   7  20     5 fr2-25
-->    0  126   all    0   7  20     5 fr3-25
-->   32  122  some    0   7  24     8 frb-32
-->    1  127  some    0   7  24     9 fri-33
-->   11  126  some    0   7  20     5 fri1-25
-->   32  122  some    0   7  30     5 ger-s35
-->   32  122  some    0   7  20     5 grk-s25
-->   65  122  some    0   7  26     5 grk-s30
-->    2  121  some    0   7  32    13 hbr-s25
-->   38   90  some    0   7  50    14 hbr-s40
-->    1  127  some    0   7  20     5 ipa-s25
--> * 33 *116  some 8481   7  12     2 k14
-->   33   95   all   32   7  12     2 kana14
-->   32  127  some    0   7  50    50 krivo
-->    1  127  some    0   7  25     5 lat-s30
-->    0  126  some    0   7  21     9 met25
-->    0  127   all    0   7   5     0 micro
-->   65   67   all    0   7 143     2 mit
-->   32  127  some    0   7   9     6 oldera
-->    0  125  some    0   7  21     9 plunk
-->    1  126  some   32   7  12     2 r14
-->    1  127  some    0   7  16     0 rot-s16
-->    0  127  some    0   7   3     0 runlen
-->    2  126   all    0   7  11     3 sans12
-->    2  126   all    0   7  11     3 sansb12
-->    2  126   all    0   7  11     3 sansi12
```

continued...

...from previous page

```
-->    2  126   all    0    7  10     3 serif10
-->    2  126   all    0    7  11     3 serif12
-->    2  126   all    0    7  10     3 serifb10
-->    2  126   all    0    7  11     3 serifb12
-->    2  126   all    0    7  10     3 serifi10
-->    2  126   all    0    7  11     3 serifi12
-->   83   84   all    0    7 108   108 stan
-->   32   90   some   0    7  28     0 stempl
-->    1  126   some   0    7   9    12 sub
-->    1  126   some   0    7   0    14 subsub
-->    1  126   some   0    7  28    -7 sup
-->   18  126   all    0    7  36   -22 supsup
-->    1  127   all    0    7  25     5 swd-s30
-->    1  122   some   0    7  20     5 sym-s25
-->   18  125   some   0    7  35    18 sym-s53
-->    1  126   all    0    7  11     3 variable
-->   32  122   some   0    7  29     7 vbee-36
-->    1  126   some   0    7  19     6 vctl-25
-->    1  126   some   0    7  11     2 vg-13
-->    1  126   some   0    7  16     4 vg-20
-->    0  127   all    0    7  20     5 vg-25
-->    2  127   some   0    7  24     7 vg-31
-->    1  127   all    0    7  32     8 vg-40
-->    1  126   some   0    7  20     5 vgb-25
-->    2  127   some   0    7  24     7 vgb-31
-->   16  126   some   0    7  20     5 vgbc-25
-->    1  126   some   0    7  20     5 vgh-25
-->   32  122   some   0    7  16     4 vgi-20
-->    0  127   all    0    7  20     5 vgi-25
-->    2  127   some   0    7  24     7 vgi-31
-->    1  126   some   0    7  32     8 vgl-40
-->    2  127   some   0    7  24     7 vgvb-31
-->    1  127   some   0    7  20     5 vmic-25
-->   26  122   some   0    7  27     9 vply-36
-->    0  126   some   0    7  15     5 vr-20
-->    1  126   some   0    7  21     4 vr-25
-->    1  127   some   0    7  20     7 vr-27
-->    1  127   some   0    7  22     8 vr-30
-->    1  127   all    0    7  25     6 vr-31
-->    1  126   some   0    7  30    10 vr-40
-->    1  126   some   0    7  20     5 vrb-25
-->    1  126   some   0    7  22     8 vrb-30
-->    1  127   some   0    7  25     6 vrb-31
-->    1  126   some   0    7  26     9 vrb-35
-->   14  127   some   0    7  27    10 vrb-37
-->    1  126   some   0    7  20     5 vri-25
-->    1  126   some   0    7  22     8 vri-30
-->    1  127   some   0    7  25     6 vri-31
-->    1  126   some   0    7  33     7 vri-40
-->   24  114   some   0    7 100    12 vsg-114
```

continued...

...from previous page

```
-->   24  114  some   0   7  50   7 vsgn-57
-->   23   96  some   0   7  32   8 vshd-40
-->    0  127   all   0   7  10   3 vtbold
-->    0  127   all   0   7  10   3 vtsingle
-->   32  122  some   0   7  28   9 vxms-37
-->   32  122  some   0   7  35   8 vxms-43
-->    0  127   all   0   7  20   5 xif-s25
```

The previous list names the fonts that should be available on every workstation (the list was taken from an Apple Macintosh IIx); however, while most systems have the font files, not all systems have correctly set up all these fonts. Usually, the problem lies with the font path—for example, the directories that the X server is told to check to find the fonts is not set up for all the fonts. Another problem occurs when font "aliases" are not set up correctly (you'll need to talk to the person who installed X on your workstation to check this one out). Some fonts that seem to be universal are **8x13**, a fixed-width font where each character fits a 8-by-13 pixel cell, **9x15**, and **variable**, a proportional-width font that resembles Helvetica.

An X application called `xfd` (X font displayer) will display the characters in a particular font. Normally, if `xfd` cannot find the font, then your program will not be able to find it either. The following command will create a window and display the characters in the font named "variable."

```
% xfd variable
```

Limited X Server Resources

Some servers, especially for X terminals, simply won't have the resources (mainly enough RAM) to load many different fonts; remember that the X server is a shared resource. X terminals are a brand new class of computers that exist mainly to provide an inexpensive hardware entry point to the X Window System. An X terminal acts much like an ASCII terminal, using another computer for the processing power and the terminal's smarts just for the display—except that the X terminals have a lot more smarts than traditional ASCII terminals. Due to cost constraints, though, most X terminals have a limited amount of RAM. Fonts, like any other X resource, use up RAM. In an X terminal environment, using the least amount of resources is a good idea.

The best advice on the question of fonts is to let the user decide which fonts to use—after all, the customer knows best. If you allow the user to specify the font to use through a command-line argument (covered in more depth in Chapter 8), then it is the user's problem to choose the right font from the user's available fonts. Typically, the command-line option is `-font fontname` (or `-fn fontname`) where "`fontname`" is the actual name of an X font.

Letting the user decide the font is especially useful because X runs on such a variety of hardware. A color Sun 386i, for example, comes with either a 16" or 19" color monitor—both at the same pixel resolution. This means that the dots are much smaller on the 16" monitor. The standard X default font, 8x13, looks tiny on a 16" monitor and is more acceptable on the 19" screen. Users with the smaller screen may opt to use a larger font, such as 9x15, just to be able to read the text. An Apple Macintosh IIx, on the other hand, has a 640-by-480 pixel resolution. On this screen, users typically want to use the smallest fonts available, due to the lower screen resolution.

EXAMPLE PROGRAM

The example program that follows creates a window and then displays some shapes and text in the window. It shows the two main X text routines, `XDrawString` and `XDrawImageString`. The output of `XDrawString` appears only in areas where a shape is not located because `XDrawString` only draws the foreground bits of a character. `XDrawImage String`, on the other hand, draws both the foreground and background bits, so its output is always visible (unless you have the foreground and background pixels set the same).

Example Program Source Code

A new file, `textx.c`, loads a font and sets a window's graphics context to use that font. It returns a pointer to an `XFontStruct` for use in other routines.

The contents of the file `textx.c` are as follows:

```
/*
**      textx.c
**
**      Text Drawing Routines
**
*/

#include   <X11/Xlib.h>

/*
**      GLOBAL display
*/

Display  *theDisplay;

/*
**      initFont()
**
**      Initializes a font for drawing text in for a given graphics
**      context.  If you just use this font for a given GC, then you
**      no longer have to worry about the font.
**
*/

XFontStruct     *
initFont( theGC, fontName )

GC      theGC;
char    fontName[];

{        /* -- function initFont */
        XFontStruct     *fontStruct;

        fontStruct      = XLoadQueryFont( theDisplay, fontName );

        if ( fontStruct != 0 )
                {
                XSetFont( theDisplay, theGC, fontStruct->fid );
                }

        return( fontStruct );

}       /* -- function initFont */

/*
**      end of file textx.c
*/
```

The contents of the test file `test4.c` are as follows:

```
/*
**      Chapter 4, Example 1
**
**      This program pops up a window and then draws into it.
**
*/

#include   <X11/Xlib.h>

/*
**      external GLOBALS from initx.c
*/

extern  Display         *theDisplay;


main()

{
        Window          theWindow, openWindow();
        GC              theGC;
        XFontStruct     *initFont(), *fontStruct;

        /*
        **      Set up our connection to X
        */

        initX();

        /*
        **      Get some info on the display and print it
        */

        getXInfo();

        /*
        **      Set up colors
        */

        initDefaultColors();

        /*
        **      Open a window
        */

        theWindow = openWindow( 100, 100,       /* -- x, y location       */
                                300, 300,       /* -- width, height       */
                                0,              /* -- This is NOT a pop-up */
                                &theGC );       /* -- Graphics Context    */
```

continued...

...from previous page

```
/*
**      Draw into the Window
*/


setColor( theGC, 28 );   /* -- LimeGreen */

drawOval( theWindow, theGC,
        10, 10,          /* -- Starting location in x, y  */
        100, 100 );      /* -- width and height           */

fillRectangle( theWindow, theGC,
        100, 100,        /* -- Starting location in x, y  */
        100, 100 );      /* -- width and height           */


/*
**      Now draw out some text.
*/

fontStruct = initFont( theGC, "variable" );
XDrawImageString( theDisplay,
        theWindow,
        theGC,
        90, 105,
        "Hello there!",
        strlen( "Hello there!" ) );

/*
** XDrawImageString draws both the background and the
** foreground bits of the font.  XDrawString just draws the
** foreground bits. In the example below, the XDrawString will
** be partially obscured.
*/

XDrawString( theDisplay,
        theWindow,
        theGC,
        90, 204,
        "Hello there!",
        strlen( "Hello there!" ) );

/*
**      Send all output to the screen
*/

XFlush( theDisplay );

/*
**      Wait awhile
*/
```

continued...

...from previous page

```
        sleep( 10 );

        /*
        **      Close the connection to the X server.
        */
        XDestroyWindow( theDisplay, theWindow );
        XFreeFont( theDisplay, fontStruct );
        quitX();

}


/*
**      end of file.
*/
```

The contents of the new Makefile are as follows:

```
##      X Project Makefile for Chapter 4, example 1
##
EXEC=   test4
##
## DEFINES
##
##
##      -g = Debugging info
##      -O = optimize (cannot use -g then)
CFLAGS= -O
##
##
##      Libraries
##      X11     X11 graphics library
##
LIBS=   -lX11
##
##
OBJECTS=        initx.o         \
                colorx.o        \
                drawx.o         \
                quitx.o         \
                textx.o         \
                windowx.o       \
                test4.o
```

continued...

...from previous page

```
##
##      Command to compile and link objects together
##
$(EXEC):        $(OBJECTS)
                cc -o $(EXEC) $(OBJECTS) $(LIBS)
##
##
##      end of make file
##
```

SUMMARY

- The X Window System has the ability to use many different typefaces, sizes, and styles, which X calls **text fonts**. X fonts are bitmap images of each character in the font.
- Before using a font, load it into the X server with `XLoadQueryFont` or `XLoadFont`. When finished with the font, free it with `XFreeFont` or `XUnloadFont` (if you used `XloadQueryFont` or `XLoadFont`, respectively).
- To draw with a font in a given window, set the graphics context for the window to use the font, with `XSetFont`.
- `XDrawString` will draw a character string to a given pixel position in a given window on the display. `XDrawImageString` does the same, but it also draws in a background for the characters.
- Unless you are writing a ransom note, avoid abusing fonts. When used correctly, fonts and typefaces can make your user interface cleaner, easier to read, and exciting.

Xlib Functions and Macros Introduced in This Chapter

```
XDrawImageString
XDrawString
XFreeFont
XLoadFont
XLoadQueryFont
XSetFont
XTextWidth
XUnloadFont
```

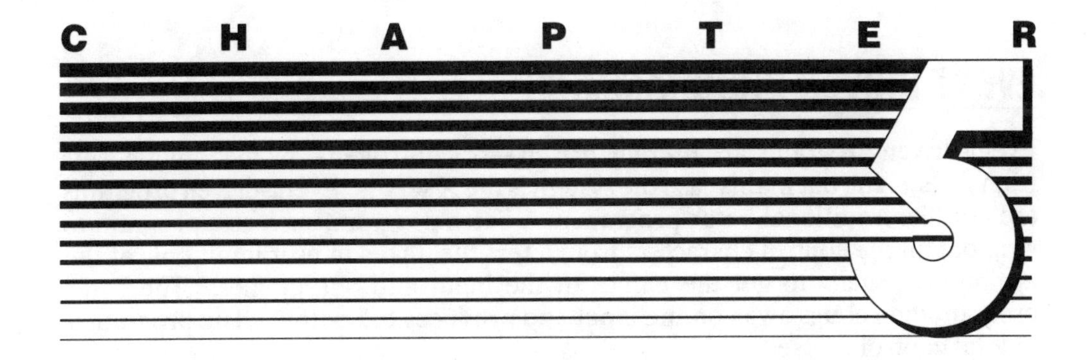

EVENTS

This chapter discusses the concept of **events** in X. In X, an event occurs when the user presses a key on the keyboard. An event also occurs when a mouse button is pressed. Another event occurs when the mouse button is released. An event occurs when a window manager program works with the user to change the size of a window on the screen. And an event occurs when one program sends an event to another program.

X uses the concept of events to let your application programs know what is happening on the display screen. More technically, an event is a packet of information sent to your program by the X server. Many different types of events exist and each one interprets the contents of the data packet differently. X uses these events to such an extent that your programs will become driven by these events.

EVENT-DRIVEN PROGRAMMING

Event-driven programs are literally driven—or controlled—by incoming events from the system, but in this case the system is the X server. Event-driven programs are not like traditional batch programs. A batch program, such as a program to strip out all the control characters from a text file, takes in user input only at the beginning, usually to get the names of the input and output files. The batch program then chugs away on the input and produces the output. The program is in total control of itself.

In an event-driven program, however, the program cedes control to the user. The user drives the actions of the program through a series of events. The program is really still in control, but it gives users the feeling they are running the show. The big difference with event-driven programming is that events can come in at any time and in any order. This places the meat of most event-driven programs in a central loop that takes each event as it comes in and responds to that event in some way.

It is very important when designing the event-driven user interface to provide some feedback for each user-initiated event. The user needs to know that your program received the event and is doing something. Highlighting a choice or beeping the speaker are two common ways to provide the feedback. This feedback must appear as soon as possible, even if the action to be taken on the event will take a long time. You need to let the user know that the event is received and understood—otherwise the user will probably try the event again and again until a response is seen.

Typical event-driven programs have an initialization section in the beginning, followed by an event loop, and, finally, a section to perform any necessary clean-ups at the end. Programmers experienced with Microsoft Windows, IBM Presentation Manager, or the Apple Macintosh will feel right at home with event-driven programming.

THE X EVENT MODEL

Events in X are generated from windows, which means an X program without any windows normally has a hard time receiving events from the X server. The X server provides each connection (i.e., each application program) with an event **queue**. This is a first-in first-out list of all events generated for the program's windows. Application programs read events from this queue and respond to them in some way. A word-processor application, for example, receives key press events and then displays each character pressed in the word processor's window or windows.

Keys pressed on the keyboard go to whichever window currently has the keyboard focus. This window is normally the window the mouse pointer is currently in. Moving the mouse pointer into a window will "focus" the keyboard to that window. X, though (again providing the mechanism for user-interface design without the policy), allows this feature to be changed. Window managers may focus the keyboard on a window that does not have the mouse pointer inside. Application programs may also grab control of the keyboard or grab control of individual keys. Grabbing control of individual keys is particularly dangerous.

A program that provides a consistent help system may want to grab control of a key labeled "help," for example. But a program that takes over the "e" key would make most word-processing tasks nearly impossible, except those written for certain French writers who produce whole novels without a single use of a given letter. Most of your users will probably not be avant-garde writers, so be careful when using this feature.

ASKING FOR EVENTS

When learning X, you will come across a number of statements that clearly show the design goals of X's creators. One such statement is "In X, your program will only receive the events that you ask for." This is another example of X providing the mechanism, not the policy, for user-interface design. In this case, the statement is not completely true, but it does pan out for the most part. In general, your program will only receive events it asked for, with a few exceptions.

To ask for events in X, use the `XSelectInput` function.

```
Display         *theDisplay;
Window          theWindow;
unsigned long   theEventMask;
.
.
.
XSelectInput( theDisplay,
      theWindow,
      theEventMask );
```

`XSelectInput` tells X that you are interested in receiving events for a given window, which can mean a given window and all its child windows beneath it in the window hierarchy.

Unless explicitly commanded otherwise, X events normally propagate up through the hierarchy of windows. An event will go to the lowest-level window in the hierarchy that asked for it if the events are allowed to propagate upward. If a child window does not handle events, the event will propagate up one level to the child's parent window to see if the parent will handle the event, and so on. If the event propagates all the way up to the `RootWindow`, chances are it will not be dealt with.

That means you can call `XSelectInput` on only the parent (highest level) window for your application and still receive all events (all the events asked for) for your program's child windows if those child windows did not have an `XSelectInput` call made on them. You could also call `XSelectInput` on all child windows as well.

THE EVENT MASK

As part of the `XSelectInput` call, you must pass an event mask. This mask has certain bits set that tell the X server which events your program is interested in receiving. Typically, you can "or" these mask bits together to create the full mask, such as

```
theEventMask = ButtonPressMask | KeyPressMask;
```

to ask for just keyboard and mouse button pressings.

When your program starts looking for more events, the previous expression can get rather complicated. And, because this event mask may be used in more than one place (for some special event-checking functions that follow), you may, for consistency's sake, want to place the event mask in a globally accessible format. Using the C preprocessor's `define` command can ensure that any changes to the event mask will propagrate throughout your program. This is the method used by the example programs in this chapter.

```
#define EV_MASK (ButtonPressMask      | \
        KeyPressMask                  | \
        ExposureMask                  | \
        StructureNotifyMask)
```

`XSelectInput` tells the X server that your program is interested in receiving certain types of events. Next, your program must actively pick up those events that it is interested in.

RECEIVING EVENTS FROM THE X SERVER

There are two main methods for picking up events from the X server: Block your program awaiting an event, or poll the server to check if any events are available. If your program performs background processing, you will have no choice—your program cannot block awaiting events from X. In most cases, though, your program can simply wait until X sends in an event. Blocking in this manner is a lot friendlier to your host computer and local area network—polling takes up a lot of CPU resources, and it pounds on the network.

The main blocking event function is `XNextEvent`. `XNextEvent` checks to see if any events are in the program's event queue. If so, it returns the first event in line. If not, it waits until an event appears in the queue.

```
Display        *theDisplay;
XEvent         theEvent;
.
.
.
XNextEvent( theDisplay, &theEvent );
```

To determine what type of event was received, you can check the event's type:

```
switch( theEvent.type )
        {
        .
        .
        .
        }
```

Other block-on-input event calls include the following:

XWindowEvent	Returns the next event for a given window that matches a given event mask.
XMaskEvent	Returns the next event for a given application that matches a given event mask.
XPeekEvent	"Peeks" at the next event in the event queue but does not remove that event. It allows an application to look ahead into the event queue.

Note the following examples:

```
Display          *theDisplay;
XEvent           theEvent;
unsigned long    theEventMask;
Window           theWindow;

XWindowEvent( theDisplay,
        theWindow,
        theEventMask,
        &theEvent );

XMaskEvent( theDisplay,
        theEventMask,
        &theEvent );

   XPeekEvent( theDisplay,
        &theEvent );
```

In general, use XNextEvent unless you are looking for a particular type of event (XMaskEvent) or an event for just one window (XWindowEvent). XPeekEvent can be used with the nonblocking function XPending (see the next section in this chapter) to check ahead for a set of incoming events (such as Expose events).

POLLING FOR EVENTS

The other method of X event checking is polling for events—checking to see if an event is available, but not waiting for one. As stated earlier in this chapter, most programs can wait for events, and therefore should because polling is very expensive, taking up a lot of CPU time and creating a lot of network traffic. If your application needs to perform work in the background, or if it handles more than one X server (such as a program to allow users to "chat" with other users on different displays), then you probably need to poll for incoming events.

You can check if events are pending in the event queue with the function XPending. XPending returns the number of events remaining in the event queue.

```
int             numEvents;
Display         *theDisplay;
.
.
.
numEvents = XPending( theDisplay );
```

Note that XPending does not check for specific types of events so that even if XPending returns that a number of events wait in the queue, a call for a specific event (using XMaskEvent, for example) may still cause your program to wait. In addition, XPending only checks your program's internal queue. While XPending may return 0, meaning no events remaining in the queue, the X server may have queued up events for your application. The way to get these events placed into your program's internal queue is to periodically call the XFlush function. XFlush flushes out the application's internal buffer of X commands and takes in any input waiting in the X server (XFlush was introduced earlier in Chapter 1).

Other polling routines correspond to the waiting event routines just mentioned. These polling routines return a value of True if such an event is available and False if no such event is available. You will notice the correspondence in that the only difference in some of the function names is that the word "Check" is added. For example, `XCheckWindowEvent` acts like `XWindowEvent`, but `XCheckWindowEvent` does not wait until an event comes in. It will return right away with either an event (returning True) or no event (returning False).

`XCheckWindowEvent`	Returns True if an event is pending for the given window and matches the given event mask.
`XCheckMaskEvent`	Returns True if an event is pending that matches the given event mask.
`XCheckTypedEvent`	Returns True if an event of a given type awaits in the event queue. Note that some event mask values may return more than one type of event.
`XCheckTypedWindowEvent`	Returns True if an event in the queue has the given type and is for the given window.

Note the following examples:

```
Display         *theDisplay;
Window          theWindow;
int             theType;
unsigned long   theEventMask;
XEvent          theEvent;

XCheckWindowEvent( theDisplay,
        theWindow,
        theEventMask,
        &theEvent );

XCheckMaskEvent( theDisplay,
        theEventMask,
        &theEvent );
```

continued...

...from previous page

```
XCheckTypedEvent( theDisplay,
        theType,
        &theEvent );

XCheckTypedWindowEvent( theDisplay,
        theWindow,
        theType,
        &theEvent );
```

These `XCheckSomethingEvent` routines can be used in an if statement to check whether any events have arrived, as in the following:

```
if ( XCheckWindowEvent( theDisplay, theWindow, theEventMask,
        &theEvent ) == True )
                {
                /* -- handle the event here */
                .
                .
                .
                }
```

EVENT TYPES

The `XEvent` type is a C language union, a union of C structures. Each type of event has its own structure—its own interpretation of the `XEvent` data.

The first element of the `XEvent` union is the **type**. The type field tells, surprisingly enough, what type of event has been received. Each bit in the event mask corresponds to at least one type of event (with a few exceptions).

Appendix B, "X Event Types and Structures" contains a full list of the X event types and structures. Following is an example of code to handle events:

```
Display         *theDisplay;
XEvent          theEvent;
.
.
.
XNextEvent( theDisplay, &theEvent );

switch( theEvent.type )
        {
        case Expose:   ...
        case MapNotify:   ...
        case ButtonPress: ...
        case KeyPress: ...
        case ConfigureNotify: ...
        .
        .
        .
        }
```

MOUSE BUTTON EVENTS

X, like most recent computer graphics packages, is very mouse-oriented. In fact, most X software seems to assume a three-button mouse (which means users of Hewlett-Packard or Apple products, for example, must emulate the extra mouse buttons with some interesting contortions). X itself defines up to five mouse or pointer buttons (in this book anywhere the word "mouse" is used, you could replace it with "trackball," "joystick," or whatever pointing device your system has), but most software only assumes a left, middle, and right mouse button.

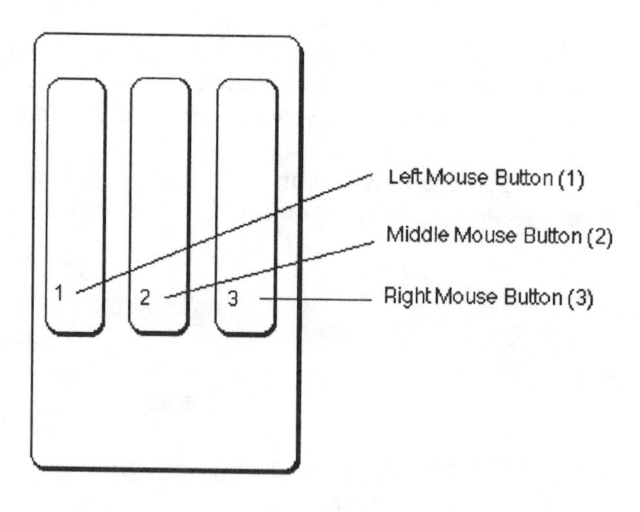

Figure 5.1 The X mouse buttons.

X mouse button events are generated under the following circumstances:

- when the user presses down a particular mouse button
- when the user releases the button
- when the user moves the mouse pointer
- when the user moves the mouse pointer while holding down a mouse button within a window in which your program has called `XSelectInput`
- when the user moves the mouse pointer while holding down a mouse button within a child of a window in which your program has called `XSelectInput`

Depending on the style of user interface you want to develop, you may want to check for one or more of these events. Unless you really need to, though, try to skip checking for the mouse movement events—each pixel of motion generates a `MotionNotify` event, and on a 1,024-by-1,024-pixel-wide monitor, that can mean a lot of events coming in very fast.

The masks to request mouse pointer events include the following:

`ButtonMotionMask`	The mouse is moved while a button is pressed.
`Button1MotionMask`	The mouse is moved while button 1 is pressed.
`Button2MotionMask`	The mouse is moved while button 2 is pressed.
`Button3MotionMask`	The mouse is moved while button 3 is pressed.
`Button4MotionMask`	The mouse is moved while button 4 is pressed.

`Button5MotionMask`	The mouse is moved while button 5 is pressed.
`ButtonPressMask`	A mouse pointer button is pressed down.
`ButtonReleaseMask`	A mouse pointer button that was pressed down was released.
`PointerMotionMask`	The mouse pointer was moved (which happens very often).
`PointerMotionHintMask`	Special mask that asks X to compress a number of mouse movements into one event.

The events your program will receive will be as follows:

`ButtonPress`	for button pressing
`ButtonRelease`	for releasing buttons that were pressed
`MotionNotify`	for any of the motion masks

The key to these mouse events includes the following three steps:

- determining which window the event took place in
- determining the x, y location of the event
- determining which mouse buttons were pressed at the time of the event

The answer to the first step is found in the `XEvent` union. The window in which the event took place is found in the window field for button events:

```
Window  theEventWindow;
XEvent  theEvent;

theEventWindow = theEvent.xbutton.window;
```

For motion events, the window in which the event took place is found as follows:

```
theEventWindow = theEvent.xmotion.window;
```

The x, y location (step 2) is in the x and y fields, as shown in the following examples:

```
int       theEventX, theEventY;

theEventX  = theEvent.xbutton.x;
theEventY  = theEvent.xbutton.y;
```

or

```
theEventX  = theEvent.xmotion.x;
theEventY  = theEvent.xmotion.y;
```

And finally, step 3—finding out which button was pressed or released—is a bit more complicated. In a `ButtonPress` event, the state field will normally be 0 (if no other modifer keys are pressed). The button field will contain which button caused the event (`Button1`, `Button2`, `Button3`, `Button4`, or `Button5`).

For a `ButtonRelease` event, the state field will contain the state just before the event (e.g., containing the button that was pressed and then released) and so will the button field.

For a `MotionNotify` event, only the state field will be available. This state field tells not only the state of the mouse pointer buttons, but also the state of any modifier keys, such as the Shift, Caps (Shift) Lock, Control, or meta keys. A meta key is typically a key that performs an alternate function and is often labeled as the "Alt" key. Most meta keys are located next to the space bar on the keyboard.

On the Sun 386i, the meta key is the left diamond-shaped key next to the space bar and not the key labeled "Alt." On a Sun 3, the meta keys are the Left or Right keys. On the HP 9000 Series 300, the Extend Char key performs this function, and on the Apple Macintosh IIx, the meta key is the Command key (labeled with an apple outline and a cloverleaf symbol). You can use the standard X client program `xev` (see Appendix D) to find out the special mappings on your keyboard.

To check for these keys, check for certain bits in the state field by using the following masks:

`Button1Mask`	The first mouse button was pressed.
`Button2Mask`	The second mouse button was pressed.
`Button3Mask`	The third mouse button was pressed.
`Button4Mask`	The fourth mouse button was pressed (usually not available).
`Button5Mask`	The fifth mouse button was pressed (usually not available).
`ShiftMask`	A Shift key was pressed.
`ControlMask`	The Control key was pressed.
`LockMask`	The Caps Lock key was pressed.
`Mod1Mask`	The typical meta key was pressed.
`Mod2Mask`	The second meta key was pressed.
`Mod3Mask`	Another meta key often not found on the keyboard was pressed.
`Mod4Mask`	Another meta key often not found on the keyboard was pressed.
`Mod5Mask`	Another meta key often not found on the keyboard was pressed.

Sample code to check for meta keys would look like the following:

```
if ( theEvent.xbutton.state & Button1Mask )
        {
        /*
        **      Handle Button 1 down
        */
        }
```

For user-interface design, a quick `ButtonPress` then `ButtonRelease` is usually referred to as a button "click." When checking for these events, it is a good idea to provide some user feedback when the first event comes in, e.g., the `ButtonPress` so the user doesn't repeatedly press the mouse button (or hold it down for a long time) under the mistaken impression that the application didn't notice the `ButtonPress`.

KEYBOARD EVENTS

As with the mouse button events, you can check when a keyboard key is pressed and when it is released. Most software, though, needs only to worry about when a key is pressed. If you wait for a key to be released, then you run the same dangers described in the previous section, "Mouse Button Events."

Each X workstation from each vendor uses a different keyboard. X abstracted various keyboard keys, using the concept of a `KeySym`. `KeySyms` allow your program to map various proprietary keyboard schemes into portable code.

The basic task of the `KeySym` is to convert a machine-specific key code into a generic letter, such as the letter "A." X also allows for the ability of some keyboards to program a given key to send a string of characters—sort of a keyboard macro. X does this by having each normal QWERTY key send back an ASCII character string, even if the string is only one letter long, such as "A."

The Xlib function `XLookupString` converts a `KeyPress` event into the ASCII character string that was "pressed" on the keyboard, basing this conversion on the keyboard mapping. With `XLookupString`, you must pass a character buffer, a buffer that is large enough to hold most returned strings, as well as the length of your buffer. In the following examples, a 65-character buffer was arbitrarily chosen. If you think this length is too small, make it larger. Chances are, though, that the length is far larger than you will need.

```
XKeyEvent       theEvent;
XComposeStatus  theComposeStatus;
KeySym          theKeySym;
int             theKeyBufferMaxLen = 64;  /* -- arbitrary number */
char            theKeyBuffer[ 65 ];
int             numChars;

numChars = XLookupString( &theEvent,
                theKeyBuffer,
                theKeyBufferMaxLen,
                &theKeySym,
                &theComposeStatus );
```

`numChars` is the length of `theKeyBuffer` as returned by `XLookupString`. It can be 0 (for no ASCII string bound to the given key) or 1 (for most keys, such as the "g" key), or > 1 if a key has been bound to a character string.

`theKeySym` is the returned `KeySym`. You can use this value to check for keys like the F1 function key, the Help key, or the Page Down key. How to do this will be described in Chapter 6.

`theComposeStatus` is not implemented on all revisions of X 11. For most applications, you can ignore the `XComposeStatus` value.

```
Display         *theDisplay;
XEvent          theEvent;
XComposeStatus  theComposeStatus;
KeySym          theKeySym;

/*
**      You must declare storage for the incoming key strokes.
*/
int             theKeyBufferMaxLen = 64;  /* -- arbitrary number */
char            theKeyBuffer[ 65 ];
.
.
.
XNextEvent( theDisplay, &theEvent );
```

continued...

...from previous page

```
switch( theEvent.type )
        {
        case KeyPress:
                XLookupString( &theEvent,
                        theKeyBuffer,
                        theKeyBufferMaxLen,
                        &theKeySym,
                        &theComposeStatus );

                printf( "A <%s> key was pressed\n", theKeyBuffer );
                break;

/*
**      Handle other event types...
*/
.
.
.
}
```

ENTER/LEAVE EVENTS

Normally in X, any keystrokes typed at the keyboard go to the window where the mouse pointer is located. Moving the mouse pointer to another window changes the keyboard focus (under normal conditions) to the new window. When this happens, the X server generates a `LeaveNotify` event for the window the mouse just left and an `EnterNotify` for the window the mouse pointer enters. If the keyboard focus changes (which normally occurs with the mouse pointer motion, but doesn't have to), your applications get a `FocusOut` event on the window that lost the keyboard focus and a `FocusIn` event on the window that is the new focus of the keyboard.

Some X client programs, like `xterm`, may fill in the text cursor on a `FocusIn` and convert the cursor to an outline on a `FocusOut`. This just provides an added visual cue to the user (who is probably having a hard time with all this) for which window "owns" the keyboard.

That part sounds easy, but X adds in a quirk. The quirk is that the X server will generate `EnterNotify/LeaveNotify` and `FocusIn/FocusOut` events on windows that are virtually crossed. When the keyboard focus or the mouse pointer is arbitrarily moved from one window to another across the screen, some of the windows in between are "virtually" crossed. It is easier to simply treat each `EnterNotify/LeaveNotify` and `FocusIn/FocusOut` event in good faith rather than design a virtual event-handler routine.

You ask for EnterNotify/LeaveNotify events with an EnterWindowMask or a LeaveWindowMask, respectively, as a parameter to an XSelectInput call. Focus change events are selected with the FocusChangeMask.

The only relevant portion of the XEvent union is the window on which the event was generated. For EnterNotify/LeaveNotify events, this window looks like the following:

```
Window          theWindow;
XEvent          theEvent;

theWindow = theEvent.xcrossing.window;
```

For focus events, the window looks like the following:

```
theWindow = theEvent.xfocus.window;
```

These types of events are checked like any other event, as in the following examples:

```
Display         *theDisplay;
XEvent          theEvent;

XNextEvent( theDisplay, &theEvent );

switch( theEvent.type )
        {
        case EnterNotify:
                .
                .
                .
        case LeaveNotify:
                .
                .
                .
        case FocusIn     :
                .
                .
                .
        case FocusOut    :
        .
        .
        .
        }
```

EXPOSURE EVENTS

Exposure events are one type of window-related events generated by X. An exposure event is generated when one of your application's windows is exposed (or partially exposed) to the world. Because windows can overlap in X, it is very likely that another program's window will at some time overlap your application's window (or windows). If this overlapping window is moved away so that it no longer covers your window, the part of your window that was covered up has been **exposed**.

When your program receives an exposure event, it should redraw the area that was previously covered up. Each `Expose` event comes with a rectangle (x, y, width, height) that identifies the exposed area. For a complex window movement, a number of `Expose` events may be sent to your application. These events should all arrive in a batch (contiguously), and each event has a counter that counts down. When the counter equals zero, you have received the last `Expose` event.

You therefore have a choice: redraw just the area that was exposed, or wait for all the exposure events and redraw the entire exposed area (or the whole window if your routine is lazy). Most of the example programs in the book are lazy and will just redraw the whole window. For large windows, though, this is obviously inefficient.

To help avoid `Expose` events, you can ask the X server to save the area underneath obscuring windows. In such a case, the server then replaces the original pixel pattern when your window is exposed. Your program will not receive an `Expose` event. This backing-store operation is transparent to your program. Unfortunately, not all servers support backing-stores. And even those that do rarely have enough RAM to handle backing-stores for every program, so if you ask the X server to save the area under obscuring windows, your program must still be prepared for `Expose` events to come in at any time. Backing-store will be covered further in Chapter 8.

You select `Expose` events with the `ExposureMask`, in a call to `XSelectInput`. The event type received is an `Expose` event, with a structure of `XExposeEvent`. Note the following examples:

```
Display         *theDisplay;
Window          theWindow;
XEvent          theEvent;
int             x, y, width, height;
int             theCount;

XNextEvent( theDisplay, &theEvent );

switch( theEvent.type )
        {
        case Expose:
                /*
                **      Get window that was exposed
                */
                theWindow = theEvent.xexpose.window;

                /*
                **      If theCount == 0, then last Expose
                **      event in sequence is received.
                **
                */
                theCount = theEvent.xexpose.count;

                /*
                **      Get area of the exposure
                */
                x       = theEvent.xexpose.x;
                y       = theEvent.xexpose.y;
                width   = theEvent.xexpose.width;
                height  = theEvent.xexpose.height;
                .
                .
                .
                }
```

EXAMPLE 1: A PROGRAM TO CHECK EVENTS

The first example program is an example of the lazy approach to `Expose` events. It simply calls a `refreshWindow` function to redraw the contents of the window whenever an `Expose` event comes in.

This example program places a window on the display and then responds to mouse pointer and keyboard events. It exits when the user types a "q" for quit. This is a rather simple introduction to events in X. Example 2 will use events to do a bit more.

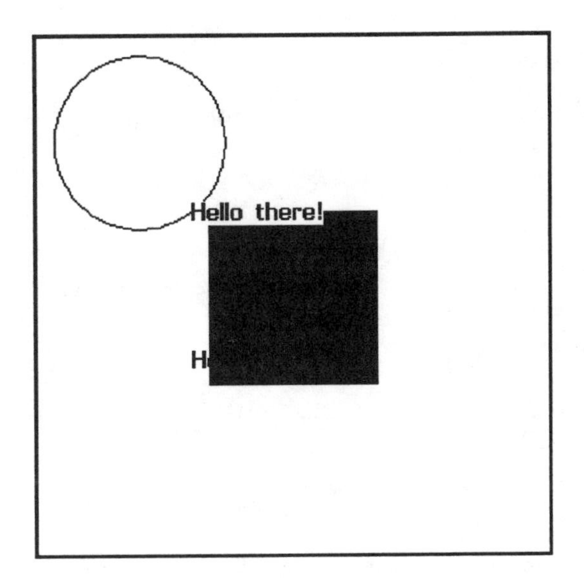

Figure 5.2 *The test program's window*

A new file, `eventx.c`, is added. This file contains the main event loop—the meat of the program (and the meat of all the programs to come)—in the function `eventLoop`. `eventLoop` calls `XNextEvent` to wait for an event from the X server. When an event comes, `eventLoop` checks the type of the event and then acts on a few basic types (usually just printing out a message). `eventLoop` returns a 1 unless the user presses the "q" key, in which case it returns a 0, which causes the program to exit.

The function `initEvents` calls `XSelectInput` on a given window so that the X server will send the application events that happen on the window.

The test file `test5.c` is modified to call `initEvents` after it creates a window on the display. Then, the main function calls `eventLoop` to handle all events.

Running this program should give you an initial feel for the way X uses events. Virtually all X applications will need to deal with events in some way.

Example 1 Source Code

The contents of the file `eventx.c` are as follows:

```
/*
**      eventx.c
**
**      Contains the event loop (where the major action of most
**      X-based programs occurs).
**
*/

#include   <X11/Xlib.h>
#include   <X11/Xutil.h>

extern  Display     *theDisplay;

/*
**      Under X, a window will never receive an event that it
**      hasn't asked for.  The way to ask for events is to set up
**      a mask indicating those events for which your window is
**      interested in.  This mask is then passed to XSelectInput
**      along with a window id and a display pointer.
*/

#define EV_MASK (ButtonPressMask  | \
                KeyPressMask      | \
                ExposureMask      | \
                StructureNotifyMask)

/*
**      eventLoop blocks awaiting an event from X.  When an event comes in,
**      it is decoded and processed.
**
**      When the user types a "q" the program will quit.
**
*/


eventLoop()

{       /* -- function eventLoop */
        XEvent          theEvent;
        XComposeStatus  theComposeStatus;
        KeySym          theKeySym;

        /*
        **      You must declare storage for the incoming key strokes.
        */
        int             theKeyBufferMaxLen = 64;  /* -- arbitrary number */
        char            theKeyBuffer[ 65 ];
```

continued...

...from previous page

```
/*
**       Block on input, awaiting an event from X
*/

XNextEvent( theDisplay, &theEvent );

/*
**      Decode the event and call a specific routine to
**      handle it
*/

switch( theEvent.type )
        {
        /*
        **      Part or all of the Window has been exposed to the
        **      world.  That part should be redrawn here.
        **      Also redraw if the window is mapped.
        */
        case Expose:
                printf( "Window is exposed\n" );

                /*
                **      The XEvent structure is really a big union
                **      of many structures, all of the
                **      same size.  The generic part of the
                **      structure is the xany part.
                **/
                refreshWindow( theEvent.xany.window );

                break;

        case MapNotify: printf( "Window is mapped\n" );
                refreshWindow( theEvent.xany.window );
                break;

        /*
        **      A Mouse button has been pressed.
        **      Note: some interface styles may want to look
        **      for ButtonRelease events, which essentially look
        **      for mouse "clicks".
        */
        case ButtonPress:
                printf( "A Mouse button was pressed\n" ); break;

        /*
        **      A key on the keyboard was hit.  This one checks
        **      for KeyPress as most people want to see feedback
        **      right away for a KeyPress.
        */
```

continued...

...from previous page

```
                case KeyPress:
                        XLookupString( &theEvent,
                                theKeyBuffer,
                                theKeyBufferMaxLen,
                                &theKeySym,
                                &theComposeStatus );

                        printf( "A <%s> key was pressed\n", theKeyBuffer );

                        /*
                        **      Quit if a "q" is hit.
                        */
                        if ( theKeyBuffer[ 0 ] == 'q' )
                                {
                                return( 0 );
                                }
                        break;


                /*
                **      The window has been sized or changed.
                */
                case ConfigureNotify:
                        printf( "The window configuration has changed\n");
                        refreshWindow( theEvent.xany.window );
                        break;
                }

        /*
        **      Return a 0 to quit, a 1 to keep going
        */
        return( 1 );
}       /* -- function eventLoop */


/*
**      initEvents
**      Selects input for the given window, with the default
**      event mask.
**
*/

initEvents( theWindow )

Window  theWindow;
```

continued...

...from previous page

```
{       /* -- function initEvents */

        XSelectInput( theDisplay,
                      theWindow,
                      EV_MASK );

}       /* -- function initEvents */

/*
**      end of file eventx.c
*/
```

The contents of the test file `test5.c` are as follows:

```
/*
**      Chapter 5, Example 1
**
**      This program pops up a window and then draws into it.
**
*/

#include   <X11/Xlib.h>

/*
**      external GLOBALS from initx.c
*/

extern          Display         *theDisplay;


/*
**      GLOBALS defined here.
*/

GC              theGC;
XFontStruct     *fontStruct;

main()

{
        Window          theWindow, openWindow();
        XFontStruct     *initFont();

        /*
        **      Set up our connection to X
        */
```

continued...

...from previous page

```
initX();

/*
**      Get some info on the display and print it
*/

getXInfo();

/*
**      Set up colors
*/

initDefaultColors();

/*
**      Open a window
*/

theWindow = openWindow(  100, 100,       /* -- x, y location       */
                         300, 300,       /* -- width, height       */
                         0,              /* -- This is NOT a pop-up */
                         &theGC );       /* -- Graphics Context     */


/*
** Load in a font
*/
fontStruct = initFont( theGC, "variable" );


/*
**      Set up the window to receive events from X.
*/
initEvents( theWindow );

/*
**      Draw initial items to window.  Normally, you should
**      await an Expose event
*/

refreshWindow( theWindow );

XFlush( theDisplay );

/*
**      Handle events
*/

while( eventLoop() );
```

continued...

...from previous page

```
        /*
        **      Close the connection to the X server.
        */

        XDestroyWindow( theDisplay, theWindow );
        XFreeFont( theDisplay, fontStruct );
        XFlush( theDisplay );

        quitX();

}


/*
**      refreshWindow is called when an Expose event comes in from X.
**      It redraws the whole contents of the window (since there is not
**      much to draw.  A more efficient program would check for the
**      region and only refresh that region.
**
*/

refreshWindow( theExposedWindow )

Window  theExposedWindow;

{       /* -- function refreshWindow */

        /*
        **      Draw into the Window
        */

        setColor( theGC, 28 );    /* -- lime green */

        drawOval( theExposedWindow, theGC,
                10, 10,         /* -- Starting location in x, y  */
                100, 100 );     /* -- width and height           */

        fillRectangle( theExposedWindow, theGC,
                100, 100,       /* -- Starting location in x, y  */
                100, 100 );     /* -- width and height           */

        /*
        **       Now draw out some text.
        */
```

continued...

...from previous page

```
        XDrawImageString( theDisplay,
                theExposedWindow,
                theGC,
                90, 105,
                "Hello there!",
                strlen( "Hello there!" ) );

        /*
        ** XDrawImageString draws both the background and the foreground
        ** bits of the font.  XDrawString just draws the foreground bits.
        ** In the example below, the XDrawString will be partially obscured.
        */

        XDrawString( theDisplay,
                theExposedWindow,
                theGC,
                90, 203,
                "Hello there!",
                strlen( "Hello there!" ) );

        /*
        **      Send all output to the screen
        */

        XFlush( theDisplay );

}       /* -- function refreshWindow */


/*
**      end of file.
*/
```

The contents of the Makefile are as follows:

```
##      X Project Makefile for Chapter 5, example 1
##
EXEC=   test5
##
## DEFINES
##
##
##      -g = Debugging info
##      -O = optimize (cannot use -g then)
CFLAGS=         -O
##
##
##      Libraries
##      X11     X11 graphics library
##
LIBS=   -lX11
##
##
OBJECTS=        initx.o         \
                colorx.o        \
                drawx.o         \
                eventx.o        \
                quitx.o         \
                textx.o         \
                windowx.o       \
                test5.o
##
##      Command to compile and link objects together
##
$(EXEC):        $(OBJECTS)
                cc -o $(EXEC) $(OBJECTS) $(LIBS)
##
##
##      end of make file
##
```

EXAMPLE 2: A MOUSE-BASED DRAWING PROGRAM

This chapter's second example program provides a very simple mouse-based drawing program. Whenever the program gets two button press events (from any button), it draws a line between the two positions. It is a primitive example of a drawing program that is described in Section II of this book.

The meat of the program changes are to the file **eventx.c**. This file now saves the mouse pointer coordinates on a **ButtonPress** event. When two **ButtonPress** events are received, the program merely draws a line. It also clears the window every time an **Expose** event comes in so that you have a clean slate to experiment with. The **eventLoop** function's calling parameters are also changed, adding a window and a graphics context so the function can draw the lines. Changing the calling parameters requires changing the file **test5.c**, although the changes are minor.

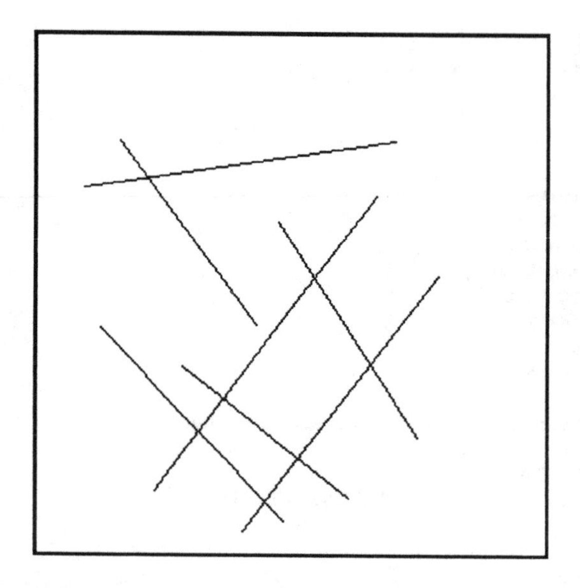

Figure 5.3 Mouse-based drawing

Example 2 Source Code

The revised contents of the file **eventx.c** are as follows:

```
/*
**      eventx.c
**
**      Contains the event loop (where the major action of most
**      X-based programs occurs).
**
*/

#include   <X11/Xlib.h>
#include   <X11/Xutil.h>

extern          Display         *theDisplay;

/*
**      Globals for current and last position.
**
*/

int     currentX = 0, currentY = 0;
int     lastX = 0, lastY = 0;

/*
**      Under X, a window will never receive an event that it
**      hasn't asked for.  The way to ask for events is to set up
**      a mask indicating those events for which your window is
**      interested in.  This mask is then passed to XSelectInput
**      along with a window id and a display pointer.
*/

#define EV_MASK (ButtonPressMask  | \
                KeyPressMask      | \
                ExposureMask      | \
                StructureNotifyMask)

/*
**      eventLoop blocks awaiting an event from X.  When an event comes in,
**      it is decoded and processed.
**
**      This function is passed a Window and a GC so that drawing may
**      take place.
**
**      When the user types a "q" the program will quit.
**
*/

eventLoop( theWindow, theGC )
```

continued...

...from previous page

```
Window  theWindow;
GC      theGC;

{       /* -- function eventLoop */
        XEvent            theEvent;
        XComposeStatus    theComposeStatus;
        KeySym            theKeySym;

        /*
        **      You must declare storage for the incoming key strokes.
        */
        int               theKeyBufferMaxLen = 64;  /* -- arbitrary number */
        char              theKeyBuffer[ 65 ];

        /*
        **      Block on input, awaiting an event from X
        */

        XNextEvent( theDisplay, &theEvent );

        /*
        **      Decode the event and call a specific routine to
        **      handle it
        */

        switch( theEvent.type )
                {
                /*
                **      Part or all of the Window has been exposed to the
                **      world.  That part should be redrawn here.
                */
                case Expose:

                        /*
                        **      The XEvent structure is really a big union
                        **      of many structures, all of the
                        **      same size.  The generic part of the
                        **      structure is the xany part.
                        **/
                        XClearWindow( theDisplay,
                                theEvent.xany.window );

                        break;

                case MapNotify:
                        refreshWindow( theEvent.xany.window );
                        break;
```

continued...

...from previous page

```
/*
**      A Mouse button has been pressed.
*/
case ButtonPress:
        if ( ( lastX == currentX ) && ( lastY == currentY ) )
                {
                /* -- Initial point */
                lastX     = theEvent.xkey.x;
                lastY     = theEvent.xkey.y;
                }
        else
                {
                currentX = theEvent.xkey.x;
                currentY = theEvent.xkey.y;

                drawLine( theEvent.xany.window,
                        theGC,
                        lastX, lastY,
                        currentX, currentY );
                XFlush( theDisplay );
                lastX = currentX;
                lastY = currentY;
                        }
                ; break;

/*
**      A key on the keyboard was hit.
*/
case KeyPress:
        XLookupString( &theEvent,
                        theKeyBuffer,
                        theKeyBufferMaxLen,
                        &theKeySym,
                        &theComposeStatus );

        /*
        **      Quit if a "q" is hit.
        */
        if ( theKeyBuffer[ 0 ] == 'q' )
                {
                return( 0 );
                }
        break;


/*
**      The window has been sized or changed.
*/
case ConfigureNotify:
        break;
}
```

continued...

...from previous page

```
        /*
        **      Return a 0 to quit, a 1 to keep going
        */
        return( 1 );
}       /* -- function eventLoop */


/*
**      initEvents
**      Selects input for the given window, with the default
**      event mask.
**
*/

initEvents( theWindow )

Window  theWindow;

{       /* -- function initEvents */

        XSelectInput( theDisplay,
                theWindow,
                EV_MASK );

}       /* -- function initEvents */

/*
**      end of file eventx.c
*/
```

The revised contents of the test file `test5.c` are as follows:

```
/*
**       test5b.c
**
**      Chapter 5, Example 2
**
**      This program pops up a window and then draws into it.
**      On every mouse click, it draws a line from the previous
**      position to the new position.
**
*/

#include   <X11/Xlib.h>

/*
**      external GLOBALS from initx.c
*/

extern          Display         *theDisplay;


/*
**      GLOBALS defined here.
*/

GC              theGC;
XFontStruct     *fontStruct;

main()

{
        Window          theWindow;
        XFontStruct     *initFont();

        /*
        **      Set up our connection to X
        */

        initX();

        /*
        **      Get some info on the display and print it
        */

        getXInfo();

        /*
        **      Set up colors
        */

        initDefaultColors();
```

continued...

...from previous page

```
        /*
        **      Open a window
        */

        theWindow = openWindow( 100, 100,          /* -- x, y location       */
                                300, 300,          /* -- width, height       */
                                0,                 /* -- This is NOT a pop-up */
                                &theGC );          /* -- Graphics Context    */


        /*
        ** Load in a font
        */
        fontStruct = initFont( theGC, "variable" );

        /*
        **      Set up the window to receive events from X.
        */
        initEvents( theWindow );


        XFlush( theDisplay );

        /*
        **      Handle events
        */

        while( eventLoop( theWindow, theGC ) );

        /*
        **      Close the connection to the X server.
        */

        XDestroyWindow( theDisplay, theWindow );
        XFreeFont( theDisplay, fontStruct );
        XFlush( theDisplay );
        quitX();

}


/*
**      refreshWindow is called when an Expose event comes in from X.
**      It redraws the whole contents of the window (since there is not
**      much to draw.  A more efficient program would check for the
**      region and only refresh that region.
**
*/

refreshWindow( theExposedWindow )
```

continued...

...from previous page

```
Window  theExposedWindow;

{       /* -- function refreshWindow */

        /*
        **      Draw into the Window
        */

        setColor( theGC, 28 );  /* -- Lime Green */
        drawOval( theExposedWindow, theGC,
                10, 10,         /* -- Starting location in x, y */
                100, 100 );     /* -- width and height          */

        fillRectangle( theExposedWindow, theGC,
                100, 100,               /* -- Starting location in x, y */
                100, 100 );     /* -- width and height          */

        /*
        **      Now draw out some text.
        */

        XDrawImageString( theDisplay,
                theExposedWindow,
                theGC,
                90, 105,
                "Hello there!",
                strlen( "Hello there!" ) );

        /*
        ** XDrawImageString draws both the background and the foreground
        ** bits of the font.  XDrawString just draws the foreground bits.
        ** In the example below, the XDrawString will be partially obscured.
        */

        XDrawString( theDisplay,
                theExposedWindow,
                theGC,
                90, 203,
                "Hello there!",
                strlen( "Hello there!" ) );

        /*
        **      Send all output to the screen
        */

        XFlush( theDisplay );
```

continued...

...*from previous page*

```
}       /* -- function refreshWindow */


/*
**      end of file test5b.c.
*/
```

MORE ABOUT THE X EVENT MODEL WITH THE XEV PROGRAM

After running these examples, you should have a good idea how events in X work. The standard X client program, `xev`, can also help you get a feel for X events. The `xev` program is covered in Appendix D.

SUMMARY

- X uses events to tell your application program something happened. That something includes keyboard-generated events, such as key presses; mouse-generated events, such as moving the mouse pointer; and window-generated events, such as moving your window to the top of the heap, thereby exposing contents that were previously hidden.

- X only sends your application the event types you ask for (except for a few types that X requires). The `XSelectInput` function allows your program to ask for events. When calling `XSelectInput`, you pass a value whose bit-pattern contains the set of masks for the events you want. These masks are defined in the X include header files with descriptive names like `KeyPressMask`.

- To actually receive events from the X server, your application can poll the server or wait for the server to send an event. In most cases, waiting for an event is just fine and is kinder to the system's resources.

- Once your application has an event, the program needs to determine the event's type and react to the event (if the program wants to).

- Two example programs in this chapter show the use of event-checking routines in X and provide a very simple mouse-based line-drawing program to demonstrate how such a program could be created.

Xlib Functions and Macros Introduced in This Chapter

```
XCheckMaskEvent
XCheckTypedEvent
XCheckTypedWindowEvent
XCheckWindowEvent
XClearWindow
XLookupString
XMaskEvent
XNextEvent
XPeekEvent
XPending
XSelectInput
XWindowEvent
```

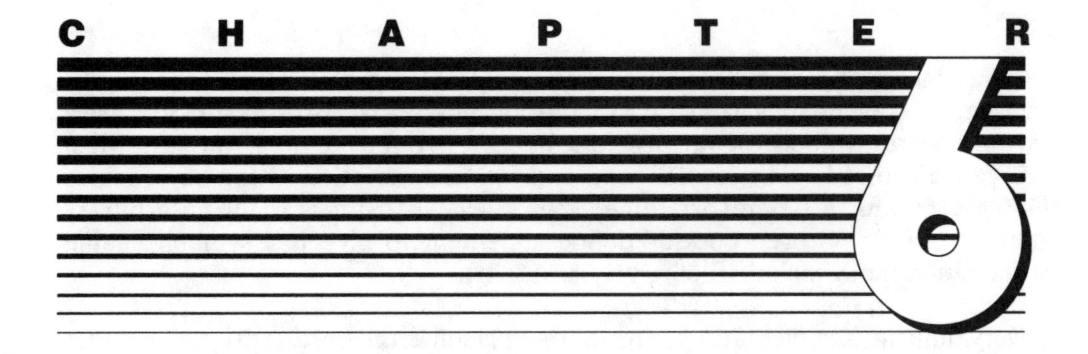

KEYBOARD EVENTS

As described in Chapter 5, almost every computer manufacturer uses a different keyboard. Some manufacturers even sell a number of different keyboards for their own products.

Most of these keyboards will have special keys, including arrow keys, a numeric keypad, function keys, and Page Up and Page Down keys. Users tend to like being able to use their up arrow key, among others. The problem addressed in this chapter is how to handle keyboard events in a generic way that will work on all (or virtually all) keyboards.

The designers of X were faced with the same problem with keyboard events. To solve this problem, they came up with the concept of KeySyms. KeySyms are a set of generic symbols for various keys, like XK_Up for the up arrow key. Most KeySym names begin with XK_ and end with a description of the key, such as XK_Begin for a Begin (or Home) key. Each KeySym is really an arbitrary number with a C preprocessor define statement to give it a symbolic name (defined in the X include file keysymdef.h).

Every time the X server is ported to another machine, the porting process includes having the server translate the native keyboard format into these KeySyms; therefore, using the KeySyms to identify these special keys will help make your code portable to other X workstations. And, because portability is the primary benefit of X, using KeySyms is a good idea.

When a KeyPress event is detected, use the function XLookupString to get the KeySym associated with the key that was pressed.

```
XLookupString( theEvent,

        theKeyBuffer,
        theKeyBufferMaxLen,
        theKeySym,
        theComposeStatus );

XKeyEvent        *theEvent;
                 char          theKeyBuffer[ MAX_LEN + 1 ];

/* -- (always allocate extra storage for character strings) */

int              theKeyBufferMaxLen = MAX_LEN;

KeySym           *theKeySym;
                 XComposeStatus       *theComposeStatus;
```

theEvent is the XEvent structure passed back from X.

theKeyBuffer is a character array in which ASCII keys will be placed. If the user types an "a" key, then theKeyBuffer will contain the NULL-terminated string "a" for that key. On some computers, the function keys (or other keys) can be programmed to enter in a whole string, such as "LOAD," when a key is pressed, so theKeyBuffer character string should be made large enough to handle these occurrences.

theKeyBufferMaxLen tells X how many characters it can put into theKeyBuffer; you are responsible for allocating the storage for theKeyBuffer.

For most ASCII-printable characters (e.g., the QWERTY keys on the keyboard), simply checking if theKeyBuffer[0] is an ASCII-printable character, or checking if the KeySym value is an ASCII-printable character, will be fine. This avoids a lot of KeySym processing for the most commonly pressed keys. XLookupString returns the number of bytes placed into theKeyBuffer, so check to be sure the number is at least greater than 0 (otherwise, theKeyBuffer's contents are undefined).

For the function keys, and the other special keys on the keyboard, the KeySym must be checked. The KeySyms are defined in the X header file keysymdef.h (Note that X header files are normally in the /usr/include/X11 directory; if your header files are not in that directory, check with your system administrator.) One look in that file will show how many possible KeySyms there are. Normally, you only need to worry about the ones that make sense for a particular application. Skip the rest.

The value in theComposeStatus is not implemented in many versions of X11, so it is best to ignore this value.

Following is an example showing how to process keyboard events:

```
#include  <X11/Xlib.h>
#include  <X11/Xutil.h>
#include  <X11/keysym.h>
#include  <X11/keysymdef.h>

        .
        .
        .
        XEvent          theEvent;
        Display         *theDisplay;
        .
        .
        .

        /*
        **      Block on input, awaiting an event from X
        */

        XNextEvent( theDisplay, &theEvent );
```

continued...

...from previous page

```
        /*
        **      Decode the event and call a specific routine to
        **      handle it
        */

        switch( theEvent.type )
                {
                /*
                **      A key on the keyboard was hit.
                */
                case KeyPress:
                        return( processKeyPress( &theEvent ) );
                        break;

                .
                .
                .
                }

        .
        .
        .

processKeyPress( theEvent )

XKeyEvent       *theEvent;

/*
**      Note how the XEvent above is passed down into
**      an XKeyEvent here.  X defines the XEvent type as a union
**      of many other event types.  All the data occupies the
**      same number of bytes.
*/

{       /* -- function processKeyPress */
        int             length;
        int             theKeyBufferMaxLen = 64;
        char            theKeyBuffer[ 65 ];
        KeySym          theKeySym;
        XComposeStatus  theComposeStatus;

        length = XLookupString( theEvent,

                        theKeyBuffer,
                        theKeyBufferMaxLen,
                        &theKeySym,
                        &theComposeStatus );
```

continued...

...from previous page

```
/*
**      Check if theKeySym is within the standard ASCII
**      printable character range.  This avoids a lot of
**      KeySym checking below.
**
*/

if ( ( theKeySym >= ' ' ) &&       /* -- ASCII 32 is a space  */
   ( theKeySym <= '~' )   &&       /* -- ASCII 126 is a Tilde */
   ( length > 0 ) )                /* -- We have char input   */
        {
        printf( "ASCII key was hit: [%s]\n", theKeyBuffer );
        }
else
        {
        /*
        **      Check for special keys on the keyboard.
        */
        switch( theKeySym )
                {
                case XK_Return   : printf( "Return\n" ); break;
                case XK_BackSpace: printf( "BackSpace\n" ); break;
                case XK_Escape   : printf( "ESCAPE\n" ); break;
                case XK_Delete   : printf( "Delete\n" ); break;
                case XK_Up       : printf( "Up\n" ); break;
                case XK_Down     : printf( "Down\n" ); break;
                case XK_Right    : printf( "Right\n" ); break;
                case XK_Left     : printf( "Left\n" ); break;
                .
                .
                .
                /*
                **      function Keys
                */
                case XK_F1       : printf( "F1\n" ); break;
                case XK_F2       : printf( "F2\n" ); break;
                case XK_F3       : printf( "F3\n" ); break;
                .
                .
                .
                /*
                **      Keypad Keys
                */
                case XK_KP_Enter : printf( "Keypad Enter\n" ); break;
                case XK_KP_Equal : printf( "Keypad =\n" ); break;
                case XK_KP_Multiply: printf( "Keypad *\n" ); break;
                case XK_KP_Add   : printf( "Keypad +\n" ); break;
                case XK_KP_0     : printf( "Keypad 0\n" ); break;
                case XK_KP_1     : printf( "Keypad 1\n" ); break;
```

continued...

...from previous page

```
                .
                .
                .
                case XK_KP_9      : printf( "Keypad 9\n" ); break;
                }
        }
.
.
. }     /* -- function processKeyPress */
```

The method used for handling the KeyPress events is as follows: First, call XLookupString to get a KeySym for the event and any ASCII string associated with the event. Second, check if the KeySym is an ASCII-printable character (e.g., between an ASCII space, char 32, and an ASCII tilde, char 126) and that the ASCII string actually has characters in it (based on the length value returned by XLookupString). If all this is true, then you have a straight ASCII character input. Otherwise, check the KeySym for a known value, such as XK_Up for the up arrow key.

When looking through the example program for this chapter and through the file keysymdef.h, you will notice that many of the function keys are defined to have double meanings. Most keyboards label function keys by starting with F1 for the first function key, F2 for the second one, and so on. Sun Microsystem keyboards, though, have function keys labeled F1 to F*n* across the top of the keyboard, as well as right and left function keys labeled R1 to R*n* and L1 to L*n*, respectively, along the sides of the keyboard (where *n* is the maximum number of function keys). Because many of the designers and early users of the X Window System use Sun workstations, these KeySyms became a part of X. Because most other keyboards do not have the left and right function keys but do have a large number of regular function keys, keysymdef.h defines XK_R1, the first right function key, for example, to be the same as XK_F21, the twenty-first regular function key.

To further complicate matters, the Sun 386i workstation has a keypad with the right function key labels as well as IBM PC keypad labels, such as Page Up, Page Down, Home, and End. Unfortunately, users may want to use the R9 key as the Page Up key—because the key does have the PgUp label—and there goes portability, at least with X11 R3 from the MIT X Consortium. Later in this chapter, some of the special Sun 386i mappings are listed, along with the KeySyms that match the labels on the keys. If you want to handle this nonportable key processing, the XK_Prior KeySym (often called the Page Up key) and the XK_R9 key should be treated the same. After running the example program in this chapter and trying out all the keys available, you might find some subtle incompatibilities on your keyboard.

In general, though, the KeySym concept aids portability and hides most of the details of specific keyboards.

META KEYS

In many menu-based interfaces, users can choose items in a menu through keyboard shortcuts. A common shortcut is allowing the user to hold down a meta (or Alt) key and simultaneously press a standard keyboard key. Meta-Q, for example, often means quit.

These meta-key shortcuts are often preferred by expert users, the so-called "power users" who use a given application program day in and day out. The only problem is that different keyboards, of course, use different keys for the meta key. (And some keyboards have more than one meta key—each meta key with a different meaning.) As stated in Chapter 5, on many IBM-compatible keyboards, the meta key is labeled "Alt." Macintoshes use a cloverleaf-shaped symbol and an apple symbol to mark this key, which is called the Command key. The Sun 386i has an Alt key, but under X11 R3 (from MIT), the 386i meta key is right next to the Alt key—the diamond-shaped key. On a Sun 3, the meta key is simply labeled "Left." Hewlett-Packards use the left "Extend Char" key.

Note that these cases are highlighted not to nitpick the X Window System's wonderful designers but to show that while the grand idea of portability is laudable, it doesn't always shine through fully in practice. There are subtle "gotchas" even in a system as remarkably portable as X. It is simply amazing, though, to see the same graphical interface run on a Hewlett-Packard and an Apollo and to watch the output of a program on a Cray supercomputer appear on the display screen of a DEC. X is the only widely available system to provide even the hope of a consistent interface across a multiple-vendor landscape.

In most cases, the meta key is located near the bottom left of the keyboard, in the vicinity of the space bar. Like the KeySyms, X abstracts all these keys into the meta key. X also allows for up to five meta keys to be available on the keyboard.

To detect when the first meta key is held down, check the state field of the XKeyEvent to see if the Mod1Mask bit is a one. This state field also contains information on the status of the Control and Shift keys. Few keyboards really have (or use) more than one meta key, so, in most cases, checking Mod1Mask (and perhaps Mod2Mask) should do the trick.

```
.
.
.
/*
**      Check for the first META key.  Many programs use keyboard
**      shortcuts for menu choices.  Such code would go here.
**
*/

if ( theEvent->state & Mod1Mask )      /* --  META Keys */

        {
        printf( "META [%s]\n", theKeyBuffer );
        }
```

As shown in Chapter 5, you can compare other masks against the state field to see which keys are held down at the same time a KeyPress event comes in, including the following:

Button1Mask	The first mouse button was down.
Button2Mask	The second mouse button was down.
Button3Mask	The third mouse button was down.
Button4Mask	The fourth mouse button was down (usually not available).
Button5Mask	The fifth mouse button was down (usually not available).
ShiftMask	A Shift key was down.
ControlMask	The Control key was down.
LockMask	The Caps Lock key was down.

`Mod1Mask`	The typical meta key was down.
`Mod2Mask`	The second meta key was down.
`Mod3Mask`	Another meta key often not found on the keyboard was down.
`Mod4Mask`	Another meta key often not found on the keyboard was down.
`Mod5Mask`	Another meta key often not found on the keyboard was down.

MOUSE BUTTONS

X11 assumes that most workstations include a mouse or other pointing device and that each mouse has three buttons, though up to five buttons are allowed. Some vendors, such as Hewlett-Packard and Apple, use a mouse with less than three buttons. In those cases, the missing mouse buttons are usually simulated by other means. On a Hewlett-Packard with a two-button mouse, the "middle" mouse button is simulated by pressing both mouse buttons at the same time. On a Macintosh II with a one-button mouse, two other mouse buttons are simulated with special keys on the keyboard (which differ depending on what type of keyboard is in use).

When designing user interfaces, it is a good idea to consider what types of machines will be running the software. To be the most generic, assume only one mouse button (or treat all mouse buttons the same). If your company has standardized on a given workstation vendor (or all workstations have the same type of mouse), this won't be a problem.

To determine which mouse button was pressed on a `ButtonPress` event, check the button field. (The state field can also be checked, as shown previously.) `ButtonRelease` events work the same way but signify that a button previously pressed has been released.

```
/*
**      Definitions for identifying which mouse or pointer button
**      was hit.
*/
#define LEFT_BUTTON     1
#define MIDDLE_BUTTON   2
#define RIGHT_BUTTON    3

        .
        .
        .

        switch( theEvent.type )
                {
                /*
                **      A Mouse button has been pressed.
                */
                case ButtonPress:

                        switch( theEvent.xbutton.button )
                                {
                                case LEFT_BUTTON  : printf( "Left mouse\n" );
                                                    break;
                                case MIDDLE_BUTTON: printf( "Middle mouse\n" );
                                                    break;
                                case RIGHT_BUTTON : printf( "Right mouse\n" );
                                                    break;
                                }
                        break;
                .
                .
                .
                }
```

EXAMPLE PROGRAM

The program that follows uses the same test file used in Chapter 5. A new file, `keyx.c`, handles the keyboard input, and `eventx.c` was modified to call the routine in `keyx.c`. The rest of the files are reused from Chapter 5.

The file keyx.c contains the routine processKeyPress, which takes a key event passed to it and then prints some information about the event. Most of the code handles the special keys that seem to populate modern keyboards, such as the Help, Page Up, and Delete keys. Your programs will need to look for the keys that are needed—looking for all the possible keys is generally a waste of time. For even more KeySyms, check the include file keysymdef.h. Run this program and try pressing each key on the keyboard. The "q" key quits the program, as before. The first meta key, the function keys, and most special keys should be included in the KeySym switch statement in the example program that follows. You can add any keys you need, or take out the keys that don't concern your application.

Example Program Source Code

Pressing the "q" key quits the program. The contents of the file keyx.c are as follows:

```
/*
**      keyx.c **
**      Handles keyboard events for the example X programs. **
*/

#include  <X11/Xlib.h>
#include  <X11/Xutil.h>
#include  <X11/keysym.h>
#include  <X11/keysymdef.h>

extern          Display         *theDisplay;

/*
**      processKeyPress handles the keyboard input for the
**      example X programs.

**
**      Note that it is passed a pointer to an XKeyEvent structure,
**      even though the event was originally placed in an XEvent union
**      structure.  X overlays the various structure types into
**      a union of structures.  By using the XKeyEvent, we can access
**      the keyboard elements more easily. **
*/

processKeyPress( theEvent )

XKeyEvent       *theEvent;
```

continued...

...from previous page

```
{       /* -- function processKeyPress */
        int                 length;
        int                 theKeyBufferMaxLen = 64;
        char                theKeyBuffer[ 65 ];
        KeySym              theKeySym;
        XComposeStatus      theComposeStatus;

        length = XLookupString( theEvent,
                            theKeyBuffer,
                            theKeyBufferMaxLen,
                            &theKeySym,
                            &theComposeStatus );

        /*
        **      Check for META keys.  Many programs use keyboard
        **      shortcuts for menu choices.  Such code would go here.
        **
        */

        if ( theEvent->state & Mod1Mask )      /* --  META Key */

                {
                switch( theKeyBuffer[ 0 ] )
                        {
                        case  'Q' :
                        case  'q' : printf( "META-Q hit\n" );
                                    return( 0 );
                                    break;
                        }
                printf( "META [%s]\n", theKeyBuffer );
                return( 1 );
                }

        /*
        **      Check if theKeySym is within the standard ASCII
        **      printable character range.
        **
        */

        if ( ( theKeySym >= ' ' ) &&       /* -- ASCII 32 is a space  */
           ( theKeySym <= '~' )   &&       /* -- ASCII 126 is a Tilde */
           ( length > 0 ) )                /* -- We have char input   */
                {
                printf( "ASCII key was hit: [%s]\n", theKeyBuffer );
```

continued...

...from previous page

```
        /*
        **      On Q, Quit the application
        */
        if ( ( theKeyBuffer[ 0 ] == 'q' ) ||
           ( theKeyBuffer[ 0 ] == 'Q' ) )
                {
                return( 0 );
                }
        }
else
        {
        /*
        **      Check for special keys on the keyboard.
        **      there are many more definitions in the header
        **      file keysymdef.h (probably in /usr/include/X11).
        **
        */
        switch( theKeySym )
                {
                case XK_Return   : printf( "Return\n" ); break;
                case XK_BackSpace: printf( "BackSpace\n" ); break;
                case XK_Escape   : printf( "ESCAPE\n" ); break;
                case XK_Delete   : printf( "Delete\n" ); break;
                case XK_Up       : printf( "Up\n" ); break;
                case XK_Down     : printf( "Down\n" ); break;
                case XK_Right    : printf( "Right\n" ); break;
                case XK_Left     : printf( "Left\n" ); break;
                case XK_R9       : /* -- Sun 386i Mapping */
                case XK_Prior    : printf( "Prior\n" ); break;
                case XK_R15      :
                case XK_Next     : printf( "Next\n" ); break;
                case XK_R13      : /* -- Sun 386i Mapping */
                case XK_End      : printf( "End\n" ); break;
                case XK_R7       : /* -- Sun 386i Mapping */
                case XK_Begin    : printf( "Begin\n" ); break;
                case XK_Insert   : printf( "Insert\n" ); break;
                case XK_Help     : printf( "Help\n" ); break;
                /*
                **      function Keys
                */
                case XK_F1       : printf( "F1\n" ); break;
                case XK_F2       : printf( "F2\n" ); break;
                case XK_F3       : printf( "F3\n" ); break;
                case XK_F4       : printf( "F4\n" ); break;
                case XK_F5       : printf( "F5\n" ); break;
                case XK_F6       : printf( "F6\n" ); break;
                case XK_F7       : printf( "F7\n" ); break;
                case XK_F8       : printf( "F8\n" ); break;
                case XK_F9       : printf( "F9\n" ); break;
                case XK_F10      : printf( "F10\n" ); break;
```

continued...

...from previous page

```
                        case XK_F11      : printf( "F11\n" ); break;
                        case XK_F12      : printf( "F12\n" ); break;
                        case XK_F13      : printf( "F13\n" ); break;
                        case XK_F14      : printf( "F14\n" ); break;
                        case XK_F15      : printf( "F15\n" ); break;
                        /*
                        **      Keypad Keys
                        */
                        case XK_KP_Enter : printf( "Keypad Enter\n" ); break;
                        case XK_KP_Equal : printf( "Keypad Equal\n" ); break;
                        case XK_KP_Multiply: printf( "Keypad *\n" ); break;
                        case XK_KP_Add   : printf( "Keypad +\n" ); break;
                        case XK_KP_Subtract:printf( "Keypad -\n" ); break;
                        case XK_KP_Decimal:printf( "Keypad .\n" ); break;
                        case XK_KP_Divide: printf( "Keypad / \n" ); break;
                        case XK_KP_0     : printf( "Keypad 0\n" ); break;
                        case XK_KP_1     : printf( "Keypad 1\n" ); break;
                        case XK_KP_2     : printf( "Keypad 2\n" ); break;
                        case XK_KP_3     : printf( "Keypad 3\n" ); break;
                        case XK_KP_4     : printf( "Keypad 4\n" ); break;
                        case XK_KP_5     : printf( "Keypad 5\n" ); break;
                        case XK_KP_6     : printf( "Keypad 6\n" ); break;
                        case XK_KP_7     : printf( "Keypad 7\n" ); break;
                        case XK_KP_8     : printf( "Keypad 8\n" ); break;
                        case XK_KP_9     : printf( "Keypad 9\n" ); break;
                        default          : ;
                        }
                }

        return( 1 );    /* -- continue processing */

}       /* -- function processKeyPress */


/* **   end of file keyx.c ** */
```

The contents of the file `eventx.c` are as follows:

```
/*
**      eventx.c
**
**      Contains the event loop (where the major action of most
**      X-based programs occurs).
**
*/

#include   <X11/Xlib.h>
#include   <X11/Xutil.h>

/*
**      Definitions for identifying which mouse or pointer button
**      was hit.
*/
#define LEFT_BUTTON       1
#define MIDDLE_BUTTON     2
#define RIGHT_BUTTON      3

extern  Display         *theDisplay;

/*
**      Under X, a window will never receive an event that it
**      hasn't asked for.  The way to ask for events is to set up
**      a mask indicating those events for which your window is
**      interested in. This mask is then passed to XSelectInput
**      along with a window id and a display pointer.
*/

#define EV_MASK (ButtonPressMask        | \
                 KeyPressMask           | \
                 ExposureMask           | \
                 StructureNotifyMask)

/*
**      eventLoop blocks awaiting an event from X.  When an event comes in,
**      it is decoded and processed.
**
**      This function is passed a Window and a GC so that drawing may
**      take place.
**
**      When the user presses a mouse button or types a "q",
**      the program will quit.
**
**
*/


eventLoop( theWindow, theGC )
```

continued...

...from previous page

```
Window  theWindow;
GC      theGC;

{       /* -- function eventLoop */
        XEvent          theEvent;

        /*
        **      Block on input, awaiting an event from X
        */

        XNextEvent( theDisplay, &theEvent );

        /*
        **      Decode the event and call a specific routine to
        **      handle it
        */
        switch( theEvent.type )
                {
                /*
                **      Part or all of the Window has been exposed to the
                **      world.  That part should be redrawn here.
                */
                case Expose:

                        /*
                        **      The XEvent structure is really a big union
                        **      of many structures, all of the
                        **      same size.  The generic part of the
                        **      structure is the xany part.
                        **/
                        refreshWindow( theEvent.xany.window );

                        break;

                case MapNotify:
                        refreshWindow( theEvent.xany.window );
                        break;

                /*
                **      A Mouse button has been pressed.
                */
                case ButtonPress:
                        switch( theEvent.xbutton.button )
                                {
                                case LEFT_BUTTON  : printf( "Left mouse\n" );
                                                    break;
                                case MIDDLE_BUTTON: printf( "Middle mouse\n" );
                                                    break;
                                case RIGHT_BUTTON : printf( "Right mouse\n" );
                                                    break;
                                }
```

continued...

...from previous page

```
                        /*
                        **      Quit on any mouse button in this example
                        **
                        */
                        return( 0 );
                        break;

                /*
                **      A key on the keyboard was hit.
                */
                case KeyPress:
                        /*
                        **      Quit if a "q" is hit.
                        */
                        return( processKeyPress( &theEvent ) );
                        break;


                /*
                **      The window has been sized or changed.
                */
                case ConfigureNotify:
                        break;
                }

        /*
        **      Return a 0 to quit, a 1 to keep going
        */
        return( 1 );
}       /* -- function eventLoop */

/*
**      initEvents
**      Selects input for the given window, with the default
**      event mask.
**
*/

initEvents( theWindow )

Window  theWindow;

{       /* -- function initEvents */

        XSelectInput( theDisplay,
                      theWindow,
                      EV_MASK );

}       /* -- function initEvents */

/*
**      end of file eventx.c
*/
```

The new Makefile is as follows:

```
##      X Project Makefile for Chapter 6, Example 1
##
EXEC=   test6
##
##
DEFINES
##
##
##      -g = Debugging info
##      -O = optimize (cannot use -g then)
CFLAGS=         -O
##
##
##      Libraries
##      X11     X11 graphics library
##
LIBS= -lX11
##
##
OBJECTS=        initx.o         \
                colorx.o        \
                drawx.o         \
                eventx.o        \
                keyx.o          \
                quitx.o         \
                textx.o         \
                windowx.o       \
                test5.o
##
##      Command to compile and link objects together
##
$(EXEC):        $(OBJECTS)
                cc -o $(EXEC) $(OBJECTS) $(LIBS)
##
##
##      end of make file
##
```

WHEN THE KEYBOARD MAPPING CHANGES

X allows the keyboard mapping to be dynamically changed. For example, some users may want to program the F2 key to enter the word "SAVE" when the F2 key is pressed. When the keyboard mapping has been changed, for whatever reason, X will send out a `MappingNotify` event. Your application will receive this event regardless of any event mask setting in a call to `XSelectInput` (i.e., it will receive `MappingNotify` events no matter what). **Note**: Do not confuse a `MappingNotify` event with a `MapNotify` event. The former refers to a keyboard-mapping change, and the latter refers to a window being mapped to the screen.

When a `MappingNotify` event comes in, the best bet is to call the function `XRefreshKeyboardMapping` to update the internal (i.e., within your application program) mapping information for the keyboard.

```
XEvent          theEvent;
Display         *theDisplay;
.
.
.
XNextEvent( theDisplay, &theEvent );

switch( theEvent.type )
        {
        .
        .
        .
        /*
        **      MappingNotify events come event without the
        **      event type listed in the event mask EV_MASK.
        **      When such an event occurs, it means that the
        **      keyboard has been re-mapped somehow.
        **      call XRefreshKeyboardMapping to keep up with
        **      the changes.  Do not confues this with MapNotify,
        **      above.
        */
        case MappingNotify:
                XRefreshKeyboardMapping( &theEvent ); break;
        }
```

SUMMARY

- X generalizes keyboard event processing, using the concept of KeySyms. KeySyms provide a symbolic way of identifying the various special keys on the keyboard, independent of the actual make and model of keyboard in use. Using KeySyms can help make your code portable to multiple platforms and help avoid issues specific to any one keyboard.

- Because many, many KeySyms are defined in keysymdef.h, and because most of the keys pressed will be QWERTY-type alphanumeric keys, you probably want to check for a KeyPress event of those types of keys first. This will optimize performance for the most common cases. After checking for the standard keys, then check for the special keyboard keys, such as the Prior (or Page Up) key and the Help key.

- You'll also want to check for meta keys, most often used in conjunction with other keys (such as an Alt-A combination) to extend the keyboard's capabilities.

- Also, different vendors provide different pointing devices; X assumes the user has three mouse buttons, while it allows up to five. Unless there are special circumstances—for example, if you're porting or designing an application that will be run only on workstations from a single vendor—it's best to assume the user only has access to one button.

Xlib Functions and Macros Introduced in This Chapter

XRefreshKeyboardMapping

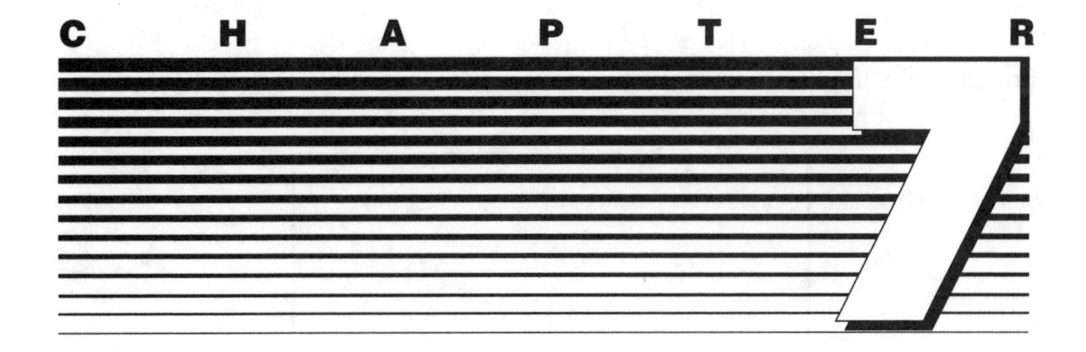

RUBBER-BAND LINES

This chapter discusses rubber-band lines, which are commonly used to provide feedback when users draw lines with a mouse. The term "rubber-band" is used because the lines look like there is a rubber band connecting the starting and current ending points. As the user moves the mouse, the ending point is constantly shifting. The rubber-band effect provides feedback.

For example, if a line were locked in now, it would resemble Figure 7.1:

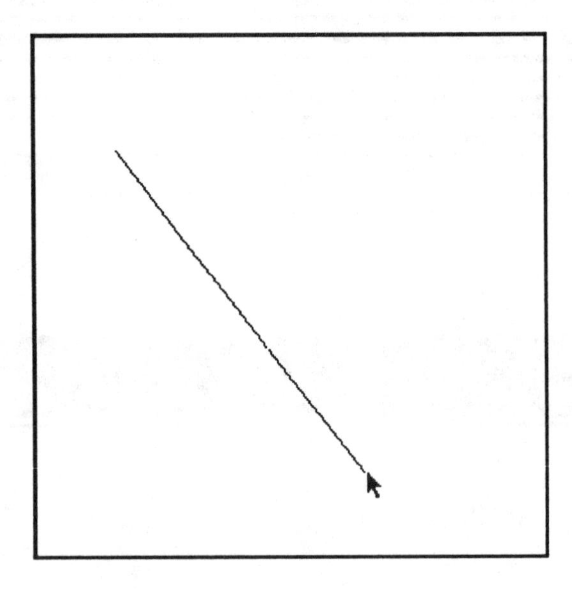

Figure 7.1. A rubber-band line.

The easiest way to create this rubber-band effect in X is to create a special graphics context for rubber-banding. Each GC (graphics context) has a graphics function field that determines its mode for drawing. The term "function" here doesn't mean an Xlib C function, but actually the name of the mode, or operation, identifier stored in the "function" field of the GC. Using the term "function" for both Xlib C language functions and a drawing mode is a bit confusing, but that is the offical X terminology. Once this graphics context is created, the drawing function (mode) should be changed so that it draws in `exclusive-or` (`xor`) mode.

RASTER OPERATION FUNCTIONS

X provides 16 drawing modes, often called raster operations, or **raster ops**. (Raster operations gained popularity in the SmallTalk-80 system, developed at the Xerox Palo Alto Research Center and used in the Apple Macintosh.) The basic idea behind raster ops is to control the output of a drawing operation, based on the bits you want to draw and the bits already on the screen in the area in which you want to draw. The xor mode takes advantage of a neat feature of exclusive-or: If you apply an exclusive-or operation when drawing once, you can restore the original picture by redrawing the same items, again applying an exclusive-or operation when drawing.

Each raster op follows the same approach. There is a set of pixels you want to draw, called the **source**. And there is a set of pixels already on the screen, called the **destination**, in the area in which you want to draw. X applies the GC raster function to the source and the destination to produce the result. The result is then drawn to the screen. (This sounds a lot more complicated than it really is.)

The default GC raster function is called GXcopy(see Figure 7.2), and it operates the way you would expect most graphics operations to operate: GXcopy ignores the destination bits. GXcopy takes the source pixels and splats them across the destination, wiping out the destination pixels underneath the source; that is, if you draw a black line on top of a blank white background, you see the black line.

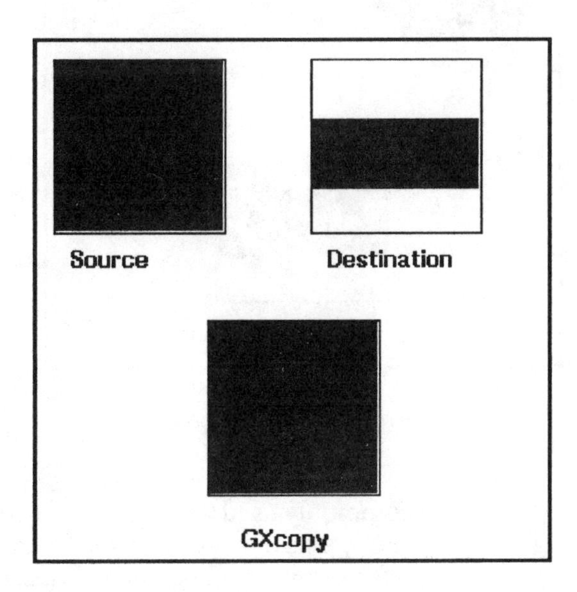

Figure 7.2 GXcopy

GXcopy is the default value for a GC's function field when you first create the graphics context. The opposite of GXcopy is an operation that leaves the destination area alone. Normally, this operation is called not drawing in the first place, but in X it is called GXnoop (for no-operation).

GXnoop (see Figure 7.3) is like not drawing, but you get the added benefit of sending an X packet over the network to the X server and forcing the X server to interpret the packet. Unless you are porting the X server to run on a new hardware platform and want to test the server, you will probably never use GXnoop.

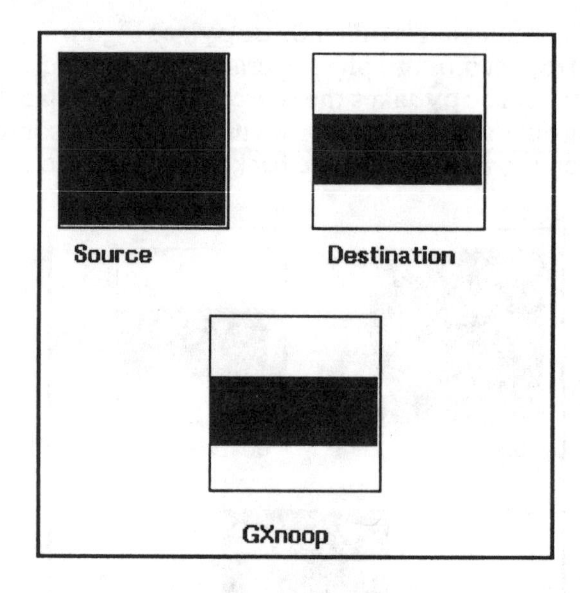

Figure 7.3 GXnoop

Aside from GXcopy, the most commonly used GC graphics function will probably be GXxor (see Figure 7.4), the exclusive-or mode introduced in this chapter. GXxor is used mainly for drawing rubber-band lines, boxes, and ovals. (Note the spelling of GXxor. There is also a GXor and a GXnor.)

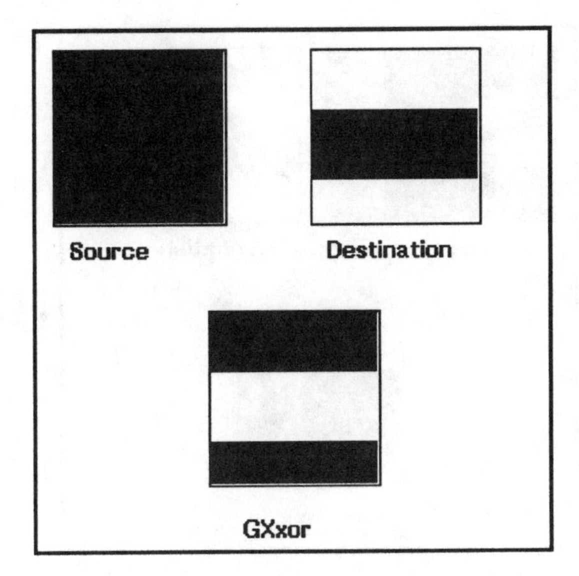

Figure 7.4 *GXxor*

The rest of the GC graphics functions are for the most part self-explanatory, as they seem to cover every possible variation you could ever think of. Most users will never need to use any of these functions, but just in case, the diagrams for the remaining graphics functions (Figures 7.5-7.17) are included on the following pages.

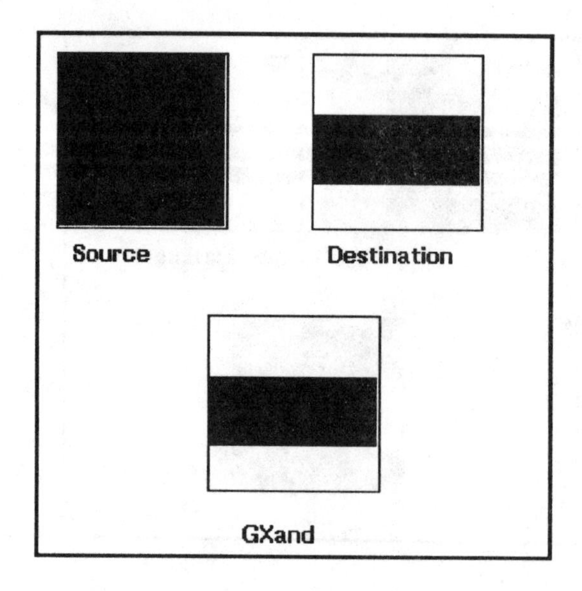

Figure 7.5 GXand

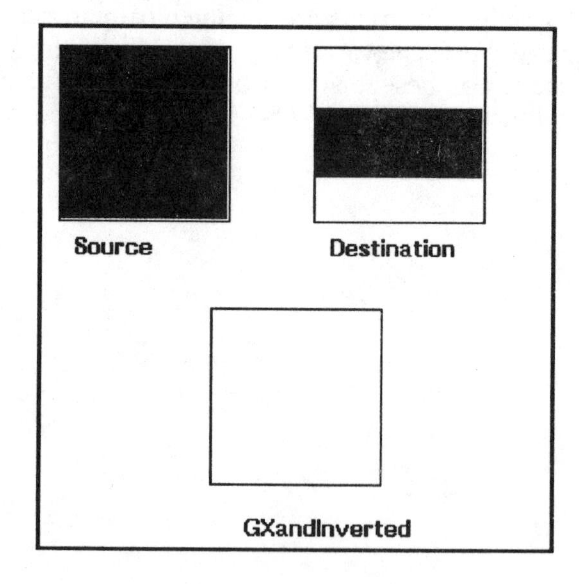

Figure 7.6 GXandInverted

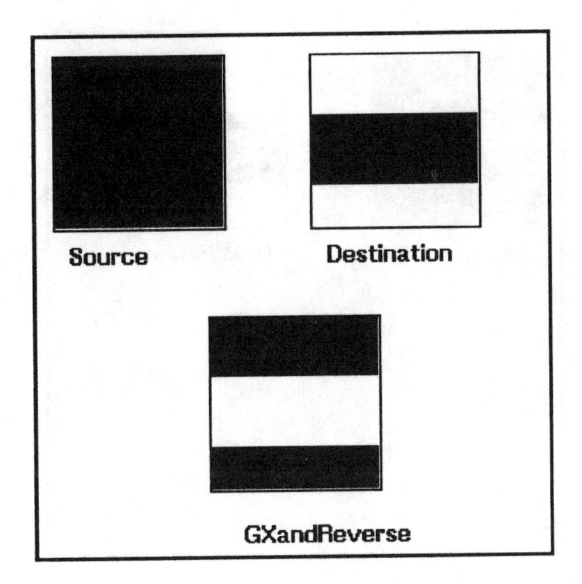

Figure 7.7 *GXandReverse*

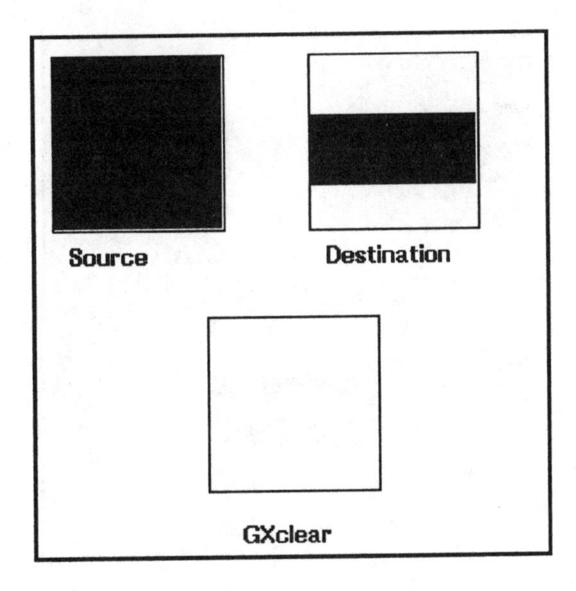

Figure 7.8 *GXclear*

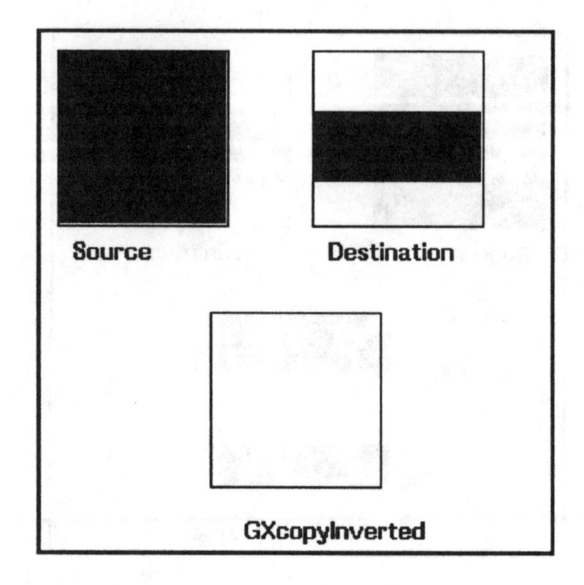

Figure 7.9 *GXcopyInverted*

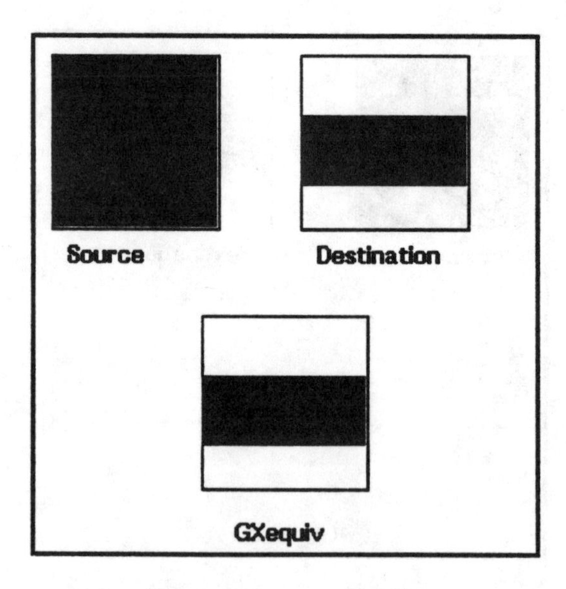

Figure 7.10 *GXequiv*

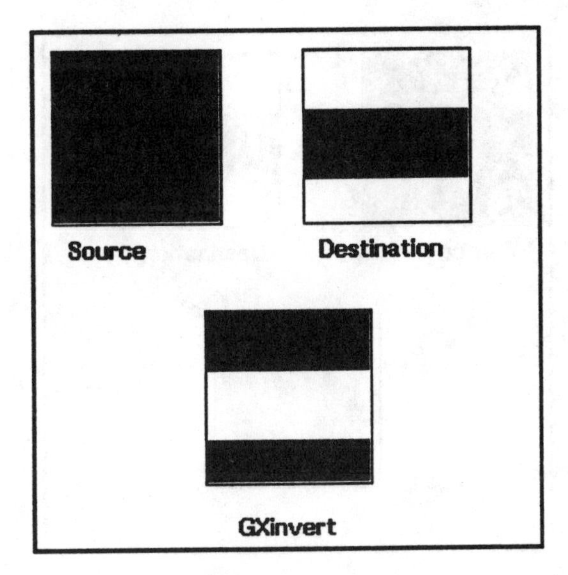

Figure 7.11 GXinvert

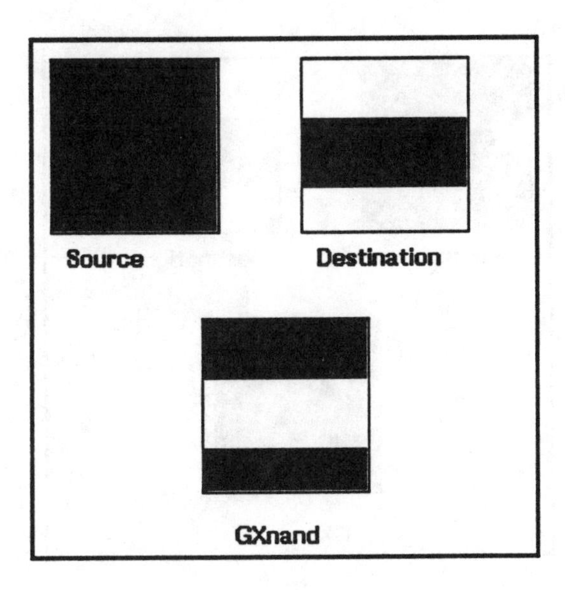

Figure 7.12 GXnand

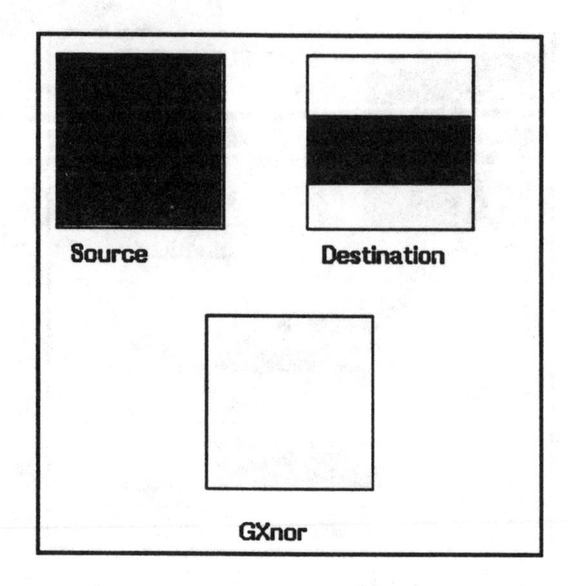

Figure 7.13 GXnor

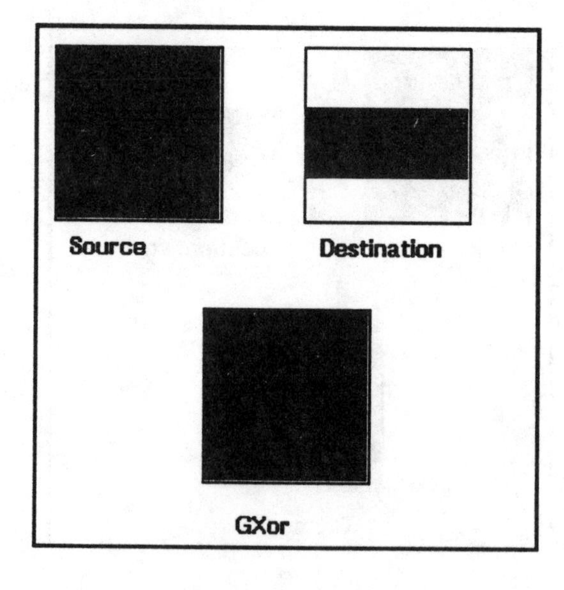

Figure 7.14 GXor

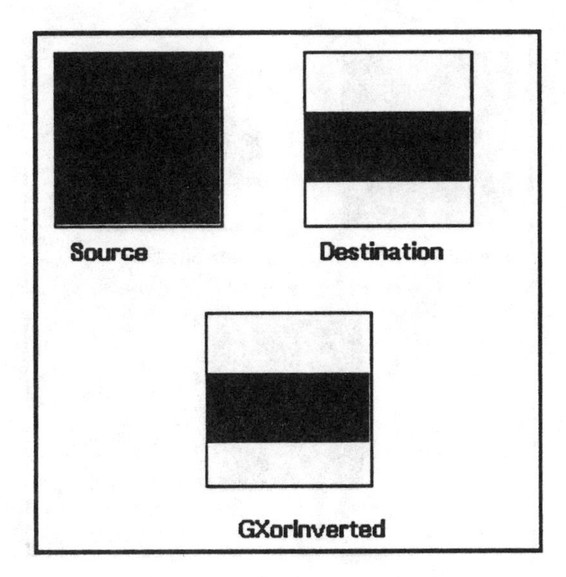

Figure 7.15 *GXorInverted*

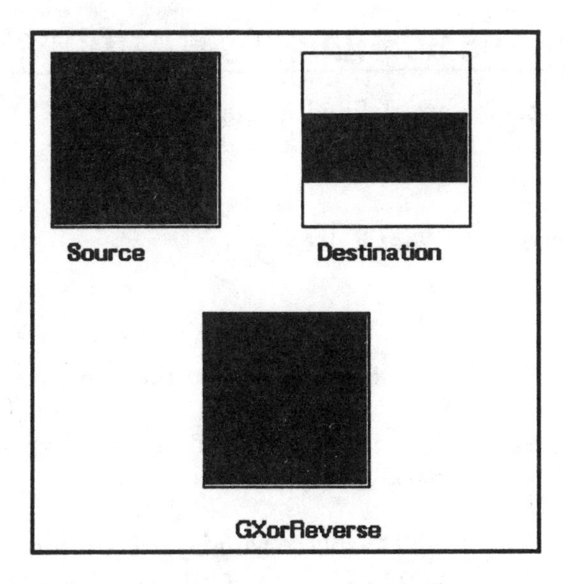

Figure 7.16 *GXorReverse*

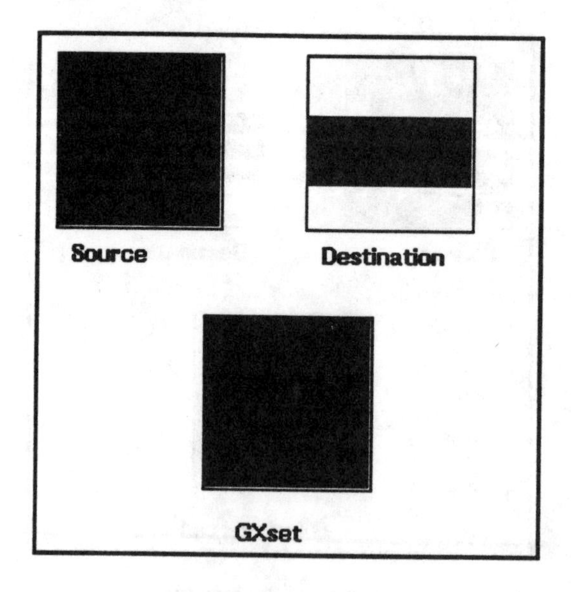

Figure 7.17 GXset

SUMMARY OF THE GC GRAPHICS FUNCTIONS

The `GC` function names are defined in the include file `X.h` (usually included automatically from the file `Xlib.h`).

GC Function Name	What it does	Value in X.h (in hexidecimal)
`GXand`	ANDS source and destination bits.	0x1
`GXandInverted`	Inverts source (NOT source), then ANDS with destination bits.	0x4
`GXandReverse`	ANDS source with inverted destination bits ((NOT dest) AND source).	0x2
`GXclear`	Clears out area (not portable).	0x0

`GXcopy`	Places down source, wipes out destination bits (default).	0x3
`GXcopyInverted`	Inverts the source (NOT source), wipes out destination bits.	0xC
`GXequiv`	Inverts the source (NOT source), then XORS with destination bits ((NOT source) XOR dest).	0x9
`GXinvert`	Inverts the desination bits (NOT dest).	0xA
`GXnand`	Inverts the source (NOT source), inverts the destination (NOT dest), then ors the two ((NOT source) OR (NOT dest)).	0xE
`GXnoop`	Leaves the destination bits alone.	0x5
`GXnor`	Inverts the source (NOT source), Inverts the destination (NOT dest), and ands the two together ((NOT source) AND (NOT dest)).	0x8
`GXor`	Ors the source and the destination bits (source OR dest).	0x7
`GXorInverted`	Inverts the source (NOT source), then ors with the destination bits ((NOT source) OR dest).	0xD
`GXorReverse`	Ors the source with the inverted destination bits (source OR (NOT dest)).	0xB
`GXset`	Sets all the bits in the drawing area (not portable).	0xF
`GXxor`	Exclusive-ors the source and the destination bits (used for rubber-band lines).	0x6

Be careful when using the GC functions GXclear and GXset, as these functions do not necessarily work the same on every machine. What they depend on is the use of 1 and 0 for the values of BlackPixel and WhitePixel – and these values may not hold through on all X servers. In general, it is best to avoid these modes if possible. Actually, the only modes most people will ever use are GXcopy and GXxor.

EXAMPLE 1: RUBBER-BAND LINES

Now, back to the original task of drawing rubber-band lines. If drawn twice, a line drawn in exclusive-or mode will disappear, leaving the original drawing intact. So the basic method for drawing rubber-band lines is as follows:

1. Create a new GC for the rubber-band effect, in addition to the regular GC used for drawing normal items.
2. Set the new GC's (graphics) function field to xor mode (GXxor), with the XSetFunction Xlib function.
3. Select an x, y coordinate location as an **anchor point** (the first point selected for the line). The goal is now to have the user select the second anchor point (the other end point for the line).
4. Draw an initial line in xor mode (using the new GC), saving the line coordinates.
5. Each time the pointer (mouse) moves, redraw the old line, using the xor GC. This makes the old line disappear. Adjust the coordinates to the new mouse position, and then draw the line to the new location, again in xor mode. Save these line coordinates.
6. When the user selects the line's end point, redraw the line, using the xor GC, to erase it. Then, draw the line, using the normal drawing GC (and not the GXxor GC) so the line appears on the display in its permanent likeness.

The first example program follows the above six steps. It takes the C program files from the last chapter and adds a new file: xor.c. This file contains two simple functions: xorSetUp and xorShutDown.

The function `xorSetUp` creates the new `GC` for a given window, using the previously written `createGC` function. It then uses the Xlib function `XSetFunction`, which sets the `GC`'s (drawing) function field to `GXxor`:

```
xorSetUp( theWindow, theXorGC )

Window  theWindow;
GC      *theXorGC;

{       /* -- function xorSetUp */

        createGC( theWindow, theXorGC );

        XSetFunction( theDisplay,
                *theXorGC,
                GXxor );

}       /* -- function xorSetUp */
```

`XSetFunction` officially looks like the following:

```
Display         *theDisplay;
GC              theGC;
int             theFunction;

XSetFunction( theDisplay,
        theGC,
        theFunction );
```

The function `xorShutDown` frees the `GC` used in rubber-banding so that the X server no longer must maintain the resource.

```
Display         *theDisplay;
.
.
.
xorShutDown( theXorGC )

GC      theXorGC;

{       /* -- function xorShutDown */

        XFreeGC( theDisplay, theXorGC );

}       /* -- function xorShutDown */
```

There are two strategies for xorSetUp and xorShutDown. The first would be to call xorSetUp every time a rubber-band line is needed. Then, xorShutDown would be called afterward to free up the resource. The second strategy is simpler and more efficient. Instead of constantly creating and freeing the rubber-band GC, create it once and store it in a global variable. Then, free it by calling xorShutDown at the end of the program.

The GC is tied to a window, so if you have one main window for most drawing, use the second strategy. In all the example programs so far in this book, only one window is used. Most applications will also use only one main window for drawing (other windows will probably be in use, but most user-driven drawing using rubber-banding will be centered in one window).

Once the rubber-band GC is set up, use the normal drawing functions created in earlier examples, such as drawLine, drawRectangle, and drawOval (from the file drawx.c, introduced in Chapter 2). Be sure to pass the new rubber-band xor GC as the GC parameter when drawing rubber-band lines.

One warning for using the GXxor GC function: If other drawing takes place between the time the line is first drawn in xor mode and the time the line is redrawn (to clear it out), the original picture may not be restored. This method of using GXxor depends on the original picture not changing between calls. Now, normally, no other program will be drawing to your windows, so this shouldn't be a problem. But if you intend to draw using GXxor over other windows, you should be aware of this limitation. Window managers typically allow you to move windows about the screen. These window managers often use GXxor to draw a ghost outline of the window, showing its size and shape, so you had better place it. These window managers need to stop all other graphics output while this takes place, or the screen will tend to look messy. All graphics output from other programs can be held up by the window manager "grabbing" the X server exclusively for your program during this time.

Example 1 Source Code

The contents of the file xor.c are as follows:

```
/*
**      xor.c
**
**      XOR (or rubber-banding) functions.  These functions make a user
**      interface look a lot better for drawing lines and boxes.
**
*/

#include    <X11/Xlib.h>
#include    <X11/Xutil.h>


extern  Display         *theDisplay;

/*
**      xorSetUp
**      Sets up the given window with a Xor Graphics Context
*/

xorSetUp( theWindow, theXorGC )

Window  theWindow;

GC      *theXorGC;

{       /* -- function xorSetUp */

        createGC( theWindow, theXorGC );

        XSetFunction( theDisplay,
                *theXorGC,
                GXxor );


        XFlush( theDisplay );

}       /* -- function xorSetUp */



/*
**      Frees up the Graphics Context storage in the server.
**
*/

xorShutDown( theXorGC )

GC      theXorGC;

{       /* -- function xorShutDown */

        XFreeGC( theDisplay, theXorGC );

}       /* -- function xorShutDown */
```

The contents of the file `eventx.c` are as follows:

```
/*
**      eventx.c
**
**      Contains the event loop (where the major action of most
**      X-based programs occurs).
*/

#include    <X11/Xlib.h>
#include    <X11/Xutil.h>

extern  Display         *theDisplay;

/*
**      Globals for current and last position.  A flag to specify
**      if the user is drawing something, and a GC for the rubber-band
**      mode.
**
*/

#define NOT_DRAWING_ON          0
#define DRAWING_ON              1

int     currentX = 0, currentY = 0;
int     lastX = 0, lastY = 0;
int     drawingOn = NOT_DRAWING_ON;
GC      theXorGC;

/*
**      Under X, a window will never receive an event that it
**      hasn't asked for.  The way to ask for events is to set up
**      a mask indicating those events for which your window is
**      interested in. This mask is then passed to XSelectInput
**      along with a window id and a display pointer.
*/

#define EV_MASK (ButtonPressMask            | \
                KeyPressMask                | \
                ExposureMask                | \
                PointerMotionMask           | \
                StructureNotifyMask)
```

continued...

...from previous page

```
/*
**      eventLoop blocks awaiting an event from X.  When an event
**      comes in, it is decoded and processed.
**
**      This function is passed a Window and a GC so that drawing may
**      take place.
**
**      When the user types a "q" the program will quit.
**
*/


eventLoop( theWindow, theGC )

Window  theWindow;
GC      theGC;

{       /* -- function eventLoop */
        XEvent          theEvent;

        /*
        **      Block on input, awaiting an event from X
        */

        XNextEvent( theDisplay, &theEvent );

        /*
        **      Decode the event and call a specific routine to
        **      handle it
        */

        switch( theEvent.type )
                {
                /*
                **      Part or all of the Window has been exposed to the
                **      world.  That part should be redrawn here.
                */
                case Expose:

                        /*
                        **      The XEvent structure is really a big union
                        **      of many structures, all of the
                        **      same size.  The generic part of the
                        **      structure is the xany part.
                        **/
                        XClearWindow( theDisplay,
                                theEvent.xany.window );

                        break;
```

continued...

...from previous page

```
case MapNotify:
        XClearWindow( theDisplay,
                theEvent.xany.window );
        break;

/*
**      A Mouse button has been pressed.
*/
case ButtonPress:
        if ( drawingOn == NOT_DRAWING_ON )
        {
        /* -- Initial point */
        lastX    = theEvent.xkey.x;
        lastY    = theEvent.xkey.y;
        currentX = lastX;
        currentY = lastY;

        drawingOn = DRAWING_ON;

        drawLine( theEvent.xany.window,
                theXorGC,
                lastX, lastY,
                currentX, currentY );
        }
else
        {
        /*
        **      Redraw line to clear it out
        */
        drawLine( theEvent.xany.window,
                theXorGC,
                lastX, lastY,
                currentX, currentY );

        currentX = theEvent.xkey.x;
        currentY = theEvent.xkey.y;

        drawLine( theEvent.xany.window,
                theGC,
                lastX, lastY,
                currentX, currentY );
        XFlush( theDisplay );
        lastX = currentX;
        lastY = currentY;

        drawingOn = NOT_DRAWING_ON;
        }
break;
```

continued...

...from previous page

```
                case MotionNotify:
                        if ( drawingOn == DRAWING_ON )
                               {
                               /*
                               **      Undraw last line
                               */
                               drawLine( theEvent.xany.window,
                                       theXorGC,
                                       lastX, lastY,
                                       currentX, currentY );

                               /*
                               **      Change Coords and draw new line
                               */
                               currentX = theEvent.xmotion.x;
                               currentY = theEvent.xmotion.y;

                               drawLine( theEvent.xany.window,
                                       theXorGC,
                                       lastX, lastY,
                                       currentX, currentY );
                               XFlush( theDisplay );
                               }
                        break;

                /*
                **      A key on the keyboard was hit.
                */
                case KeyPress:
                        return( processKeyPress( &theEvent ) );
                        break;

                /*
                **      The window has been sized or changed.
                */
                case ConfigureNotify:
                        break;
                }

        /*
        **      Return a 0 to quit, a 1 to keep going
        */
        return( 1 );
}       /* -- function eventLoop */


/*
**      initEvents
**      Selects input for the given window, with the default
**      event mask.
**
*/
```

continued...

...from previous page

```
initEvents( theWindow )

Window  theWindow;

{       /* -- function initEvents */


                        theWindow,
                        EV_MASK );

        /*
        **      Set Up rubber-banding Graphics Context
        */
        xorSetUp( theWindow, &theXorGC );

        /*
        **      Initialize drawing state variable
        */

        drawingOn = NOT_DRAWING_ON;

}       /* -- function initEvents */

/*
**      end of file eventx.c
*/
```

The contents of the revised `test.c` file are as follows:

```
/*
**      Chapter 7, Example 1
**
**      This program pops up a window and then draws into it.
**      On every mouse click, it draws a line from the previous
**      position to the new position.
**
**
*/

#include   <X11/Xlib.h>

/*
**      external GLOBALS
*/
```

continued...

...from previous page

```
extern          Display         *theDisplay;
extern          GC              theXorGC;
/*
**      GLOBALS defined here.
*/

GC              theGC;
XFontStruct     *fontStruct;

main()

{
        Window          theWindow, openWindow();
        XFontStruct     *initFont();

        /*
        **      Set up our connection to X
        */

        initX();

        /*
        **      Get some info on the display and print it
        */

        getXInfo();

        /*
        **      Set up colors
        */

        initDefaultColors();

        /*
        **      Open a window
        */

        theWindow = openWindow( 100, 100,       /* -- x, y location       */
                                300, 300,       /* -- width, height       */
                                0,              /* -- This is NOT a pop-up */
                                &theGC );       /* -- Graphics Context    */

        /*
        **      Set up the window to receive events from X.
        */
        initEvents( theWindow );
```

continued...

...from previous page

```
        /*
        ** Load in a font
        */
        fontStruct = initFont( theGC, "variable" );


        XFlush( theDisplay );

        /*
        **      Handle events
        */

        while( eventLoop( theWindow, theGC ) );

        /*
        **      Close the connection to the X server.
        */
        xorShutDown( theXorGC );
        XFreeFont( theDisplay, fontStruct );
        XDestroyWindow( the Display, theWindow );
        XFlush( theDisplay );
        quitX();

}


/*
**      refreshWindow is called when an Expose event comes in from X.
**      It redraws the whole contents of the window (since there is
**      not much to draw.  A more effient program would check for the
**      region and only refresh that region.
**
*/

refreshWindow( theExposedWindow )

Window  theExposedWindow;


{       /* -- function refreshWindow */

        /*
        **      Not needed for example
        */

}       /* -- function refreshWindow */


/*
**      end of file.
*/
```

The contents of the revised Makefile are as follows:

```
##      X Project Makefile for Chapter 7, Example 1
##
EXEC=   test7
##
## DEFINES
##
##
##      -g = Debugging info
##      -O = optimize (cannot use -g then)
CFLAGS= -O
##
##
##      Libraries
##      X11     X11 graphics library
##
LIBS=   -lX11
##
##
OBJECTS=        initx.o         \
                colorx.o        \
                drawx.o         \
                eventx.o        \
                keyx.o          \
                quitx.o         \
                textx.o         \
                windowx.o       \
                xor.o           \
                test7.o
##
##      Command to compile and link objects together
##
$(EXEC):        $(OBJECTS)
                cc -o $(EXEC) $(OBJECTS) $(LIBS)
##
##
##      end of make file
##
```

EXAMPLE 2: RUBBER-BAND OVALS

The second example program performs the same type of task as the first example program, except that the second example draws rubber-band ovals instead of rubber-band lines. The only file modified is the file `eventx.c`, which has the line-drawing code changed to oval-drawing routines.

Note that ovals need to have a bounding rectangle, i.e., a rectangle that ends up at a lower position than where it starts, meaning that the first point must have X and Y coordinate values lower than the second point's X and Y coordinate values. This is based on the way X draws ovals with a bounding rectangle; therefore, if you move the mouse pointer up after selecting the first point, the example program will stop drawing rubber-band ovals until the mouse is moved to a point lower than the starting location. This code had to be added to create the second example program.

Ovals, because they are made by the function `XDrawArc`, also take much longer to draw than rubber-band lines or rectangles. Try replacing all `drawOval` functions with `drawRectangle`, and you will see just how long the drawing of ovals takes. Note that this program reuses all the files except `eventx.c`.

Example 2 Source Code

The revised contents of the file `eventx.c` are as follows:

```
/*
**      eventx.c
**
**      Contains the event loop (where the major action of most
**      X-based programs occurs).
**
*/

#include   <X11/Xlib.h>
#include   <X11/Xutil.h>

extern  Display         *theDisplay;

/*
**      Globals for current and last position. A flag to specify
**      if the user is drawing something, and a GC for the rubber-band
**      mode.
**
*/
```

continued...

...from previous page

```
#define NOT_DRAWING_ON          0
#define DRAWING_ON              1

int     currentX = 0, currentY = 0;
int     lastX = 0, lastY = 0;
int     drawingOn = NOT_DRAWING_ON;
GC      theXorGC;

/*
**      Under X, a window will never receive an event that it
**      hasn't asked for.  The way to ask for events is to set up
**      a mask indicating those events for which your window is
**      interested in. This mask is then passed to XSelectInput
**      along with a window id and a display pointer.
*/

#define EV_MASK (ButtonPressMask            | \
                KeyPressMask                | \
                ExposureMask                | \
                PointerMotionMask           | \
                StructureNotifyMask)

/*
**      eventLoop blocks awaiting an event from X.  When an event
**      comes in, this function is passed a Window and a GC so that
**      drawing may take place.
**
**      When the user types a "q" the program will quit.
**
*/


eventLoop( theWindow, theGC )

Window  theWindow;
GC      theGC;

{       /* -- function eventLoop */
        XEvent          theEvent;


        /*
        **      Block on input, awaiting an event from X
        */

        XNextEvent( theDisplay, &theEvent );
        /*
        **      Decode the event and call a specific routine to
        **      handle it
        */
```

continued...

...from previous page

```
switch( theEvent.type )
        {
        /*
        **      Part or all of the Window has been exposed to the
        **      world.  That part should be redrawn here.
        */
        case Expose:

                /*
                **      The XEvent structure is really a big union
                **      of many structures, all of the
                **      same size.  The generic part of the
                **      structure is the xany part.
                **/
                XClearWindow( theDisplay,
                        theEvent.xany.window );

                break;

        case MapNotify:
                XClearWindow( theDisplay,
                        theEvent.xany.window );
                break;

        /*
        **      A Mouse button has been pressed.
        */
        case ButtonPress:
                /*
                **      Set up starting point for item
                */
                if ( drawingOn == NOT_DRAWING_ON )
                        {
                        /* -- Initial point */
                        lastX    = theEvent.xkey.x;
                        lastY    = theEvent.xkey.y;
                        currentX = lastX;
                        currentY = lastY;

                        drawingOn = DRAWING_ON;

                        drawOval( theEvent.xany.window,
                                theXorGC,
                                lastX, lastY,
                                currentX - lastX,
                                currentY - lastY );
                        }
```

continued...

...from previous page

```
                /*
                **      Get ending point and draw item
                */
                else
                        {
                        if ( ( theEvent.xkey.x > lastX ) &&
                           ( theEvent.xkey.y   > lastY ) )
                                {
                                /*
                                **      Redraw item to clear it out
                                */
                                drawOval( theEvent.xany.window,
                                        theXorGC,
                                        lastX, lastY,
                                        currentX - lastX,
                                        currentY - lastY );

                                currentX = theEvent.xkey.x;
                                currentY = theEvent.xkey.y;

                                drawOval( theEvent.xany.window,
                                        theGC,
                                        lastX, lastY,
                                        currentX - lastX,
                                        currentY - lastY );

                                XFlush( theDisplay );
                                lastX = currentX;
                                lastY = currentY;

                                drawingOn = NOT_DRAWING_ON;
                                }
                        }
                break;

        case MotionNotify:
                if ( drawingOn == DRAWING_ON )
                        {

                        /*
                        **      Ovals look rather stange if
                        **      the width or height is < 0.
                        **      Therefore, only draw if the
                        **      current point > last point
                        */
```

continued...

...from previous page

```
                        if ( ( theEvent.xmotion.x > lastX ) &&
                          ( theEvent.xmotion.y   > lastY ) )
                            {
                            /*
                            **      Undraw last line
                            */
                            drawOval( theEvent.xany.window,
                                    theXorGC,
                                    lastX, lastY,
                                    currentX - lastX,
                                    currentY - lastY );

                            /*
                            **      Change Coords and draw new line
                            */
                            currentX = theEvent.xmotion.x;
                            currentY = theEvent.xmotion.y;

                            drawOval( theEvent.xany.window,
                                    theXorGC,
                                    lastX, lastY,
                                    currentX - lastX,
                                    currentY - lastY );
                            }

                        XFlush( theDisplay );
                        }
                break;

        /*
        **      A key on the keyboard was hit.
        */
        case KeyPress:
                return( processKeyPress( &theEvent ) );
                break;

          /*
          **      The window has been sized or changed.
          */
          case ConfigureNotify:
                  break;
          }

    /*
    **      Return a 0 to quit, a 1 to keep going
    */
    return( 1 );
}       /* -- function eventLoop */
```

continued...

...from previous page

```
/*
**      initEvents
**      Selects input for the given window, with the default
**      event mask.
**
*/

initEvents( theWindow )

Window  theWindow;

{       /* -- function initEvents */

        XSelectInput( theDisplay,
                      theWindow,
                      EV_MASK );

        /*
        **      Set Up rubber-banding Graphics Context
        */
        xorSetUp( theWindow, &theXorGC );

        /*
        **      Initialize drawing state variable
        */

        drawingOn = NOT_DRAWING_ON;

}       /* -- function initEvents */

/*
**      end of file eventx.c
*/
```

EXAMPLE 3: SHOWING THE RASTER OP FUNCTIONS

When writing the previous section on the X raster op functions, such as GXcopy, the authors put together a little test program to display these GC functions. The figures at the beginning of this chapter were made from actual screen dumps of the output of this simple test program. Because that program was so useful for understanding the 16 GC functions, it will be included here as an example.

This test program was created by taking the files from the second example program and then modifying small parts to perform certain tasks. This is an easy way to put together test programs, and you are encouraged to test out any area of X you are unsure of by quickly putting together a test program and using the base routines described in this book to get you started.

This third example program places the same window on the screen as before, but it displays three rectangles inside. The first rectangle shows the source for a drawing operation and is a filled rectangle. The second rectangle shows the destination where the drawing will take place. The third rectangle shows what happens when you draw the source onto the destination by using a particular GC graphics function, such as GXxor. The program uses a different raster op function each time a mouse button is pressed.

For this test program, two files were changed. First, the window needed to display only one raster op function at a time to be as clear as possible. So the file eventx.c was modified to clear the window and draw a new raster op example on each ButtonPress event. Then, all the code for drawing rubber-band ovals and lines was cut out because it simply got in the way of showing example raster ops.

Second, the test file test7.c was modified to add a number of new functions for displaying a raster op example.

The function srcRectangle fills the rectangle for the source part of the drawing. This simulates what you would be drawing while using a given GC graphics function. This function merely fills a rectangle, based on a given starting X and Y coordinate location. The reason the srcRectangle and destRectangle functions were created was to make sure that each time the "source" part was drawn, it was drawn in the same way. The same is true for the "destination" part. Otherwise, the program would not accurately simulate the various GC graphics functions.

```
srcRectangle( theWindow, theGC, startX, startY )

Window  theWindow;
GC      theGC;
int     startX, startY;

{       /* -- function srcRectangle */

        fillRectangle( theWindow, theGC,
                startX + 1, startY + 1,
                98, 98 );

}       /* -- function srcRectangle */
```

The function destRectangle draws a smaller, horizontal rectangle so that some of the bits in the destination are on and others are off. This way, GC functions such as GXxor and GXnand will be shown more clearly.

```
destRectangle( theWindow, theGC, startX, startY )

Window  theWindow;
GC              theGC;
int             startX, startY;

{       /* -- function destRectangle */

        fillRectangle( theWindow, theGC,
                startX + 1, startY + 35,
                98, 40 );

}       /* -- function destRectangle */
```

The meat of the test is the function refreshWindow. It is based on the refreshWindow used in Chapter 5, but this one draws the three test rectangles. In this example, refreshWindow first clears the window and then sets the graphics context, theGC, to draw in the normal mode, GXcopy. The GXcopy mode is used to draw all static data. Only at the end, when drawing the source rectangle over the destination rectangle, will the new GC graphics function, theFunction, be used. theFunctionName is the name of the GC graphics function, such as "GXor" for the GXor function. theFunctionName is for display purposes only.

```
refreshWindow( theWindow, theGC, theFunction, theFunctionName )

Window  theWindow;
GC      theGC;
int     theFunction;
char    theFunctionName[];

{       /* -- function refreshWindow */

        /*
        **      First clear the window
        */
        XClearWindow( theDisplay,
                theWindow );
```

continued...

...from previous page

```
/*
**      Set the GC's graphics function to the default, GXcopy
*/
XSetFunction( theDisplay,
        theGC,
        GXcopy );

/*
**      Draw the Source test rectangle.
**      The Source is a solid filled rectangle.
**
*/

drawRectangle( theWindow, theGC,
        10, 10,
        100, 100 );

srcRectangle( theWindow, theGC, 10, 10 );

XDrawImageString( theDisplay,
        theWindow,
        theGC,
        20, 130,
        "Source", strlen( "Source" ) );

/*
**      Draw the Destination test rectangle.
**      The Destination is a filled horizontal rectangle.
**
*/

drawRectangle( theWindow, theGC,
        160, 10,
        100, 100 );

destRectangle( theWindow, theGC, 160, 10 );

XDrawImageString( theDisplay,
        theWindow,
        theGC,
        170, 130,
        "Destination", strlen( "Destination" ) );

/*
**      Draw the Function test rectangle, exactly as the
**      Destination rectangle.
*/
```

continued...

...from previous page

```
        drawRectangle( theWindow, theGC,
                100, 160,
                100, 100 );

        destRectangle( theWindow, theGC, 100, 160 );

        XDrawImageString( theDisplay,
                theWindow,
                theGC,
                120, 290,
                theFunctionName, strlen( theFunctionName ) );

        /*
        **      Now, apply the test GC function, by drawing the
        **      Source rectangle on top of the Destination
        **      rectangle already drawn.
        */

        XSetFunction( theDisplay,
                theGC,
                theFunction );

        srcRectangle( theWindow, theGC, 100, 160 );

        /*
        **      Send all output to the screen
        */

        XFlush( theDisplay );

}       /* -- function refreshWindow */
```

The test program needed some way to change from one GC graphics function to another. The new function `getGCFunction` accomplished this task. `getGCFunction` is passed a pointer to an integer and a pointer to a character string. The integer is incremented from 0 to 16 and then back to 0 again to start over. After the increment, the character string is set to a string that describes the GC graphics function, such as "GXnand" for the function `GXnand`.

```
getGCFunction( theFunction, theName )

int     *theFunction;
char    theName[];

{       /* -- function getGCFunction */

        /*
        **      Increment the function
        */

        *theFunction = *theFunction + 1;

        if ( *theFunction > 0x0F )
                *theFunction = 0x00;

        /*
        **      Get new name
        */
        switch( *theFunction )
                {
                case  0x00: strcpy( theName, "GXclear" ); break;
                case  0x01: strcpy( theName, "GXand" ); break;
                case  0x02: strcpy( theName, "GXandReverse" ); break;
                case  0x03: strcpy( theName, "GXcopy" ); break;
                case  0x04: strcpy( theName, "GXandInverted" ); break;
                case  0x05: strcpy( theName, "GXnoop" ); break;
                case  0x06: strcpy( theName, "GXxor" ); break;
                case  0x07: strcpy( theName, "GXor" ); break;
                case  0x08: strcpy( theName, "GXnor" ); break;
                case  0x09: strcpy( theName, "GXequiv" ); break;
                case  0x0A: strcpy( theName, "GXinvert" ); break;
                case  0x0B: strcpy( theName, "GXorReverse" ); break;
                case  0x0C: strcpy( theName, "GXcopyInverted" ); break;
                case  0x0D: strcpy( theName, "GXorInverted" ); break;
                case  0x0E: strcpy( theName, "GXnand" ); break;
                case  0x0F: strcpy( theName, "GXset" ); break;
                }

}       /* -- function getGCFunction */
```

To switch the GC graphics function (mode) on each `ButtonPress` event, the file `eventx.c` was modified to handle the actual switching. It keeps two global variables, one (an integer) for the GC graphics function and the other (a character array) for a text string describing the function.

```
/*
**      Globals to increment the graphics GC function, from 0
**      to 16.
*/

int     theGCFunction = 0x00;    /* -- 0 in hexidecimal */

/*
**      theFunctionName holds a text string with the name of the
**      function
*/
char    theGCFunctionName[ 30 ];
```

Then, in the `eventLoop` function, what happens when a `ButtonPress` event is received was changed to the following:

```
        .
        .
        .
        case ButtonPress:
                getGCFunction( &theGCFunction,
                        theGCFunctionName );
                refreshWindow( theEvent.xany.window,
                        theGC,
                        theGCFunction,
                        theGCFunctionName );
                break;
```

This ties the whole test program together. It took a lot less time to put together this test program than it did to make the 16 images for printing the figures in this chapter. Note that a number of GC raster ops gave different results when run on a color and a monochrome system. The GC functions `GXcopyInverted`, `GXequiv`, `GXinvert`, `GXnand`, `GXnor`, `GXorInverted`, and `GXorReverse` all output some variety of green or tan on a color system. The difference was between an X server with eight color planes and an X server with one color plane. When inverting colored pixels, you normally get other colored pixels (note that black and white are colors in X). When inverting on a monochrome system, the only choices are black and white. Before using any GC modes other than `GXcopy` or `GXxor`, test them out and experiment to find the mode you want.

Example 3 Source Code

The revised contents of the test file `test7.c` are as follows:

```
/*
**      Chapter 7, Example 3
**
**      This simple add-on displays a raster-op mode in a window.
**
**
*/

#include        <X11/Xlib.h>

/*
**      external GLOBALS from initx.c
*/

extern          Display         *theDisplay;


/*
**      GLOBALS defined here.
*/

GC              theGC;
XFontStruct     *fontStruct;

main()

{
        Window          theWindow, openWindow();
        XFontStruct     *initFont();

        /*
        **      Set up our connection to X
        */

        initX();

        /*
        **      Get some info on the display and print it
        */

        getXInfo();

        /*
        **      Set up colors
        */

        initDefaultColors();
```

continued...

...from previous page

```
        /*
        **      Open a window
        */

        theWindow = openWindow( 100, 100,         /* -- x, y location          */
                                300, 300,         /* -- width, height          */
                                0,                /* -- This is NOT a pop-up   */
                                &theGC );         /* -- Graphics Context       */


        /*
        ** Load in a font
        */
        fontStruct = initFont( theGC, "variable" );


        refreshWindow( theWindow, theGC, GXxor, "GXxor" );

        /*
        **      Set up the window to receive events from X.
        */
        initEvents( theWindow );

        XFlush( theDisplay );

        /*
        **      Handle events
        */

        while( eventLoop( theWindow, theGC ) );

        /*
        **      Close the connection to the X server.
        */

        XFreeFont( theDisplay, fontStruct );
        XDestroyWindow( theDisplay, theWindow );
        XFlush( theDisplay );
        quitX();

}


/*
**      refreshWindow is called to draw a sample of a given graphics
**      function.  This is a special version of this function for
**      chapter 7, example 3.  It is passed a window to draw in, a
**      Graphics Context and a display function to test out.  It draws
**      two regular rectangles (with the GXcopy, the default, graphics
**      GC function) and then a test rectangle in the given GC
**      function.
**
```

continued...

...from previous page

```
**      Since this is a function for test purposes only, it assumes
**      a window size of 300 by 300 pixels.  Normally, you shouldn't
**      assume things like this.
**
**
*/

refreshWindow( theWindow, theGC, theFunction, theFunctionName )

Window  theWindow;
GC      theGC;
int     theFunction;
char    theFunctionName[];

{       /* -- function refreshWindow */

        /*
        **      First clear the window
        */
        XClearWindow( theDisplay,
                theWindow );

        /*
        **      Set the GC's graphics function to the default, GXcopy
        */
        XSetFunction( theDisplay,
                theGC,
                GXcopy );

        /*
        **      Draw the Source test rectangle.
        **      The Source is a solid filled rectangle.
        **
        */

        drawRectangle( theWindow, theGC,
                10, 10,
                100, 100 );

        srcRectangle( theWindow, theGC, 10, 10 );

        XDrawImageString( theDisplay,
                theWindow,
                theGC,
                20, 130,
                "Source", strlen( "Source" ) );
```

continued...

...from previous page

```
/*
**      Draw the Destination test rectangle.
**      The Destination is a filled horizontal rectangle.
**
*/

drawRectangle( theWindow, theGC,
        160, 10,
        100, 100 );

destRectangle( theWindow, theGC, 160, 10 );

XDrawImageString( theDisplay,
        theWindow,
        theGC,
        170, 130,
        "Destination", strlen( "Destination" ) );

/*
**      Draw the Function test rectangle, exactly as the
**      Destination rectangle.
*/

drawRectangle( theWindow, theGC,
        100, 160,
        100, 100 );

destRectangle( theWindow, theGC, 100, 160 );

XDrawImageString( theDisplay,
        theWindow,
        theGC,
        120, 290,
        theFunctionName, strlen( theFunctionName ) );

/*
**      Now, apply the test GC function, by drawing the
**      Source rectangle on top of the Destination
**      rectangle already drawn.
*/

XSetFunction( theDisplay,
        theGC,
        theFunction );

srcRectangle( theWindow, theGC, 100, 160 );

/*
**      Send all output to the screen
*/
```

continued...

...from previous page

```
        XFlush( theDisplay );


}       /* -- function refreshWindow */

/*
**      getGCFunction increments the graphics context function
**      and sets up[ a string with the function's name.
**
*/

getGCFunction( theFunction, theName )

int     *theFunction;
char    theName[];

{       /* -- function getGCFunction */

        /*
        **      Increment the function
        */

        *theFunction = *theFunction + 1;

        if ( *theFunction > 0x0F )
                *theFunction = 0x00;

        /*
        **      Get new name
        */
        switch( *theFunction )
                {
                case  0x00: strcpy( theName, "GXclear" ); break;
                case  0x01: strcpy( theName, "GXand" ); break;
                case  0x02: strcpy( theName, "GXandReverse" ); break;
                case  0x03: strcpy( theName, "GXcopy" ); break;
                case  0x04: strcpy( theName, "GXandInverted" ); break;
                case  0x05: strcpy( theName, "GXnoop" ); break;
                case  0x06: strcpy( theName, "GXxor" ); break;
                case  0x07: strcpy( theName, "GXor" ); break;
                case  0x08: strcpy( theName, "GXnor" ); break;
                case  0x09: strcpy( theName, "GXequiv" ); break;
                case  0x0A: strcpy( theName, "GXinvert" ); break;
                case  0x0B: strcpy( theName, "GXorReverse" ); break;
                case  0x0C: strcpy( theName, "GXcopyInverted" ); break;
                case  0x0D: strcpy( theName, "GXorInverted" ); break;
                case  0x0E: strcpy( theName, "GXnand" ); break;
                case  0x0F: strcpy( theName, "GXset" ); break;
                }
```

continued...

...from previous page

```
}       /* -- function getGCFunction */

/*
**      srcRectangle fills a rectangle for the source GC function
**      part of the test.  It is passed a window, a GC and the
**      starting coords of the rectangle to draw in.  The srcRectangle
**      fills a 98-pixel wide rectangle.
**
*/

srcRectangle( theWindow, theGC, startX, startY )

Window  theWindow;
GC      theGC;
int     startX, startY;

{       /* -- function srcRectangle */

        fillRectangle( theWindow, theGC,
                startX + 1, startY + 1,
                98, 98 );

}       /* -- function srcRectangle */


/*
**      destRectangle fills a rectangle for the source GC function
**      part of the test.  It is passed a window, a GC and the
**      starting coords of the rectangle to draw in. The destRectangle
**      fills a horizontal rectangle starting at 35 pixels
**      down from startY and going down 40 more pixels.  It fills
**      the rectangle across from startX + 1 to startX + 98.
**
*/

destRectangle( theWindow, theGC, startX, startY )

Window  theWindow;
GC      theGC;
int     startX, startY;

{       /* -- function destRectangle */

        fillRectangle( theWindow, theGC,
                startX + 1, startY + 35,
                98, 40 );

}       /* -- function destRectangle */
/*
**      end of file.
*/
```

The revised contents of the file `eventx.c` are as follows:

```
/*
**      eventx.c
**
**      Contains the event loop (where the major action of most
**      X-based programs occurs).
**
**      This is a specially-modified version for Chapter 7, example
**      3. All it basically does is show another raster op mode on
**      each mouse button press.  If a q key is hit, though, it will
**      quit the program.
**
*/

#include        <X11/Xlib.h>
#include        <X11/Xutil.h>

extern          Display         *theDisplay;

/*
**      Globals to increment the graphics GC function, from 0
**      to 16.
*/

int     theGCFunction = 0x00;    /* -- 0 in hexidecimal */

/*
**      theFunctionName holds a text string with the name of the
**      function
*/
char    theGCFunctionName[ 30 ];

/*
**      Under X, a window will never receive an event that it
**      hasn't asked for.  The way to ask for events is to set up
**      a mask indicating those events for which your window is
**      interested in. This mask is then passed to XSelectInput
**      along with a window id and a display pointer.
*/

#define EV_MASK (ButtonPressMask        | \
                KeyPressMask            | \
                ExposureMask            | \
                PointerMotionMask       | \
                StructureNotifyMask)

/*
**      eventLoop blocks awaiting an event from X.  When an event
**      comes in, it is decoded and processed.
**
```

continued...

...from previous page

```
**      This function is passed a Window and a GC so that drawing may
**      take place.
**
**      When the user types a "q" the program will quit.
**
*/


eventLoop( theWindow, theGC )

Window  theWindow;
GC      theGC;

{       /* -- function eventLoop */
        XEvent          theEvent;


        /*
        **      Block on input, awaiting an event from X
        */

        XNextEvent( theDisplay, &theEvent );

        /*
        **      Decode the event and call a specific routine to
        **      handle it
        */

        switch( theEvent.type )
                {
                /*
                **      Part or all of the Window has been exposed to the
                **      world.  That part should be redrawn here.
                */
                case Expose:

                        /*
                        **      The XEvent structure is really a big union
                        **      of many structures, all of the
                        **      same size.  The generic part of the
                        **      structure is the xany part.
                        */
                        getGCFunction( &theGCFunction,
                                theGCFunctionName );

                        refreshWindow( theEvent.xany.window,
                                theGC,
                                theGCFunction,
                                theGCFunctionName );
                        break;
```

continued...

...from previous page

```
                /*
                **      A Mouse button has been pressed.
                */
                case ButtonPress:
                        getGCFunction( &theGCFunction,
                                theGCFunctionName );
                        refreshWindow( theEvent.xany.window,
                                theGC,
                                theGCFunction,
                                theGCFunctionName );
                        break;
                /*
                **      A key on the keyboard was hit.
                */
                case KeyPress:
                        return( processKeyPress( &theEvent ) );
                        break;
                }

        /*
        **      Return a 0 to quit, a 1 to keep going
        */
        return( 1 );
}       /* -- function eventLoop */


/*
**      initEvents
**      Selects input for the given window, with the default
**      event mask.
**
*/

initEvents( theWindow )

Window  theWindow;

{       /* -- function initEvents */

        XSelectInput( theDisplay,
                        theWindow,
                        EV_MASK );

}       /* -- function initEvents */

/*
**      end of file eventx.c
*/
```

SUMMARY

- Rubber-band lines are the cornerstone of any mouse-based drawing application. To create rubber-band lines in X Window, you need to create a special graphics context (GC), which then gains you access to the 16 drawing modes (or raster operations) provided under X.

- Each raster operation has the same structure: The **source** (a desired set of pixels) and the **destination** (a set of pixels already on the screen) are joined by the GC raster function to the source and the destination to produce the result, which is then drawn to the screen. The default GC raster function is called `GXcopy`, and it is the function you'll use most often.

- The process for creating rubber-band lines can be summarized in the following six steps:

  1. Create a new GC for the rubber-band effect.

  2. Set the new GC's (graphics) function field to `xor` mode (`GXxor`) with the `XSetFunction` Xlib function.

  3. Select an x, y coordinate location as an anchor point, and have the user select the second anchor point.

  4. Draw an initial line in `xor` mode (using the new GC), saving the line coordinates.

  5. Each time the pointer (mouse) moves, redraw the old line, using the `xor` GC. This makes the old line disappear. Adjust the coordinates to the new mouse position, and then draw the line to the new location, again in `xor` mode. Save these line coordinates.

  6. When the user selects the line's end point, redraw the line, using the `xor` GC, to erase it. Then, draw the line, using the normal drawing GC (and not the `GXxor` GC) so that the line appears on the display in its permanent likeness.

- Drawing rubber-band ovals is more complicated, as they are created by joining arcs. For this task, you use the function `XDrawArc`.

Xlib Functions and Macros Introduced in This Chapter

```
XFreeGC
XSetFunction
XDrawArc
```

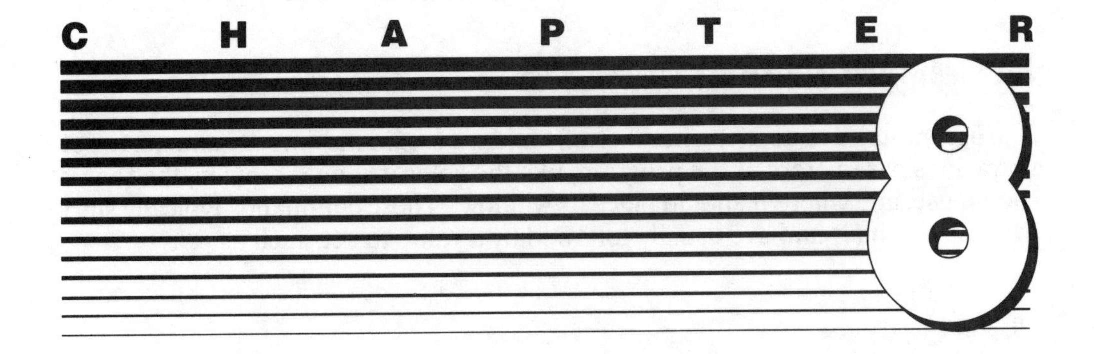

X STANDARDS AND INTERACTING WITH WINDOW MANAGERS

Most X programs are expected to follow certain minimal standards, especially for placing the program's top-level windows. Window managers also require more information about your application's requests for screen real estate. It is a good idea to provide this information because window managers essentially control the screen real estate and the placement of windows on the screen. This chapter covers some of these extended topics needed to round out your applications.

X COMMAND-LINE ARGUMENTS

X programs tend to accept a number of standard command-line arguments to set up various parameters of the program, like the color it should draw in, the font it should use, and where it should place its window. These commands typically start with a hyphen (-) and are usually followed by a value to set, such as

```
-display DisplayName
```

to specify on which display the program should open its windows. The network transparency built into X allows a program to be run on one machine and display its output on another.

Some command-line arguments can be abbreviated, such as `-fn` for `-font`. Following is a list of some standard arguments:

Command	Value (if needed)	Meaning
`-background`	`ColorName`	set background color
`-bg`	`ColorName`	set background color
`-bd`	`ColorName`	set border color
`-bordercolor`	`ColorName`	set border color
`-borderwidth`	`ColorName`	set the width of the top-level window's border
`-bw`	`BorderWidth`	set the width of the top-level window's border
`-display`	`DisplayName`	use given display and screen
`-fg`	`ColorName`	set foreground color
`-foreground`	`ColorName`	set foreground color

Command	Value (if needed)	Meaning
`-fn`	`FontName`	use this font
`-font`	`FontName`	use this font
`-geom`	`=WidthxHeight+X+Y`	set window's initial position and/or size
`-geometry`	`=WidthxHeight+X+Y`	set window's initial position and/or size
`-h`		print help message
`-help`		print help message
`-iconic`		begin in iconic state
`-name`	`WindowTitle`	use the window title for the window
`-title`	`WindowTitle`	use the window title for the window

You will need to choose which, if any, of these options your programs will support. For example, some of the options just don't make sense for an electronic publishing program or an industrial-control application.

DISPLAY NAMES

The X standard for display names is

```
host:server.screen
```

where the `host` is the machine's host name. The `server` is a number for which server is to be used (if multiple servers are running on one machine). And the `screen` is a number for which screen to use (provided the server supports more than one screen).

The default UNIX server is

```
unix:0.0
```

or

```
unix:0
```

If you call `XOpenDisplay` with a NULL display name parameter, chances are `unix:0.0` will be the server name used.

X GEOMETRY

While most learners (or victims) of high school mathematics probably remember geometry as Pythagoras' Theorem and right triangles, X defines geometry as

```
[=] [Width x Height ] [{+/-}XOffset{+/-}YOffset]
```

This geometry typically specifies the size and location of an application's main window (the top-level window). The best way to figure out these geometries is through examples.

For a 100-by-200 pixel window, to place the window at coordinates +5, +5, from the upper left corner (origin) of the window, you could use the following geometry (the equal sign is optional):

```
=100x200+5+5
```

To simply make the window 100 by 200 pixels in size, you could use the following:

```
100x200
```

To position the 100-by-200 pixel window with the right edge of the window 35 pixels in from the right edge of the screen and five pixels down from the top of the screen, you could use the geometry in the next example—note that a negative `YOffset` value would mean that the window's lower edge should be positioned relative to the lower edge of the screen, rather than the upper edge:

```
=100x200-35+5
```

If your program takes in a geometry spec as a character string, you can use the function `XParseGeometry` to parse out the x, y, width, and height values from the string:

```
#include  <X11/Xutil.h>
        .
        .
        .
        int     geometryStatus;
        int     x, y, width, height;
        char    theGeometry[ 120 ];       /* -- 120 is an arbitrary number */

        /*
        **      parse geometry spec
        */
        geometryStatus = XParseGeometry( theGeometry,
                &x,
                &y,
                &width,
                &height );

        /*
        **      Check which values were actually set
        */
        if ( !( geometryStatus & XValue ) )
                x = 10;                         /* -- default X value */
        if ( !( geometryStatus & YValue ) )
                y = 10;                         /* -- default Y value */
        if ( !( geometryStatus & WidthValue ) )
                width  = 300;                   /* -- default Width value */
        if ( !( geometryStatus & HeightValue ) )
                height = 300;                   /* -- default Height value */

        /*
        **      and so on for XNegtive and YNegative returns
        */
        .
        .
        .
```

XParseGeometry returns a geometryStatus value (an integer) that contains bit patterns for whichever (if any) of the values x, y, width, or height were set in the geometry string theGeometry. The status value can be checked against the following bit patterns: XValue (the x value was set), YValue (the y value was set), WidthValue (the width value was set), HeightValue (the height value was set), XNegative (x is negative, i.e., specified from the right side of the screen, rather than the left), and YNegative (y is negative, i.e., the window's bottom edge is specified relative to the bottom of the screen).

CREATING CURSORS FOR WINDOWS

X supports many different cursor shapes, such as the ubiquitious left-pointing arrow, the watch (letting you know the system is busy), and the pointing hand. Our favorite, though, is the waving Gumby cursor.

Figure 8.1 The waving Gumby cursor.

In X, each window can be associated with a cursor shape. Whenever the mouse pointer is in the window, the pointer shape is set to the shape of the cursor defined for that window. If you do not define a cursor, the cursor will be inherited from the parent window. (The root window's cursor is a big X. If you do not define a cursor for your window, it will most likely inherit the big X cursor.)

You can set the cursor you want for a window when you first create the window with the XCreateWindow function. The cursor is part of the XSetWindow-Attributes structure.

```
Cursor                  theCursor;
XSetWindowAttributes    theWindowAttributes;
.
.
.
theWindowAttributes.cursor     = theCursor;

theWindowMask                  = CWCursor;
.
.
.
/*
**      Create the window...
*/
```

The structure `theWindowAttributes` will then be passed to an `XCreate-Window` call, as in the `openWindow` function in the file `windowx.c`, listed later in this chapter. You can also define a cursor for an already-created window with the `XDefineCursor` function:

```
Display         *theDisplay;
Window          theWindow;
Cursor          theCursor;

XDefineCursor( theDisplay,
        theWindow,
        theCursor );
```

You can undo the cursor definition with the `XUndefineCursor` function:

```
Display         *theDisplay;
Window          theWindow;

XUndefineCursor( theDisplay,
        theWindow );
```

Calling `XUndefineCursor` means the window will now use the cursor of its parent.

Cursors as Text

X follows a rather clever notion that cursors are characters in a font: Each character in a font is really a symbolic picture, so why can't a cursor be the same thing?

Actually, in X, cursors are *two* characters in a font. The first character is the outline of the cursor, the second character of the pair is the mask, which defines the shape of the cursor. An entire font, the cursor font contains a standard set of X cursors. If you don't like the shapes in the cursor font, you can still create your own (see the next section "Creating Your Own Cursor," but it is easiest to use the standard shapes).

To get a good look at the available cursors in the cursor font, use the X program `xfd` to display the fonts. Simply type

```
% xfd cursor
```

at the command prompt (on a UNIX workstation) and the `xfd` client program will pop up a window with the cursor shapes (and their masks), as in Figure 8.2.

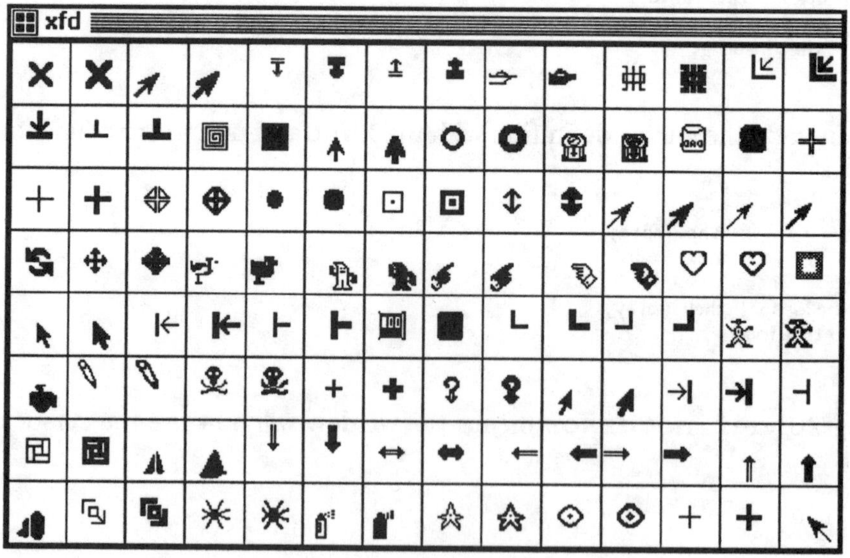

Figure 8.2 Part of the cursor font.

To use one of the cursor font cursors for your application's window, you must first create the cursor. Use `XCreateFontCursor` to create a cursor from the standard cursor font.

```
#include  <X11/cursorfont.h>
        .
        .
        .
        Display         *theDisplay;
        unsigned int    theCursorShape;
        Cursor          theCursor;

        /*
        **      Create a Gumby cursor
        */
        theCursorShape = XC_Gumby;

        theCursor      = XCreateFontCursor( theDisplay,
                                    theCursorShape );
```

`XCreateFontCursor` returns a Cursor ID of the new cursor. The include file `cursorfont.h` contains 77 different cursor names—each of which corresponds to an even-numbered character in the cursor font (the odd-numbered characters are the masks).

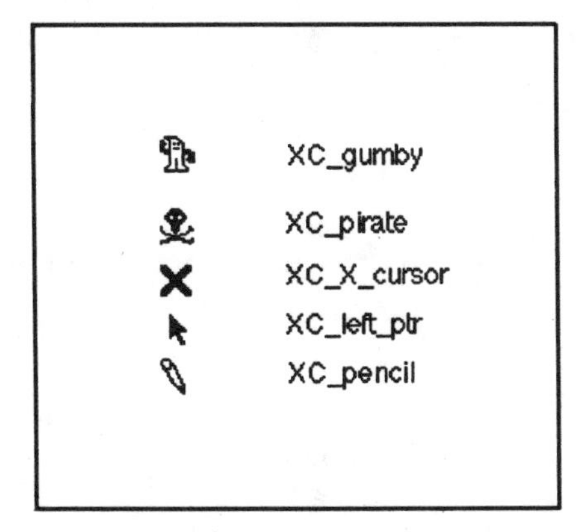

Figure 8.3 Cursors and their shape IDs.

Following is the list of different cursor names and corresponding numbers.

Cursor	Number
XC_XCursor	0
XC_arrow	2
XC_based_arrow_down	4
XC_based_arrow_up	6
XC_boat	8
XC_bogosity	10
XC_bottom_left_corner	12
XC_bottom_right_corner	14
XC_bottom_side	16
XC_bottom_tee	18
XC_box_spiral	20
XC_center_ptr	22
XC_circle	24
XC_clock	26
XC_coffee_mug	28
XC_cross	30
XC_cross_reverse	32
XC_crosshair	34
XC_diamond_cross	36
XC_dot	38
XC_dotbox	40
XC_double_arrow	42
XC_draft_large	44
XC_draft_small	46
XC_draped_box	48
XC_exchange	50
XC_fleur	52
XC_gobbler	54
XC_gumby	56
XC_hand1	58
XC_hand2	60
XC_heart	62
XC_icon	64
XC_iron_cross	66
XC_left_ptr	68
XC_left_side	70
XC_left_tee	72

continued...

```
XC_leftbutton              74
XC_ll_angle                76
XC_lr_angle                78
XC_man                     80
XC_middlebutton            82
XC_mouse                   84
XC_pencil                  86
XC_pirate                  88
XC_plus                    90
XC_question_arrow          92
XC_right_ptr               94
XC_right_side              96
XC_right_tee               98
XC_rightbutton             100
XC_rtl_logo                102
XC_sailboat                104
XC_sb_down_arrow           106
XC_sb_h_double_arrow       108
XC_sb_left_arrow           110
XC_sb_right_arrow          112
XC_sb_up_arrow             114
XC_sb_v_double_arrow       116
XC_shuttle                 118
XC_sizing                  120
XC_spider                  122
XC_spraycan                124
XC_star                    126
XC_target                  128
XC_tcross                  130
XC_top_left_arrow          132
XC_top_left_corner         134
XC_top_right_corner        136
XC_top_side                138
XC_top_tee                 140
XC_trek                    142
XC_ul_angle                144
XC_umbrella                146
XC_ur_angle                148
XC_watch                   150
XC_xterm                   152
```

Creating Your Own Cursors

You can create your own cursors out of bitmaps (single-plane pixmaps) or other fonts—one font character or bitmap for the cursor mask, and one font character or bitmap for the cursor itself. Each cursor created in this manner needs a "hot" point, the point that is considered the x, y location of the cursor. With an arrow cursor, for example, you want the hot spot to be at the tip of the arrow. With a watch cursor, a good hot spot is the center of the watch. You can also specify the color of the cursor foreground and background if you want a colored cursor.

Use `XCreatePixmapCursor` to create a cursor from two pixmaps:

```
Display         *theDisplay;
Pixmap          theCursorPixmap;
Pixmap          theMaskPixmap;
XColor          theForegroundColor;
XColor          theBackgroundColor;
unsigned int    hotX, hotY;             /* -- "hot" spot */

Cursor          theCursor;

theCursor = XCreatePixmapCursor( theDisplay,
                    theCursorPixmap,
                    theMaskPixmap,
                    &theForegroundColor,
                    &theBackgroundColor,
                    hotX, hotY );
```

Normally, cursors fit in a 16-by-16 pixel cell. Both the cursor and the mask pixmaps must have a depth of one plane. The colors are the `XColor` structures defined in Chapter 3.

To create a cursor from a character—called a glyph—in a font, use the `X-CreateGlyphCursor` function:

```
Display         *theDisplay;
Font            theCursorFont;
Font            theMaskFont;
XColor          theForegroundColor;
XColor          theBackgroundColor;
unsigned int    theCursorChar, theMaskChar;
unsigned int    hotX, hotY;             /* -- "hot" spot */

Cursor          theCursor;

theCursor = XCreateGlyphCursor( theDisplay,
                    theCursorFont,
                    theMaskFont,
                    theCursorChar,
                    theMaskChar,
                    &theForegroundColor,
                    &theBackgroundColor );
```

In this case, the "hot" spot is formed by the origins of the characters. These origins are placed at the same position in the new cursor.

The values for `theCursorChar` and `theMaskChar` define which characters in the respective fonts are actually to be used for creating the cursor. More information on loading fonts can be found in Chapter 4.

Freeing Up the Cursor Resources

Cursors do take up space (RAM storage) in the X server, so it is a good idea to free them up when you are finished with the cursor. Use `XFreeCursor` to do this.

```
Display         *theDisplay;
Cursor          theCursor;

XFreeCursor( theDisplay,
        theCursor );
```

EXAMPLE 1: TAKING IN COMMAND-LINE ARGUMENTS AND SETTING UP A CURSOR

The first example program acts like the programs in Chapter 7—it draws rubber-band ovals based on mouse `ButtonPress` and `MotionNotify` events. The program quits when the user types a "q."

This example program differs from the Chapter 7 programs in that it takes in certain command-line arguments and sets up a cursor for its window. To take in the command-line arguments and parse them, the file `argsx.c` was added.

This file contains a function `getArguments` that parses the `argc`, `argv` command-line arguments into (possibly) a display name, a window geometry, a font name, and a window title. The function `getArguments` returns a 1 if the user wants the window to appear in an iconic state (`-iconic`) or a 0 if the user did not specify the `-iconic` option. Note that a window manager, if one is running, may not support window icons, so this option is merely a request for a window manager to start the application's top-level windows as icons.

```
getArguments( argc, argv, theDisplayName, theGeometry, theFont-
Name, theTitle )

int     argc;
char    *argv[];
char    theDisplayName[];
char    theGeometry[];
char    theFontName[];
char    theTitle[];
```

`getArguments` goes through the command-line arguments to see if any match the options it is looking for.

The parameters to the `openWindow` function in `windowx.c` are modified to support an initial iconic window state and the window's title. `openWindow` also uses an application-wide cursor for the window:

```
Window
openWindow( x, y, width, height, flag, theTitle, iconicState, theNewGC )

int     x, y;            /* -- Where the window should go        */
int     width, height;   /* -- Size of the window                */
int     flag;            /* -- if > 0 then the window is a pop-up */
char    theTitle[];      /* -- Title for Window                  */
int     iconicState;     /* -- == 1 if start as icon, ==0 if not  */
GC      *theNewGC;       /* -- Returned Graphics Context         */
```

The following code sets the iconic state and the window's name:

```
.
.
.
Display         *theDisplay;
XWMHints        theWMHints;
Window          theNewWindow;
.
.
.
/*
**      4) Send "Hints" to the Window Manager.
**      Before this window will appear on the display,
**      an X window manager may intecept the call and
**      place the window where it wants to.  This next section
**      tells the window manager "hints" as to where the
**      window should go.
**
*/
if ( iconicState == 0 )
        {
        theWMHints.initial_state = NormalState;
        }
else
        {
        /*
        **      Not all window managers will support an iconic
        **      initial state -- or even icons at all, but at
        **      least we tried.
        */
        theWMHints.initial_state = IconicState;
        }

theWMHints.icon_pixmap    = theIconPixmap;
theWMHints.flags          = IconPixmapHint | StateHint;

XSetWMHints( theDisplay, theNewWindow, &theWMHints );

/*
**      Store Window Name
*/
XStoreName( theDisplay, theNewWindow, theTitle );
```

You can define a cursor for each window. This example sets the cursor in the `XSetWindowAttributes` structure, which is passed to the call to `XCreateWindow`, which actually creates the window. Thus, at window creation time, the cursor is defined for the window.

```
.
.
.
XSetWindowAttributes     theWindowAttributes;
.
.
.
theWindowAttributes.border_pixel      = theBlackPixel;
theWindowAttributes.background_pixel  = theWhitePixel;
theWindowAttributes.cursor            = theCursor;
theWindowAttributes.override_redirect = False;

theWindowMask =  CWBackPixel       |
                 CWBorderPixel     |
                 CWCursor          |
                 CWOverrideRedirect;
```

The cursor is created in `initx.c` and uses the standard cursor font to create its cursor with the `XCreateFontCursor` function.

```
.
.
.
#include  <X11/cursorfont.h>

Display          *theDisplay;
Cursor           theCursor;       /* -- Application program's cursor    */
        .
        .
        .
        theCursor      = XCreateFontCursor( theDisplay,
                                    XC_crosshair );
        .
        .
        .
```

This cursor is a cross-hair cursor. You may want to try a few other cursor shapes mentioned earlier and listed in the include file `cursorfont.h`.

The function `initX` also now takes a display name parameter to allow it to open its window on another display, if the user wants.

```
.
.
.
initX( theDisplayName )

char    *theDisplayName;

{       /* -- function initX  */

        /*
        **      1) Establish a connection to the X Server.
        **
        */

        theDisplay = XOpenDisplay( theDisplayName );
        .
        .
        .
```

The file `quitx.c` frees the cursor resource created in `initx.c`, above, before quitting.

```
.
.
.
extern  Display         *theDisplay;
extern  Cursor          theCursor;
        .
        .
        .
        XFreeCursor( theDisplay,
                theCursor );
```

The test file `test8.c` now calls `getArguments` to parse the command-line arguments. Then, it calls `initX`, passing a display name (which might be NULL for the default display), and then parses the window geometry with `XParseGeometry`. It opens the window, passing the new iconic state and window title parameters.

```
.
.
.
/*
**      Parse the command line parameters
*/
iconicState = getArguments( argc, argv,
                        theDisplayName,
                        theGeometry,
                        theFontName,
                        theTitle );
/*
**      Set up our connection to X
*/

initX( theDisplayName );
.
.
.
/*
**      Open a window
*/

theWindow = openWindow( x, y,           /* -- x, y location          */
                        width, height,  /* -- width, height          */
                        0,              /* -- This is NOT a pop-up   */
                        theTitle,       /* -- Window Title           */
                        iconicState,    /* -- Initial state          */
                        &theGC );       /* -- Graphics Context       */
```

Example 1 Source Code

The file `argx.c` is new. The files `test8.c`, `initx.c`, `quitx.c`, and `windowx.c` are modified. The rest of the files are reused from Chapter 7, Example 2 (*not* from Chapter 7, Example 3, the example on the graphics context drawing modes).

The contents of the new file `argsx.c` are as follows:

```
/*
**      argsx.c
**
**      Functions to handle command-line arguments to an X program.
**
*/

#include   <stdio.h>

/*
**      Default Values
**
*/

#define DEFAULT_DISPLAY         NULL
#define DEFAULT_GEOMETRY        NULL
#define DEFAULT_FONT            "variable"
#define DEFAULT_TITLE           "test8"

/*
**      GLOBALS for the arguments
**
*/


/*
**      getArguments sets up a set of text strings with either default
**      values or the values entered in by the user on the command line.
**
**      it handles the following arguments:
**      -h
**      -help              print help message
**      -display           use the display name following to display the
**                         program on
**      -geom
**      -geometry          accept user location and/or size for the window
**      -fn
**      -font              use the font name that follows, instead of the
**                         default
**      -iconic            begin in iconic state. This function will
**                         return a 1 for iconic state, 0 for normal
**                         state.
**      -name
**      -title             user the text following as the window's title,
**                         rather than the default
*/

getArguments( argc, argv, theDisplayName, theGeometry, theFontName, theTitle )

int     argc;
char    *argv[];
char    theDisplayName[];
```

continued...

...from previous page

```
char     theGeometry[];
char     theFontName[];
char     theTitle[];

{        /* -- function getArguments */
         int      argCounter;
         int      iconicState;

         /*
         **       set up defaults
         */
         theDisplayName[ 0 ] = '\0';
         theGeometry    [ 0 ] = '\0';
         strcpy( theFontName,     DEFAULT_FONT );
         strcpy( theTitle,        DEFAULT_TITLE );

         iconicState = 0;    /* -- NOT iconic to start out */

         /*
         **       Override defaults if there is a command-line argument to
         **       do so
         */
         for( argCounter = 0; argCounter < argc; argCounter++ )
                  {
                  /*
                  **       Check if user wants help message
                  */
                  if ( strncmp( argv[ argCounter ], "-h", 2 ) == 0 )
                           {
                           printHelpMessage();
                           exit( 1 );
                           }

                  /*
                  **       Check if user wants a different display
                  */
                  if ( strncmp( argv[ argCounter ], "-display", 8 ) == 0 )
                           {
                           argCounter++;
                           if ( argCounter < argc )
                                    {
                                    strcpy( theDisplayName, argv[ argCounter ] );
                                    }
                           else
                                    {
                                    fprintf( stderr,
                                       "ERROR: the -display option should be %s\n",
                                       "followed by a display name." );
                                    }
                           }
```

continued...

...from previous page

```
/*
**      Check if user wants to specify a window size/loc
*/
if ( strncmp( argv[ argCounter ], "-geom", 5 ) == 0 )
        {
        argCounter++;
        if ( argCounter < argc )
                {
                strcpy( theGeometry, argv[ argCounter ] );
                }
        else
                {
                fprintf( stderr,
                   "ERROR: the -geometry option should be %s\n",
                   "followed by a geometry spec," );
                fprintf( stderr,
                   "e.g, 100x100+200+200 for \n%s\n%s\n",
                   "location 100,100",
                   "size 200 by 200." );
                }
        }

/*
**      Check if user wants to specify a window title
*/
if ( ( strncmp( argv[ argCounter ], "-title", 6 ) == 0 ) ||
   ( strncmp( argv[ argCounter ], "-name", 5 ) == 0 ) )
        {
        argCounter++;
        if ( argCounter < argc )
                {
                strcpy( theTitle, argv[ argCounter ] );
                }
        else
                {
                fprintf( stderr,
                   "ERROR: the -title option should be %s\n",
                   "be followed by a window title" );
                }
        }

/*
**      Check if user wants to begin prog as an icon.
*/
if ( strncmp( argv[ argCounter ], "-iconic", 7 ) == 0 )
        {
        iconicState = 1;   /* -- as an icon */
        }
}
```

continued...

...from previous page

```
        /*
        **      These defaults = NULL
        */
        if ( strlen( theDisplayName ) < 1 )
                theDisplayName = NULL;

        if ( strlen( theGeometry ) < 1 )
                theGeometry = NULL;

        return( iconicState );

}       /* -- function getArguments */



/*
**      printHelpMessage prints a short, terse, Unix-style help
**      message.  Most applications should come with a manual
**      (and on-line man pages) as well as on-line help
**      from within the application.
**
*/

printHelpMessage()

{       /* -- function printHelpMessage */

        fprintf( stderr, "The allowable command line options are:\n" );
        fprintf( stderr, "\t-display displayname \n" );
        fprintf( stderr, "\tUse a different display for output\n" );
        fprintf( stderr, "\t-geometry geometryspec \n" );
        fprintf( stderr, "\tSpecify window location and size\n" );
        fprintf( stderr, "\t-font fontname \n" );
        fprintf( stderr, "\tUse the given font name for text\n" );
        fprintf( stderr, "\t-title windowtitle\n" );
        fprintf( stderr, "\tUse the given name for the window title \n" );
        fprintf( stderr, "\t-iconic\n" );
        fprintf( stderr, "\tStart with the window in iconic state \n" );

}       /* -- function printHelpMessage */



/*
**      end of file argsx.c
*/
```

The contents of the revised test file `test8.c` are as follows:

```
/*
**      Chapter 8, Example 1 Test program for command-line arguments
**
*/

#include   <stdio.h>
#include   <X11/Xlib.h>
#include   <X11/Xutil.h>

/*
**      external GLOBALS from initx.c
*/

extern  Display         *theDisplay;


/*
**      GLOBALS defined here.
*/

GC                      theGC;
XFontStruct             *fontStruct;

main( argc, argv )

int     argc;
char    *argv[];

{
        Window          theWindow, openWindow();
        XFontStruct     *initFont();
        int             iconicState;
        int             geometryStatus;
        int             x, y, width, height;
        char            theDisplayName[ 120 ];
        char            theGeometry[ 120 ];
        char            theTitle[ 120 ];
        char            theFontName[ 120 ];

        /*
        **      Parse the command line parameters
        */
        iconicState = getArguments( argc, argv,
                                theDisplayName,
                                theGeometry,
                                theFontName,
                                theTitle );
```

continued...

...from previous page

```
/*
**      Set up our connection to X
*/

initX( theDisplayName );

/*
**      Get some info on the display and print it
*/

getXInfo();

/*
**      Set up colors
*/

initDefaultColors();

/*
**      parse geometry spec
*/
geometryStatus = XParseGeometry( theGeometry, &x, &y, &width, &height );

/*
**      Check which values were actually set
*/
if ( !( geometryStatus & XValue ) )
        x = 10;
if ( !( geometryStatus & YValue ) )
        y = 10;
if ( !( geometryStatus & WidthValue ) )
        width  = 300;
if ( !( geometryStatus & HeightValue ) )
        height = 300;


/*
**      Open a window
*/

theWindow = openWindow( x, y,           /* -- x, y location        */
                        width, height,  /* -- width, height        */
                        0,              /* -- This is NOT a pop-up */
                        theTitle,       /* -- Window Title         */
                        iconicState,    /* -- Initial state        */
                        &theGC );       /* -- Graphics Context     */
```

continued...

...from previous page

```
        /*
        **      Set up the window to receive events from X.
        */
        initEvents( theWindow );

        /*
        ** Load in a font
        */
        fontStruct = initFont( theGC, theFontName );
        if ( fontStruct == NULL )
                {
                fontStruct = initFont( theGC, "variable" );
                }

        XFlush( theDisplay );

        /*
        **      Handle events
        */

        while( eventLoop( theWindow, theGC ) );

        /*
        **      Close the connection to the X server.
        */

        XFreeFont( theDisplay, fontStruct );
        XDestroyWindow( theDisplay, theWindow );
        XFlush( theDisplay );
        quitX();

}


/*
**      refreshWindow is called when an Expose event comes in from X.
**
*/

refreshWindow( theExposedWindow )

Window  theExposedWindow;


{       /* -- function refreshWindow */


}       /* -- function refreshWindow */


/*
**      end of file.
*/
```

The files `initx.c`, `quitx.c`, and `windowx.c` were modified to set up a special cursor for the test window.

The revised contents of the file `windowx.c` are as follows:

```
/*
**      windowx.c
**
**      Window opening routine
*/

#include  <X11/Xlib.h>
#include  <X11/Xutil.h>
#include  <stdio.h>

/*
**      The bitmap file "theIcon" is a file made from the
**      X11 program bitmap, which is a general-purpose bitmap
**      editor.  You can use the bitmap file as presented, or
**      create your own.
**
*/

#include  "theIcon"

/*
**      Program-wide Globals.
**
*/

extern  Display          *theDisplay;      /* -- Which display  */
extern  int              theScreen;        /* -- Which screen on the display */
extern  int              theDepth;         /* -- Number of color planes  */
extern  unsigned long    theBlackPixel;    /* -- System "Black" color    */
extern  unsigned long    theWhitePixel;    /* -- System "White" color    */
extern  Cursor           theCursor;        /* -- Arrow Cursor            */

#define          BORDER_WIDTH     2

/*
**      openWindow
**
**      This function takes a x, y pixel location for the upper
**      left corner of the window, as well as a width and height
**      for the size of the window.
**      It opens a window on the X display, and returns the window
**      id. It is also passed a flag that specifies whether the
**      window is to be a pop-up window (such as a menu) or
**      not.  This initial version does not implement that feature.
```

continued...

...from previous page

```
**      The GC theNewGC is a graphics context that is created for the
**      window, and returned to the caller.  The GC is necessary for
**      drawing into the window.
**
**      1) Set up the attributes desired for the window.
**      2) Open a window on the display.
**      3) Set up an icon for the window.
**      4) Send "Hints" to the Window Manager.
**      5) Now tell the window manager about the size and location.
**      6) Create a graphics context for the window.
**      7) Ask X to place the window visibly on the screen.
**      8) Flush out all the queued up X requests to the X server
**
**      Note: with this program, you can either be friendly or
**      unfriendly to the window manager, if one is running.
**      See the section on override_redirect below. If you
**      set override_redirect to True, you are being unfriendly
**      to the window manager.
**
*/


Window
openWindow( x, y, width, height, flag, theTitle, iconicState, theNewGC )

int     x, y;           /* -- Where the window should go        */
int     width, height;  /* -- Size of the window                */
int     flag;           /* -- if > 0 then the window is a pop-up */
char    theTitle[];     /* -- Title for Window                  */
int     iconicState;    /* -- == 1 if start as icon, ==0 if not */
GC      *theNewGC;      /* -- Returned Graphics Context         */


{       /* -- function openWindow */
        XSetWindowAttributes    theWindowAttributes;
        XSizeHints                      theSizeHints;
        unsigned        long            theWindowMask;
        Window                          theNewWindow;
        Pixmap                          theIconPixmap;
        XWMHints                        theWMHints;

        /*
        **      1) Set up the attributes desired for the window.
        **      Note that window managers may deny us some of
        **      these resources.  Note also that setting override_redirect
        **      to True will tell the window manager to leave our
        **      window alone.  Try this program by setting
        **      override_redirect to False.
        **
        **      Add-on: Define a cursor for the window
        */
```

continued...

...from previous page

```
theWindowAttributes.border_pixel      = theBlackPixel;
theWindowAttributes.background_pixel  = theWhitePixel;
theWindowAttributes.cursor            = theCursor;
theWindowAttributes.override_redirect = False;

theWindowMask = CWBackPixel        |
                CWBorderPixel      |
                CWCursor           |
                CWOverrideRedirect;


/*
**      2) Open a window on the display.
**
*/

theNewWindow = XCreateWindow( theDisplay,
                RootWindow( theDisplay , theScreen ),
                x, y,
                width, height,
                BORDER_WIDTH,
                theDepth,
                InputOutput,
                CopyFromParent,
                theWindowMask,
                &theWindowAttributes );

/*
**      3) Set up an icon for the window.
**      Each window should also register an Icon with the
**      window manager.  This icon is used if the window
**      is shrunk down to an iconic form by the user
**      (through interaction with a window manager).
**
*/

theIconPixmap = XCreateBitmapFromData( theDisplay,
                        theNewWindow,
                        theIcon_bits,
                        theIcon_width,
                        theIcon_height );

/*
**      4) Send "Hints" to the Window Manager.
**      Before this window will appear on the display,
**      an X window manager may intecept the call and
**      place the window where it wants to. This next section
**      tells the window manager "hints" as to where the
**      window should go.
```

continued...

...from previous page

```
**
*/
if ( iconicState == 0 )
        {
        theWMHints.initial_state = NormalState;
        }
else
        {
        /*
        **      Not all window managers will support an iconic
        **      initial state -- or even icons at all, but at
        **      least we tried.
        */
        theWMHints.initial_state = IconicState;
        }

theWMHints.icon_pixmap   = theIconPixmap;
theWMHints.flags         = IconPixmapHint | StateHint;

XSetWMHints( theDisplay, theNewWindow, &theWMHints );

/*
**      Store Window Name
*/
XStoreName( theDisplay, theNewWindow, theTitle );

/*
**      5) Now tell the window manager about the size and location.
**      we want for our windows.  USPosition means we are
**      stating the User choose the position, same with the
**      size.
**
*/

theSizeHints.flags      = USPosition | USSize;      /* -- what we want */
theSizeHints.x          = x;
theSizeHints.y          = y;
theSizeHints.width      = width;
theSizeHints.height     = height;

XSetNormalHints( theDisplay, theNewWindow, &theSizeHints );


/*
**      6) Create a graphics context for the window.
**
*/
```

continued...

...from previous page

```
        if ( createGC( theNewWindow, theNewGC ) == 0 )
                {
                XDestroyWindow( theDisplay, theNewWindow );
                return( (Window) 0 );
                }


        /*
        **      7) Ask X to place the window visibly on the screen.
        **      Up to now, the window has been created but has not
        **      appeared on the screen. Mapping the window places it
        **      visibly on the screen.
        **
        */

        XMapWindow( theDisplay, theNewWindow );

        /*
        **      8) Flush out all the queued up X requests to the X server
        **
        */

        XFlush( theDisplay );

        /*
        **      9) Return the window ID, which is needed to specify
        **      which window to draw to.
        **
        */

        return( theNewWindow );

}       /* -- function openWindow */


/*
**      createGC creates a graphics context for the given window.
**      A graphics context is necessary to draw into the window.
**
**      Returns 0 if there was an error, 1 if all is A-OK.
**
*/

createGC( theNewWindow, theNewGC )

Window  theNewWindow;
GC      *theNewGC;
```

continued...

...from previous page

```
{       /* -- function createGC */
        XGCValues       theGCValues;

        *theNewGC = XCreateGC( theDisplay,
                        theNewWindow,
                        (unsigned long) 0,
                        &theGCValues );

        if ( *theNewGC == 0 )           /* -- Unable to create a GC */
                {
                return( 0 );            /* -- Error                 */
                }
        else
                {
                /* --  Set Foreground and Background defaults for the new GC */
                XSetForeground( theDisplay,
                                *theNewGC,
                                theBlackPixel );

                XSetBackground( theDisplay,
                                *theNewGC,
                                theWhitePixel );

                return( 1 );            /* -- A-OK                  */
                }

}       /* -- function createGC */

/*
**      end of file windowx.c
**
*/
```

The revised contents of the file `initx.c` are as follows:

```
/*
**      initx.c
**
**      Initialization code to talk to the X server
**
*/

#include <X11/Xlib.h>
#include <X11/Xutil.h>
#include <X11/cursorfont.h>

#include <stdio.h>
```

continued...

...from previous page

```
/*
**      Program-wide Globals.
**
*/

Display         *theDisplay;            /* -- Which display              */
int             theScreen;              /* -- Which screen on the display */
int             theDepth;               /* -- Number of color planes     */
unsigned long   theBlackPixel;          /* -- System "Black" color       */
unsigned long   theWhitePixel;          /* -- System "White" color       */
Colormap        theColormap;            /* -- default System color map   */
Cursor          theCursor;              /* -- Application program's cursor*/


/*
**      initX
**      Sets up the connection to the X server and stores information
**      about the environment.
**
*/

initX( theDisplayName )

char    *theDisplayName;

{       /* -- function initX  */

        /*
        **      1) Establish a connection to the X Server.
        **
        */

        theDisplay = XOpenDisplay( theDisplayName );

        /* -- Check if the connection was made */
        if ( theDisplay == NULL )
                {
                fprintf( stderr,
                   "ERROR: Cannot establish a connection to the X Server %s\n",
                   XDisplayName( theDisplayName ) );
                exit( 1 );
                }

        /*
        **      2) Check for the default screen and color plane depth.
        **      If theDepth == 1, then we have a monochrome system.
        **
        */
```

continued...

...from previous page

```
        theScreen     = DefaultScreen( theDisplay );
        theDepth      = DefaultDepth( theDisplay, theScreen );
        theBlackPixel = BlackPixel( theDisplay, theScreen );
        theWhitePixel = WhitePixel( theDisplay, theScreen );
        theColormap   = DefaultColormap( theDisplay, theScreen );

        /*
        **      3) Create a cursor for all the program's windows.
        */

        theCursor     = XCreateFontCursor( theDisplay, XC_crosshair );

}       /* -- function initX  */


/*
**      getXInfo prints information to the starting terminal
**      (usually an xterm) about the current X Window display
**      and screen.
*/

getXInfo()

{       /* -- function getXInfo */

        /*
        **      You will find many funny values when you check the X
        **      information below.  It should be something to the tune of:
        **      MIT X Consortium (vendor)
        **      3 (vendor release)
        **      X11 R3 (or R2, the Version and Revision numbers).
        **      But, on most implementations, this information
        **      does not seem to jibe.
        **      On the generic MIT X Consortium release for
        **      X11R3, you might see X11R0, with a vendor release # of 3
        **
        */

        printf( "%s version %d of the X Window System, X%d R%d\n",
                ServerVendor( theDisplay ),
                VendorRelease( theDisplay ),
                ProtocolVersion( theDisplay ),
                ProtocolRevision( theDisplay ) );

        /*
        **      Now, print some more detailed information about the
        **      display.
        **
        */
```

continued...

...from previous page

```
        if ( theDepth == 1 )
                {
                printf( "Color plane depth.............%d (monochrome)\n",
                        theDepth );
                }
        else
                {
                printf( "Color plane depth.............%d\n",
                        theDepth );
                }

        printf( "Display Width.................%d\n",
                 DisplayWidth( theDisplay, theScreen ) );
        printf( "Display Height................%d\n",
                 DisplayHeight( theDisplay, theScreen ) );


        printf( "The display %s\n", XDisplayName( theDisplay ) );

}       /* -- function getXInfo */

/*
**      end of file initx.c
**
*/
```

The revised contents of the file `quitx.c` are as follows:

```
/*
**      quitx.c
**
**      routines to close down X
**
*/

#include  <X11/Xlib.h>
#include  <X11/Xutil.h>

extern  Display         *theDisplay;
extern  Cursor          theCursor;


/*
**      quitX()
**
**      closes the connection to the X server
**
*/
```

continued...

...from previous page

```
quitX()

{       /* -- function quitX  */

        XFreeCursor( theDisplay, theCursor );

        XCloseDisplay( theDisplay );

}       /* -- function quitX  */

/*
**      end of file quitx.c
**
*/
```

Following is the Makefile for Example 1:

```
##      X Project Makefile for Chapter 8, Example 1
##
EXEC=   test8
##
## DEFINES
##
##
##      -g = Debugging info
##      -O = optimize (cannot use -g then)
CFLAGS= -O
##
##
##      Libraries
##      X11     X11 graphics library
##
LIBS=   -lX11
##
##
OBJECTS=        initx.o         \
                argsx.o         \
                colorx.o        \
                drawx.o         \
                eventx.o        \
                keyx.o          \
                quitx.o         \
                textx.o         \
                windowx.o       \
                xor.o           \
                test8.o
```

continued...

...from previous page

```
##
##      Command to compile and link objects together
##
$(EXEC):        $(OBJECTS)
                cc -o $(EXEC) $(OBJECTS) $(LIBS)
##
##
##      end of make file
##
```

EXAMPLE 2: SENDING MORE INFORMATION TO THE WINDOW MANAGER

In X, the window manager is simply another client program, albeit a special client program. The basic idea of a window manager is that the window manager controls the screen. It can specify where applications place their windows and what sizes those windows are allowed to be. Some window managers ensure that windows never overlap, creating a tiled window manager. Others allow for overlapping windows.

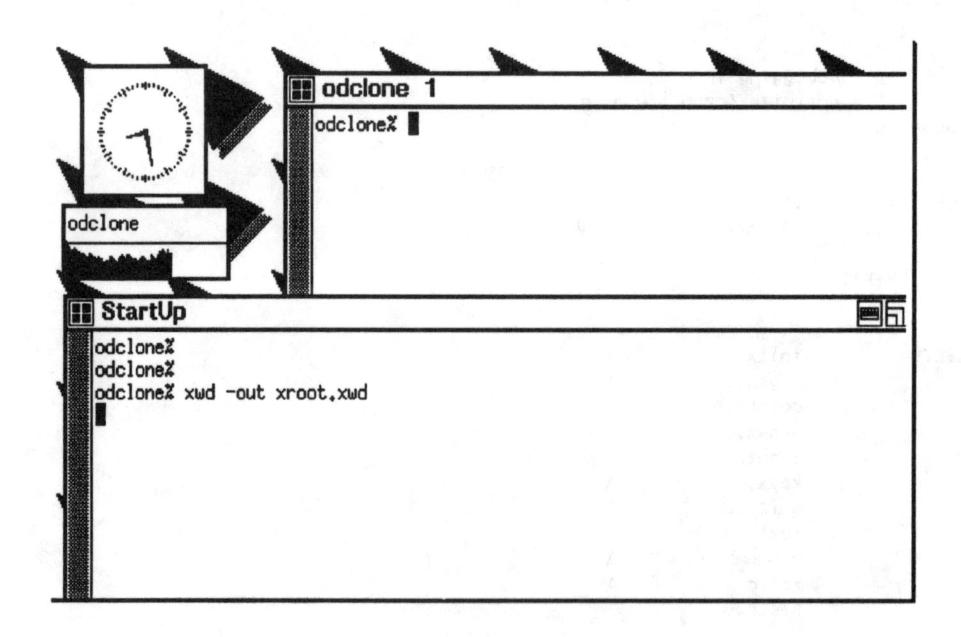

Figure 8.4 Window manager title bars.

Some window managers place title bars or other "decorations" on a window (see Figure 8.4). Thus, it is important to register a window's title with the window manager. Some window managers also provide the ability to collapse a window into an icon, so applications should register an icon name with the window manager, too. In all cases, because the window manager can mess with your application's windows, it is a good idea to tell the window manager what you want (and hope for the best).

The Class Property

Windows in X can have a class property. Window managers may use the class property to associate a number of programs together. Some programs may look for windows owned by other programs—windows of a certain class—so it is a good idea to set the class hint property. To set this property, you need to fill in an XClassHint structure:

```
typedef struct
        {
        char    *res_name;
        char    *res_class;
        } XClassHint;
```

The res_name field should resemble the name of the program. The res_class field should be something like "editor" or "manager" or whatever describes the class of the application. These strings should be relatively short.

You set the class hints with the Xlib function XSetClassHint. You can get the class hints for a window (even if it is not your own window) with XGetClassHint.

```
Display         *theDisplay;
Window          theWindow;
XClassHint      theClassHint;

theClassHint.res_name  = "test8";
theClassHint.res_class = "foo";

XSetClassHint( theDisplay,
        theWindow,
        &theClassHint );
```

Sizing Windows

Because window managers generally control how a window can be sized, you want to tell the window manager as much information as possible about how you want your windows to be sized. An `xterm` window dealing entirely with text, for example, wants its window to be resized only in increments of lines or columns of text (because it only uses space in increments of lines and columns). Other windows, like the `xclock` clock face, can be resized to effectively any size.

The window's size hints, already introduced, can set "hints" (or requests) for a window's minimum and maximum size, the window's increments for sizing, and the aspect ratios. The `XSizeHints` structure contains the following:

```
typedef struct
        {
        long    flags;
        int     x, y;
        int     width, height;
        int     min_width, min_height;
        int     max_width, max_height;
        int     width_inc, height_inc;
        struct  {
                int     x;      /* -- the numerator part */
                int     y;      /* -- the denominator part */
                } min_aspect, max_aspect;
        } XSizeHints;
```

The `flags` field needs to be set to the logical or of the field identifiers you are using. These field identifiers are bit patterns (as are all X flag items):

`USPosition`	The user has specified the position.
`USSize`	The user has specified the size.
`PPosition`	The program has specified the position.
`PSize`	The program has specified the size.
`PMinSize`	The minimum size for the window.
`PMaxSize`	The maximum size for the window.

continued...

`PResizeInc` The sizing increments.

`PAspect` The sizing aspect ratios.

`PAllHints` All fields are set.

The following example says that the user sets the size and position and the program sets the minimum and maximum sizes for the given window.

```
.
.
.
Display         *theDisplay;
Window          theWindow;
XSizeHints      theSizeHints;
.
.
.
theSizeHints.flags      = USPosition | USSize | PMinSize | PMaxSize;
theSizeHints.x          = x;
theSizeHints.y          = y;
theSizeHints.width      = width;
theSizeHints.height     = height;
theSizeHints.min_width  = 150;
theSizeHints.max_width  = 450;
theSizeHints.min_height = 150;
theSizeHints.max_height = 300;

XSetNormalHints( theDisplay,
        theWindow,
        &theSizeHints );
```

Icon Names

Icons can have names, too. When a window manager collapses a window into an icon, it can display the icon name beneath the icon picture (usually a pixmap) so that the user has some hope of figuring out which icon corresponds to which program. The `XSetIconName` function registers an icon name for a window. The following example sets the icon name for a window to "wombat."

```
Display         *theDisplay;
Window          theWindow;
char            *theIconName = "wombat";

XSetIconName( theDisplay,
        theWindow,
        theIconName );
```

Ideally, the icon name has something to do with the program name or window name.

Example 2 Source Code

The second example just modifies the file `windowx.c` to send more information to the window manager, if one is running. Normally, programs should not have to worry which window manager, if any, is running.

The revised contents of the file `windowx.c` are as follows:

```
/*
**      windowx.c
**
**      Window opening routine
**
*/

#include  <X11/Xlib.h>
#include  <X11/Xutil.h>
#include  <stdio.h>

/*
**      The bitmap file "theIcon" is a file made from the
**      X11 program bitmap, which is a general-purpose bitmap
**      editor.  You can use the bitmap file as presented, or
**      create your own.
**
*/

#include  "theIcon"

/*
**      Program-wide Globals.
**
*/
```

continued...

...from previous page

```
extern  Display         *theDisplay;     /* -- Which display                       */
extern  int             theScreen;       /* -- Which screen on the display         */
extern  int             theDepth;        /* -- Number of color planes              */
extern  unsigned long   theBlackPixel;   /* -- System "Black" color                */
extern  unsigned long   theWhitePixel;   /* -- System "White" color                */
extern  Cursor          theCursor;       /* -- Arrow Cursor                        */

#define         BORDER_WIDTH    2
#define         RES_NAME        "test"   /* -- Resource Name                       */
#define         RES_CLASS       "foo"    /* -- Resource Class, e.g.," Editor"      */

/*
**      openWindow
**
**      This function takes a x, y pixel location for the upper
**      left corner of the window, as well as a width and height
**      for the size of the window.
**      It opens a window on the X display, and returns the window
**      id. It is also passed a flag that specifies whether the
**      window is to be a pop-up window (such as a menu) or
**      not.  This initial version does not implement that feature.
**      The GC theNewGC is a graphics context that is created for the
**      window, and returned to the caller.  The GC is necessary for
**      drawing into the window.
**
**      1) Set up the attributes desired for the window.
**      2) Open a window on the display.
**      3) Set up an icon for the window.
**      4) Send "Hints" to the Window Manager.
**      5) Store the Window, Icon and Class Names with the X Server.
**      6) Now tell the window manager about the size and location.
**      7) Create a graphics context for the window.
**      8) Ask X to place the window visibly on the screen.
**      9) Flush out all the queued up X requests to the X server
**
**      Note: with this program, you can either be friendly or
**      unfriendly to the window manager, if one is running.
**      See the section on override_redirect below. If you
**      set override_redirect to True, you are being unfriendly
**      to the window manager.
**
*/


Window
openWindow( x, y, width, height, flag, theTitle, iconicState, theNewGC )


int     x, y;           /* -- Where the window should go        */
int     width, height;  /* -- Size of the window                */
int     flag;           /* -- if > 0 then the window is a pop-up */
```

continued...

...from previous page

```
char     theTitle[];       /* -- Title for Window                      */
int      iconicState;      /* -- == 1 if start as icon, ==0 if not     */
GC       *theNewGC;        /* -- Returned Graphics Context             */

{        /* -- function openWindow */
         XSetWindowAttributes    theWindowAttributes;
         XSizeHints              theSizeHints;
         unsigned        long    theWindowMask;
         Window                  theNewWindow;
         Pixmap                  theIconPixmap;
         XWMHints                theWMHints;
         XClassHint              theClassHint;

         /*
         **      1) Set up the attributes desired for the window.
         **      Note that window managers may deny us some of
         **      these resources.  Note also that setting
         **      override_redirect to True will tell the window manager
         **      to leave our window alone.  Try this program by setting
         **      override_redirect to False.
         **
         */

         theWindowAttributes.border_pixel       = theBlackPixel;
         theWindowAttributes.background_pixel   = theWhitePixel;
         theWindowAttributes.cursor             = theCursor;
         theWindowAttributes.override_redirect = False;

         theWindowMask = CWBackPixel        |
                         CWBorderPixel      |
                         CWCursor           |
                         CWOverrideRedirect;


         /*
         **      2) Open a window on the display.
         **
         */

         theNewWindow = XCreateWindow( theDisplay,
                         RootWindow( theDisplay , theScreen ),
                         x, y,
                         width, height,
                         BORDER_WIDTH,
                         theDepth,
                         InputOutput,
                         CopyFromParent,
                         theWindowMask,
                         &theWindowAttributes );
```

continued...

...from previous page

```
/*
**      3) Set up an icon for the window.
**      Each window should also register an Icon with the
**      window manager.  This icon is used if the window
**      is shrunk down to an iconic form by the user
**      (through interaction with a window manager).
**
*/

theIconPixmap = XCreateBitmapFromData( theDisplay,
                        theNewWindow,
                        theIcon_bits,
                        theIcon_width,
                        theIcon_height );

/*
**      4) Send "Hints" to the Window Manager.
**      Before this window will appear on the display,
**      an X window manager may intecept the call and
**      place the window where it wants to.  This next section
**      tells the window manager "hints" as to where the
**      window should go.
**
*/
if ( iconicState == 0 )
        {
        theWMHints.initial_state = NormalState;
        }
else
        {
        /*
        **      Not all window managers will support an iconic
        **      initial state -- or even icons at all, but at
        **      least we tried.
        */
        theWMHints.initial_state = IconicState;
        }

theWMHints.icon_pixmap    = theIconPixmap;
theWMHints.flags          = IconPixmapHint | StateHint;

XSetWMHints( theDisplay, theNewWindow, &theWMHints );



/*
**      5) Store the Window, Icon and Class Names with the X
**      Server.
*/
```

continued...

...from previous page

```
XStoreName( theDisplay, theNewWindow, theTitle );
XSetIconName( theDisplay, theNewWindow, RES_NAME );

theClassHint.res_name  = RES_NAME;
theClassHint.res_class = RES_CLASS;

XSetClassHint( theDisplay, theNewWindow, &theClassHint );

/*
**      6) Now tell the window manager about the size and
**      location we want for our windows.  USPosition means we
**      are stating the User choose the position, same with the
**      size.  PPosition and PSize would mean that the program
**      choose the size.  Try to make the window smaller
**      than the minimum sizes if you are running a window
**      manager.
**
*/

theSizeHints.flags      = USPosition | USSize | PMinSize | PMaxSize;
theSizeHints.x          = x;
theSizeHints.y          = y;
theSizeHints.width      = width;
theSizeHints.height     = height;
theSizeHints.min_width  = 150;
theSizeHints.max_width  = 450;
theSizeHints.min_height = 150;
theSizeHints.max_height = 300;

XSetNormalHints( theDisplay, theNewWindow, &theSizeHints );


/*
**      7) Create a graphics context for the window.
**
*/

if ( createGC( theNewWindow, theNewGC ) == 0 )
        {
        XDestroyWindow( theDisplay, theNewWindow );
        return( (Window) 0 );
        }


/*
**      8) Ask X to place the window visibly on the screen.
**      Up to now, the window has been created but has not
**      appeared on the screen. Mapping the window places it
**      visibly on the screen.
**
*/
```

continued...

...from previous page

```
        XMapWindow( theDisplay, theNewWindow );

        /*
        **      9) Flush out all the queued up X requests to the X server
        **
        */

        XFlush( theDisplay );

        /*
        **      10) Return the window ID, which is needed to specify
        **      which window to draw to.
        **
        */

        return( theNewWindow );

}       /* -- function openWindow */



/*
**      createGC creates a graphics context for the given window.
**      A graphics context is necessary to draw into the window.
**
**      Returns 0 if there was an error, 1 if all is A-OK.
**
*/

createGC( theNewWindow, theNewGC )

Window  theNewWindow;
GC              *theNewGC;

{       /* -- function createGC */
        XGCValues       theGCValues;

        *theNewGC = XCreateGC( theDisplay,
                        theNewWindow,
                        (unsigned long) 0,
                        &theGCValues );

        if ( *theNewGC == 0 )   /* -- Unable to create a GC */
                {
                return( 0 );    /* -- Error                 */
                }
        else
                {
```

continued...

...from previous page

```
                /* --  Set Foreground and Background defaults for the new GC */
                XSetForeground( theDisplay,
                                *theNewGC,
                                theBlackPixel );

                XSetBackground( theDisplay,
                                *theNewGC,
                                theWhitePixel );

                return( 1 );    /* -- A-OK                      */
                }

}       /* -- function createGC */

/*
**      end of file windowx.c
**
*/
```

SUMMARY

Making sure your program interacts properly with an X window manager is important. This chapter covers the extended topics you need to make sure this interraction occurs.

- When setting up your program's parameters (such as the color, font, and cursor), you need to use a number of command-line arguments. These are prefixed by a hyphen (-) and are listed earlier in this chapter.

- Because X is designed to run on a number of different systems, you must include the display name. The default UNIX server is

  ```
  unix:0.0
  ```

- Using X's geometry, you specify the size and location of an application's main window. X defines this geometry as

  ```
  [=][Width x Height][{+/-}Xoffset{+/-}Yoffset]
  ```

  where the `[Width x Height]` refers to the pixel dimensions of the display, and the x, y coordinates are computed from the top right of the screen. Negative x, y coordinates mean that the window's lower edge should be positioned relative to the lower edge of the screen.

- Different cursors are used for different applications. To maintain flexibility, X defines cursors as two characters in a font, which means cursors are essentially defined as text. You can create your own cursors, or you can call on a standard cursor font that contains 77 different cursor names, including the waving Gumby cursor.

- Because the window manager controls the screen and sometimes needs information for title bars, it is important that you register a window's title with a window manager. In addition, you need to set up a class hint property because programs sometimes look only for windows owned by other programs.

- You need to tell a window manager how a window can be resized (with maximum and minimum sizes, for example), and you need to tell it an icon's name.

Xlib Functions and Macros Introduced in This Chapter

```
XCreateFontCursor
XCreateGlyphCursor
XCreatePixmapCursor
XDefineCursor
XFreeCursor
XParseGeometry
XSetClassHint
XSetIconName
XStoreName
XUndefineCursor
```

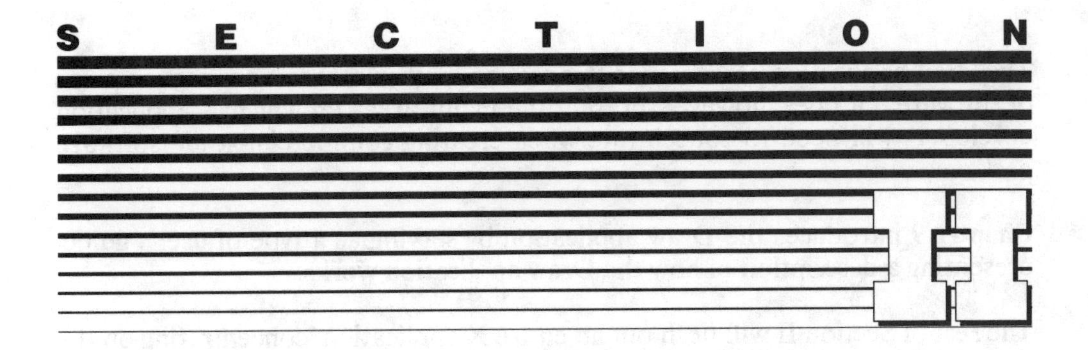

BUILDING AN X WINDOW SYSTEM APPLICATION

The simple Draw application introduced in this section will contain code to handle the following items:

- Multiple windows in one application, including subwindows
- Pop-up windows
- Floating selection palettes
- The ability to undo an operation
- Pixmap operations
- Critical error handling

These are precisely the attributes needed to produce commercial-quality software that runs under the X Window System.

The Draw application presented in this section is by no means a production piece of software—it does, however, present the major areas on which X application developers will need to concentrate when creating commercial-grade software packages.

Chapter 9 introduces the Draw application by serving as a type of user's guide, presenting a description of how the Draw application works.

The rest of Section II will flesh out an entire X application, concentrating on the areas necessary to produce a commercial-grade application.

Chapter 10 will cover the concepts of applications having many (sometimes many, many) windows all controlled by one program. Most major X applications will have multiple windows because windows in X provide many nice features, such as clipping and hit detection. Chapter 10 will describe how to create a "floating" palette of the type that is currently all the rage in microcomputer software. It will go on to cover more information about cursors, the similarities between Windows and Pixmaps in X, and how you can take advantage of these similarities, especially in a drawing program.

Chapter 11 will describe event-processing in the Draw application. The various accepted events will be described, as well as a set of "power user" keyboard shortcuts.

Chapter 12 will show the almost trivial changes needed to implement a pop-up style window. It will detail the creation of a user dialog box to be used for asking the user which file to load in. Dialog boxes can also be multi-windowed.

Chapter 13 will focus in detail on the Draw application and provides the complete source code for the entire application.

Chapter 14 presents some ideas on how you could enhance the Draw application and make it into a commercial-quality application through the use of vendor-supplied toolkits.

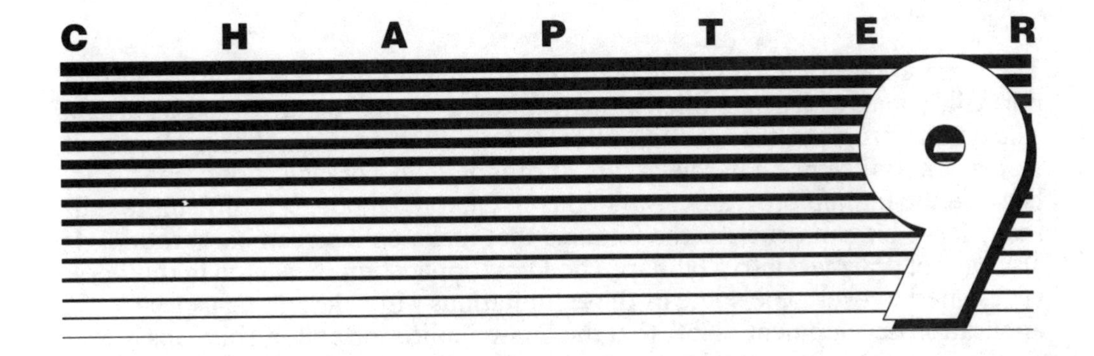

INTRODUCING THE DRAW APPLICATION: A USER'S GUIDE

It is usually a good idea to start out with a user guide to help you describe what you plan to accomplish. Chapter 9 presents a description of how the Draw application works.

The Draw application is a simple real-size bitmap editor. The X Window System normally comes with a magnified bitmap editor, a client program called `bitmap`. The bitmap program, though fun, suffers from a number of drawbacks. It cannot load in a new file once it has been run. It cannot undo a drawing operation. And, because the bitmap program always edits in enlarged mode, it is difficult to edit really large bitmaps, such as the bitmaps that make up a screen background. It also cannot draw text into a bitmap. The Draw application presented in this book is designed to overcome some of those limitations while describing aspects of X application development. Note that the Draw application edits all bitmaps in real size; it does not enlarge the bitmap in any way—even though this would be a very nice additional feature.

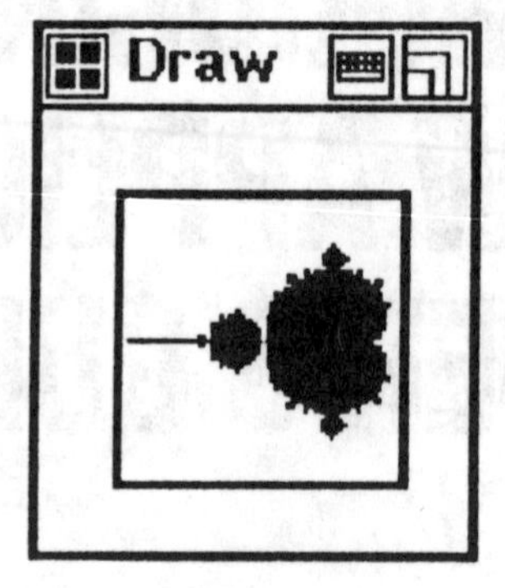

Figure 9.1 The Draw application.

THE FLOATING SELECTION PALETTE

The Draw application uses a "floating" palette to allow the user to choose what kind of item to draw—text, lines, points, or ovals.

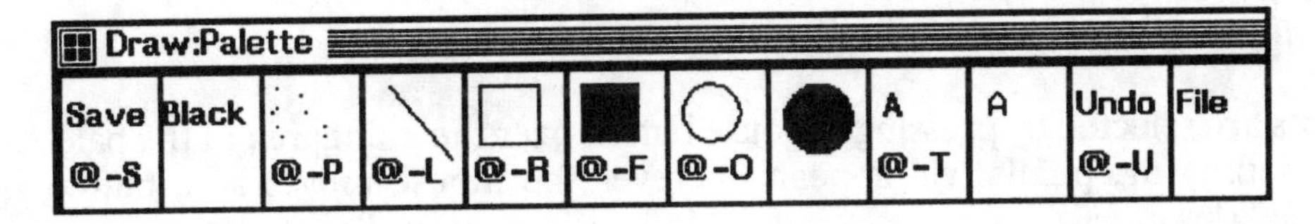

Figure 9.2 *A floating palette.*

This palette allows the user to do the following:

- Save the current drawing file.
- Draw in black or draw in white.
- Draw points.
- Draw lines.
- Draw rectangles.
- Fill rectangles in the current drawing color.
- Draw ovals.
- Fill ovals in the current drawing color.
- Draw text in the "variable" font.
- Draw text in the "9x15" (or any user-requested) font.
- Undo the last drawing operation.
- Load in a new bitmap file to edit.
- Wipe out (clear) the current drawing area (to start completely over).
- Quit the program.

Each item is selected when a cursor is positioned over the given area of the palette window and a button is pressed. To start drawing lines, for example, the user clicks the mouse over the line part of the palette. Then, to actually draw a line, the user moves the mouse pointer over the draw window. The line is started when a mouse button is held down. The line ends when the user lifts the mouse button. As the button is held down, the line will follow the cursor, like a rubber-band.

Points

Points are selected by pressing a mouse button over the point area of the palette. When drawing, points will appear wherever the mouse moves as a button is pressed down.

Text

To draw text, the user clicks in one of the two text areas of the palette, since this application supports two fonts. Then, the mouse pointer is moved over the draw window. A simple click of a mouse button specifies where the text starts. Any `KeyPress` events that follow will be interpreted as text input, and the text will be drawn starting where the mouse pointer was when the mouse button was pressed. The Backspace key or the Delete key will remove the last character typed.

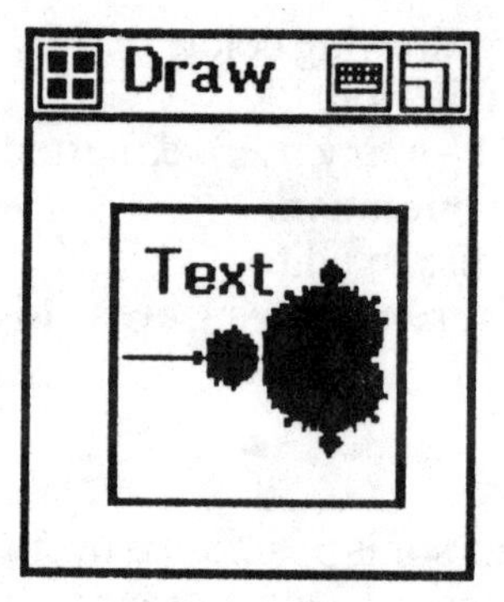

Figure 9.3 *Drawing text in a bitmap.*

Other items are drawn in much the same way. This is a simple application, so it should be easy to pick up.

Loading In New Files

A mouse button press over the file area of the palette will signal that the user wants to load in a new file. A file dialog box will appear. The user can enter the name of a bitmap-style file to load and then choose to cancel the dialog box (and skip loading any file) or accept the file name by pressing a mouse button over the OK box.

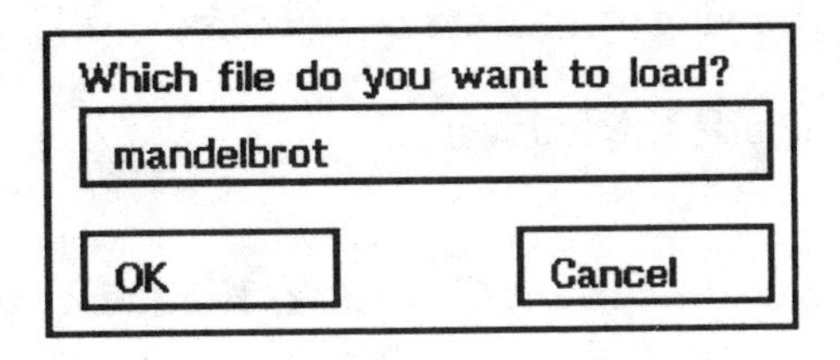

Figure 9.4 *The file dialog box.*

These files are in the same format as files created by the `bitmap` program. This format uses an ASCII-encoding for the bitmap data and is actual C source code. Following is a sample bitmap file:

```
#define fi_width 16
#define fi_height 16
static char fi_bits[] = {
   0xff, 0xff, 0xff, 0xff, 0x07, 0xff, 0x73, 0xfe, 0x73, 0xfe, 0x03, 0xfe,
   0xf3, 0xff, 0x73, 0xfe, 0x07, 0xff, 0xff, 0xff, 0xff, 0xff, 0xff, 0xff,
   0xff, 0xff, 0xff, 0xff, 0xff, 0xff, 0xff, 0xff};
```

You can include this file into a C program and compile in a bitmap definition, or you can use an X function (described later) to load in the file to an X client.

Undoing Drawing Operations

Any time the user presses a mouse button over the Undo palette choice (or presses the Meta-U key combination), the drawing area is filled with what was there before the last drawing took place. This means you can undo any drawing operation, but you can only undo one level deep—you cannot undo all the way back to the beginning, for example.

Undo is a very handy feature, especially for people who are not used to drawing with something akin to the shape of a bar of soap. Undo also allows for a less worried user environment: The user doesn't have to worry about making a mistake because any drawing can always be undone.

Other palette items include the following:

- Save, which saves the current file to disk. Frequent saves are encouraged.
- Black/White, which toggles between drawing in black or drawing in white (bitmap files are monochrome). The color name displayed is the color currently in use.
- Rectangles and filled rectangles.
- Ovals and filled ovals.
- Wipe, which wipes out the bitmap so that it is a clear white rectangle.
- Quit, which quits the program.

COMMAND-LINE PARAMETERS

Users on a UNIX machine can pass command-line parameters to an X program, as described in Chapter 8. The Draw application will accept a number of command-line parameters:

Option	Argument	Description
`-display`	`displayname`	Makes the output appear on a different server.
`-fn` `-font`	`fontname` `fontname`	Loads up a font other than 9x15.
`-geom` `-geometry`	`geometryspec`	Specifies the window geometry for the draw window.
`-h` `-help`		Provides a help message.
`-iconic`		Asks the window manager to start program as an icon.
`-name`	`Title`	Sets window name.
`-size`	`WidthxHeight`	Sets size for a new bitmap.
`-title`	`Title`	Sets window name.
`FileName`		Loads in the given bitmap file.

POWER-USER META-KEY SHORTCUTS

The so-called power users often like the ability to use shortcut commands on the keyboard, instead of moving the mouse over to the right section of the palette and clicking the mouse buttons.

The Draw application supports the use of the first meta key (often the only meta key on a keyboard) to provide keyboard shortcuts. The most common keyboard shortcut is Meta-S, which saves the current drawing file to disk. Meta-Q, another favorite, quits the Draw application. The keyboard shortcuts used in the Draw application are summarized in the following table.

Key	Function
Meta-F	`Filled Rect`
Meta-L	`Line`
Meta-O	`Oval`
Meta-P	`Point`
Meta-Q	`Quit`
Meta-R	`Rect`
Meta-S	`Save`
Meta-T	`Text 1`
Meta-U	`Undo`

CRITICAL ERROR HANDLING

One of the first steps in producing commercial-quality software is making sure the program doesn't crash. X programs will terminate on any X-related error, such as a bad window parameter – unless a critical error handler is installed. An error handler will intercept the X error and allow your routine to process the error rather than force a nasty program termination.

```
#include    <X11/Xlib.h>
#include    <X11/Xutil.h>
#include    <X11/Xproto.h>
        .
        .
        .
        int     errorHandler();
        .
        .
        .
        /*
        **      Set up the normal error handler, for things like
        **      bad window IDs, etc.
        */
        XSetErrorHandler( errorHandler );
        .
        .
        .
```

XSetErrorHandler is passed one parameter, a pointer to an error handler function. The actual error handler function should take two parameters: a Display pointer (for the display server in which the error occurred) and a pointer to an XErrorEvent structure.

```
errorHandler( theDisplay, theErrorEvent )

Display          *theDisplay;
XErrorEvent      *theErrorEvent;

{       /* -- function errorHandler */
        .
        .
        .

}       /* -- function errorHandler */
```

The XErrorEvent structure will contain information about the error, including a major and minor code describing the problem. The XErrorEvent structure contains seven fields and is described in the include file Xlib.h:

```
typedef struct
        {
        int             type;
        Display         *theDisplay;
        XID             resourceid;
        unsigned long   serial;
        char            error_code;
        char            request_code;
        char            minor_code;
        } XErrorEvent;
```

The resourceid, an XID, is the ID of the offending resource, such as a Window or Pixmap. It is usually defined as an unsigned long (check the include file X.h to see what your system has it defined as). The serial field is the serial number of the request, which usually isn't very helpful unless you are debugging an X server.

The error code is normally more helpful, as it can be passed to the `XGetErrorText` function to get a text string describing the error.

```
Display         *theDisplay;
XErrorEvent     *theErrorEvent;
char            theBuffer[ MAX_LENGTH ];
int             bufferLength;

bufferLength = MAX_LENGTH - 1;

XGetErrorText( theDisplay,
        theErrorEvent->error_code,
        theBuffer,
        bufferLength );
```

`XGetErrorText` pulls out a line of text that helps describe the error. It puts this text in a character-string buffer that you must allocate space for. You also need to pass the maximum length for a buffer that your code can accept.

The `request_code` is the major op-code of the failed request, and the `minor_code` is, appropriately enough, the minor op-code of the failed X request.

The error handler function itself should look something like the following:

```
errorHandler( theDisplay, theErrorEvent )

Display         *theDisplay;
XErrorEvent     *theErrorEvent;

{       /* -- function errorHandler */
        int     bufferLength = 120;
        char    theBuffer[ 130 ];

        XGetErrorText( theDisplay,
                theErrorEvent->error_code,
                theBuffer,
                bufferLength );

        fprintf( stderr,
                "X Error: %s\n", theBuffer );

        fprintf( stderr,
```

continued...

...from previous page

```
        "Serial number of reuqest: %ld Op Code: %d.%d Error Code: %d\n",
        theErrorEvent->serial,
        theErrorEvent->request_code,
        theErrorEvent->minor_code,
        theErrorEvent->error_code );

    fprintf( stderr, "Resource ID of failed request: %ld on display %s.\n",
        theErrorEvent->resourceid,
        DisplayString( theDisplay ) );

}       /* -- function errorHandler */
```

This error handler does nothing more than merely report the error to `stderr`.

Because X errors are typically generated by bad parameters passed to an Xlib function, and because X resources are usually used over and over again, one error will probably generate many errors because the error handler function `errorHandler` does not deal with the error in any way except to report it. In your code, you probably want to put in something to deal with the error. This code just shows how to set the function up.

HANDLING FATAL IO ERRORS

The `XSetErrorHandler` sets up a function that will be called for any regular X error, such as when a bad window `ID` is passed to a drawing function. Other X errors, though, are fatal to an X program, especially errors involving loss of the server connection. This type of error could happen if the server program itself tipped over or if the network communication went down.

X calls these fatal errors IO errors. If one occurs, your program will be terminated by the Xlib, whether you like it or not. You can, however, set up a fatal error handler function, much like the regular error handler function. This fatal error handler, though, will be the last routine that your program executes. Even with a fatal error handler, the program will still terminate. Therefore, it is a good idea to save files or generally clean up the system as much as possible in the little time remaining.

From a fatal error handler, you cannot use any Xlib routines that would generate a request of the X server (an IO error means that the link to the X server is severed). You can register your fatal error handler function with X by calling the `XSetIOErrorHandler` function and passing the address of your fatal error handler routine.

```
#include    <X11/Xlib.h>
#include    <X11/Xutil.h>
#include    <X11/Xproto.h>
        .
        .
        .
        int      fatalErrorHandler();

        .
        .
        .
        /*
        **       Set up the fatal error handler for a broken connection
        **       with the X server, and other nasties.
        **
        */
        XSetIOErrorHandler( fatalErrorHandler );
```

The actual `fatalErrorHandler` function takes one parameter, a `Display` pointer showing on which display the error was generated.

```
/*
**      fatalErrorHandler takes care of fatal X errors, like a broken
**      connection to the X server.  If this routine does not exit,
**      and returns, the Xlib will exit anyway.  Thus, in this
**      function you need to save all important data and get ready for
**      a fatal termination.  Note: Do not call Xlib routines from a
**      fatal X error handler.
**
**      This function is registered with X by use of the
**      XSetIOErrorHandler Xlib function.
**
*/

fatalErrorHandler( theDisplay )

Display         *theDisplay;

{       /* -- function fatalErrorHandler */

        fprintf( stderr, "X Error: Fatal IO error on display %s.\n",
                DisplayString( theDisplay ) );
        fprintf( stderr, "Bailing out near line one.\n" );

        /*
        **      Put any clean-up code here.
        **
        */
```

continued...

...from previous page

```
        /*
        **      Thus terminates another program
        */

        exit( 1 );

}       /* -- function fatalErrorHandler */
```

Again, in this sample `fatalErrorHandler` function, not much is accomplished except reporting the error to the user. In the Draw application to be presented in the following chapters, saving the file involves an Xlib call, as does most of the program. The `fatalErrorHandler` function cannot really do all that much. In a computer-aided design (CAD) program or an industrial process-control program, though, the story would probably be different. It seems rather arrogant for X to decide that it will terminate your program on a fatal IO error when it might be better if you could try to reopen a display connection at a later time, but that's what you have to live with. In any case, most commercial X applications will probably want to include error-handling routines like those just described.

SUMMARY

This chapter serves as a short introduction to the Draw application. A real-size bitmap editor, Draw improves on the X `bitmap` editor by allowing users to load in new files, undo drawing operations, draw text into a bitmap and edit large bitmaps.

- Draw is built around a floating palette, a typical feature of window-based systems. By pressing mouse buttons when the cursor is positioned over different areas of the palette, the user can import existing files and draw lines, points, text, and other items.

- The Draw application also supports meta keys intended for use by "power users." The Undo command found on the palette, for example, can be called through the keyboard by the Meta-U combination.

- The Draw application also introduces you to error handling in the X Window System. Unless a critical error handler is installed in your programs, you may never know exactly where an error occurred. In addition, you can set up fatal error handler functions that will clean up the system or save active files before the program terminates.

Xlib Functions and Macros Introduced in This Chapter

XGetErrorText
XSetErrorHandler
XSetIOErrorHandler

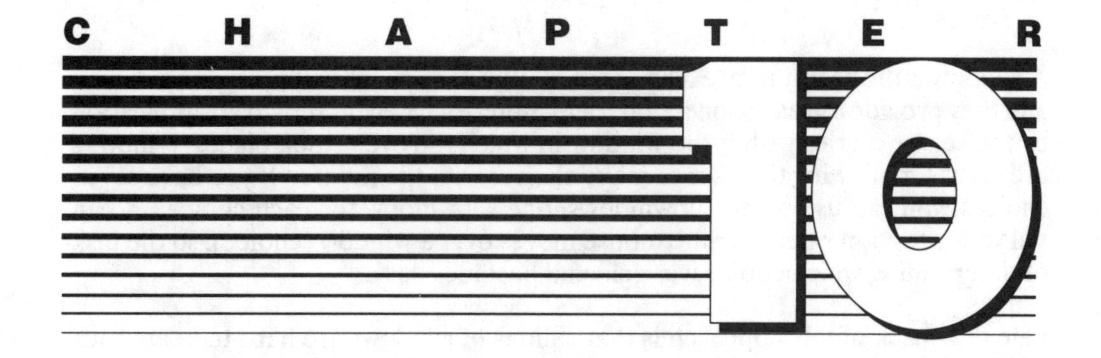

MULTIPLE-WINDOW APPLICATIONS

Each of the example programs discussed so far has only used one window. Most X applications, though, use two, three, or zillions of windows as part of the program's interface. In this chapter, you will learn how to create the multiple windows used in the Draw application, along with learning the advantages and difficulties of using multiple windows.

A window is the base unit of exchange in X. Windows provide clipping boundaries, and they provide a great boon to "hit" detection: Every event sent to an application by the server carries with it the window in which the event took place. Windows are great for allowing the user to make choices with the mouse. If you have seven choices, you can use seven subwindows, one subwindow for each choice. X can tell your program whenever the mouse moves over a window (choice), so the task of determining which choice was selected becomes easy.

One drawback of this approach is that zillions of windows are hard to keep track of. Each window needs a variable ID of type `Window` and perhaps a graphics context (`GC`) or two. You may need to set up fonts for the windows, draw different text, and make sure each window is updated properly. In addition, as shown in Chapter 1, window creation is not a simple task. Window creation can also slow down the response time of your program. Finally, windows take up scarce resources on the server and in your system. Especially with limited-RAM X terminals, you need to be careful not to blow out the server's memory.

There is no clear-cut way to determine the correct number of windows for an application. Most applications start with one top-level parent window and then create subwindows for various interface elements. Remember that each window can have a different cursor associated with it, so if you need different cursor shapes over different areas, you may want to create a few more windows. The best advice is to carefully examine what your interface needs and how the user will interact with it. Use the number of windows that naturally fits the application. Over 100 windows is probably a bit too much; under 20 is much better. Windows are perfect for interface components such as floating palettes with a limited number of choices.

FLOATING PALETTES

Floating palettes seem to be the latest rage in graphical user interfaces. These palettes provide a set—or "palette"—of available options. The "floating" part means that the user can move these palettes around the screen as needed—usually either up close to the action, allowing for rapid selections, or far out of the way.

An easy way to create a floating palette is to diverge from most X programs. Most X programs start with one top-level window. All the programs' other windows then become child windows of the parent top-level window. All these child windows are clipped to the boundaries of the parent. The way to diverge from this common practice is to create two top-level windows: One for the application's main window and the other for the floating palette's main window.

X window managers normally leave application child windows alone but provide a mechanism to move, size, and iconify all top-level windows on the screen. Thus, a floating palette can be moved around the screen in the same way that all main windows can, depending on which window manager you are running. The neat thing about these floating palettes is the ability to position them where you want — over the application or far away, in whatever location is convenient.

The floating palette presented here has a top-level window and a number of child windows, or subwindows. Each child window provides one choice for the user. When a mouse `ButtonPress` event is detected in a child window, the user has chosen the option associated with that window.

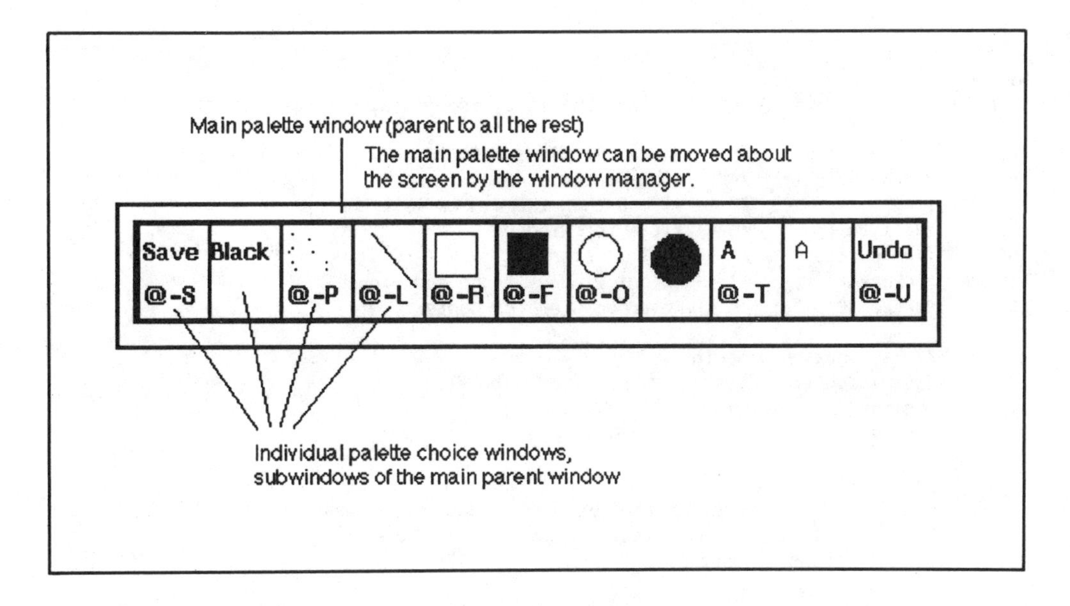

Figure 10.1 Floating palettes.

In previous chapters, the function `openWindow` was created to hide a lot of the messy details needed to open a window. To create a subwindow, you need to go back into this function and change one parameter — the parent window. The Xlib function `XCreateWindow` takes a parent window as a parameter. Up to this point, the parent has always been the screen's root window. Now, the parent will be the floating palette main window, as in the following:

```
/*
**      from windowx.c
*/

#include  <X11/Xlib.h>
#include  <X11/Xutil.h>

extern  Display         *theDisplay;     /* -- Which display                     */
extern  int             theScreen;       /* -- Which screen on the display       */
extern  int             theDepth;        /* -- Number of color planes            */
extern  unsigned long   theBlackPixel;   /* -- System "Black" color              */
extern  unsigned long   theWhitePixel;   /* -- System "White" color              */
extern  Pixmap          theIconPixmap;   /* -- Icon pixmap for windows           */

#define         BORDER_WIDTH    2
.
.
.
Window
openWindow( x, y, width, height, flag, theTitle, iconicState, theParent, theNewGC )

int     x, y;           /* -- Where the window should go        */
int     width, height;  /* -- Size of the window                */
int     flag;           /* -- if > 0 then the window is a pop-up */
char    theTitle[];     /* -- Title for Window                  */
int     iconicState;    /* -- == 1 if start as icon, ==0 if not  */
Window  theParent;      /* -- Parent Window of the new window   */
GC      *theNewGC;      /* -- Returned Graphics Context         */

{       /* -- function openWindow */
        XSetWindowAttributes    theWindowAttributes;
        unsigned        long    theWindowMask;
        Window                  theNewWindow;

        /*
        **      1) Set up the attributes desired for the window.
        **      Note that window managers may deny us some of
        **      these resources.


        **
        */

        theWindowAttributes.border_pixel      = theBlackPixel;
        theWindowAttributes.background_pixel  = theWhitePixel;

        theWindowMask = CWBackPixel | CWBorderPixel;


        /*
        **      2) Open a window on the display.
        **
        */
```

continued...

...from previous page

```
        theNewWindow = XCreateWindow( theDisplay,
                            theParent,
                            x, y,
                            width, height,
                            BORDER_WIDTH,
                            theDepth,
                            InputOutput,
                            CopyFromParent,
                            theWindowMask,
                            &theWindowAttributes );

        .
        .
        .
```

The above modifications to the `openWindow` function in `windowx.c` allow for the creation of subwindows. To actually put together the floating palette, you need a number of subwindows. The function `initWindows` in the file `drawapp.c` creates all the Draw application windows, including the floating palette. Each palette subwindow is the same size and is therefore created with an x coordinate incremented by the subwindow width each time.

```
/*
**      from drawapp.c */

#include    <X11/Xlib.h>
#include    <X11/Xutil.h>

#include    "drawapp.h"

/*
**      External GLOBALS
**
*/

extern  Display         *theDisplay;
extern  Window          theRootWindow;
extern  unsigned long   theBlackPixel;  /* -- System "Black" color */
extern  unsigned long   theWhitePixel;  /* -- System "White" color */

Window          thePaletteWindow;
```

continued...

...from previous page

```
/*
**      Subwindows of the palette window
*/
Window          theColorWindow;
Window          theFileWindow;
Window          theFilledOvalWindow;
Window          theFilledRectWindow;
Window          theLineWindow;
Window          theOvalWindow;
Window          thePointWindow;
Window          theQuitWindow;
Window          theRectWindow;
Window          theSaveWindow;
Window          theText1Window;
Window          theText2Window;
Window          theUndoWindow;
Window          theWipeOutWindow;

/*
**      Graphic Contexts for all windows
*/

GC              theBorderGC;            /* -- Border window GC    */
GC              theWhiteGC;             /* -- Draw White bits     */
GC              theBlackGC;             /* -- Draw Black bits     */
GC              theXorGC;               /* -- Rubber-band drawing */

GC              thePaletteGC;

/*
**      Subwindows of the palette window
*/

GC              theColorGC;
GC              theFileGC;
GC              theFilledOvalGC;
GC              theFilledRectGC;
GC              theLineGC;
GC              theOvalGC;
GC              thePointGC;
GC              theQuitGC;
GC              theRectGC;
GC              theSaveGC;
GC              theText1GC;
GC              theText2GC;
GC              theUndoGC;
GC              theWipeOutGC;
```

continued...

...from previous page

```
/*
**      Width and height for each small window in the palette.
*/
#define PALETTE_HEIGHT   56
#define PALETTE_WIDTH   42
#define NUM_ITEMS        14       /* -- 14 Windows in palette window */
#define PALETTE_FULL_WIDTH        (PALETTE_WIDTH * NUM_ITEMS)

/*
**      initWindows
*/

initWindows( theGeometry, theTitle, iconicState )

char    theGeometry[];
char    theTitle[];
int     iconicState;

{       /* -- function initWindows */
        int             geometryStatus;
        int             x, y, x1, y1, width, height;
        Window          openWindow();
        char            thePaletteTitle[ 120 ];
        .
        .
        .
        /*
        **      Create thePaletteWindow--where all choices are made.
        **      thePaletteWindow starts with a fixed size.
        **
        */
        if ( strlen( theTitle ) < 100 )
                {
                strcpy( thePaletteTitle, theTitle );
                strcat( thePaletteTitle, ":Palette" );
                }

        y     += ( height + 5 );
        width  = PALETTE_FULL_WIDTH;
        height = PALETTE_HEIGHT;
        thePaletteWindow = openWindow( x, y, width, height,
                            NORMAL_WINDOW, thePaletteTitle,
                            iconicState, theRootWindow, &thePaletteGC );

        initEvents( thePaletteWindow, IN_PALETTE );
        XFlush( theDisplay );
        .
        .
        .
```

After the initial palette main window is created, each subwindow is created as well. These subwindows could have been made as arrays, but for clarity each one has been given a name that corresponds to its function.

```
.
.
.
/*
**      Create all thePaletteWindow's subwindows; thePaletteWindow
**      is now the parent window.
*/
width   = PALETTE_WIDTH;
x       = 0;
y       = 0;

/*
**      theSaveWindow;
*/
theSaveWindow = openWindow( x, y, width, height,
                        NORMAL_WINDOW, thePaletteTitle,
                        NORMAL_STATE, thePaletteWindow, &theSaveGC );

initEvents( theSaveWindow, IN_PALETTE );
associateFont( theSaveGC, TEXT1_FONT );

/*
**      theColorWindow;
*/
x += PALETTE_WIDTH;
theColorWindow = openWindow( x, y, width, height,
                        NORMAL_WINDOW, thePaletteTitle,
                        NORMAL_STATE, thePaletteWindow, &theColorGC );

initEvents( theColorWindow, IN_PALETTE );
associateFont( theColorGC, TEXT1_FONT );

/*
**      thePointWindow;
*/
x += PALETTE_WIDTH;
thePointWindow = openWindow( x, y, width, height,
                        NORMAL_WINDOW, thePaletteTitle,
                        NORMAL_STATE, thePaletteWindow, &thePointGC );

initEvents( thePointWindow, IN_PALETTE );
associateFont( thePointGC, TEXT1_FONT );
```

continued...

...from previous page

```
/*
**      theLineWindow;
*/
x += PALETTE_WIDTH;
theLineWindow = openWindow( x, y, width, height,
                            NORMAL_WINDOW, thePaletteTitle,
                            NORMAL_STATE, thePaletteWindow, &theLineGC );

initEvents( theLineWindow, IN_PALETTE );
associateFont( theLineGC, TEXT1_FONT );

/*
**      theRectWindow;
*/
x += PALETTE_WIDTH;
theRectWindow = openWindow( x, y, width, height,
                            NORMAL_WINDOW, thePaletteTitle,
                            NORMAL_STATE, thePaletteWindow, &theRectGC );

initEvents( theRectWindow, IN_PALETTE );
associateFont( theRectGC, TEXT1_FONT );

/*
**      theFilledRectWindow;
*/
x += PALETTE_WIDTH;
theFilledRectWindow = openWindow( x, y, width, height,
                            NORMAL_WINDOW, thePaletteTitle,
                            NORMAL_STATE, thePaletteWindow, &theFilledRectGC );
initEvents( theFilledRectWindow, IN_PALETTE );
associateFont( theFilledRectGC, TEXT1_FONT );

/*
**      theOvalWindow;
*/
x += PALETTE_WIDTH;
theOvalWindow = openWindow( x, y, width, height,
                            NORMAL_WINDOW, thePaletteTitle,
                            NORMAL_STATE, thePaletteWindow, &theOvalGC );

initEvents( theOvalWindow, IN_PALETTE );
associateFont( theOvalGC, TEXT1_FONT );

/*
**      theFilledOvalWindow;
*/
x += PALETTE_WIDTH;
theFilledOvalWindow = openWindow( x, y, width, height,
                            NORMAL_WINDOW, thePaletteTitle,
                            NORMAL_STATE, thePaletteWindow, &theFilledOvalGC );
```

continued...

...from previous page

```
initEvents( theFilledOvalWindow, IN_PALETTE );
associateFont( theFilledOvalGC, TEXT1_FONT );

/*
**      theText1Window;
*/
x += PALETTE_WIDTH;
theText1Window = openWindow( x, y, width, height,
                        NORMAL_WINDOW, thePaletteTitle,
                        NORMAL_STATE, thePaletteWindow, &theText1GC );

initEvents( theText1Window, IN_PALETTE );
associateFont( theText1GC, TEXT1_FONT );

/*
**      theText2Window;
*/
x += PALETTE_WIDTH;
theText2Window = openWindow( x, y, width, height,
                        NORMAL_WINDOW, thePaletteTitle,
                        NORMAL_STATE, thePaletteWindow, &theText2GC );

initEvents( theText2Window, IN_PALETTE );
associateFont( theText2GC, TEXT2_FONT );

/*
**      theUndoWindow;
*/
x += PALETTE_WIDTH;
theUndoWindow = openWindow( x, y, width, height,
                        NORMAL_WINDOW, thePaletteTitle,
                        NORMAL_STATE, thePaletteWindow, &theUndoGC );

initEvents( theUndoWindow, IN_PALETTE );
associateFont( theUndoGC, TEXT1_FONT );

/*
**      theFileWindow;
*/
x += PALETTE_WIDTH;
theFileWindow = openWindow( x, y, width, height,
                        NORMAL_WINDOW, thePaletteTitle,
                        NORMAL_STATE, thePaletteWindow, &theFileGC );

initEvents( theFileWindow, IN_PALETTE );
associateFont( theFileGC, TEXT1_FONT );
```

continued...

...from previous page

```
/*
**      theWipeOutWindow;
*/
x += PALETTE_WIDTH;
theWipeOutWindow = openWindow( x, y, width, height,
                        NORMAL_WINDOW, thePaletteTitle,
                        NORMAL_STATE, thePaletteWindow, &theWipeOutGC );

initEvents( theWipeOutWindow, IN_PALETTE );
associateFont( theWipeOutGC, TEXT1_FONT );

/*
**      theQuitWindow;
*/
x += PALETTE_WIDTH;
theQuitWindow = openWindow( x, y, width, height,
                        NORMAL_WINDOW, thePaletteTitle,
                        NORMAL_STATE, thePaletteWindow, &theQuitGC );

initEvents( theQuitWindow, IN_PALETTE );
associateFont( theQuitGC, TEXT1_FONT );
.
.
.
```

Fourteen subwindows are created for the palette, one for each choice:

`theSaveWindow`	to save the current bitmap file to disk
`theColorWindow`	to select black or white drawing
`thePointWindow`	to select drawing points
`theLineWindow`	to select drawing lines
`theRectWindow`	to select drawing rectangles
`theFilledRectWindow`	to select drawing filled rectangles
`theOvalWindow`	to select drawing ovals
`theFilledOvalWindow`	to select drawing filled ovals

continued...

`theText1Window`	to select drawing in the first text font
`theText2Window`	to select drawing in the second text font
`theUndoWindow`	to undo the last drawing command
`theFileWindow`	to load in a new file
`theWipeWindow`	to wipe the drawing clean and start over
`theQuitWindow`	to quit the program

Fourteen graphics contexts are also created, one for each choice's window:

```
GC          theColorGC;
GC          theFileGC;
GC          theFilledOvalGC;
GC          theFilledRectGC;
GC          theLineGC;
GC          theOvalGC;
GC          thePointGC;
GC          theQuitGC;
GC          theRectGC;
GC          theSaveGC;
GC          theText1GC;
GC          theText2GC;
GC          theUndoGC;
GC          theWipeOutGC;
```

Highlighting a Palette Choice

Whenever a mouse `ButtonPress` event is received on a palette subwindow, the user has made a choice. To let the user know the program knows this, the palette subwindow in question is flashed to provide feedback to the user. This "flashing" is accomplished by filling the window with a black rectangle and then clearing the window and redrawing its old contents.

```
/*
**      highlightChoice highlights a palette window
**      when the user clicks a mouse button in the window.
**      Then, it refreshes the given window.
*/

highlightChoice( theWindow )

Window  theWindow;

{       /* -- function highlightChoice */
        XExposeEvent    theEvent;

        /*
        **      Fill the window to highlight the selection.
        */
        fillRectangle( theWindow, thePaletteGC,
                0, 0, PALETTE_WIDTH, PALETTE_HEIGHT );

        XFlush( theDisplay );

        /*
        **      Clear the window
        */
        XClearWindow( theDisplay, theWindow );

        /*
        **      allow processExpose() to redraw the original
        **      contents of the window.
        */

        theEvent.window = theWindow;
        processExpose( &theEvent );

        XFlush( theDisplay );

}       /* -- function highlightChoice */
```

The function `highlightChoice` is passed a window ID for the window in the palette that was selected. To refresh the contents of the window, `highlight-Choice` fakes an expose event by placing the window ID into an `XExpose-Event` structure, passing that structure to the function `processExpose`. `processExpose` handles the refreshing of all the Draw application windows for expose events. Because there are 14 different palette windows to choose from, the program was designed so only one routine took care of refreshing the contents of windows.

Refreshing the Palette Window

In the normal course of events, certain windows will be covered, partially obscured, and then exposed later. When a window is exposed, its contents normally need to be redrawn. By using many small palette windows, only the parts of the palette that actually were obscured will be redrawn just because each obscured window will get a refresh event when it is exposed again.

The function `processExpose` (in `drawapp.c`) takes an `XExposeEvent` (or a faked event, as detailed above), and redraws the window that was exposed. This program again uses the lazy refresh method—it redraws the entire window that was obscured. For really large windows (such as when you are editing a 1,000-by-800-pixel Godzilla bitmap), redrawing the entire window is extremely inefficient.

```
        .
        .
        .
/*
**      processExpose redraws a given window if it gets an Expose
**      event. This is another example of "lazy" Expose event
**      handling,as this routine redraws the whole window on each
**      Expose event.
**
*/

processExpose( theEvent )

XExposeEvent     *theEvent;

{       /* -- function processExpose */

        /*
        **      redraw the bitmap image
        */
        if ( theEvent->window == theDrawWindow )
                {
                refreshDrawWindow();
                return;
                }

        if ( theEvent->window == theSaveWindow )
                {
                XDrawString( theDisplay, theSaveWindow, theSaveGC,
                                2, 20, "Save", strlen( "Save" ) );
```

continued...

...from previous page

```
                XDrawString( theDisplay, theSaveWindow, theSaveGC,
                                2, 45, "@-S", strlen( "@-S" ) );
                return;
                }

        if ( theEvent->window == theColorWindow )
                {
                if ( theDrawingColor == BLACK )
                        {
                        XDrawString( theDisplay, theColorWindow, theColorGC,
                                0, 20, "Black", strlen( "Black" ) );
                        }
                else
                        {
                        XDrawString( theDisplay, theColorWindow, theColorGC,
                                0, 20, "White", strlen( "White" ) );
                        }
                return;
                }
        if ( theEvent->window == thePointWindow )
                {
                XDrawPoint( theDisplay, thePointWindow, thePointGC, 5, 5 );
                XDrawPoint( theDisplay, thePointWindow, thePointGC, 15, 8 );
                XDrawPoint( theDisplay, thePointWindow, thePointGC, 3, 15 );
                XDrawPoint( theDisplay, thePointWindow, thePointGC, 25, 25 );
                XDrawPoint( theDisplay, thePointWindow, thePointGC, 5, 21 );
                XDrawPoint( theDisplay, thePointWindow, thePointGC, 7, 25 );
                XDrawPoint( theDisplay, thePointWindow, thePointGC, 25, 21 );
                XDrawPoint( theDisplay, thePointWindow, thePointGC, 5, 13 );
                XDrawPoint( theDisplay, thePointWindow, thePointGC, 17, 15 );

                XDrawString( theDisplay, thePointWindow, thePointGC,
                                2, 45, "@-P", strlen( "@-P" ) );
                return;
                }

        if ( theEvent->window == theLineWindow )
                {
                drawLine( theLineWindow, theLineGC,
                        10, 5, 35, 35 );
                XDrawString( theDisplay, theLineWindow, theLineGC,
                                2, 45, "@-L", strlen( "@-L" ) );
                return;
                }

        if ( theEvent->window == theRectWindow )
                {
                drawRectangle( theRectWindow, theRectGC,
                        5, 5, 24, 24 );
                XDrawString( theDisplay, theRectWindow, theRectGC,
                                2, 45, "@-R", strlen( "@-R" ) );
```

continued...

...from previous page

```
                return;
                }

        if ( theEvent->window == theFilledRectWindow )
                {
                fillRectangle( theFilledRectWindow, theFilledRectGC,
                        5, 5, 24, 24 );
                XDrawString( theDisplay, theFilledRectWindow, theFilledRectGC,
                                2, 45, "@-F", strlen( "@-F" ) );
                return;
                }

        if ( theEvent->window == theOvalWindow )
                {
                drawOval( theOvalWindow, theOvalGC,
                        5, 5, 24, 24 );
                XDrawString( theDisplay, theOvalWindow, theOvalGC,
                                2, 45, "@-O", strlen( "@-O" ) );
                return;
                }

        if ( theEvent->window == theFilledOvalWindow )
                {
                fillOval( theFilledOvalWindow, theFilledOvalGC,
                        5, 5, 30, 30 );
                return;
                }

        if ( theEvent->window == theText1Window )
                {
                XDrawString( theDisplay, theText1Window, theText1GC,
                                5, 20, "A", strlen( "A" ) );
                XDrawString( theDisplay, theText1Window, theText1GC,
                                2, 45, "@-T", strlen( "@-T" ) );
                return;
                }

        if ( theEvent->window == theText2Window )
                {
                XDrawString( theDisplay, theText2Window, theText2GC,
                                5, 20, "A", strlen( "A" ) );
                return;
                }

        if ( theEvent->window == theUndoWindow )
                {
                XDrawString( theDisplay, theUndoWindow, theUndoGC,
                                2, 20, "Undo", strlen( "Undo" ) );
                XDrawString( theDisplay, theUndoWindow, theUndoGC,
                                2, 45, "@-U", strlen( "@-U" ) );
                return;
                }
```

continued...

...from previous page

```
	if ( theEvent->window == theFileWindow )
		{
		XDrawString( theDisplay, theFileWindow, theFileGC,
				2, 20, "File", strlen( "File" ) );
		return;
		}

	if ( theEvent->window == theWipeOutWindow )
		{
		XDrawString( theDisplay, theWipeOutWindow, theWipeOutGC,
				2, 20, "Wipe", strlen( "Wipe" ) );
		return;
		}

	if ( theEvent->window == theQuitWindow )
		{
		XDrawString( theDisplay, theQuitWindow, theQuitGC,
				2, 20, "Quit", strlen( "Quit" ) );
		XDrawString( theDisplay, theQuitWindow, theQuitGC,
				2, 45, "@-Q", strlen( "@-Q" ) );
		return;
		}

}	/* -- function processExpose */
```

`processExpose` checks the window field of the `XExposeEvent` structure and then draws something different in each window. Most of the palette windows have either a shape, e.g., a line or rectangle, or a text string to describe the function (which proves a little difficult sometimes; for example, how do you describe the concept of Undo with an icon shape?). Some choices have keyboard shortcuts (using the meta key), and for those windows, the keyboard shortcut is drawn underneath the picture or word describing the choice. For example, the Save palette choice (and window) has the word "Save" on top to describe its function, as well as "@-S" underneath to show that Meta-S also will save the file. The "@" was arbitrarily chosen to represent the meta key, as no consistent meta key symbol exists on all keyboards.

Cursors for the Palette

To further help the user identify which drawing function is in effect, most windows on the palette have a unique cursor.

The Save, Line, and File choices all use a left-pointing arrow cursor (XC_top_left_arrow). The rectangular-bounded shapes (rectangles and ovals) use a crosshair cursor (XC_crosshair). The text items use a text cursor (XC_xterm), and the Color and Undo choices use a cursor that has two arrows pointing at each other, symbolizing a swap (XC_exchange). The draw Points choice uses a pencil cursor (XC_pencil), and the Wipe-out choice uses a skull and crossbones (XC_pirate). Finally, the Quit choices use the Gumby cursor waving goodbye (XC_gumby).

The function initCursors in the file cursorx.c sets up the cursors just discussed.

```
#include    <X11/Xlib.h>
#include    <X11/cursorfont.h>

#include    "drawapp.h"

/*
**      GLOBAL Cursor ids.
**
*/

Cursor  theArrowCursor;         /* -- XC_top_left_arrow, for line drawing */
Cursor  theBusyCursor;          /* -- XC_watch, used while writing to disk*/
Cursor  theCornerCursor;        /* -- XC_bottom_right_corner, for rects   */
Cursor  theCrossCursor;         /* -- XC_crosshair, for rects and ovals   */
Cursor  thePointCursor;         /* -- XC_pencil, for points               */
Cursor  theQuitCursor;          /* -- XC_gumby, waving bye-bye            */
Cursor  theSkullCursor;         /* -- XC_pirate, for the Wipe out cmd     */
Cursor  theTextCursor;          /* -- XC_xterm, for text drawing          */
Cursor  theUndoCursor;          /* -- XC_exchange, for undo-ing           */
        .
        .
        .
initCursors()

{       /* -- function initCursors */

        theArrowCursor  = XCreateFontCursor( theDisplay,
                                XC_top_left_arrow );
        theBusyCursor   = XCreateFontCursor( theDisplay,
                                XC_watch );
        theCornerCursor = XCreateFontCursor( theDisplay,
                                XC_bottom_right_corner );
        theCrossCursor  = XCreateFontCursor( theDisplay,
                                XC_crosshair );
        thePointCursor  = XCreateFontCursor( theDisplay,
                                XC_pencil );
```

continued...

...from previous page

```
        theQuitCursor    = XCreateFontCursor( theDisplay,
                                      XC_gumby );
        theSkullCursor   = XCreateFontCursor( theDisplay,
                                      XC_pirate );
        theTextCursor    = XCreateFontCursor( theDisplay,
                                      XC_xterm );
        theUndoCursor    = XCreateFontCursor( theDisplay,
                                      XC_exchange );

}       /* -- function initCursors */
```

The function **associateCursors** takes all these created cursors and sets up (or restores) all the necessary cursors for the Draw application windows.

```
/*
**      associateCursors associates all the windows in the DrawApp
**      application with their default cursors.  This routine MUST
**      not be called until all the above listed windows have been
**      created and the function initCursors(), below has been called.
**
**      The parameter drawingCommand specifies which drawing command
**      is in effect, which in turn determines the cursor for the
**      main drawing window, theDrawWindow.
**
**      This function is called at the beginning of DrawApp, as well
**      as to restore the cursors after a call to makeAllBusyCursor().
**
*/

associateCursors( drawingCommand )

int     drawingCommand;

{       /* -- function associateCursors */

        /*
        **      Set theDrawWindow to the proper cursor
        */
        setCmdCursor( drawingCommand, FIRST_POINT );

        XDefineCursor( theDisplay, theBorderWindow, theArrowCursor );

        /*
        **      Set up the rest of the cursors to their defaults
        **
        */
        XDefineCursor( theDisplay, thePaletteWindow, theArrowCursor );
        XDefineCursor( theDisplay, theColorWindow, theUndoCursor );
```

continued...

...from previous page

```
        XDefineCursor( theDisplay, theFileWindow, theArrowCursor );
        XDefineCursor( theDisplay, theFilledOvalWindow, theCrossCursor );
        XDefineCursor( theDisplay, theFilledRectWindow, theCrossCursor );
        XDefineCursor( theDisplay, theLineWindow, theArrowCursor );
        XDefineCursor( theDisplay, theOvalWindow, theCrossCursor );
        XDefineCursor( theDisplay, thePointWindow, thePointCursor );
        XDefineCursor( theDisplay, theQuitWindow, theQuitCursor );
        XDefineCursor( theDisplay, theRectWindow, theCrossCursor );
        XDefineCursor( theDisplay, theSaveWindow, theArrowCursor );
        XDefineCursor( theDisplay, theText1Window, theTextCursor );
        XDefineCursor( theDisplay, theText2Window, theTextCursor );
        XDefineCursor( theDisplay, theUndoWindow, theUndoCursor );
        XDefineCursor( theDisplay, theWipeOutWindow, theSkullCursor );

}       /* -- function associateCursors */
```

Waiting for Godot (or Setting a "Busy" Cursor)

Saving a file to disk can make users feel like waiting for Godot—it sometimes takes too long. To let the user know that the program is busy writing to disk (or reading from disk), all the cursors in the Draw application windows are set to `theBusyCursor`, before writing to disk. This cursor looks like a watch (`XC_watch`) to symbolize waiting. The function `makeAllBusyCursor` handles this task.

```
makeAllBusyCursor()

{       /* -- function makeAllBusyCursor */

        XDefineCursor( theDisplay, theBorderWindow, theBusyCursor );
        XDefineCursor( theDisplay, theDrawWindow, theBusyCursor );
        XDefineCursor( theDisplay, thePaletteWindow, theBusyCursor );
        XDefineCursor( theDisplay, theColorWindow, theBusyCursor );
        XDefineCursor( theDisplay, theFileWindow, theBusyCursor );
        XDefineCursor( theDisplay, theFilledOvalWindow, theBusyCursor );
        XDefineCursor( theDisplay, theFilledRectWindow, theBusyCursor );
        XDefineCursor( theDisplay, theLineWindow, theBusyCursor );
        XDefineCursor( theDisplay, theOvalWindow, theBusyCursor );
        XDefineCursor( theDisplay, thePointWindow, theBusyCursor );
        XDefineCursor( theDisplay, theQuitWindow, theBusyCursor );
        XDefineCursor( theDisplay, theRectWindow, theBusyCursor );
        XDefineCursor( theDisplay, theSaveWindow, theBusyCursor );
        XDefineCursor( theDisplay, theText1Window, theBusyCursor );
        XDefineCursor( theDisplay, theText2Window, theBusyCursor );
        XDefineCursor( theDisplay, theUndoWindow, theBusyCursor );
        XDefineCursor( theDisplay, theWipeOutWindow, theBusyCursor );
```

continued...

...from previous page

```
        XFlush( theDisplay );

}       /* -- function makeAllBusyCursor */
```

The cursors are restored to their normal values when the function **associateCursors** is called again after the disk-intensive operation is complete, to show that the wait is over.

Setting the Cursor for the Drawing Window

The drawing window (where all the work actually takes place) has its cursor set up to follow the current drawing item. If the user is drawing points, for example, the drawing window cursor will be the pencil cursor. This way, the user has a better idea of what the program thinks the user wants. The **setCmdCursor** function sets the cursor up.

```
/*
**      setCmdCursor sets up the cursor for the main drawing window,
**      theDrawWindow, based on the current drawing command.  The
**      routine takes two parameters, the new drawing command and
**      which point is being drawn.  The rectangle and oval commands
**      have a different cursor depending whether the first or the
**      second point is being drawn.
**
*/

setCmdCursor( drawingCommand, whichPoint )

int     drawingCommand;
int     whichPoint;

{       /* -- function setCmdCursor */

        switch( drawingCommand )
                {
                case DRAW_POINT         :
                        XDefineCursor( theDisplay, theDrawWindow,
                                thePointCursor );
                        break;
                case DRAW_LINE          :
                        XDefineCursor( theDisplay, theDrawWindow,
                                theArrowCursor );
                        break;
```

continued...

...from previous page

```
            case DRAW_TEXT1      :
            case DRAW_TEXT2      :
                XDefineCursor( theDisplay, theDrawWindow,
                        theTextCursor );
                break;
            case DRAW_RECT       :
            case DRAW_FILLED_RECT:
            case DRAW_OVAL       :
            case DRAW_FILLED_OVAL:
                if ( whichPoint == FIRST_POINT )
                        {
                        XDefineCursor( theDisplay, theDrawWindow,
                                theCrossCursor );
                        }
                else
                        {
                        XDefineCursor( theDisplay, theDrawWindow,
                                theCornerCursor );
                        }
                break;
            }

        XFlush( theDisplay );

}       /* -- function setCmdCursor */
```

Freeing Up the Cursor Resources

Just before the program quits, it frees up the cursor resources it used with the function `freeCursors`:

```
freeCursors()

{       /* -- function freeCursors */

        XFreeCursor( theDisplay, theArrowCursor );
        XFreeCursor( theDisplay, theBusyCursor );
        XFreeCursor( theDisplay, theCornerCursor );
        XFreeCursor( theDisplay, theCrossCursor );
        XFreeCursor( theDisplay, thePointCursor );
        XFreeCursor( theDisplay, theQuitCursor );
        XFreeCursor( theDisplay, theSkullCursor );
        XFreeCursor( theDisplay, theTextCursor );
        XFreeCursor( theDisplay, theUndoCursor );

        XFlush( theDisplay );

}       /* -- function freeCursors */
```

THE DRAWING WINDOW

The drawing window is the main application window where all the action is. It is in the drawing window that the user will actually be drawing X bitmap shapes to be used for icons or screen backgrounds or whatever. This draw window is independent of the floating palette so that it too can be moved around the screen. This drawing window is set up to be the size of the bitmap to be edited or a default size if none is specified.

Users may want to edit tiny bitmaps though, such as 16-by-16 pixels, and the draw window would be too small to be usable if it were 16-by-16 pixels (try locating a 16-by-16 pixel window on a 1,024-by-1,024 pixel display). So the same approach as the one used for the palette window is needed: A larger frame window will outline the drawing window and enable the user to actually see the drawing.

The drawing window will be a child of the framing border window. These two windows are also created in the function `initWindows` in `drawapp.c`:

```
char            theDrawName[ MAX_TEXT_LENGTH + 5 ];
Window          theBorderWindow;
Window          theDrawWindow;

/*
**      Graphic Contexts for all windows
*/

GC              theBorderGC;              /* -- Border window GC    */
GC              theWhiteGC;               /* -- Draw White bits     */
GC              theBlackGC;               /* -- Draw Black bits     */
GC              theXorGC;                 /* -- Rubber-band drawing */
.
.
.

/*
**      initWindows
*/

initWindows( theGeometry, theTitle, iconicState )

char    theGeometry[];
char    theTitle[];
int     iconicState;
```

continued...

...from previous page

```
{       /* -- function initWindows */
        int             geometryStatus;
        int             x, y, x1, y1, width, height;
        Window          openWindow();
        char            thePaletteTitle[ 120 ];

        /*
        **      parse geometry spec
        */
        geometryStatus = XParseGeometry( theGeometry, &x, &y, &width, &height );

        /*
        **      Check which values were actually set
        */
        if ( !( geometryStatus & XValue ) )
                x = 10;
        if ( !( geometryStatus & YValue ) )
                y = 10;
        if ( !( geometryStatus & WidthValue ) )
                width  = 100;
        if ( !( geometryStatus & HeightValue ) )
                height = 100;

        /*
        **      Create theBorderWindow--to frame the drawing window
        */
        if ( strlen( theTitle ) < 100 )
                {
                strcpy( theDrawName, theTitle );
                }

        theBorderWindow = openWindow( x, y, width, height,
                                NORMAL_WINDOW, theTitle,
                                iconicState, theRootWindow, &theBorderGC );
        initEvents( theBorderWindow, IN_PALETTE );  /* -- Not really in palette*/

        /*
        **      Create theDrawWindow--where all drawing takes place
        */
        x1 = ( width / 2 ) - ( theDrawWidth / 2 );
        y1 = ( height / 2 ) - ( theDrawHeight / 2 );

        if ( x1 < 0 ) x1 = 0;
        if ( y1 < 0 ) y1 = 0;

        theDrawWindow = openWindow( x1, y1,
                                theDrawWidth, theDrawHeight,
                                NORMAL_WINDOW, theTitle,
                                NORMAL_STATE, theBorderWindow, &theBlackGC );

        initEvents( theDrawWindow, NOT_IN_PALETTE );
```

continued...

...from previous page

```
/*
**      Create a GC for drawing in white
*/
createGC( theDrawWindow, &theWhiteGC );
XSetForeground( theDisplay,
        theWhiteGC,
        theWhitePixel );

/*
**      Create a GC for xor-ing rubber-band items
*/
xorSetUp( theDrawWindow, &theXorGC );
.
.
.
```

The drawing window, `theDrawWindow`, gets three graphics contexts, one for drawing in black (`theBlackGC`), one for drawing in white (`theWhiteGC`), and one for the rubber-band lines (`theXorGC`).

CLEANING UP THE X WINDOW AND GC RESOURCES

Like any good X program, the Draw application tries to free up the server resources it devoured while running. The function `freeWindowsAndGCs` in `drawapp.c` handles this task:

```
.
.
.
/*
**      Releases all window and GC resources used by the DrawApp
**      application.
*/

freeWindowsAndGCs()

{       /* -- function freeWindowsAndGCs */

        /*
        **      Free up all Graphics Contexts
        */
        XFreeGC( theDisplay, theBorderGC );
        XFreeGC( theDisplay, theBlackGC );
        XFreeGC( theDisplay, theWhiteGC );
```

continued...

...from previous page

```
        XFreeGC( theDisplay, theXorGC );
        XFreeGC( theDisplay, thePaletteGC );
        XFreeGC( theDisplay, theColorGC );
        XFreeGC( theDisplay, theFileGC );
        XFreeGC( theDisplay, theFilledOvalGC );
        XFreeGC( theDisplay, theFilledRectGC );
        XFreeGC( theDisplay, theLineGC );
        XFreeGC( theDisplay, theOvalGC );
        XFreeGC( theDisplay, thePointGC );
        XFreeGC( theDisplay, theQuitGC );
        XFreeGC( theDisplay, theRectGC );
        XFreeGC( theDisplay, theSaveGC );
        XFreeGC( theDisplay, theText1GC );
        XFreeGC( theDisplay, theText2GC );
        XFreeGC( theDisplay, theUndoGC );
        XFreeGC( theDisplay, theWipeOutGC );

        /*
        **      Destroy all windows
        */
        XDestroySubwindows( theDisplay,
                thePaletteWindow );
        XDestroyWindow( theDisplay, thePaletteWindow );

        XDestroySubwindows( theDisplay,
                theBorderWindow );
        XDestroyWindow( theDisplay, theBorderWindow );

        XFlush( theDisplay );

}       /* -- function freeWindowsAndGCs */
```

FILE FORMAT FOR THE DRAW APPLICATION

The Draw application uses the same file format as the `bitmap` program—an ASCII C language format—which is an ideal format for two main reasons: `XReadBitmapFile` and `XWriteBitmapFile`. These two Xlib routines provide a handy way to read in and save bitmap-format files from and to the disk. Files in this format can be used by the `bitmap` program and can be included directly in C programs.

`XReadBitmapFile` reads in a bitmap-format ASCII file into an X `Pixmap` structure (bitmaps are `Pixmaps` with a depth of one, i.e., monochrome). `XReadBitmapFile` takes a `Drawable` parameter, but this drawable is used just to determine what screen the `Pixmap` should be created on. In this case, the screen's root window is used:

```
Display *theDisplay;
Window  theRootWindow;
Pixmap  tempPixmap;
int     status;
int     width, height;
int     xHotSpot, yHotSpot;
char    *theFileName;    /* -- Contains the name of the file to load */

status = XReadBitmapFile( theDisplay,
        theRootWindow,
        theFileName,
        &width, &height,
        &tempPixmap,
        &xHotSpot, &yHotSpot );
```

This call is successful if the status returned equals `BitmapSuccess`.

```
if ( status == BitmapSuccess )
        {
        /*
        **      Process Pixmap
        */
        .
        .
        .
        }
```

Once the file is into a pixmap, you can then use `XCopyPlane` (see the next section in this chapter) to display the pixmap in a window. You can also save one-depth pixmaps to disk (into bitmap ASCII files), using the `XWriteBitmapFile` Xlib function. In the following example, the function `saveFile` (from `filex.c`) calls `XWriteBitmapFile`:

```
Display         *theDisplay;
Pixmap          theDrawPixmap;          /* -- The pixmap in use */
unsigned int    theDrawWidth;           /* -- The width of the pixmap */
unsigned int    theDrawHeight;          /* -- the height of the pixmap */

/*
**      saveFile saves the current pixmap to the given file name
**
*/

saveFile( theFileName )

char    theFileName[];
```

continued...

...from previous page

```
{       /* -- function saveFile */
        int     status;

        status = XWriteBitmapFile( theDisplay,
                                  theFileName,
                                  theDrawPixmap,
                                  theDrawWidth,
                                  theDrawHeight,
                                  (-1), (-1) );    /* -- Hot spots for cursors */

        if ( status != BitmapSuccess )
                {
                fprintf( stderr, "ERROR: Could not save file %s.\n",
                                  theFileName );
                }

        XFlush( theDisplay );

}       /* -- function saveFile */
```

`saveFile` is passed the name of the file to save the `Pixmap` to on disk.

`Pixmaps` in X are very handy beasts. Not only can they be loaded from and saved to ASCII bitmap files, they can also be treated as windows for most drawing functions.

PIXMAPS AND WINDOWS

Most drawing functions in the Xlib can draw onto drawables, i.e., windows or pixmaps. `Pixmaps` are resources internal to the X server. They are effectively drawing areas that exist off screen. You can use `XDrawLine`, for example, to draw to a pixmap. No pixels will be drawn on the screen unless you copy the contents of the off-screen pixmap to a window on the screen.

XCopyPlane

The Xlib function `XCopyPlane` copies one plane of a drawable onto another drawable, which may have more than one plane. In the Draw application, all `Pixmap` drawables have one-plane depth, but the windows used inherit the number of planes of the root window. `XCopyPlane` can copy pixels between pixmaps and pixmaps or between pixmaps and windows (or between windows and windows).

`XCopyPlane` looks like the following:

```
Display         *theDisplay;
Drawable        theSource;
Drawable        theDestination;
GC              theDestinationGC;
int             sourceX, sourceY;             /* -- starting location */
unsigned int    width, height;                /* -- size of area copied */
int             destinationX, destinationY;
unsigned long   thePlane;                     /* -- which plane to copy */

XCopyPlane( theDisplay,
        theSource,
        theDestination,
        theDestinationGC,
        sourcesX, sourceY,
        width, height,
        destinationX, destinationY,
        thePlane );
```

In the Draw application, `thePlane` is set to 0x01 so that it copies only a monochrome plane with `BlackPixel` and `WhitePixel` (the pixmaps in use all only have one plane).

The function `copyPixmap` (in `pixmapx.c`) is used by the Draw application to copy the contents of a pixmap to the drawing window (`theDrawWindow`) and to save a copy of the current pixmap (into `theUndoPixmap`) so that the drawing operation can be undone (by copying the original pixmap back).

```
/*
**      Copies the contents of one pixmap (or window) into another,
**      used for the undo routines.
**
*/

copyPixmap( srcPixmap, destPixmap, destGC, width, height )

Drawable        srcPixmap;
Drawable        destPixmap;
GC              destGC;
unsigned int    width, height;

{       /* -- function copyPixmap */
```

continued...

...from previous page

```
        /*
        **      XCopyArea would work on a monochrome
        **      system, but not a color system.
        */
        XCopyPlane( theDisplay,
                srcPixmap,
                destPixmap,
                destGC,
                0, 0,           /* -- X, Y */
                width, height,
                0, 0,
                0x01 );         /* -- Plane */

        XFlush( theDisplay );

}       /* -- function copyPixmap */
```

Undo with Pixmaps

`Pixmaps` are used in the Draw application to store the contents of the window before saving to disk with the `XWriteBitmapFile` function. `Pixmaps` are also used to undo drawing commands. The undo method used by the Draw application works as follows:

1. Before any drawing, save a copy of the current pixmap, `theDrawPixmap`, to `theUndoPixmap`.

2. Draw each item twice: once to the window on the display and once to `theDrawPixmap`. That way, `theDrawWindow` and `theDrawPixmap` should have matching contents.

3. To undo, copy the contents of `theUndoPixmap` to `theDrawWindow` and `theDrawPixmap`.

This gives the Draw application one level of undo, but it cannot go back farther than that. The `undo` function handles the undoing:

```
/*
**      undo undoes the draw display back to the last-saved
**      pixmap (which is maintained by the maintainUndo() function).
**
*/

undo()

{       /* -- function undo */

        copyPixmap( theUndoPixmap, theDrawPixmap, theBlackPixGC,
                        theDrawWidth, theDrawHeight );

        refreshDrawWindow();     /* -- copy contents to theDrawWindow */

}       /* -- function undo */
```

Before any drawing takes place, the function `maintainUndo` is called in `pixmapx.c`. This function copies `theDrawPixmap` to `theUndoPixmap` so that whatever drawing operation comes after this can be undone.

```
/*
**      maintainUndo saves a copy of the current pixmap so that
**      any drawing operations can be undone.
**
*/

maintainUndo()

{       /* -- function maintainUndo */

        copyPixmap( theDrawPixmap,      /* -- Source */
                        theUndoPixmap,  /* -- Dest   */
                        theUndoPixGC,
                        theDrawWidth,
                        theDrawHeight );

}       /* -- function maintainUndo */
```

And, finally, the function `refreshDrawWindow` is called any time the contents of `theDrawWindow` need to be redrawn.

```
/*
**      refreshDrawWindow refreshes the picture in the draw window.
**
*/

refreshDrawWindow()

{       /* -- function refreshDrawWindow */

        XClearWindow( theDisplay, theDrawWindow );

        copyPixmap( theDrawPixmap,
                theDrawWindow,
                theBlackGC,
                theDrawWidth, theDrawHeight );

        XFlush( theDisplay );

}       /* -- function refreshDrawWindow */
```

All these pixmaps are created originally with the `XCreatePixmap` function:

```
Display         *theDisplay;
Drawable        theRootWindow;
unsigned int    theDrawWidth, theDrawHeight;
unsigned int    thePixmapDepth = 1;             /* -- monochrome */
Pixmap          thePixmap;

thePixmap = XCreatePixmap( theDisplay,
                theRootWindow,
                theDrawWidth,
                theDrawHeight,
                thePixmapDepth );
```

`XCreatePixmap` uses the `Drawable` parameter (`theRootWindow`) to specify which screen the `Pixmap` should be associated with (these functions really should take a screen parameter rather than a `Drawable`). The `Pixmap` will be created on the same screen as the `Drawable`. In this case, the screen's root window is used as a convenient `Drawable` on the screen.

SUMMARY

This chapter shows you how the multiple windows used in the Draw application were created.

- Multiple windows allow many advantages for both users and programmers. However, multiple windows are also complicated. Each window requires a certain amount of system overhead, and each requires that you set up such things as variable `ID` and fonts. Plus, as you saw in Chapter 1, it's not as easy as you might think to set up a window in a windowing system, which is why it's important that you do some planning before you set up your window design. Don't try to get too fancy and set up more windows than your user needs.

- A good place to start your window design is to use floating palettes to show the user available options. This means you need to diverge from the usual X window design. In the Draw application, the application is one top-level window, and the floating palette is the other main window, with the different choices within the floating palette treated as subwindows. This gives the user the flexibility to move the floating palette around the screen and place it anywhere.

- When a user chooses a function on the floating palette, you will want to provide feedback—a key element of any software design (for example, a watch cursor is incorporated to let the user know that a disk is being read from or written to). This feedback is accomplished in the Draw application by filling the window with a black rectangle and then clearing the window and redrawing its old contents.

- So the user will know what function was chosen, different cursors are assigned to represent different drawing functions. For example, the Save, Line, and File choices use a left-pointing arrow, much like every other windowing system. The erasing or Wipe-out function is represented by a skull and crossbones. The Quit function is represented by a waving Gumby.

- Design features discussed in earlier chapters are also incorporated into the Draw application. For example, the program frees up cursor resources before it quits. It also frees up server resources before it quits.

- Pixmaps are used to store the contents of the window before saving to disk and are used to undo drawing commands. This is quite a simple process, involving saving copies of the current pixmap to `theUndoPixmap`, and drawing each item twice. This gives the Draw application one level to revert to, but no more.

Xlib Functions and Macros Introduced in This Chapter

XCopyPlane
XCreatePixmap
XReadBitmapFile
XWriteBitmapFile

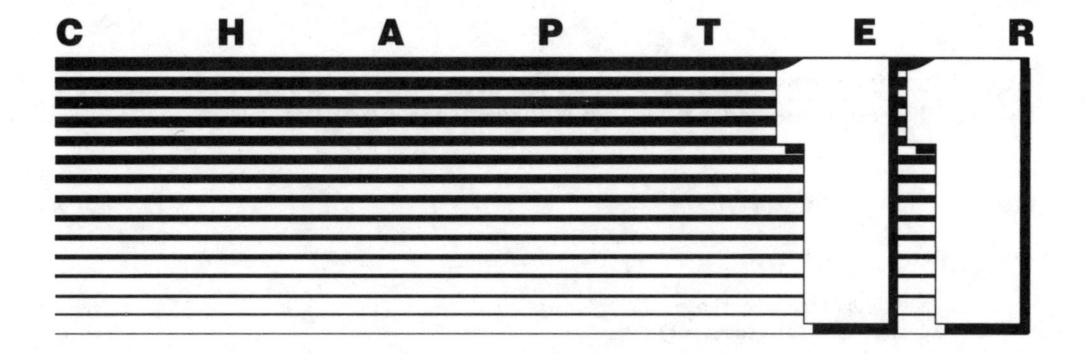

EVENT PROCESSING IN THE DRAW APPLICATION

This chapter explains event processing in the Draw application. The Draw application accepts five kinds of events:

- Drawing events
- Palette-selection events
- Text-entry events
- Keyboard shortcut events
- X server-generated events

The main event loop handles these five types of events for the Draw application. The function `eventLoop`, introduced in Chapter 5, is modified in this chapter to distribute more of the event processing to special routines, resulting in a cleaner, leaner `eventLoop` function.

eventLoop returns a value of 0 when the user wants to quit the program and a value of 1 to continue. eventLoop still resides in eventx.c:

```
Display         *theDisplay;

eventLoop()

{       /* -- function eventLoop */
        XEvent          theEvent;

        /*
        **      Block on input, awaiting an event from X
        */

        XNextEvent( theDisplay, &theEvent );

        /*
        **      Decode the event and call a specific routine to
        **      handle it
        */

        switch( theEvent.type )
                {
                /*
                **      Part or all of the Window has been exposed to the
                **      world, or the window is mapped, or its size has
                **      changed.
                */
                case ConfigureNotify:
                case Expose:
                case MapNotify:
                        processExpose( &theEvent );
                        break;
                /*
                **      A Mouse button has been pressed.
                */
                case ButtonPress:
                        return( processButton( &theEvent ) );
                        break;

                /*
                **      A Mouse button has been pressed, then
                **      released.
                */
                case ButtonRelease:
                        processRelease( &theEvent );
                        break;

                case MotionNotify:
                        processMotion( &theEvent );
                        break;
```

continued...

...from previous page

```
            /*
            **      A key on the keyboard was hit.
            */
            case KeyPress:
                    return( processKeyPress( &theEvent ) );
                    break;
            }

        /*
        **      Return a 0 to quit, a 1 to keep going
        */
        return( 1 );

}       /* -- function eventLoop */
```

THE EVENT MASK AND SELECTING EVENTS

In X, events will be sent to only those windows that ask for events. In addition, you must ask for the specific kinds of events your program's windows want to accept. Draw has two basic types of windows: those that the user draws in (in this case, there is just one — the main draw window) and those that the user does not draw in. The user does not draw in the floating selection palette and the two background windows, which leaves only the main draw window (named, precisely enough, `theDrawWindow`).

Thus, there are two sets of events to request. In this case, only the drawing window receives extra events beyond what the other windows receive. Consequently, the event mask used to request events is shared, with the drawing window adding two more elements.

The event mask sent to the X server with an `XSelectInput` call determines which events are to be sent to the window by the X server. The basic event mask for the Draw application is defined in `eventx.c`:

```
#include    <X11/Xlib.h>
        .
        .
        .
#define EV_MASK (ButtonPressMask        | \
                 KeyPressMask           | \
                 ExposureMask           | \
                 StructureNotifyMask)
```

This event mask is used to ask for the following events to be sent from the X server:

- `ButtonPress`
- `CirculateNotify`
- `ConfigureNotify`
- `DestroyNotify`
- `Expose`
- `GravityNotify`
- `KeyPress`
- `MapNotify`
- `ReparentNotify`
- `UnmapNotify`

(Actually, from the `StructureNotifyMask`, only the `ConfigureNotify` and `MapNotify` events are used in the application.)

After each window is created, the function `XSelectInput` is called for the new window and passed the event mask. This is accomplished in Draw with the `initEvents` function. `initEvents` takes two parameters: the window `ID` and a flag specifying if the window is part of the palette or is the drawing window. The windows considered part of the palette use the basic event mask. The draw window, however, adds `ButtonMotionMask` and `ButtonReleaseMask` to the mask—without these, of course, the user would not be able to draw anything. This means that the draw window receives `ButtonRelease` events when a mouse button is released (after being pressed down), and also receives `MotionNotify` events if the mouse position moves while a mouse button is held down.

The drawing window uses these events for the main drawing. Lines, for example, are drawn in rubber-band fashion while a mouse button is held down in the drawing window, and the line is locked in place when the mouse button is released. An undo can cancel the operation if the resulting line is not wanted.

The function `initEvents` is defined in `eventx.c`:

```
        .
        .
        .
initEvents( theWindow, inPalette )

Window  theWindow;
int     inPalette;

{       /* -- function initEvents */

        if ( inPalette == IN_PALETTE )
                {
                XSelectInput( theDisplay,
                        theWindow,
                        EV_MASK );
                }
        else
                {
                XSelectInput( theDisplay,
                        theWindow,
                        ( EV_MASK | ButtonMotionMask | ButtonReleaseMask ) );
                }

}       /* -- function initEvents */
```

DRAWING EVENTS

Drawing in the Draw application is a three-step process:

1. The user presses a mouse button, generating a `ButtonPress` event. The application sets a flag that drawing has started and draws the first item in `xor` mode (for the rubber-banding effect).
2. The user holds down the mouse button and moves the mouse around to draw a line, rectangle, oval, or a number of points. With each movement of the mouse, the application redraws the items in the old position (using `xor` mode) and then draws the items in the new position (again using `xor` mode).
3. Finally, the user releases the mouse button, locking in the line, rectangle, or oval. The item is redrawn in `xor` mode to erase it, and then drawn to the window using the current `GC` (drawing in either black or white).

All these events are detected in the function `eventLoop` in `eventx.c`.

```
Display         *theDisplay;

eventLoop()

{       /* -- function eventLoop */
        XEvent          theEvent;

        /*
        **      Block on input, awaiting an event from X
        */

        XNextEvent( theDisplay, &theEvent );

        /*
        **      Decode the event and call a specific routine to
        **      handle it
        */

        switch( theEvent.type )
                {
                .
                .
                .
                /*
                **      A Mouse button has been pressed.
                */
                case ButtonPress:
                        return( processButton( &theEvent ) );
                        break;

                /*
                **      A Mouse button has been pressed, then
                **      released.
                */
                case ButtonRelease:
                        processRelease( &theEvent );
                        break;

                case MotionNotify:
                        processMotion( &theEvent );
                        break;
                .
                .
                .
                }
        .
        .

}       /* -- function eventLoop */
```

When the user presses a mouse button, generating a `ButtonPress` event, the application needs to set a flag that specifies that drawing has started. This is handled in the function `processButton`.

```
/*
**      GLOBALS for drawing
*/

int     theDrawingCommand  = DRAW_POINT;
int     theDrawingColor    = BLACK;
int     theDrawingMode     = DRAWING_OFF;

char    theDrawingText[ MAX_TEXT_LENGTH + 5 ];

int     theDrawX           = 0;
int     theDrawY           = 0;
int     theLastDrawX       = 0;
int     theLastDrawY       = 0;

.
.
.
processButton( theEvent )

XButtonPressedEvent     *theEvent;

{       /* -- function processButton */
        int     status = 1;
        int     choice;
        int     x, y;
        char    theFileName[ 120 ];

        /*
        **      if theDrawingMode == DRAWING_ON, undo rubber-band item.
        */
        restoreXorItem();

        /*
        **      If a ButtonPress event in theDrawWindow, then
        **      draw something.
        */
        if ( theEvent->window == theDrawWindow )
                {
                /*
                **      If not drawing yet
                */
```

continued...

...from previous page

```
        /*
        **      Save item for Undo
        */
        maintainUndo();


        /*
        **      if a point, draw the point; if text
        **      set up text; if line or rect, set that up
        */
        switch( theDrawingCommand )
                {
                case    DRAW_POINT:
                        drawItem( theDrawingCommand,
                                theDrawingColor,
                                theEvent->x, theEvent->y,
                                0, 0, " ");
                        break;

                case    DRAW_TEXT1:
                case    DRAW_TEXT2:
                        theDrawX       = theEvent->x;
                        theDrawY       = theEvent->y;
                        theDrawingMode = DRAWING_TEXT;
                        theDrawingText[ 0 ] = '\0';
                        break;

                case    DRAW_LINE:
                case    DRAW_RECT:
                case    DRAW_FILLED_RECT:
                case    DRAW_OVAL:
                case    DRAW_FILLED_OVAL:
                        theDrawingMode = DRAWING_ON;
                        theLastDrawX   = theEvent->x;
                        theLastDrawY   = theEvent->y;
                        theDrawX       = theEvent->x + 1;
                        theDrawY       = theEvent->y + 1;
                        drawItem( theDrawingCommand, XOR,
                                theLastDrawX, theLastDrawY,
                                1, 1, " " );
                        break;
                }
        return ( status );
        }

    .
    .
    .

}       /* -- function processButton */
```

The flag that was set is called theDrawingMode. It can have a value of DRAWING_ON, for when the user is drawing a rubber-band item and DRAWING_OFF for when the user is done drawing and for before the user starts. (DRAWING_ON and DRAWING_OFF are defined in drawapp.h.)

processButton calls restoreXorItem to undraw (using GXxor mode) any drawing item that was previously drawn in GXxor mode.

```
restoreXorItem()

{       /* -- function restoreXorItem */

        if ( theDrawingMode == DRAWING_ON )
                {
                drawItem( theDrawingCommand, XOR,
                        theLastDrawX, theLastDrawY,
                        theDrawX - theLastDrawX,
                        theDrawY - theLastDrawY,
                        " " );          /* -- no text */
                }

}       /* -- function restoreXorItem */
```

The MotionNotify events occur only in theDrawWindow (because only theDrawWindow had the ButtonMotionMask specified in the call to XSelectInput) and only when the user holds down a mouse button and moves the position of the mouse. When a MotionNotify event comes in, the function processMotion is called. This function checks to be sure that the event is for theDrawWindow, and then checks that theDrawingMode is DRAWING_ON. If so, it will redraw any rubber-band item that is being drawn or draw a point at the mouse location on the screen, if the user is drawing points.

```
processMotion( theEvent )

XPointerMovedEvent      *theEvent;

{       /* -- function processMotion */

        if ( theEvent->window == theDrawWindow )
                {
                if ( theDrawingMode == DRAWING_ON )
```

continued...

...from previous page

```
                    {
                    if ( ( ( theEvent->x > theLastDrawX ) &&
                       ( theEvent->y > theLastDrawY ) ) ||
                       ( theDrawingCommand == DRAW_LINE ) )
                        {
                        /*
                        **      Undraw last item
                        */
                        drawItem( theDrawingCommand, XOR,
                                theLastDrawX, theLastDrawY,
                                theDrawX - theLastDrawX,
                                theDrawY - theLastDrawY, " " );

                        /*
                        **      Update Coords
                        */
                        theDrawX = theEvent->x;
                        theDrawY = theEvent->y;

                        /*
                        **      Draw item in new position
                        */
                        drawItem( theDrawingCommand, XOR,
                                theLastDrawX, theLastDrawY,
                                theDrawX - theLastDrawX,
                                theDrawY - theLastDrawY, " " );

                        }
                    }

                /*
                **      If the Button is down and the user wants to
                **      draw points, keep drawing.
                */
                if ( theDrawingCommand == DRAW_POINT )
                    {
                    /*
                    **      Save item for Undo
                    */
                    maintainUndo();

                    theDrawX = theEvent->x;
                    theDrawY = theEvent->y;
                    drawItem( theDrawingCommand, theDrawingColor,
                            theDrawX, theDrawY, 0, 0, " " );
                    }
                }

        XFlush( theDisplay );

}       /* -- function processMotion */
```

When the user releases a mouse button that was previously held down, a rubber-band item (such as a line, rectangle, or oval) is undrawn, the position is locked in, and the item is drawn "permanently," but not permanently enough to prevent an undo. This is done by using the GXcopy mode rather than the GXxor mode.

```
/*
**      processRelease processes the ButtonRelease events, if the
**      user has been drawing an item like a rectangle.
**
*/

processRelease( theEvent )

XButtonReleasedEvent     *theEvent;

{       /* -- function processRelease */

        if ( ( theEvent->window == theDrawWindow ) &&
           ( theDrawingMode == DRAWING_ON ) )
                {
                /*
                **      Save item for Undo
                */
                maintainUndo();

                /*
                **      Draw final item on window
                */
                switch( theDrawingCommand )
                        {
                        case    DRAW_RECT:
                        case    DRAW_FILLED_RECT:
                        case    DRAW_OVAL:
                        case    DRAW_FILLED_OVAL:
                                /*
                                **      Be sure the bounding rect
                                **      goes down
                                */
                                if ( ( theEvent->x <= theLastDrawX ) ||
                                   ( theEvent->y <= theLastDrawY ) )
                                        {
                                        break;
                                        }
                                /*
                                **      If so, go on
                                */
```

continued...

...from previous page

```
                        default         :
                                theDrawX = theEvent->x;
                                theDrawY = theEvent->y;
                                drawItem( theDrawingCommand,
                                        theDrawingColor,
                                        theLastDrawX, theLastDrawY,
                                        theDrawX - theLastDrawX,
                                        theDrawY - theLastDrawY,
                                        " " );
                                theDrawingMode = DRAWING_OFF;
                        }
                }

}       /* -- function processRelease */
```

To be generic, all of the previous functions use one function to draw—called `drawItem`. `drawItem` takes a drawing command, a variable that specifies what to draw (such as a command `DRAW_LINE`), the color to draw it in (`BLACK`, `WHITE`, or `XOR`), the location for the item, its size (width and height), and a character string (only used if the user is drawing text; otherwise, it can be a NULL string).

```
/*
**      drawitem.c
**
**      Draws items like lines, rectangles and ovals for the
**      DrawApp application.
**
*/

#include    <X11/Xlib.h>
#include    <X11/Xutil.h>

#include    "drawapp.h"

/*
**      External GLOBALS
*/

extern  Display         *theDisplay;
extern  Window          theDrawWindow;
extern  Pixmap          theDrawPixmap;

/*
**      Graphic Contexts for theDrawWindow
*/
```

continued...

...from previous page

```
extern  GC      theWhiteGC;                 /* -- Draw White bits     */
extern  GC      theBlackGC;                 /* -- Draw Black bits     */
extern  GC      theXorGC;                   /* -- Rubber-band drawing */
extern  GC      theBlackPixGC;              /* -- Draw Pixmap GC      */
extern  GC      theWhitePixGC;              /* -- Draw Pixmap GC      */

/*
**      drawItem draws a given item
*/

drawItem( theCommand, theColor, x, y, width, height, theText )

int     theCommand;     /* -- what to draw, from drawapp.h */
int     theColor;       /* -- what color to draw in        */
int     x, y;           /* -- where to draw it             */
int     width, height;  /* -- how big to draw it           */
char    theText[];      /* -- text for DRAW_TEXT1, _TEXT2  */

{       /* -- function drawItem */

        switch( theColor )
                {
                case BLACK:
                        drawIt( theDrawWindow, theBlackGC, theCommand,
                                x, y, width, height, theText );
                        drawIt( theDrawPixmap, theBlackPixGC, theCommand,
                                x, y, width, height, theText );
                        break;
                case WHITE:
                        drawIt( theDrawWindow, theWhiteGC, theCommand,
                                x, y, width, height, theText );
                        drawIt( theDrawPixmap, theWhitePixGC, theCommand,
                                x, y, width, height, theText );
                        break;
                case XOR:
                        drawIt( theDrawWindow, theXorGC, theCommand,
                                x, y, width, height, theText );
                        break;
                }

        XFlush( theDisplay );

}       /* -- function drawItem */
```

You will also notice that `drawItem` draws everything twice, once to the window, `theDrawWindow`, and once to the pixmap, `theDrawPixmap`. `theDrawPixmap` stores all the graphics for refreshing the display and also handling an Undo command. `drawItem` merely determines the graphics context to be used (depending on which color) and then calls the function `drawIt` to actually draw an item in a `Drawable` (window or pixmap).

```
drawIt( theWindow, theGC, theCommand, x, y, width, height, theText )

Drawable        theWindow;
GC              theGC;
int             theCommand;
int             x, y;
int             width, height;
char            theText[];

{       /* -- function drawIt */

        switch( theCommand )
                {
                case DRAW_TEXT1:
                case DRAW_TEXT2:
                        XDrawString( theDisplay, theWindow, theGC, x, y,
                                theText, strlen( theText ) );
                        break;
                case DRAW_POINT:
                        XDrawPoint( theDisplay, theWindow, theGC, x, y );
                        break;
                case DRAW_LINE:
                        drawLine( theWindow, theGC, x, y,
                                x + width, y + height );
                        break;
                case DRAW_RECT:
                        drawRectangle( theWindow, theGC, x, y,
                                width, height );
                        break;
                case DRAW_FILLED_RECT:
                        fillRectangle( theWindow, theGC, x, y,
                                width, height );
                        break;
                case DRAW_OVAL:
                        drawOval( theWindow, theGC, x, y,
                                width, height );
                        break;
                case DRAW_FILLED_OVAL:
                        fillOval( theWindow, theGC, x, y,
                                width, height );
                        break;
                }
}       /* -- function drawIt */
```

PALETTE-SELECTION EVENTS

Palette-selection events determine what to draw in the Draw application, as well as handle user commands such as saving the file, undoing the last drawing, and perhaps wiping out the entire drawing and starting over.

Palette-selection events are easy. Because each choice in the palette window occupies a window all to itself, any `ButtonPress` event detected in one of those windows means that the user selected that choice. This automatic choice detection is the prime advantage gained in multiple-window applications.

As previously discussed, the function `processButton` is called on a `ButtonPress` event, such as when the user clicks a mouse button in the floating palette.

```
processButton( theEvent )

XButtonPressedEvent      *theEvent;

{       /* -- function processButton */
        int     status = 1;
        int     choice;
        int     x, y;
        char    theFileName[ 120 ];

        /*
        **      if theDrawingMode == DRAWING_ON, undo rubber-band item.
        */
        restoreXorItem();
        .
        .
        .
        /*
        **      If in the palette windows, then set command
        */

        if ( theEvent->window == thePointWindow )
                {
                theDrawingCommand = DRAW_POINT;
                }

        if ( theEvent->window == theLineWindow )
                {
                theDrawingCommand = DRAW_LINE;
                }

        if ( theEvent->window == theRectWindow )
                {
                theDrawingCommand = DRAW_RECT;
                }

        if ( theEvent->window == theFilledRectWindow )
                {
                theDrawingCommand = DRAW_FILLED_RECT;
                }
```

continued...

...from previous page

```
if ( theEvent->window == theOvalWindow )
        {
        theDrawingCommand = DRAW_OVAL;
        }

if ( theEvent->window == theFilledOvalWindow )
        {
        theDrawingCommand = DRAW_FILLED_OVAL;
        }

if ( theEvent->window == theText1Window )
        {
        theDrawingCommand = DRAW_TEXT1;
        associateFont( theBlackGC, TEXT1_FONT );
        associateFont( theWhiteGC, TEXT1_FONT );
        associateFont( theBlackPixGC, TEXT1_FONT );
        associateFont( theWhitePixGC, TEXT1_FONT );
        }

if ( theEvent->window == theText2Window )
        {
        theDrawingCommand = DRAW_TEXT2;
        associateFont( theBlackGC, TEXT2_FONT );
        associateFont( theWhiteGC, TEXT2_FONT );
        associateFont( theBlackPixGC, TEXT2_FONT );
        associateFont( theWhitePixGC, TEXT2_FONT );
        }

if ( theEvent->window == theColorWindow )
        {
        if ( theDrawingColor == BLACK )
                {
                theDrawingColor = WHITE;
                }
        else
                {
                theDrawingColor = BLACK;
                }
        }

if ( theEvent->window == theSaveWindow )
        {
        highlightChoice( theEvent->window );
        saveCurrentFile();
        return( status );
        }
```

continued...

...from previous page

```
	if ( theEvent->window == theUndoWindow )
		{
		highlightChoice( theEvent->window );
		undo();
		return( status );
		}

	if ( theEvent->window == theFileWindow )
		{
		highlightChoice( theEvent->window );

		/*
		**	Get Mouse coords
		*/
		findMouse( theDisplay, &x, &y );
		x -= 20;
		y -= 20;

		choice = stringDialog( x, y,
				"Which file do you want to load?",
				"OK", "Cancel", theFileName );

		if ( choice == 1 )	/* -- OK choice */
			{
			loadFile( theFileName );
			}

		return( status );
		}

	if ( theEvent->window == theWipeOutWindow )
		{
		maintainUndo();
		wipeOutPix();
		return( status );
		}

	if ( theEvent->window == theQuitWindow )
		{
		status = 0;	/* -- quit */
		}

	/*
	**	If the user chooses a different item to draw, then
	**	turn off any current drawing.
	*/
	theDrawingMode = DRAWING_OFF;

	/*
	**	Give the user some feedback on the choice
	*/
```

continued...

...from previous page

```
        highlightChoice( theEvent->window );
        setCmdCursor( theDrawingCommand, FIRST_POINT );
        XFlush( theDisplay );

        /*
        **      if status == 0, then quit program.
        */
        return( status );

}       /* -- function processButton */
```

For most palette selections, the only items that you need to set up are as follows:

- setting `theDrawingCommand` to the new drawing command
- setting `theDrawingMode` to `DRAWING_OFF` because the user is starting anew
- highlighting the palette subwindow where the event took place, to present the user with some feedback that the command was understood
- setting up the proper cursor for `theDrawingWindow`, based on the current drawing command, `theDrawingCommand`

About half of the palette choices require additional processing. The Text choices need to do everything just listed and set up the proper font into the drawing GCs so that the correct font will be drawn. The Undo choice needs to call the function `undo`, which will replace the current drawing with the drawing that was last saved by a call to the function `maintainUndo`.

The File choice will pop up the file dialog box (described in Chapter 12). The wipe-out choice clears the drawing window and the pixmap. And the Save choice calls the function `saveCurrentFile` to save the drawing to disk.

TEXT-ENTRY EVENTS

Any user typing on the keyboard generates `KeyPress` events. `KeyPress` events in the Draw application fall into three classes:

- text-entry events when the user is "drawing" text onto a bitmap
- keyboard shortcuts (see "Keyboard Shortcut Events" later in this chapter)
- spurious events (to be ignored) when the user is not drawing text

Drawing text onto the bitmap is a two-step process. First, the user selects where the text should start by clicking a mouse button. Second, the user types in the characters at the keyboard. Each typed character should appear to the right of the last, assuming you are designing software that uses English text. (Readers who design software that uses Arabic text will want to reverse this.) Because you don't know for sure what type of font will be used or how big it will be, the easiest way to make characters appear one after another is to build up a string and redraw the entire string each time a new character is added. This method works fine for editing bitmaps; if you create a word processor, though, a faster, more efficient method would be needed.

The following code handles normal QWERTY-key input when the user is drawing text via the function `processKeyPress`. The function `processKeyPress` is called from the `eventLoop` (discussed earlier in this chapter) on any `KeyPress` event.

```
#include  <X11/Xlib.h>
#include  <X11/Xutil.h>
#include  <X11/keysym.h>
#include  <X11/keysymdef.h>

processKeyPress( theEvent )

XKeyEvent        *theEvent;

{       /* -- function processKeyPress */
        int              length, l;
        int              theKeyBufferMaxLen = 64;
        char             theKeyBuffer[ 65 ];
        KeySym           theKeySym;
        XComposeStatus   theComposeStatus;
```

continued...

...from previous page

```
        length = XLookupString( theEvent,
                        theKeyBuffer,
                        theKeyBufferMaxLen,
                        &theKeySym,
                        &theComposeStatus );

        .
        .
        .
```

After looking up the character string associated with the `KeyPress` event by using `XLookupString`, the returned `KeySym` is compared to the normal ASCII values. If a normal keyboard key was pressed, and if the user is currently drawing in one of the two drawing fonts, then the character string returned by `XLookupString` is concatenated onto a global string that stores the characters entered so far. This global string, `theDrawingText`, is then drawn to the screen to reflect the new character or characters entered. (Note that `XLookupString` can return more than one character.)

```
.
.
.
/*
**      Check if theKeySym is within the standard ASCII
**      printable character range.
**
*/

if ( ( theKeySym >= ' ' ) &&      /* -- ASCII 32 is a space  */
   ( theKeySym <= '~' )  &&      /* -- ASCII 126 is a Tilde */
   ( length > 0 ) )              /* -- We have char input   */
        {
        if ( ( theDrawingCommand == DRAW_TEXT1 ) ||
           ( theDrawingCommand == DRAW_TEXT2 ) )
                {
                if ( ( strlen( theDrawingText ) +
                   strlen( theKeyBuffer ) ) < MAX_TEXT_LENGTH )
                        {
                        /*
                        **      save current display for undo
                        */
                        maintainUndo();
```

continued...

...from previous page

```
                        strncat( theDrawingText,
                                theKeyBuffer,
                                length );
                        drawItem( theDrawingCommand, theDrawingColor,
                                theDrawX, theDrawY,
                                0, 0, theDrawingText );
                        }
                }
        }
        .
        .
        .
```

If the text entered does not fit the standard QWERTY keys on the typewriter part of the keyboard, the system then checks for meta-key events (see "Keyboard Shortcut Events" later in this chapter) and for keypad keys. Keypad keys normally contain the digits 0 to 9 as well as some math symbols, such as +, -, *, and /. Because these are valid character inputs, they are allowed as well.

```
        .
        .
        .
else
        {
        /*
        **      Check for special keys on the keyboard.
        **      there are many more definitions in the header
        **      file keysymdef.h (probably in /usr/include/X11).
        **
        */
        switch( theKeySym )
                {
                /*
                **      Keypad Keys
                */
                case XK_KP_Equal :
                case XK_KP_Multiply:
                case XK_KP_Add    :
                case XK_KP_Subtract:
                case XK_KP_Decimal:
                case XK_KP_Divide:
                case XK_KP_0      :
                case XK_KP_1      :
                case XK_KP_2      :
                case XK_KP_3      :
                case XK_KP_4      :
                case XK_KP_5      :
```

continued...

...*from previous page*

```
case XK_KP_6     :
case XK_KP_7     :
case XK_KP_8     :
case XK_KP_9     :
        if ( ( length > 0 ) &&
           ( ( theDrawingCommand == DRAW_TEXT1 ) ||
           ( theDrawingCommand == DRAW_TEXT2 ) ) )
                {
                if ( ( strlen( theDrawingText ) +
                  strlen( theKeyBuffer ) )
                  < MAX_TEXT_LENGTH )
                        {
                        strcat( theDrawingText,
                                theKeyBuffer );
                        drawItem( theDrawingCommand,
                                  theDrawingColor,
                                  theDrawX, theDrawY,
                                  0, 0,
                                  theDrawingText );
                        }
                }
        break;

   .
   .
   .
   .
```

It is a sad fact of life that users are not very good at keyboard input, or at least not consistently so. People frequently make mistakes or change their minds. In such cases, most people want to be able to edit the text they are entering. In Draw, users can always undo the last thing drawn—in this case, the last letter—but most people are already familiar with the Backspace and Delete keys on a keyboard. Because Draw keeps a character string with all the input characters, it is easy to remove the last character that was entered. The next step, then, is to clean up the display so the last character is wiped out from the window.

The `undo` function could be called to clear out the last item drawn, but this approach only works for one character. If the user presses the Delete key again, `undo` won't work because the Draw application only provides one level of undo. Instead, the string must be cleared out by redrawing the string in the opposite color. Then, the new string (minus the last character) is drawn again, using the normal color. This method can leave pixel "droppings," but in general it cleans up after itself. A much better method would be to provide for undoing operations back to the beginning, but that could eat up a lot of memory—especially if you edit a large, full-screen picture of Godzilla or the moon, for example.

```
.
.
.
/*
**      The BackSpace and the Delete key operate
**      the same in this program, and they take
**      advantage of the fact that we are using
**      XDrawString to draw the text (XDrawImageString
**      would work differently).  The method is
**      as follows:  first, draw the text string
**      over again in the opposite color (wiping
**      it out).  Then, redraw the text string
**      in the normal color, so that only the
**      last character is wiped out.  This can
**      still leave some pixel "droppings," but
**      works in general.
*/
case XK_BackSpace:
case XK_Delete   :
        /*
        **      save current display for undo
        */
        maintainUndo();

        l = strlen( theDrawingText );

        if ( l >= 1 )
                {
                if ( theDrawingColor == BLACK )
                        {
                        drawItem( theDrawingCommand,
                                  WHITE,
                                  theDrawX, theDrawY,
                                  0, 0,
                                  theDrawingText );
                        }
                else
                        {
                        drawItem( theDrawingCommand,
                                  BLACK,
                                  theDrawX, theDrawY,
                                  0, 0,
                                  theDrawingText );
                        }
                l--;

                theDrawingText[ l ] = '\0';
                drawItem( theDrawingCommand,
                    theDrawingColor,
                    theDrawX, theDrawY,
                    0, 0,
                    theDrawingText );
            XFlush( theDisplay );
            }
```

continued...

...from previous page

```
                    break;
            default         : ;
            }
    }
```

And, finally, the function **processKeyPress** returns a 1 to signify that the program should not quit yet; remember, a 0 would relate a user choice to quit.

```
    .
    .
    .
    return( 1 );      /* -- continue processing */

}       /* -- function processKeyPress */
```

KEYBOARD SHORTCUT EVENTS

The so-called "power users" often like the ability to use shortcut commands on the keyboard instead of moving the mouse over to the right section of the palette and clicking the mouse buttons. If you use an application every day, constantly choosing menu or palette items becomes pure drudgery. Although you probably won't be using Draw every day, it is nice to offer friendly shortcuts to the user.

In the Draw application, a number of these shortcuts are set up through the use of the meta key. By holding the meta key down while pressing a regular key, the user makes a choice, such as pressing the meta key and the "q" key simultaneously to choose to quit the program. The keyboard shortcuts offered by Draw include the following:

Key Combination	Meaning
Meta-L	Line
Meta-S	Save
Meta-P	Point
Meta-R	Rectangle
Meta-F	Filled Rectangle
Meta-O	Oval
Meta-T	Text 1
Meta-U	Undo
Meta-Q	Quit

In keyx.c, the function processKeyPress implements the keyboard shortcuts. Most of the shortcuts set up what kind of item is to be drawn, such as drawing ovals. If the first meta key is held down and the "o" key is pressed, the application goes through five steps to set up drawing ovals:

```
.
.
.
case  'O': /* -- Draw ovals      */
case  'o': restoreXorItem();
        highlightChoice( theOvalWindow );
        theDrawingCommand = DRAW_OVAL;
        theDrawingMode    = DRAWING_OFF;
        setCmdCursor( theDrawingCommand, FIRST_POINT );
        break;
        .
        .
        .
```

First, any rubber-band drawing is restored to a normal state, by redrawing in xor mode if any rubber-band drawing occurred. Then, the Oval selection window on the floating palette is highlighted by filling the window with a black rectangle and then clearing it, causing a "flashing" effect. Next, the flag variable theDrawing-Command is set to draw ovals, and the mode (i.e., whether the user has started drawing) is set to a value indicating that no oval drawing has started yet. Finally, the drawing window's cursor is set up to the cursor used for drawing rectangles and ovals, in this case the crosshair cursor.

processKeyPress handles the oval-drawing keyboard shortcut (Meta-O) as well as all the other keyboard shortcuts:

```
Display         *theDisplay;
        .
        .
        .
processKeyPress( theEvent )

XKeyEvent       *theEvent;

{       /* -- function processKeyPress */
        int                 length, l;
        int                 theKeyBufferMaxLen = 64;
        char                theKeyBuffer[ 65 ];
        KeySym              theKeySym;
        XComposeStatus      theComposeStatus;
```

continued...

...from previous page

```
length = XLookupString( theEvent,
                theKeyBuffer,
                theKeyBufferMaxLen,
                &theKeySym,
                &theComposeStatus );

/*
**      Check for META keys.  Many programs use keyboard
**      shortcuts for menu choices.  DrawApp Meta Keys include:
**      Meta-F  Fill Rectangles
**      Meta-L  Draw Lines
**      Meta-O  Draw Ovals
**      Meta-P  Draw Points
**      Meta-Q  Quit
**      Meta-R  Draw Rectangles
**      Meta-S  Save
**      Meta-T  Draw Text in font 1
**      Meta-U  Undo
**
*/

if ( theEvent->state & Mod1Mask )      /* --  META Keys */
        {
        switch( theKeyBuffer[ 0 ] )
                {
                case  'F': /* -- Fill rectangles */
                case  'f': restoreXorItem();
                      highlightChoice( theFilledRectWindow );
                      theDrawingCommand = DRAW_FILLED_RECT;
                      theDrawingMode    = DRAWING_OFF;
                      setCmdCursor( theDrawingCommand, FIRST_POINT );
                      break;
                case  'L': /* -- Draw Lines        */
                case  'l': restoreXorItem();
                      highlightChoice( theLineWindow );
                      theDrawingCommand = DRAW_LINE;
                      theDrawingMode    = DRAWING_OFF;
                      setCmdCursor( theDrawingCommand, FIRST_POINT );
                      break;
                case  'O': /* -- Draw ovals        */
                case  'o': restoreXorItem();
                      highlightChoice( theOvalWindow );
                      theDrawingCommand = DRAW_OVAL;
                      theDrawingMode    = DRAWING_OFF;
                      setCmdCursor( theDrawingCommand, FIRST_POINT );
                      break;
```

continued...

...from previous page

```
                case  'P': /* -- Draw Points     */
                case  'p': restoreXorItem();
                     highlightChoice( thePointWindow );
                     theDrawingCommand = DRAW_POINT;
                     theDrawingMode    = DRAWING_OFF;
                     setCmdCursor( theDrawingCommand, FIRST_POINT );
                     break;
                case  'Q' :
                case  'q' :
                     return( 0 );
                     break;
                case  'R': /* -- Draw rectangles */
                case  'r': restoreXorItem();
                     highlightChoice( theRectWindow );
                     theDrawingCommand = DRAW_RECT;
                     theDrawingMode    = DRAWING_OFF;
                     setCmdCursor( theDrawingCommand, FIRST_POINT );
                     break;
                case  's': /* -- Save file */
                case  'S': saveCurrentFile();
                     break;
                case  'T': /* -- Draw text in font 1 */
                case  't': restoreXorItem();
                     associateFont( theBlackGC, TEXT1_FONT );
                     associateFont( theWhiteGC, TEXT1_FONT );
                     associateFont( theBlackPixGC, TEXT1_FONT );
                     associateFont( theWhitePixGC, TEXT1_FONT );
                     highlightChoice( theText1Window );
                     theDrawingCommand = DRAW_TEXT1;
                     theDrawingMode    = DRAWING_OFF;
                     setCmdCursor( theDrawingCommand, FIRST_POINT );
                     break;
                }
        return( 1 );
        }
        .
        .
        .
/*
**      The rest of the KeyPress event processing follows...
*/
```

X SERVER-GENERATED EVENTS

The last type of events accepted by the Draw application are X-generated events. These events occur when windows are exposed or resized (or, in general, folded, spindled, or mutilated). Like any good X program, Draw responds to exposure events. Most exposure events can be handled by merely redrawing the contents of the given window, especially for the smaller windows that make up the floating palette. In fact, that is how all exposure events are handled in Draw. This is admittedly a lazy approach, and exposure-handling slows down when the contents of very large windows are redrawn.

The function `processExpose` was described in Chapter 10. If you want to handle `Expose` events by only redrawing the exposed area instead of the whole window, you could add some code to `processExpose`. This code would clip the drawing to the boundary of the `Expose` event. (Doing this directly to the Draw application creates some problems because some routines fake an `Expose` event and send the faked event structure to the function `processExpose`. You would need to modify the code wherever `processExpose` is called and a true `XExposeEvent` is not used.)

The method for specifying a clipping area is to modify the graphics context, the GC, used for drawing. Two new functions could take care of this task, `setUpClipping` and `restoreClipping`:

```
setUpClipping( x, y, width, height, theGC )

int     x, y, width, height; GC  theGC;

{       /* -- function setUpClipping */
        XRectangle      theRectangles[ 2 ];

        /*
        **      Set up clipping rectangle
        */
        theRectangles[ 0 ].x        = theEvent->x;
        theRectangles[ 0 ].y        = theEvent->y;
        theRectangles[ 0 ].width    = theEvent->width;
        theRectangles[ 0 ].height   = theEvent->height;

        XSetClipRectangles( theDisplay,
                theGC,
                0, 0,           /* -- Use GC's window's origin */
                theRectangles,
                1,              /* -- number of rectangles    */
                Unsorted );     /* -- rectangle ordering      */

}       /* -- function setUpClipping */
```

XSetClipRectangles can be used to set up more than one rectangle to clip to. You could use this ability by keeping track of the count field of the XExposeEvent structure and adding a rectangle to the XRectangle array each time you get an Expose event. When all the Expose events are in (when the count equals zero), you could then draw, with the clipping set to the union of all the rectangles in the array passed to XSetClipRectangles. The function above, though, just sets the clipping to one rectangle.

XSetClipRectangles is passed an array of XRectangle structures. The XRectangle structure looks like the following:

```
typedef struct
        {
        short           x, y;
        unsigned short  width, height;
        } XRectangle;
```

The XRectangle structure is defined in the header file Xlib.h.

The function XSetClipRectangles looks like the following,

```
Display         *theDisplay;
GC                      theGC;
int                     xClipOrigin, yClipOrigin;
XRectangle      theRectangles[ NUM_RECTANGLES ];
int                     numberOfRectangles;
int                     rectangleOrdering;

XSetClipRectangles( theDisplay,
        theGC,
        xClipOrigin, yClipOrigin,
        theRectangles,
        numberOfRectangles,
        rectangleOrdering );
```

where NUM_RECTANGLES is a constant used to specify how many elements have been filled in and used in the XRectangle array.

The `rectangleOrdering` parameter can be one of the following:

`Unsorted` The rectangles in the array are not sorted.

`YSorted` The rectangles are sorted by their Y origin, with Ys increasing.

`YXSorted` `YSorted`, and all rectangles with equal Y origin are sorted in increasing X origin order.

`YXBanded` `YXSorted`. With every possible Y scanline (rows across the window), all rectangles that appear on the scanline have the same Y origin and heights.

If that wasn't complex enough, failure to properly sort the rectangles can generate a `BadMatch` error. It's probably easiest to declare the rectangles `Unsorted` and not worry about sorting errors at all.

After the clip rectangle is set up for the GC, redraw the contents of the given window (the drawing will be clipped to the bounds of the clip rectangle). When the drawing is complete, you probably want to reset the clip mask back to the full window so the next time you draw, you don't need to worry if any clipping has been set up.

The easiest way to do this is to call the function `XSetClipMask` and pass a null clip mask, which explicitly sets the clipping mask to the full area of the window.

```
/*
**      Restores the clip area of a GC back to normal
*/

restoreClipping( theGC )

GC      theGC;

{       /* -- function restoreClipping */

        XSetClipMask( theDisplay,
                theGC,
                None );

}       /* -- function restoreClipping */
```

XSetClipMask formally looks like the following:

```
Display         *theDisplay;
GC              theGC;
Pixmap          thePixmap;

XSetClipMask( theDisplay,
        theGC,
        thePixmap );
```

Instead of passing None for the Pixmap, you can pass any Pixmap with a single bit-plane of depth (depth = 1). You can have a lot of fun with this, especially if you want to implement the SmallTalk language under X.

There are many ways you can handle Expose events. The easiest way is to simply redraw the entire window. This method is perfectly fine for small palette windows. For larger windows, you may want to set up a clip mask or clip rectangles.

SUMMARY

This chapter explains event processing in the Draw application. This processing is handled with five kinds of events: drawing events, palette-selection events, text-entry events, keyboard shortcut events, and X server-generated events. The main-event loop handles the five types of events for the Draw application.

- With X, events are sent only to windows that ask for events, much like a pizza-delivery person delivering pizzas only to houses that ordered them. In addition to reqesting events, you must also specify the events your program's windows want to accept—like ordering different toppings on your pizza. In Draw, the main window—that is, the window the user will use for actual drawing—receives extra events. The event mask sent to the X server with an XSelectInput call determines which events are to be sent to the window by the X server.

- In Draw, ButtonMotionMask and ButtonReleaseMask were added to the mask because without mouse input, a drawing application would be fairly useless. The draw window receives ButtonRelease events when a mouse button is released and MotionNotify events if the mouse position moves while a mouse button is held down.

- Once X knows what to expect, the user can begin drawing, which is a three-step process: First, the user presses a mouse button, telling Draw to begin drawing; second, with the button held down, the user moves the mouse to create a line, rectangle, or oval; and third, when the user releases the mouse button, the drawing is locked in by using `GXcopy` mode rather than `GXxor` mode. Of course, this operation can be undone by the user.

- The other windows in Draw are used by the floating palette. The palette-selection events are easy to process because a `ButtonPress` event in a floating-palette window can only mean that the user has selected that choice.

- In addition to drawing, the Draw application allows users to type in text, generating `KeyPress` events. Drawing text onto a bitmap is a simple two-step process: The user clicks a mouse button to show where the text should start, and then the user bangs away at a QWERTY keyboard, including meta-key events and numerical signs. (Meta keys are also included so that a user won't have to make a palette-selection event to perform simple tasks.) A string is built, and the entire string is redrawn each time a new character is added. Note that this method works well enough for a bitmap, but it would be highly inefficient if you were designing a word processor.

- Finally, there are X-generated events, such as when windows are exposed or resized. Draw takes a somewhat lazy approach in processing these events. Most exposure events can be handled by merely redrawing the contents of the given window, especially for the smaller windows that make up the floating palette, and that's exactly how Draw does it.

Xlib Functions and Macros Introduced in This Chapter

```
XSetClipMask
XSetClipRectangles
```

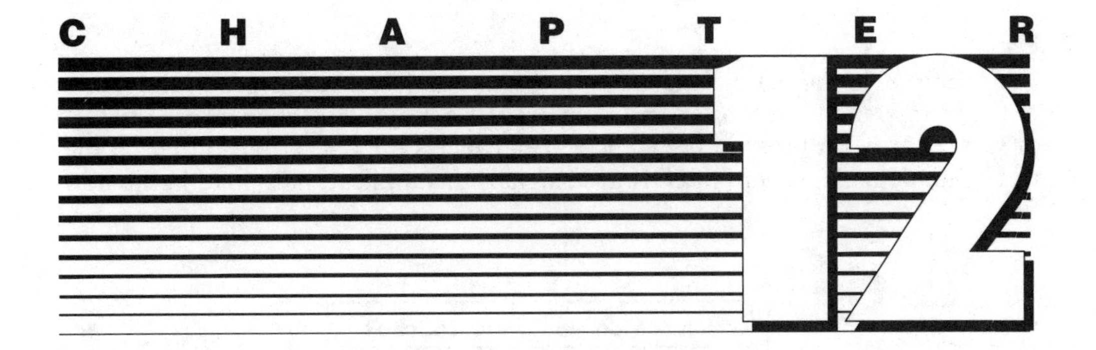

POP-UP WINDOWS AND DIALOG BOXES

This chapter discusses how to create pop-up windows and dialog boxes. A pop-up window is a window that pops up for a short period of time. Usually, pop-up windows are used for menus, warning messages, or requests for data from the user. A dialog box typically handles a dialog with the user in which the application asks the user to enter in a piece of data.

For example, in the dialog box shown in Figure 12.1, the user types in the name of the bitmap file to be loaded and then presses a mouse button in either the OK or Cancel area. A press in the Cancel area cancels the operation so that no file will be loaded. A press in the OK area signals the application to load in the new file.

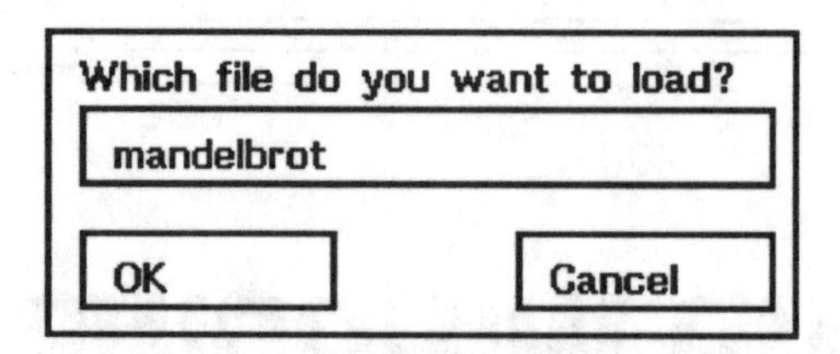

Figure 12.1 Load file dialog box.

Pop-up windows are meant to appear instantly, or as instantly as possible, and as near as possible to the area of interest on the screen (even though the exact area of interest may be impossible to determine).

Pop-up windows should be small because larger windows will usually take longer to appear and will certainly take longer disappear if you count in the time it takes to refresh the display.

SETTING UP A POP-UP WINDOW IN X

Setting up a pop-up window in X is fairly easy. You create it just as you would any other window, but you add a request to save the pixels under the window and to override any window redirection the window manager might have in mind. You can do this by setting the appropriate fields in an `XSetWindowAttributes` structure and setting up the proper flag before calling the function `XCreateWindow`.

In the Draw application, the pop-up window flag mentioned earlier is finally being used in the `openWindow` function (in the file `windowx.c`).

```
Window openWindow( x, y, width, height, flag, theTitle, iconicState, theParent, theNewGC )

int     x, y;           /* -- Where the window should go         */
int     width, height;  /* -- Size of the window                 */
int     flag;           /* -- if > 0 then the window is a pop-up */
char    theTitle[];     /* -- Title for Window                   */
int     iconicState;    /* -- == 1 if start as icon, ==0 if not  */
Window  theParent;      /* -- Parent Window of the new window    */
GC      *theNewGC;      /* -- Returned Graphics Context          */

{       /* -- function openWindow */
        XSetWindowAttributes        theWindowAttributes;
        XSizeHints                  theSizeHints;
        unsigned        long        theWindowMask;
        Window                      theNewWindow;
        XWMHints                    theWMHints;
        XClassHint                  theClassHint;

        /*
        **      1) Set up the attributes desired for the window.
        **      Note that window managers may deny us some of
        **      these resources.
        **
        */

        theWindowAttributes.border_pixel       = theBlackPixel;
        theWindowAttributes.background_pixel   = theWhitePixel;

        if ( flag == POP_UP_WINDOW )
                {
                theWindowAttributes.override_redirect = True;
                theWindowAttributes.save_under        = True;
                theWindowMask = ( CWBackPixel      |
                                  CWBorderPixel    |
                                  CWSaveUnder      |
                                  CWOverrideRedirect );
                }
        else
                {
                theWindowMask = CWBackPixel    | CWBorderPixel;
                }
        .
        .
        .
```

If the window is a pop-up window, then Draw asks the X server to save the pixels underneath the window's location (`save_under = True`) and asks that any window manager leave this pop-up window alone (`override_redirect = True`). The `XSetWindowAttributes` structure is passed in an `XCreateWindow` call.

```
        .
        .
        .
        /*
        **      2) Open a window on the display.
        **
        */

        theNewWindow = XCreateWindow( theDisplay,
                        theParent,
                        x, y,
                        width, height,
                        BORDER_WIDTH,
                        theDepth,
                        InputOutput,
                        CopyFromParent,
                        theWindowMask,
                        &theWindowAttributes );
        .
        .
        .
}       /* -- function openWindow */
```

The `override_redirect` request has previously been discussed. The `save_under` request, though, is new. Setting the `save_under` field to `True` requests that the X server save the pixels underneath the new window. The assumption here is that the new window will only appear for a short time, so the interface will respond more quickly if the X server can replace the pixels when the pop-up window goes away. If this works, the server will avoid `Expose` events and speed up the refresh of the screen because the server won't have to send `Expose` events to a number of applications and then wait for the applications to refresh their windows.

The `save_under` field is just a request, though. And with all requests, it may be denied. Not all X servers support "save-unders." And, even if the X server supports save-unders, the server may not have enough memory to do so for your window. Even so, X will take care of it.

Because you cannot guarantee that X can save the area under your pop-up window, don't worry about it. The worst thing that can happen is that each window under your pop-up window will get `Expose` events when the pop-up window goes away. The best thing that can happen is that your pop-up window goes away, with the X server refreshing the windows that were covered up, thus speeding up the interface response time. Just ask for save-unders and hope for the best.

CALLING UP THE POP-UP WINDOW FROM THE PALETTE

The pop-up window in the Draw application asks the user to enter a file name – the name of a bitmap file to edit. Thus, the dialog window is called up when a `ButtonPress` event is detected in the File selection of the floating palette. The function `processButton` in the file `buttonx.c` handles `ButtonPress` events:

```
processButton( theEvent )

XButtonPressedEvent      *theEvent;

{       /* -- function processButton */
        .
        .
        .
        if ( theEvent->window == theFileWindow )
                {
                highlightChoice( theEvent->window );

                /*
                **      Get Mouse coords
                */
                findMouse( theDisplay, &x, &y );
                x -= 20;
                y -= 20;

                choice = stringDialog( x, y,
                                "Which file do you want to load?",
                                "OK", "Cancel", theFileName );

                if ( choice == 1 )      /* -- OK choice */
                        {
                        loadFile( theFileName );
                        }

                return( status );
                }

        .
        .
        .

}       /* -- function processButton */
```

First, the routine highlights `theFileWindow` so that the user sees some feedback on the choice. Then the current mouse location is determined by a call to `findMouse`, which gets the global mouse coordinates. These mouse coordinates are used to locate the file name dialog box window. You will notice that 20 is subtracted from each coordinate. This is done so the mouse will be within the dialog box (without the mouse being moved). The value of 20 means that the window will appear so that the current position of the mouse is in 20 pixels (in both X and Y) from the top left corner of the dialog window. The value of 20 is purely arbitrary.

The function `stringDialog` calls up the dialog box and gets a file name from the user. If the user presses the OK section of the dialog box by clicking a mouse button in the area, then `stringDialog` returns a 1. If the user cancels the operation, `stringDialog` returns a 0. If the user wants to load in a new file (by choosing the OK choice), then the function `loadFile` loads in the new bitmap file, using the file name returned by `stringDialog`. The next section of this chapter will cover the new items in detail, starting with finding the mouse location.

FINDING THE MOUSE POINTER LOCATION

In the Draw application, the user can ask the program to load in another bitmap file for editing. The user does this by pressing a mouse button when the mouse pointer is over the File choice in the floating palette. When that happens, the application pops up a dialog window to get the name of the file the user wants loaded in. The program asks the X server where the mouse pointer is currently located and then pops up the dialog window so that the mouse pointer is within the dialog window. The assumption here is that the mouse pointer is located near the area the user is currently interested in. (If the system isn't too slow, this area should be over the File selection of the floating palette.)

Now, the Draw application could pop up the window anywhere on the screen and move the mouse into the window (called "warping" the mouse in X vernacular), but in general it is not a good idea to warp the mouse anywhere because warping is unexpected and can confuse the user. There are certain times, though, when you might want to warp the mouse pointer, such as in a program that allows users to zoom a window up to full-screen size and unzoom the window later on. In this case, it might be easier on the user to have the mouse pointer automatically follow the window and remain in the same relative window location as it was before the window was zoomed or unzoomed.

To move, or warp, the mouse pointer on the screen, use the Xlib function XWarpPointer.

```
Display         *theDisplay;
Window          sourceWindow;
Window          destWindow;
int             sourceX, sourceY;
unsigned int    sourceWidth, sourceHeight;
int             destX, destY;

XWarpPointer( theDisplay,
        sourceWindow,
        destWindow,
        sourceX, sourceY,
        sourceWidth, sourceHeight,
        destX, destY );
```

The parameters to XWarpPointer will take on a host of different meanings in different conditions.

The simplest way to use XWarpPointer is to set destWindow to the root window. Then, destX and destY are global coordinates and specify the new mouse location. This is a lot easier than messing with all the options. Also, set sourceWindow to None so that the source coordinates are ignored and the mouse is warped no matter what.

destWindow is the destination window. It can be None. If destWindow is None, then the destX and destY coordinates are taken to mean "Move offsets relative to the current position of the pointer."

sourceWindow is the source window. If sourceWindow is an actual window ID and not None, then XWarpPointer will only work if the mouse is within the rectangle starting at sourceX, sourceY and with size sourceWidth and sourceHeight (XWarpPointer should actually be called XMaybeWarp-Pointer). A sourceWidth of 0 specifies that the whole width of the window is to be used (this is handy if you don't know how wide the window is). Similarly, a sourceHeight of 0 specifies using the whole height of the window.

If sourceWindow is None, then it doesn't matter where the mouse is – it will be moved to the new location.

If all this doesn't make any sense, it's probably meant to be that way, because the designers of X really don't want you to use XWarpPointer – ever.

If you do warp the mouse, though, you should have a pretty good idea where the mouse coordinates are (i.e., the location to which you warped the mouse). If you haven't just warped the mouse and need to find out where the mouse pointer is located, use XQueryPointer.

```
Display         *theDisplay;
Window          theWindow;
Window          theRoot, theChild;
int             rootX, rootY;
int             wX, wY;
unsigned int    buttonState;
int             status;

status = XQueryPointer( theDisplay,
                        theWindow,
                        &theRoot,
                        &theChild,
                        &rootX, &rootY,
                        &wX, &wY,
                        &buttonState );
```

XQueryPointer returns a status of True if the mouse pointer is on the same screen as the window theWindow. Otherwise, False is returned and most of the values will not be valid, except for theRoot, rootX, and rootY.

If True is returned, the coordinates wX and wY contain the mouse pointer location, with respect to the window theWindow. If the mouse is in a subwindow of theWindow, then theChild will be set to the subwindow's ID. theRoot will contain the root window ID for the screen the mouse is in (remember X supports displays with multiple screens). rootX and rootY are the coordinates relative to theRoot.

The buttonState parameter returns the state of the mouse buttons (up to five of them) and the Control, Shift, Caps Lock, etc., keys. This is the same as the state field in an XButtonPressEvent structure.

In the following code, the function findMouse finds the global mouse coordinates, relative to the root window for the display, which are passed as a parameter to findMouse. findMouse doesn't worry about child windows or coordinates; it just concerns itself with the root window's coordinate space, which is the global coordinate space for a given screen.

```
/*
**      findMouse gets the current mouse coords in global
**      coordinates.
**
*/

findMouse( displayPtr, x, y )

Display *displayPtr; int *x, *y;

{       /* -- function findMouse */
        Window          theRoot, theChild;
        int             wX, wY, rootX, rootY, status;
        unsigned int    wButtons;

        status = XQueryPointer( displayPtr,
                RootWindow( displayPtr, DefaultScreen( displayPtr ) ),
                &theRoot,
                &theChild,
                &rootX, &rootY,
                &wX, &wY,
                &wButtons );

        if ( status == True )
                {
                *x = wX;
                *y = wY;
                }
        else
                {
                *x = 0;
                *y = 0;
                }

}       /* -- function findMouse */
```

A POP-UP FILE NAME DIALOG BOX

After determining the mouse coordinates, the Draw application pops up a dialog box that prompts the user to enter a file name.

```
        .
        .
        .
        choice = stringDialog( x, y,
                        "Which file do you want to load?",
                        "OK", "Cancel", theFileName );

        .
        .
        .
```

Actually, the function `stringDialog` is written so that you can ask the user to enter in any text string, not just file names. `stringDialog` expects the following information:

- an x, y location in which to place the dialog box main window
- a message or a question to ask the user
- the text for the OK choice
- the text for the Cancel choice
- a character string in which to return the text the user enters, if any

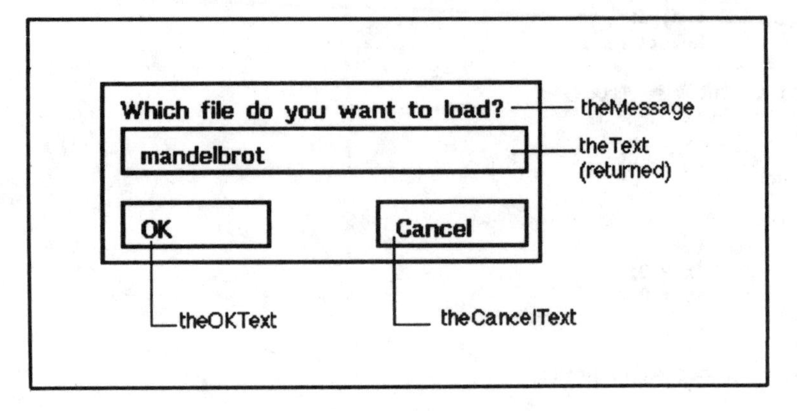

Figure 12.2 The dialog box text.

```
stringDialog( x, y, theMessage, theOKText, theCancelText, theText )

int     x, y;                 /* -- Upper left corner for dialog */
char    theMessage[];         /* -- the Prompt                   */
char    theOKText[];          /* -- the OK selection text        */
char    theCancelText[];      /* -- the Cancel selection text    */
char    theText[];            /* -- the RETURNED text string     */
```

`stringDialog` will return when the user presses a mouse button over the OK or the Cancel areas of the dialog box. The `stringDialog` function could be the base for a whole library of different types of dialog boxes.

IMPLEMENTING THE DIALOG BOX

The function `stringDialog` implements a dialog box using multiple windows. `theDialogWindow` is the main window, and it frames the rest of the windows. `theDStringWindow` contains the text the user types in. `theDOKWindow` is used for the Accept choice. `theDCancelWindow` is used for the Cancel choice.

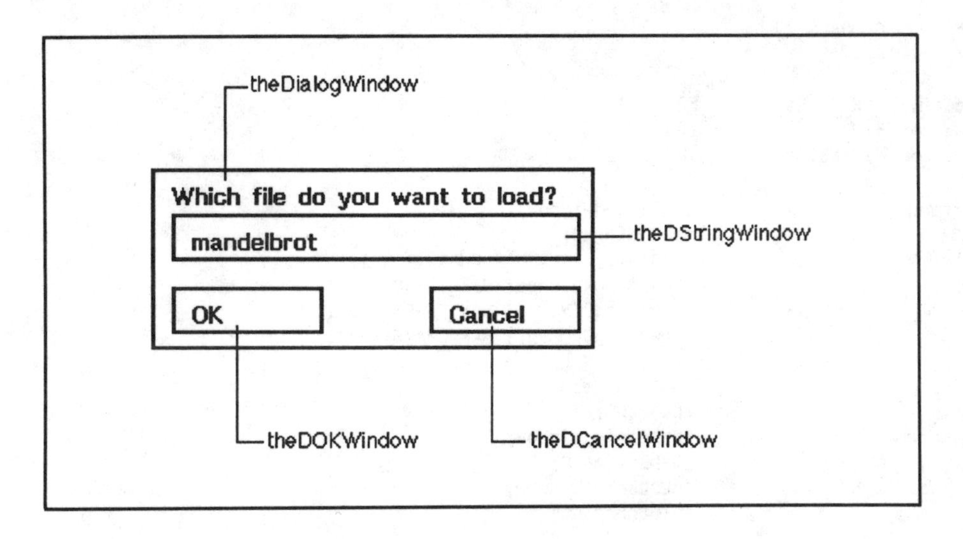

Figure 12.3 The dialog windows.

```
/*
**      dialogx.c
**
**      Pop-up Window dialog box for the DrawApp application.
**
*/

#include   <X11/Xlib.h>
#include   <X11/Xutil.h>
#include   <X11/keysym.h>
#include   <X11/keysymdef.h>

#include   "drawapp.h"

/*
**      External GLOBALS
*/
```

continued...

...from previous page

```
extern  Display         *theDisplay;
extern  Cursor          theArrowCursor;
extern  Cursor          theTextCursor;
extern  Window          theRootWindow;
extern  Window          theDrawWindow;

/*
**      GLOBALS
*/

#define MAX_CHARS       80
#define MIN_WIDTH       200
#define MIN_HEIGHT      100

Window                  theDialogWindow;
GC                      theDialogGC;
char                    theDialogText[ MAX_CHARS + 5 ];
char                    theDialogMessage[ MAX_CHARS + 5 ];
char                    theDialogOKMsg  [ MAX_CHARS + 5 ];
char                    theDialogCanMsg [ MAX_CHARS + 5 ];

Window                  theDOKWindow;
GC                      theDOKGC;
Window                  theDStringWindow;
GC                      theDStringGC;
Window                  theDCancelWindow;
GC                      theDCancelGC;

/*
**      stringDialog pops up a transient window that asks the user
**      to enter in a file name.  The user can press the OK or
**      the Cancel selection (with any mouse button), to end the
**      dialog session.
**
**      This is a modal dialog.  The program control will return
**      to the calling routine AFTER the user makes a choice to
**      Accept or Cancel.
**
**      stringDialog returns a 0 for cancel or a 1 for OK.
**
*/

stringDialog( x, y, theMessage, theOKText, theCancelText, theText )

int     x, y;                   /* -- Upper left corner for dialog */
char    theMessage[];           /* -- the Prompt                   */
char    theOKText[];            /* -- the OK selection text        */
char    theCancelText[];        /* -- the Cancel selection text    */
char    theText[];              /* -- the RETURNED text string     */
```

continued...

...from previous page

```
{       /* -- function stringDialog */
        int     theChoice = 0;          /* -- Cancel */
        int     width, height, value;

        /*
        **      Size window
        */
        value = textWidth( theMessage, TEXT1_FONT );
        if ( value > MIN_WIDTH )
                width = value + 30;
        else
                width = MIN_WIDTH;

        value = ( textHeight( TEXT1_FONT ) + 10 ) * 3;
        if ( value > MIN_HEIGHT )
                height = value;
        else
                height = MIN_HEIGHT;
        .
        .
        .
```

The first step is to determine how big the whole dialog box should be. You want the window to be small so it doesn't eat up too many X resources (specifically RAM to hold the pixels underneath the window) and take too long to draw. But you should also want the window to look nice. The width is determined by how many pixels wide the messages will be in the `TEXT1_FONT` used by the Draw application. The height is determined by how tall the `TEXT1_FONT` is.

```
        .
        .
        .
        /*
        **      Open Windows
        */
        initDialogWindows( x, y, width, height );

        /*
        **      Set up display info
        */
        if ( strlen( theMessage ) < MAX_CHARS )
                {
                strcpy( theDialogMessage, theMessage );
                }
```

continued...

...from previous page

```
else
        {
        strncpy( theDialogMessage, theMessage, MAX_CHARS );
        }

if ( strlen( theOKText  ) < MAX_CHARS )
        {
        strcpy( theDialogOKMsg, theOKText );
        }
else
        {
        strncpy( theDialogOKMsg, theOKText, MAX_CHARS );
        }

if ( strlen( theCancelText  ) < MAX_CHARS )
        {
        strcpy( theDialogCanMsg, theCancelText );
        }
else
        {
        strncpy( theDialogCanMsg, theCancelText, MAX_CHARS );
        }
.
.
.
```

All the text messages sent to `stringDialog` are copied into global variables so these text strings don't need to be passed as parameters to every routine in `dialogx.c`.

```
.
.
.
/*
**      Display Dialog Info
*/
theDialogText[ 0 ] = '\0';   /* -- NULL string to start out */

displayDialog( theDialogWindow );
displayDialog( theDStringWindow );
displayDialog( theDCancelWindow );
displayDialog( theDOKWindow );
```

continued...

...from previous page

```
        /*
        **      Handle Dialog Window Events
        */
        theChoice = (-1);

        while( theChoice == (-1) )
                {
                theChoice = dialogEventLoop();
                }

        if ( theChoice == 1 )    /* -- OK! */
                {
                strcpy( theText, theDialogText );
                }

        /*
        **      Close Window and free resources.
        */
        freeDialog();

        /*
        **      Return choice
        */

        return( theChoice );

}       /* -- function stringDialog */
```

SETTING UP THE DIALOG WINDOWS

The dialog windows are all created from the `initDialogWindows` function. This function determines the size and location of the dialog subwindows, based on the size and location of the main dialog window, `theDialogWindow`.

```
/*
**      initDialogWindows creates all the pop-up dialog box windows
**      and GCs in their correct positions
**
*/

initDialogWindows( x, y, width, height )

int     x, y, width, height;
```

continued...

...from previous page

```
{       /* -- function initDialogWindows */
        Window  openWindow();

        /*
        **      Main Dialog Box Window
        */

        theDialogWindow = openWindow( x, y, width, height,
                                POP_UP_WINDOW,   /* -- IS a POP-UP */
                                "File Requestor",
                                NORMAL_STATE,
                                theRootWindow,
                                &theDialogGC );
        .
        .
        .
```

theDialogWindow is opened as a POP_UP_WINDOW so that the X server will be asked to save the pixels underneath. Any window manager will also be asked to leave this window alone.

```
        .
        .
        .
        associateFont( theDialogGC, TEXT1_FONT );
        initEvents( theDialogWindow, IN_PALETTE );

        theDOKWindow = openWindow( 10,
                                2 * ( height / 3 ),
                                ( width / 3 ), ( height / 3 ) - 10,
                                NORMAL_WINDOW,
                                "File Requestor",
                                NORMAL_STATE,
                                theDialogWindow,
                                &theDOKGC );
        .
        .
        .
```

All the dialog subwindows are created as a NORMAL_WINDOW because they sit up on theDialogWindow and there is no need to save the pixels underneath the subwindows.

```
.
.
.
associateFont( theDOKGC, TEXT1_FONT );
initEvents( theDOKWindow, IN_PALETTE );

theDCancelWindow = openWindow( width - 10 - ( width / 3 ),
                        2 * ( height / 3 ),
                        ( width / 3 ), ( height / 3 ) - 10,
                        NORMAL_WINDOW,
                        "File Requestor",
                        NORMAL_STATE,
                        theDialogWindow,
                        &theDCancelGC );

associateFont( theDCancelGC, TEXT1_FONT );
initEvents( theDCancelWindow, IN_PALETTE );

theDStringWindow = openWindow( 10,
                        textHeight( TEXT1_FONT ) + 10,
                        width -20, ( height / 3 ) - 10,
                        NORMAL_WINDOW,
                        "File Requestor",
                        NORMAL_STATE,
                        theDialogWindow,
                        &theDStringGC );

associateFont( theDStringGC, TEXT1_FONT );
initEvents( theDStringWindow, IN_PALETTE );

/*
**      Set up cursors
*/
XDefineCursor( theDisplay, theDialogWindow,  theArrowCursor );
XDefineCursor( theDisplay, theDCancelWindow, theArrowCursor );
XDefineCursor( theDisplay, theDOKWindow,     theArrowCursor );

XDefineCursor( theDisplay, theDStringWindow, theTextCursor );
.
.
.
```

All the dialog windows use the pointing arrow cursor, except for the window in which text entry actually takes place. This window uses the text cursor.

```
    .
    .
    .
    XFlush( theDisplay );

}       /* -- function initDialogWindows */
```

DISPLAYING THE CONTENTS OF THE DIALOG WINDOWS

Once the dialog windows (also called dialog "boxes") are created, something needs to be displayed in them. Also, if any other windows cover up part of a dialog box, that dialog box may need to have its contents redisplayed.

The function `displayDialog` is called whenever any dialog windows need to be redisplayed (or actually displayed for the first time). `displayDialog` takes one parameter, the window `ID` of the dialog window to be redisplayed.

```
/*
**      displayDialog displays the current contents of the dialog
**      box, for any given window.
**
*/

displayDialog( theWindow )

Window  theWindow;

{       /* -- function displayDialog */
        int     y;

        y = textHeight( TEXT1_FONT ) + 5;

        if ( theWindow == theDialogWindow )
                {
                XDrawString( theDisplay, theWindow, theDialogGC,
                                10, y,
                                theDialogMessage,
                                strlen( theDialogMessage ) );
                }

        if ( theWindow == theDStringWindow )
                {
                XDrawString( theDisplay, theWindow, theDStringGC,
                                10, y,
                                theDialogText,
                                strlen( theDialogText ) );
                }

        if ( theWindow == theDOKWindow )
                {
                XDrawString( theDisplay, theWindow, theDOKGC,
                                10, y,
                                theDialogOKMsg,
                                strlen( theDialogOKMsg  ) );
                }
```

continued...

...from previous page

```
        if ( theWindow == theDCancelWindow )
                {
                XDrawString( theDisplay, theWindow, theDCancelGC,
                                10, y,
                                theDialogCanMsg,
                                strlen( theDialogCanMsg  ) );
                }

        XFlush( theDisplay );

}       /* -- function displayDialog */
```

DIALOG EVENTS

The dialog box presented here is called a **modal** dialog; that is, the user enters the dialog mode and must exit the mode by clicking a mouse button in either the OK or Cancel window before going on. This is implemented as one function, `stringDialog`, that only returns after the user is done with the dialog box. Because of this, the dialog needs its own event loop to handle all events for the dialog. All events for the the rest of the Draw application are ignored until the dialog box is done.

The function `dialogEventLoop` is suspiciously like the application's main `eventLoop` function.

```
        .
        .
        .
/*
**      dialogEventLoop handles all the dialog events.  It has its
**      own event handler because it is a modal dialog and does
**      not return until the user chooses OK (1) or Cancel (0)
**      buttons.  Until then, it returns (-1).
**
*/

dialogEventLoop()

{       /* -- function dialogEventLoop */
        int             status = (-1);
        XEvent          theEvent;
```

continued...

...from previous page

```
/*
**      Block on input, awaiting an event from X
*/

XNextEvent( theDisplay, &theEvent );

switch( theEvent.type )
        {
        case ConfigureNotify:
        case Expose:
        case MapNotify:
                displayDialog( theEvent.xany.window );
                break;
        .
        .
        .
```

Any X-server generated event is dealt with by merely redisplaying the contents of the affected window.

```
        .
        .
        .
        /*
        **      A Mouse button has been pressed.
        */
        case ButtonPress:
                if ( theEvent.xbutton.window == theDOKWindow )
                        {
                        fillRectangle( theDOKWindow, theDOKGC,
                                0, 0, 200, 200 );
                        displayDialog( theEvent.xbutton.window );
                        status = 1;
                        }

                if ( theEvent.xbutton.window == theDCancelWindow )
                        {
                        fillRectangle( theDCancelWindow, theDCancelGC,
                                0, 0, 200, 200 );
                        displayDialog( theEvent.xbutton.window );
                        status = 0;
                        }
                break;
        .
        .
        .
```

The only `ButtonPress` events looked for are in the OK (`theDOKWindow`) or Cancel (`theDCancelWindow`) windows. On those events, the window is filled with a black rectangle and then cleared with the text redisplayed. This provides feedback to the user.

```
                .
                .
                .
                /*
                **      A key on the keyboard was hit.
                */
                case KeyPress:
                        dialogKeyPress( &theEvent );
                        break;
                }

        return( status );

}       /* -- function dialogEventLoop */
```

Any `KeyPress` events are routed to the `dialogKeyPress` routine, which acts suspiciously like the `processKeyPress` function in the file `keyx.c` for handling keyboard input.

```
/*
**      dialogKeyPress handles keyboard input into the stringDialog
**      window.
**
*/

dialogKeyPress( theEvent )

XKeyEvent       *theEvent;

{       /* -- function dialogkeyPress */
        int             length, l;
        int             theKeyBufferMaxLen = 64;
        char            theKeyBuffer[ 65 ];
        KeySym          theKeySym;
        XComposeStatus  theComposeStatus;

        length = XLookupString( theEvent,
                        theKeyBuffer,
                        theKeyBufferMaxLen,
                        &theKeySym,
                        &theComposeStatus );
```

continued...

...from previous page

```
        /*
        **      Check if theKeySym is within the standard ASCII
        **      printable character range.
        **
        */

        l = strlen( theDialogText );

        if ( ( theKeySym >= ' ' ) &&        /* -- ASCII 32 " "  */
          ( theKeySym <= '~' )   &&         /* -- ASCII 126 "~" */
          ( length > 0 ) )                  /* -- We have input */
                {
                if( ( l + strlen( theKeyBuffer ) ) < MAX_TEXT_LENGTH )
                        {
                        strcat( theDialogText, theKeyBuffer );
                        displayDialog( theDStringWindow );
                        }
                }
        else
                {
                switch( theKeySym )
                        {
                        case XK_BackSpace:
                        case XK_Delete:
                                if ( l >= 1 )
                                        {
                                        /*
                                        **      ClearWindow
                                        */
                                        XClearWindow( theDisplay,
                                                theDStringWindow );

                                        l--;
                                        theDialogText[ l ] = '\0';
                                        displayDialog( theDStringWindow );
                                        XFlush( theDisplay );
                                        }
                                break;
                        default         : ;
                        }
                }

}       /* -- function dialogkeyPress */
```

CLEANING UP

The function `freeDialog` is called to clean up the X resources. It frees the GCs and windows associated with the dialog box (`stringDialog` uses the same font as the Draw application, so you don't need to free up the font here).

```
/*
**      freeDialog frees up all the dialog box resources.
**
*/

freeDialog()

{       /* -- function freeDialog */

        /*
        **      Free up all GCs
        */
        XFreeGC( theDisplay, theDialogGC );
        XFreeGC( theDisplay, theDOKGC );
        XFreeGC( theDisplay, theDStringGC );
        XFreeGC( theDisplay, theDCancelGC );

        /*
        **      Destroy all windows
        */
        XDestroySubwindows( theDisplay, theDialogWindow );
        XDestroyWindow( theDisplay, theDialogWindow );

        XFlush( theDisplay );

}       /* -- function freeDialog */
```

The function `XDestroySubwindows` is a handy way to get rid of any subwindows by using just one Xlib function call.

```
Display         *theDisplay;
Window          theWindow;

XDestroySubwindows( theDisplay,
                theWindow );
```

`XDestroySubwindows` wipes out all child windows of the parent `theWindow`, in one call. `theWindow` will receive any `Expose` events caused by the deletion of the subwindows.

Note that it is not a good idea to try to delete all the subwindows of the root window (which includes all windows from all applications).

HINTING ABOUT TRANSIENT WINDOWS

X seems to like a lot of hinting, rather than requiring you to come right out and say something. In most cases, though, the hints are really hints, and the X server or the window manager has the option of taking the hint or not. In X, you can set a property for a window that specifies the window is a transient window. A transient window is expected to only remain for a short time. Some window managers may treat transient windows differently from normal windows. The goal is to make all transient windows share the same characteristics as the window manager. That way, the user is presented with a consistent interface across many applications. Of course, this lofty goal is easier said than done.

In the previous dialog box, instead of hinting to X that `theDialogWindow` is a transient window, we asked X to leave the window alone, by overriding any redirection from the window manager. Instead, though, you may want your dialog boxes to share the window manager's transient window title bar—for consistency, if the window manager deals with transient windows at all. To have your dialog boxes share the same transient window title bar, use the function `XSetTransientForHint`. `XSetTransientForHint` tells an X window manager that the new window will only be around for a short time (you hope) and is a transient window for a given application.

```
Display         *theDisplay;
Window          theTransientWindow;
Window          theApplicationTopLevelWindow;

XSetTransientForHint( theDisplay,
                theTransientWindow,
                theApplicationTopLevelWindow );
```

`theTransientWindow` is the main dialog window (previously called `the-DialogWindow`). `theApplicationTopLevelWindow` is one of your application's top-level windows. `XSetTransientForHint` associates `the-TransientWindow` with your application's top-level window.

It would be a good idea to use the `XSetTransientForHint` function for any larger dialog box or other pop-up window you use (pop-up selections, pop-up help, etc.). For small dialog windows or pop-up menus, you probably want to use the `override_redirect` method. Menus, in particular, should appear instantly on the screen (or as instantly as possible) and don't really need title bars. In addition, some window managers may mandate that no top-level windows overlap. Chances are, pop-up menus wouldn't look too good if they couldn't overlap the main application window, which is yet another reason to use `override_redirect` for pop-up menus.

SUMMARY

This chapter discusses how to create pop-up windows and dialog boxes.

- A pop-up window is most often used for menus or warning messages. A dialog box typically asks the user for a piece of data, such as the name of a bitmap file to edit. In the Draw application, a dialog box was used to ask the user to enter a file name and to verify that choice with a mouse click.

- It's easy to set up a pop-up window in X: You merely create a window and ask that the pixels underneath the window are saved. You also must request that the selection overrides any window redirection that the window manager might want and since it is a request and not an order, the window redirection may take place anyway.

- As mentioned, we created a pop-up window that allows users to call bitmap files. First the user must click a mouse button in the floating-palette window for this purpose. After that, the routine highlights `theFileWindow` so that the user knows the request has been acknowledged. `findMouse` determines the current mouse location so that your window pops up underneath your mouse. The function `stringDialog` calls up the dialog box and gets the file name from the user, asking for verification.

- The window was created under the mouse. The X designers include another option, called warping the mouse, which moves ths mouse. In most circumstances, warping the mouse only serves to confuse the user. There are situations, though, where warping the mouse might be acceptable.

- After we've determined where to create the window, it pops up, asking the user for a file name. (You don't need to use dialog boxes just to call up files it can be any character string.) At this point, you also need to figure out how big the dialog box should be—anything too big will eat up precious X resources, but anything too small will be ugly.

- In this case, the dialog box is a modal dialog—the user enters the dialog mode and exits the mode by clicking a mouse button in either the OK or Cancel window. This is implemented as one function for the application, `stringDialog`, that only returns after the user is done with the dialog box. Because of this, the dialog needs its own event loop to handle all events for the dialog, which blocks out any other events until the user clears up the dialog box.

- Like any good X program, this one ends with a function, `freeDialog`, that clears X resources (GCs and windows associated with the dialog box) when through with them.

- In Draw, the X window manager overridden and essentially told to leave the dialog boxes alone. However, you can set up dialog boxes as transient windows so all pop-up windows will have the same characteristics. While this is a worthy goal, it isn't all that simple it's best to set up larger windows as transient windows and set up small dialog windows or pop-up menus to override the window manager.

Xlib Functions and Macros Introduced in This Chapter

```
XDestroySubWindows
XQueryPointer
XSetTransientForHint
XWarpPointer
```

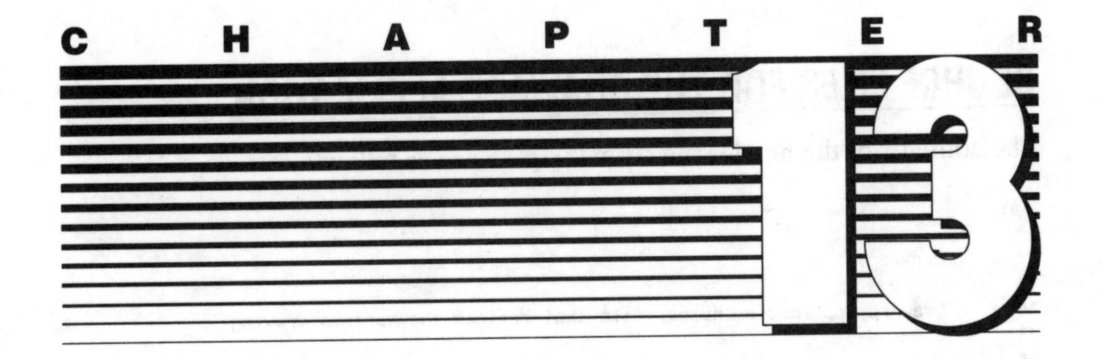

THE DRAW APPLICATION SOURCE CODE

This chapter contains the full source code for the Draw application described in Chapters 9-12. The Draw application is intended to provide a real example of what you will need to do to create a fully functional X Window application.

SOURCE FILES FOR THE DRAWAPP APPLICATION

The contents of the header file `drawapp.h` are as follows:

```
/*
**      drawapp.h
**
**      DrawApp application header file that defines the various drawing
**      commands.
**
*/

#define         DRAW_POINT              1
#define         DRAW_LINE               2
#define         DRAW_RECT               3
#define         DRAW_FILLED_RECT        4
#define         DRAW_OVAL               5
#define         DRAW_FILLED_OVAL        6
#define         DRAW_TEXT1              7
#define         DRAW_TEXT2              8

/*
**      Drawing mode, for the drawing commands that need a lower
**      right corner to finish the drawing: DRAW_RECT,
**      DRAW_FILLED_RECT, DRAW_OVAL, DRAW_FILLED_OVAL
**
*/

#define         FIRST_POINT             1
#define         SECOND_POINT            2


/*
**      The DrawApp application uses two fonts, Text1 and Text2.
**      The symbols below are used to specify which of these
**      fonts to use at a given time.
*/

#define         TEXT1_FONT              1
#define         TEXT2_FONT              2
#define         MAX_TEXT_LENGTH         120

/*
**      DrawApp's resource name and resource class
**
*/
```

continued...

...from previous page

```
#define         RES_NAME        "drawapp"
#define         RES_CLASS       "bitmap"/* -- just for fun */
#define         DEFAULT_FONT1   "variable"
#define         DEFAULT_FONT2   "9x15"
#define         DEFAULT_TITLE   "Draw"

/*
**      iconicState is ICONIC_STATE or NORMAL_STATE
**
*/

#define         NORMAL_STATE            0
#define         ICONIC_STATE            1


/*
**      Pop-up or normal windows
*/

#define         NORMAL_WINDOW           0
#define         POP_UP_WINDOW           1


/*
**      Most of the DrawApp windows are part of the "floating"
**      palette.  These windows do not need to track mouse motion.
*/

#define         IN_PALETTE              1
#define         NOT_IN_PALETTE          2

/*
**      Drawing colors
**
*/

#define         BLACK                   1
#define         WHITE                   2
#define         XOR                     3

/*
**      Drawing modes
*/
#define         DRAWING_OFF             0
#define         DRAWING_ON              1
#define         DRAWING_TEXT            2

/*
**      end of file.
*/
```

The contents of the C source file `argsx.c` are as follows:

```
/*
**      argsx.c
**
**      Functions to handle command-line arguments to an X program.
**
*/

#include   <stdio.h>

#include   "drawapp.h"

/*
**      Default Values
**
*/

#define DEFAULT_DISPLAY         NULL
#define DEFAULT_GEOMETRY        NULL

/*
**      GLOBALS for the arguments
**
*/

extern  theDrawWidth;
extern  theDrawHeight;


/*
**      getArguments sets up a set of text strings with either default
**      values or the values entered in by the user on the command line.
**
**      it handles the following arguments:
**      -h
**      -help           print help message
**      -display        use the display name following to display the program on
**      -geom
**      -geometry       accept user location and/or size for the window
**      -fn
**      -font           use the font name that follows, instead of the default
**      -iconic         begin in iconic state. This function will return a
**                      1 for iconic state, 0 for normal state.
**      -name
**      -title          user the text following as the window's title,
**                      rather than the default
**      -size           e.g., -size 64x64; size of the bitmap to edit.
**
*/
```

continued...

...from previous page

```
getArguments( argc, argv, theDisplayName, theGeometry, theFont1Name,
theFont2Name, theTitle, fileSuccess, theFileName )

int     argc;
char    *argv[];
char    theDisplayName[];
char    theGeometry[];
char    theFont1Name[];
char    theFont2Name[];
char    theTitle[];
int     *fileSuccess;
char    theFileName[];

{       /* -- function getArguments */
        int     argCounter;
        int     iconicState;
        int     foundParam;
        int     numParams, width, height;

        /*
        **      set up defaults
        */
        theDisplayName[ 0 ] = '\0';
        theGeometry   [ 0 ] = '\0';
        strcpy( theFont1Name,   DEFAULT_FONT1 );
        strcpy( theFont2Name,   DEFAULT_FONT2 );
        strcpy( theTitle,       DEFAULT_TITLE );

        iconicState = NORMAL_STATE;    /* -- NOT iconic to start out */

        /*
        **      Override defaults if there is a command-line argument to do so
        */
        for( argCounter = 0; argCounter < argc; argCounter++ )
                {
                /*
                **      Have not found any parameters yet
                */
                foundParam = 0;

                /*
                **      Check if user wants help message
                */
                if ( strncmp( argv[ argCounter ], "-h", 2 ) == 0 )
                        {
                        printHelpMessage();
                        exit( 1 );
                        }
```

continued...

...from previous page

```
/*
**      Check if user wants a different display
*/
if ( strncmp( argv[ argCounter ], "-display", 8 ) == 0 )
        {
        foundParam++;    /* -- found a parameter */

        argCounter++;
        if ( argCounter < argc )
                {
                strcpy( theDisplayName, argv[ argCounter ] );
                }
        else
                {
                fprintf( stderr,
                   "ERROR: the -display option should be %s\n",
                   "followed by a display name." );
                }
        }

/*
**      Check if user wants to specify a window size/loc
*/
if ( strncmp( argv[ argCounter ], "-geom", 5 ) == 0 )
        {
        foundParam++;    /* -- found a parameter */

        argCounter++;
        if ( argCounter < argc )
                {
                strcpy( theGeometry, argv[ argCounter ] );
                }
        else
                {
                fprintf( stderr,
                   "ERROR: the -geometry option should be %s\n",
                   "be followed by a geometry spec," );
                fprintf( stderr,
                   "e.g, 100x100+200+200 for \n%s\n%s\n",
                   "location 100,100",
                   "size 200 by 200." );
                }
        }

/*
**      Check if user wants to specify a window title
*/
if ( ( strncmp( argv[ argCounter ], "-title", 6 ) == 0 ) ||
   ( strncmp( argv[ argCounter ], "-name", 5 ) == 0 ) )
        {
        foundParam++;    /* -- found a parameter */
```

continued...

...from previous page

```
                argCounter++;
                if ( argCounter < argc )
                        {
                        strcpy( theTitle, argv[ argCounter ] );
                        }
                else
                        {
                        fprintf( stderr,
                           "ERROR: the -title option should be %s\n",
                           "be followed by a window title" );
                        }
                }

        /*
        **      Check if user wants to begin prog as an icon.
        */
        if ( strncmp( argv[ argCounter ], "-iconic", 7 ) == 0 )
                {
                foundParam++;      /* -- found a parameter */

                iconicState = ICONIC_STATE;     /* -- as an icon */
                }

        /*
        **      Check if user wants to use a different font.
        */
        if ( ( strncmp( argv[ argCounter ], "-font", 5 ) == 0 ) ||
           ( strncmp( argv[ argCounter ], "-fn", 3 ) == 0 ) )
                {
                foundParam++;      /* -- found a parameter */

                argCounter++;
                if ( argCounter < argc )
                        {
                        strcpy( theFont2Name, argv[ argCounter ] );
                        }
                else
                        {
                        fprintf( stderr,
                           "ERROR: the -font option should be %s\n",
                           "be followed by a font name." );
                        }
                }

        /*
        **      Check if user wants to specify a bitmap size
        */
        if ( strncmp( argv[ argCounter ], "-size", 5 ) == 0 )
                {
                foundParam++;      /* -- found a parameter */
```

continued...

...from previous page

```
                argCounter++;
                if ( argCounter < argc )
                        {
                        numParams = sscanf( argv[ argCounter],
                                                 " %dx%d",
                                                 &width, &height );
                        if ( numParams >= 2 )
                                {
                                printf( "Params found %d by %d\n",
                                        width, height );
                                theDrawWidth  = width;
                                theDrawHeight = height;
                                }
                        }
                else
                        {
                        fprintf( stderr,
                           "ERROR: the -size option should be %s\n",
                           "be followed by a bitmap size," );
                        fprintf( stderr,
                           "e.g, 64x64 for a 64-by64 pixel bitmap.\n");
                        }
                }

        /*
        **      If there is an argument, and we have found no
        **      parameter yet, assume it is a file name
        */
        if ( foundParam == 0 )
                {
                strcpy( theFileName, argv[ argCounter ] );
                *fileSuccess = 1;
                }
        }


/*
**      These defaults = NULL
*/
if ( strlen( theDisplayName ) < 1 )
        theDisplayName = NULL;

if ( strlen( theGeometry ) < 1 )
        theGeometry = NULL;

return( iconicState );

}       /* -- function getArguments */
```

continued...

...from previous page

```
/*
**      printHelpMessage prints a short, terse, Unix-style help
**      message.  Most applications should come with a manual
**      (and on-line man pages) as well as on-line help
**      from within the application.
**
*/

printHelpMessage()

{       /* -- function printHelpMessage */

        fprintf( stderr, "The allowable command line options are:\n" );
        fprintf( stderr, "\t-display displayname \n" );
        fprintf( stderr, "\tUse a different display for output\n" );
        fprintf( stderr, "\t-geometry geometryspec \n" );
        fprintf( stderr, "\tSpecify window location and size\n" );
        fprintf( stderr, "\t-font fontname \n" );
        fprintf( stderr, "\tUse the given font name for text\n" );
        fprintf( stderr, "\t-title windowtitle\n" );
        fprintf( stderr, "\tUse the given name for the window title \n" );
        fprintf( stderr, "\t-iconic\n" );
        fprintf( stderr, "\tStart with the window in iconic state \n" );

}       /* -- function printHelpMessage */



/*
**      end of file argsx.c
*/
```

The contents of the C source file `buttonx.c` are as follows:

```
/*
**      buttonx.c
**      Routines for processing ButtonPress events
**
*/

#include  <X11/Xlib.h>
#include  <X11/Xutil.h>

#include  "drawapp.h"
```

continued...

...from previous page

```
/*
**      GLOBALS for drawing
*/

int     theDrawingCommand   = DRAW_POINT;
int     theDrawingColor     = BLACK;
int     theDrawingMode      = DRAWING_OFF;

char    theDrawingText[ MAX_TEXT_LENGTH + 5 ];

int     theDrawX            = 0;
int     theDrawY            = 0;
int     theLastDrawX        = 0;
int     theLastDrawY        = 0;

/*
**      External GLOBALS
*/

extern  Display         *theDisplay;

extern  Window          theDrawWindow;
extern  Window          thePaletteWindow;

/*
**      Subwindows of the palette window
*/
extern  Window          theColorWindow;
extern  Window          theFileWindow;
extern  Window          theFilledOvalWindow;
extern  Window          theFilledRectWindow;
extern  Window          theLineWindow;
extern  Window          theOvalWindow;
extern  Window          thePointWindow;
extern  Window          theQuitWindow;
extern  Window          theRectWindow;
extern  Window          theSaveWindow;
extern  Window          theText1Window;
extern  Window          theText2Window;
extern  Window          theUndoWindow;
extern  Window          theWipeOutWindow;


/*
**      Graphic Contexts for theDrawWindow
*/

extern  GC              theWhiteGC;             /* -- Draw White bits       */
extern  GC              theBlackGC;             /* -- Draw Black bits       */
extern  GC              theXorGC;               /* -- Rubber-band drawing   */
```

continued...

...from previous page

```
extern  GC              theWhitePixGC;          /* -- Draw White in pixmap */
extern  GC              theBlackPixGC;          /* -- Draw Black in pixmap */

/*
**      processButton processes a ButtonPress event
**
*/

processButton( theEvent )

XButtonPressedEvent     *theEvent;

{       /* -- function processButton */
        int     status = 1;
        int     choice;
        int     x, y;
        char    theFileName[ 120 ];


        /*
        **      if theDrawingMode == DRAWING_ON, undo rubber-band item.
        */
        restoreXorItem();

        /*
        **      If a ButtonPress event in theDrawWindow, then
        **      draw something.
        */
        if ( theEvent->window == theDrawWindow )
                {
                /*
                **      If not drawing yet
                */


                /*
                **      Save item for Undo
                */
                maintainUndo();


                /*
                **      if a point, draw the point; if text
                **      set up text; if line or rect, set that up
                */
                switch( theDrawingCommand )
                        {
                        case    DRAW_POINT:
                                drawItem( theDrawingCommand,
                                        theDrawingColor,
                                        theEvent->x, theEvent->y,
                                        0, 0, " ");
```

continued...

...from previous page

```
                                break;

                        case    DRAW_TEXT1:
                        case    DRAW_TEXT2:
                                theDrawX        = theEvent->x;
                                theDrawY        = theEvent->y;
                                theDrawingMode = DRAWING_TEXT;
                                theDrawingText[ 0 ] = '\0';
                                break;

                        case    DRAW_LINE:
                        case    DRAW_RECT:
                        case    DRAW_FILLED_RECT:
                        case    DRAW_OVAL:
                        case    DRAW_FILLED_OVAL:
                                theDrawingMode = DRAWING_ON;
                                theLastDrawX    = theEvent->x;
                                theLastDrawY    = theEvent->y;
                                theDrawX        = theEvent->x + 1;
                                theDrawY        = theEvent->y + 1;
                                drawItem( theDrawingCommand, XOR,
                                        theLastDrawX, theLastDrawY,
                                        1, 1, " " );
                                break;
                        }
                return ( status );
                }

        /*
        **      If in the palette windows, then set command
        */

        if ( theEvent->window == thePointWindow )
                {
                theDrawingCommand = DRAW_POINT;
                }

        if ( theEvent->window == theLineWindow )
                {
                theDrawingCommand = DRAW_LINE;
                }

        if ( theEvent->window == theRectWindow )
                {
                theDrawingCommand = DRAW_RECT;
                }

        if ( theEvent->window == theFilledRectWindow )
                {
                theDrawingCommand = DRAW_FILLED_RECT;
                }
```

continued...

...from previous page

```
if ( theEvent->window == theOvalWindow )
        {
        theDrawingCommand = DRAW_OVAL;
        }

if ( theEvent->window == theFilledOvalWindow )
        {
        theDrawingCommand = DRAW_FILLED_OVAL;
        }

if ( theEvent->window == theText1Window )
        {
        theDrawingCommand = DRAW_TEXT1;
        associateFont( theBlackGC, TEXT1_FONT );
        associateFont( theWhiteGC, TEXT1_FONT );
        associateFont( theBlackPixGC, TEXT1_FONT );
        associateFont( theWhitePixGC, TEXT1_FONT );
        }

if ( theEvent->window == theText2Window )
        {
        theDrawingCommand = DRAW_TEXT2;
        associateFont( theBlackGC, TEXT2_FONT );
        associateFont( theWhiteGC, TEXT2_FONT );
        associateFont( theBlackPixGC, TEXT2_FONT );
        associateFont( theWhitePixGC, TEXT2_FONT );
        }

if ( theEvent->window == theColorWindow )
        {
        if ( theDrawingColor == BLACK )
                {
                theDrawingColor = WHITE;
                }
        else
                {
                theDrawingColor = BLACK;
                }
        }

if ( theEvent->window == theSaveWindow )
        {
        highlightChoice( theEvent->window );
        saveCurrentFile();
        return( status );
        }
```

continued...

...from previous page

```
	if ( theEvent->window == theUndoWindow )
		{
		highlightChoice( theEvent->window );
		undo();
		return( status );
		}

	if ( theEvent->window == theFileWindow )
		{
		highlightChoice( theEvent->window );

		/*
		**	Get Mouse coords
		*/
		findMouse( theDisplay, &x, &y );
		x -= 20;
		y -= 20;

		choice = stringDialog( x, y,
				"Which file do you want to load?",
				"OK", "Cancel", theFileName );

		if ( choice == 1 )	/* -- OK choice */
			{
			loadFile( theFileName );
			}

		return( status );
		}

	if ( theEvent->window == theWipeOutWindow )
		{
		maintainUndo();
		wipeOutPix();
		return( status );
		}

	if ( theEvent->window == theQuitWindow )
		{
		status = 0;	/* -- quit */
		}

	/*
	**	If the user chooses a different item to draw, then
	**	turn off any current drawing.
	*/
	theDrawingMode = DRAWING_OFF;

	/*
	**	Give the user some feedback on the choice
	*/
```

continued...

...from previous page

```
        highlightChoice( theEvent->window );
        setCmdCursor( theDrawingCommand, FIRST_POINT );
        XFlush( theDisplay );

        /*
        **      if status == 0, then quit program.
        */
        return( status );

}       /* -- function processButton */

/*
**      processMotion processes a MotionNotify event, an event
**      that comes in whenever the mouse pointer is moved over
**      theDrawWindow.  This routine only acts if the user is
**      picking the second point of a two-point drawing command,
**      such as draw rectangle.  If so, it draws a rubber-band item
**
*/

processMotion( theEvent )

XPointerMovedEvent      *theEvent;

{       /* -- function processMotion */

        if ( theEvent->window == theDrawWindow )
                {
                if ( theDrawingMode == DRAWING_ON )
                        {
                        if ( ( ( theEvent->x > theLastDrawX ) &&
                           ( theEvent->y > theLastDrawY ) ) ||
                           ( theDrawingCommand == DRAW_LINE ) )
                                {
                                /*
                                **      Undraw last item
                                */
                                drawItem( theDrawingCommand, XOR,
                                        theLastDrawX, theLastDrawY,
                                        theDrawX - theLastDrawX,
                                        theDrawY - theLastDrawY, " " );

                                /*
                                **      Update Coords
                                */
                                theDrawX = theEvent->x;
                                theDrawY = theEvent->y;

                                /*
                                **      Draw item in new position
                                */
```

continued...

...from previous page

```
                        drawItem( theDrawingCommand, XOR,
                              theLastDrawX, theLastDrawY,
                              theDrawX - theLastDrawX,
                              theDrawY - theLastDrawY, " " );

                        }
                  }

            /*
            **    If the Button is down and the user wants to
            **    draw points, keep drawing.
            */
            if ( theDrawingCommand == DRAW_POINT )
                  {
                  /*
                  **    Save item for Undo
                  */
                  maintainUndo();

                  theDrawX = theEvent->x;
                  theDrawY = theEvent->y;
                  drawItem( theDrawingCommand, theDrawingColor,
                        theDrawX, theDrawY, 0, 0, " " );
                  }
            }

      XFlush( theDisplay );

}     /* -- function processMotion */


/*
**    processRelease processes the ButtonRelease events, if the
**    user has been drawing an item like a rectangle.
**
*/

processRelease( theEvent )

XButtonReleasedEvent    *theEvent;

{     /* -- function processRelease */

      if ( ( theEvent->window == theDrawWindow ) &&
         ( theDrawingMode == DRAWING_ON ) )
            {
            /*
            **    Save item for Undo
            */
            maintainUndo();
```

continued...

...from previous page

```
		/*
		**	Draw final item on window
		*/
		switch( theDrawingCommand )
			{
			case	DRAW_RECT:
			case	DRAW_FILLED_RECT:
			case	DRAW_OVAL:
			case	DRAW_FILLED_OVAL:
				/*
				**	Be sure the bounding rect
				**	goes down
				*/
				if ( ( theEvent->x <= theLastDrawX ) ||
				   ( theEvent->y <= theLastDrawY ) )
					{
					break;
					}
				/*
				**	If so, go on
				*/
			default		:
				theDrawX = theEvent->x;
				theDrawY = theEvent->y;
				drawItem( theDrawingCommand,
					theDrawingColor,
					theLastDrawX, theLastDrawY,
					theDrawX - theLastDrawX,
					theDrawY - theLastDrawY,
					" " );
				theDrawingMode = DRAWING_OFF;
			}
		}
}	/* -- function processRelease */


/*
**	restoreXorItem restores an item that has been drawn in Xor mode.
**
*/

restoreXorItem()

{	/* -- function restoreXorItem */
```

continued...

...from previous page

```
        if ( theDrawingMode == DRAWING_ON )
                {
                drawItem( theDrawingCommand, XOR,
                        theLastDrawX, theLastDrawY,
                        theDrawX - theLastDrawX,
                        theDrawY - theLastDrawY,
                        " " );          /* -- no text */
                }

}       /* -- function restoreXorItem */


/*
**      end of file
*/
```

The contents of the C source file `cursorx.c` are as follows:

```
/*
**      cursorx.c
**
**      DrawApp application cursor functions.
**
**      The DrawApp subwindows each have a cursor that makes sense
**      for the window.  In addition, drawing different items, like
**      lines or points, have different cursors in the application.
**
**      functions:
**              associateCursors        sets all cursors to the proper windows
**              freeCursors             frees up all cursor resources
**              initCursors             initializes all cursors
**              makeAllBusyCursor       makes all DrawApp windows have theBusyCursor
**              setCmdCursor            sets the right cursor for a new drawing cmd
**
*/

#include   <X11/Xlib.h>
#include   <X11/cursorfont.h>

#include   "drawapp.h"

/*
**      GLOBAL Cursor ids.
**
*/
```

continued...

...from previous page

```
Cursor   theArrowCursor;          /* -- XC_top_left_arrow, for line drawing */
Cursor   theBusyCursor;           /* -- XC_watch, used while writing to disk*/
Cursor   theCornerCursor;         /* -- XC_bottom_right_corner, for rects   */
Cursor   theCrossCursor;          /* -- XC_crosshair, for rects and ovals   */
Cursor   thePointCursor;          /* -- XC_pencil, for points               */
Cursor   theQuitCursor;           /* -- XC_gumby, waving bye-bye            */
Cursor   theSkullCursor;          /* -- XC_priate, for the Wipe out cmd     */
Cursor   theTextCursor;           /* -- XC_xterm, for text drawing          */
Cursor   theUndoCursor;           /* -- XC_exchange, for undo-ing           */

/*
**       External GLOBALS
**
*/

extern   Display        *theDisplay;

extern   Window         theDrawWindow;
extern   Window         theBorderWindow;
extern   Window         thePaletteWindow;

/*
**       Subwindows of the palette window
*/
extern   Window         theColorWindow;
extern   Window         theFileWindow;
extern   Window         theFilledOvalWindow;
extern   Window         theFilledRectWindow;
extern   Window         theLineWindow;
extern   Window         theOvalWindow;
extern   Window         thePointWindow;
extern   Window         theQuitWindow;
extern   Window         theRectWindow;
extern   Window         theSaveWindow;
extern   Window         theText1Window;
extern   Window         theText2Window;
extern   Window         theUndoWindow;
extern   Window         theWipeOutWindow;

/*
**       associateCursors associates all the windows in the DrawApp
**       application with their default cursors.  This routine MUST
**       not be called until all the above listed windows have been
**       created and the function initCursors(), below hass been called.
**
```

continued...

...from previous page

```
**      The parameter drawingCommand specifies which drawing command
**      is in effect, which in turn determines the cursor for the
**      main drawing window, theDrawWindow.
**
**      This function is called at the beginning of DrawApp, as well
**      as to restore the cursors after a call to makeAllBusyCursor().
**
*/

associateCursors( drawingCommand )

int     drawingCommand;

{       /* -- function associateCursors */

        /*
        **      Set theDrawWindow to the proper cursor
        */
        setCmdCursor( drawingCommand, FIRST_POINT );

        XDefineCursor( theDisplay, theBorderWindow, theArrowCursor );

        /*
        **      Set up the rest of the cursors to their defaults
        **
        */
        XDefineCursor( theDisplay, thePaletteWindow, theArrowCursor );
        XDefineCursor( theDisplay, theColorWindow, theUndoCursor );
        XDefineCursor( theDisplay, theFileWindow, theArrowCursor );
        XDefineCursor( theDisplay, theFilledOvalWindow, theCrossCursor );
        XDefineCursor( theDisplay, theFilledRectWindow, theCrossCursor );
        XDefineCursor( theDisplay, theLineWindow, theArrowCursor );
        XDefineCursor( theDisplay, theOvalWindow, theCrossCursor );
        XDefineCursor( theDisplay, thePointWindow, thePointCursor );
        XDefineCursor( theDisplay, theQuitWindow, theQuitCursor );
        XDefineCursor( theDisplay, theRectWindow, theCrossCursor );
        XDefineCursor( theDisplay, theSaveWindow, theArrowCursor );
        XDefineCursor( theDisplay, theText1Window, theTextCursor );
        XDefineCursor( theDisplay, theText2Window, theTextCursor );
        XDefineCursor( theDisplay, theUndoWindow, theUndoCursor );
        XDefineCursor( theDisplay, theWipeOutWindow, theSkullCursor );

}       /* -- function associateCursors */


/*
**      freeCursors frees up all the cursor resources in the X server.
**      It should only be called at the end of the DrawApp
**      application, after all the windows have been destroyed.
**
*/
```

continued...

...from previous page

```
freeCursors()

{       /* -- function freeCursors */

        XFreeCursor( theDisplay, theArrowCursor );
        XFreeCursor( theDisplay, theBusyCursor );
        XFreeCursor( theDisplay, theCornerCursor );
        XFreeCursor( theDisplay, theCrossCursor );
        XFreeCursor( theDisplay, thePointCursor );
        XFreeCursor( theDisplay, theQuitCursor );
        XFreeCursor( theDisplay, theSkullCursor );
        XFreeCursor( theDisplay, theTextCursor );
        XFreeCursor( theDisplay, theUndoCursor );

        XFlush( theDisplay );

}       /* -- function freeCursors */

/*
**      initCursors creates all the proper cursors so that they can
**      be associated with the windows.
**
*/


initCursors()

{       /* -- function initCursors */

        theArrowCursor  = XCreateFontCursor( theDisplay,
                                        XC_top_left_arrow );
        theBusyCursor   = XCreateFontCursor( theDisplay,
                                        XC_watch );
        theCornerCursor = XCreateFontCursor( theDisplay,
                                        XC_bottom_right_corner );
        theCrossCursor  = XCreateFontCursor( theDisplay,
                                        XC_crosshair );
        thePointCursor  = XCreateFontCursor( theDisplay,
                                        XC_pencil );
        theQuitCursor   = XCreateFontCursor( theDisplay,
                                        XC_gumby );
        theSkullCursor  = XCreateFontCursor( theDisplay,
                                        XC_pirate );
        theTextCursor   = XCreateFontCursor( theDisplay,
                                        XC_xterm );
        theUndoCursor   = XCreateFontCursor( theDisplay,
                                        XC_exchange );

}       /* -- function initCursors */
```

continued...

...from previous page

```
/*
**      makeAllBusyCursor sets theBusyCursor as the cursor for all the
**      DrawApp windows.  This function is typically called right
**      before a disk operation to show the user that the application
**      is busy, but still functioning.
**
**      Typically, associateCursors is called after the busy task is
**      completed, to restore all the cursors to their normal values.
**
*/

makeAllBusyCursor()

{       /* -- function makeAllBusyCursor */

        XDefineCursor( theDisplay, theBorderWindow, theBusyCursor );
        XDefineCursor( theDisplay, theDrawWindow, theBusyCursor );
        XDefineCursor( theDisplay, thePaletteWindow, theBusyCursor );
        XDefineCursor( theDisplay, theColorWindow, theBusyCursor );
        XDefineCursor( theDisplay, theFileWindow, theBusyCursor );
        XDefineCursor( theDisplay, theFilledOvalWindow, theBusyCursor );
        XDefineCursor( theDisplay, theFilledRectWindow, theBusyCursor );
        XDefineCursor( theDisplay, theLineWindow, theBusyCursor );
        XDefineCursor( theDisplay, theOvalWindow, theBusyCursor );
        XDefineCursor( theDisplay, thePointWindow, theBusyCursor );
        XDefineCursor( theDisplay, theQuitWindow, theBusyCursor );
        XDefineCursor( theDisplay, theRectWindow, theBusyCursor );
        XDefineCursor( theDisplay, theSaveWindow, theBusyCursor );
        XDefineCursor( theDisplay, theText1Window, theBusyCursor );
        XDefineCursor( theDisplay, theText2Window, theBusyCursor );
        XDefineCursor( theDisplay, theUndoWindow, theBusyCursor );
        XDefineCursor( theDisplay, theWipeOutWindow, theBusyCursor );

        XFlush( theDisplay );

}       /* -- function makeAllBusyCursor */


/*
**      setCmdCursor sets up the cursor for the main drawing window,
**      theDrawWindow, based on the current drawing command. The
**      routine takes two parameters, the new drawing command and which
**      point is being drawn.  The rectangle and oval commands have
**      a different cursor depending whether the first or the second
**      point is being drawn.
**
*/

setCmdCursor( drawingCommand, whichPoint )
```

continued...

...from previous page

```
int     drawingCommand;
int     whichPoint;
{       /* -- function setCmdCursor */


        switch( drawingCommand )
                {
                case DRAW_POINT       :
                        XDefineCursor( theDisplay, theDrawWindow,
                                thePointCursor );
                        break;
                case DRAW_LINE        :
                        XDefineCursor( theDisplay, theDrawWindow,
                                theArrowCursor );
                        break;
                case DRAW_TEXT1       :
                case DRAW_TEXT2       :
                        XDefineCursor( theDisplay, theDrawWindow,
                                theTextCursor );
                        break;
                case DRAW_RECT        :
                case DRAW_FILLED_RECT:
                case DRAW_OVAL        :
                case DRAW_FILLED_OVAL:
                        if ( whichPoint == FIRST_POINT )
                                {
                                XDefineCursor( theDisplay, theDrawWindow,
                                        theCrossCursor );
                                }
                        else
                                {
                                XDefineCursor( theDisplay, theDrawWindow,
                                        theCornerCursor );
                                }
                        break;
                }


        XFlush( theDisplay );

}       /* -- function setCmdCursor */


/*
**      end of file.
*/
```

The contents of the C source file `dialogx.c` are as follows:

```
/*
**      dialogx.c
**
**      Pop-up Window dialog box for the DrawApp application.
**
*/

#include    <X11/Xlib.h>
#include    <X11/Xutil.h>
#include    <X11/keysym.h>
#include    <X11/keysymdef.h>

#include    "drawapp.h"

/*
**      External GLOBALS
*/

extern  Display         *theDisplay;
extern  Cursor          theArrowCursor;
extern  Cursor          theTextCursor;
extern  Window          theRootWindow;
extern  Window          theDrawWindow;

/*
**      GLOBALS
*/

#define MAX_CHARS       80
#define MIN_WIDTH       200
#define MIN_HEIGHT      100

Window                  theDialogWindow;
GC                      theDialogGC;
char                    theDialogText[ MAX_CHARS + 5 ];
char                    theDialogMessage[ MAX_CHARS + 5 ];
char                    theDialogOKMsg   [ MAX_CHARS + 5 ];
char                    theDialogCanMsg  [ MAX_CHARS + 5 ];

Window                  theDOKWindow;
GC                      theDOKGC;
Window                  theDStringWindow;
GC                      theDStringGC;
Window                  theDCancelWindow;
GC                      theDCancelGC;
```

continued...

...from previous page

```
/*
**      stringDialog pops up a transient window that asks the user
**      to enter in a file name.  The user can press the OK or
**      the Cancel selection (with any mouse button), to end the
**      dialog session.
**
**      This is a modal dialog.  The program control will return
**      to the calling routine AFTER the user makes a choice to
**      Accept or Cancel.
**
**      stringDialog returns a 0 for cancel or a 1 for OK.
**
*/

stringDialog( x, y, theMessage, theOKText, theCancelText, theText )

int             x, y;                   /* -- Upper left corner for dialog */
char            theMessage[];           /* -- the Prompt                   */
char            theOKText[];            /* -- the OK selection text        */
char            theCancelText[];        /* -- the Cancel selection text    */
char            theText[];              /* -- the RETURNED text string     */

{       /* -- function stringDialog */
        int     theChoice = 0;          /* -- Cancel */
        int     width, height, value;

        /*
        **      Size window
        */
        value = textWidth( theMessage, TEXT1_FONT );
        if ( value > MIN_WIDTH )
                width = value + 30;
        else
                width = MIN_WIDTH;

        value = ( textHeight( TEXT1_FONT ) + 10 ) * 3;
        if ( value > MIN_HEIGHT )
                height = value;
        else
                height = MIN_HEIGHT;

        /*
        **      Open Windows
        */
        initDialogWindows( x, y, width, height );

        /*
        **      Set up display info
        */
```

continued...

...from previous page

```
if ( strlen( theMessage ) < MAX_CHARS )
        {
        strcpy( theDialogMessage, theMessage );
        }
else
        {
        strncpy( theDialogMessage, theMessage, MAX_CHARS );
        }

if ( strlen( theOKText  ) < MAX_CHARS )
        {
        strcpy( theDialogOKMsg, theOKText );
        }
else
        {
        strncpy( theDialogOKMsg, theOKText, MAX_CHARS );
        }

if ( strlen( theCancelText  ) < MAX_CHARS )
        {
        strcpy( theDialogCanMsg, theCancelText );
        }
else
        {
        strncpy( theDialogCanMsg, theCancelText, MAX_CHARS );
        }

/*
**      Display Dialog Info
*/
theDialogText[ 0 ] = '\0';    /* -- NULL string to start out */

displayDialog( theDialogWindow );
displayDialog( theDStringWindow );
displayDialog( theDCancelWindow );
displayDialog( theDOKWindow );

/*
**      Handle Dialog Window Events
*/
theChoice = (-1);

while( theChoice == (-1) )
        {
        theChoice = dialogEventLoop();
        }

if ( theChoice == 1 )    /* -- OK! */
        {
        strcpy( theText, theDialogText );
        }
```

continued...

...from previous page

```
	/*
	**	Close Window and free resources.
	*/
	freeDialog();

	/*
	**	Return choice
	*/

	return( theChoice );

}	/* -- function stringDialog */



/*
**	initDialogWindows creates all the pop-up dialog box windows
**	and GCs in their correct positions
**
*/

initDialogWindows( x, y, width, height )

int	x, y, width, height;

{	/* -- function initDialogWindows */
	Window	openWindow();

	/*
	**	Main Dialog Box Window
	*/

	theDialogWindow = openWindow( x, y, width, height,
				POP_UP_WINDOW,	/* -- IS a POP-UP */
				"File Requestor",
				NORMAL_STATE,
				theRootWindow,
				&theDialogGC );

	associateFont( theDialogGC, TEXT1_FONT );
	initEvents( theDialogWindow, IN_PALETTE );

	theDOKWindow = openWindow( 10,
				2 * ( height / 3 ),
				( width / 3 ), ( height / 3 ) - 10,
				NORMAL_WINDOW,
				"File Requestor",
				NORMAL_STATE,
				theDialogWindow,
				&theDOKGC );
```

continued...

...from previous page

```
        associateFont( theDOKGC, TEXT1_FONT );
        initEvents( theDOKWindow, IN_PALETTE );

        theDCancelWindow = openWindow( width - 10 - ( width / 3 ),
                                2 * ( height / 3 ),
                                ( width / 3 ), ( height / 3 ) - 10,
                                NORMAL_WINDOW,
                                "File Requestor",
                                NORMAL_STATE,
                                theDialogWindow,
                                &theDCancelGC );

        associateFont( theDCancelGC, TEXT1_FONT );
        initEvents( theDCancelWindow, IN_PALETTE );

        theDStringWindow = openWindow( 10,
                                textHeight( TEXT1_FONT ) + 10,
                                width -20, ( height / 3 ) - 10,
                                NORMAL_WINDOW,
                                "File Requestor",
                                NORMAL_STATE,
                                theDialogWindow,
                                &theDStringGC );

        associateFont( theDStringGC, TEXT1_FONT );
        initEvents( theDStringWindow, IN_PALETTE );

        /*
        **      Set up cursors
        */
        XDefineCursor( theDisplay, theDialogWindow,  theArrowCursor );
        XDefineCursor( theDisplay, theDCancelWindow, theArrowCursor );
        XDefineCursor( theDisplay, theDOKWindow,     theArrowCursor );

        XDefineCursor( theDisplay, theDStringWindow, theTextCursor );

        XFlush( theDisplay );

}       /* -- function initDialogWindows */


/*
**      displayDialog displays the current contents of the dialog
**      box, for any given window.
**
*/

displayDialog( theWindow )
```

continued...

...from previous page

```
Window  theWindow;

{       /* -- function displayDialog */
        int     y;

        y = textHeight( TEXT1_FONT ) + 5;

        if ( theWindow == theDialogWindow )
                {
                XDrawString( theDisplay, theWindow, theDialogGC,
                        10, y,
                        theDialogMessage,
                        strlen( theDialogMessage ) );
                }

        if ( theWindow == theDStringWindow )
                {
                XDrawString( theDisplay, theWindow, theDStringGC,
                        10, y,
                        theDialogText,
                        strlen( theDialogText ) );
                }

        if ( theWindow == theDOKWindow )
                {
                XDrawString( theDisplay, theWindow, theDOKGC,
                        10, y,
                        theDialogOKMsg,
                        strlen( theDialogOKMsg  ) );
                }

        if ( theWindow == theDCancelWindow )
                {
                XDrawString( theDisplay, theWindow, theDCancelGC,
                        10, y,
                        theDialogCanMsg,
                        strlen( theDialogCanMsg  ) );
                }

        XFlush( theDisplay );

}       /* -- function displayDialog */


/*
**      dialogEventLoop handles all the dialog events.  It has its
**      own event handler because it is a modal dialog and does
**      not return until the user chooses OK (1) or Cancel (0)
**      buttons.  Until then, it returns (-1).
**
*/
```

continued...

...from previous page

```
dialogEventLoop()

{       /* -- function dialogEventLoop */
        int             status = (-1);
        XEvent          theEvent;

        /*
        **      Block on input, awaiting an event from X
        */

        XNextEvent( theDisplay, &theEvent );

        switch( theEvent.type )
                {
                case ConfigureNotify:
                case Expose:
                case MapNotify:
                        displayDialog( theEvent.xany.window );
                        break;
                /*
                **      A Mouse button has been pressed.
                */
                case ButtonPress:
                        if ( theEvent.xbutton.window == theDOKWindow )
                                {
                                fillRectangle( theDOKWindow, theDOKGC,
                                        0, 0, 200, 200 );
                                displayDialog( theEvent.xbutton.window );
                                status = 1;
                                }

                        if ( theEvent.xbutton.window == theDCancelWindow )
                                {
                                fillRectangle( theDCancelWindow, theDCancelGC,
                                        0, 0, 200, 200 );
                                displayDialog( theEvent.xbutton.window );
                                status = 0;
                                }
                        break;
                /*
                **      A key on the keyboard was hit.
                */
                case KeyPress:
                        dialogKeyPress( &theEvent );
                        break;
                }

        return( status );

}       /* -- function dialogEventLoop */
```

continued...

...from previous page

```
/*
**      dialogKeyPress handles keyboard input into the stringDialog
**      window.
**
*/


dialogKeyPress( theEvent )

XKeyEvent       *theEvent;

{       /* -- function dialogkeyPress */
        int             length, l;
        int             theKeyBufferMaxLen = 64;
        cha             theKeyBuffer[ 65 ];
        KeySym          theKeySym;
        XComposeStatus  theComposeStatus;

        length = XLookupString( theEvent,
                        theKeyBuffer,
                        theKeyBufferMaxLen,
                        &theKeySym,
                        &theComposeStatus );
        /*
        **      Check if theKeySym is within the standard ASCII
        **      printable character range.
        **
        */

        l = strlen( theDialogText );


        if ( ( theKeySym >= ' ' ) &&      /* -- ASCII 32 " "  */
          ( theKeySym <= '~' )   &&       /* -- ASCII 126 "~" */
          ( length > 0 ) )                /* -- We have input */
                {
                if( ( l + strlen( theKeyBuffer ) ) < MAX_TEXT_LENGTH )
                        {
                        strcat( theDialogText, theKeyBuffer );
                        displayDialog( theDStringWindow );
                        }
                }
        else
                {
                switch( theKeySym )
                        {
                        case XK_BackSpace:
                        case XK_Delete:
                                if ( l >= 1 )
```

continued...

...from previous page

```
                                        {
                                        /*
                                        **      ClearWindow
                                        */
                                        XClearWindow( theDisplay,
                                                theDStringWindow );

                                        l--;
                                        theDialogText[ l ] = '\0';
                                        displayDialog( theDStringWindow );
                                        XFlush( theDisplay );
                                        }
                                break;
                        default         : ;
                        }
                }

}       /* -- function dialogkeyPress */


/*
**      freeDialog frees up all the dialog box resources.
**
*/

freeDialog()

{       /* -- function freeDialog */

        /*
        **      Free up all GCs
        */
        XFreeGC( theDisplay, theDialogGC );
        XFreeGC( theDisplay, theDOKGC );
        XFreeGC( theDisplay, theDStringGC );
        XFreeGC( theDisplay, theDCancelGC );

        /*
        **      Destroy all windows
        */
        XDestroySubwindows( theDisplay, theDialogWindow );
        XDestroyWindow( theDisplay, theDialogWindow );

        XFlush( theDisplay );

}       /* -- function freeDialog */


/*
**      end of file
*/
```

The contents of the C source file `drawapp.c` are as follows:

```
/*
**      drawapp.c
**
**      Contains the major functions to draw and run the
**      DrawApp application.
**
*/

#include    <X11/Xlib.h>
#include    <X11/Xutil.h>

#include    "drawapp.h"

/*
**      External GLOBALS
**
*/

extern  Display         *theDisplay;
extern  Window          theRootWindow;
extern  unsigned long   theBlackPixel;  /* -- System "Black" color */
extern  unsigned long   theWhitePixel;  /* -- System "White" color */
extern  int             theDrawingColor;/* -- WHITE, BLACK, or XOR */

/*
**      GLOBALS vars for drawapp.c
**
*/

char            theDrawName[ MAX_TEXT_LENGTH + 5 ];
Window          theBorderWindow;
Window          theDrawWindow;
Window          thePaletteWindow;

/*
**      Subwindows of the palette window
*/
Window          theColorWindow;
Window          theFileWindow;
Window          theFilledOvalWindow;
Window          theFilledRectWindow;
Window          theLineWindow;
Window          theOvalWindow;
Window          thePointWindow;
Window          theQuitWindow;
Window          theRectWindow;
Window          theSaveWindow;
Window          theText1Window;
```

continued...

...from previous page

```
Window          theText2Window;
Window          theUndoWindow;
Window          theWipeOutWindow;

/*
**      Graphic Contexts for all windows
*/

GC              theBorderGC;            /* -- Border window GC    */
GC              theWhiteGC;             /* -- Draw White bits     */
GC              theBlackGC;             /* -- Draw Black bits     */
GC              theXorGC;               /* -- Rubber-band drawing */

GC              thePaletteGC;

/*
**      Subwindows of the palette window
*/

GC              theColorGC;
GC              theFileGC;
GC              theFilledOvalGC;
GC              theFilledRectGC;
GC              theLineGC;
GC              theOvalGC;
GC              thePointGC;
GC              theQuitGC;
GC              theRectGC;
GC              theSaveGC;
GC              theText1GC;
GC              theText2GC;
GC              theUndoGC;
GC              theWipeOutGC;

/*
**      Size of the bitmap to edit
*/

int     theDrawWidth    = 64;   /* -- default os 64x64 */
int     theDrawHeight   = 64;

/*
**      Width and height for each small window in the palette.
*/
#define PALETTE_HEIGHT  56
#define PALETTE_WIDTH   42
#define NUM_ITEMS       14      /* -- 14 Windows in palette window */
#define PALETTE_FULL_WIDTH      (PALETTE_WIDTH * NUM_ITEMS)
```

continued...

...from previous page

```
/*
**      initWindows
**      Initializes the windows needed for the DrawApp application.
**      The routine is given a geometry spec that may contain the
**      desired window location and size for the DrawApp drawing window,
**      a window title and a state for whether the windows are to start
**      iconic or not.
**
*/

initWindows( theGeometry, theTitle, iconicState )

char    theGeometry[];
char    theTitle[];
int     iconicState;

{       /* -- function initWindows */
        int             geometryStatus;
        int             x, y, x1, y1, width, height;
        Window          openWindow();
        char            thePaletteTitle[ 120 ];

        /*
        **      parse geometry spec
        */
        geometryStatus = XParseGeometry( theGeometry, &x, &y, &width, &height );

        /*
        **      Check which values were actually set
        */
        if ( !( geometryStatus & XValue ) )
                x = 10;
        if ( !( geometryStatus & YValue ) )
                y = 10;
        if ( !( geometryStatus & WidthValue ) )
                width  = 100;
        if ( !( geometryStatus & HeightValue ) )
                height = 100;


        /*
        **      Create theDrawWindow--where all drawing takes place
        */
        if ( strlen( theTitle ) < 100 )
                {
                strcpy( theDrawName, theTitle );
                }
```

continued...

...from previous page

```
	theBorderWindow = openWindow( x, y, width, height,
				NORMAL_WINDOW, theTitle,
				iconicState, theRootWindow, &theBorderGC );
	initEvents( theBorderWindow, IN_PALETTE );  /* -- Not really in palette*/

	/*
	**	Create theDrawWindow--where all drawing takes place
	*/
	x1 = ( width / 2 ) - ( theDrawWidth / 2 );
	y1 = ( height / 2 ) - ( theDrawHeight / 2 );

	if ( x1 < 0 ) x1 = 0;
	if ( y1 < 0 ) y1 = 0;

	theDrawWindow = openWindow( x1, y1,
				theDrawWidth, theDrawHeight,
				NORMAL_WINDOW, theTitle,
				NORMAL_STATE, theBorderWindow, &theBlackGC );

	initEvents( theDrawWindow, NOT_IN_PALETTE );

	/*
	**	Create a GC for drawing in white
	*/
	createGC( theDrawWindow, &theWhiteGC );
	XSetForeground( theDisplay,
		theWhiteGC,
		theWhitePixel );

	/*
	**	Create a GC for xor-ing rubber-band items
	*/
	xorSetUp( theDrawWindow, &theXorGC );


	/*
	**	Create thePaletteWindow--where all choices are made.
	**	thePaletteWindow starts with a fixed size.
	**
	*/
	if ( strlen( theTitle ) < 100 )
		{
		strcpy( thePaletteTitle, theTitle );
		strcat( thePaletteTitle, ":Palette" );
		}


	y      += ( height + 5 );
	width  = PALETTE_FULL_WIDTH;
	height = PALETTE_HEIGHT;
	thePaletteWindow = openWindow( x, y, width, height,
				NORMAL_WINDOW, thePaletteTitle,
				iconicState, theRootWindow, &thePaletteGC );
```

continued...

...from previous page

```
initEvents( thePaletteWindow, IN_PALETTE );
XFlush( theDisplay );

/*
**      Create all thePaletteWindow's subwindows; thePaletteWindow
**      is now the parent window.
*/
width   = PALETTE_WIDTH;
x       = 0;
y       = 0;

/*
**      theSaveWindow;
*/
theSaveWindow = openWindow( x, y, width, height,
                            NORMAL_WINDOW, thePaletteTitle,
                            NORMAL_STATE, thePaletteWindow, &theSaveGC );

initEvents( theSaveWindow, IN_PALETTE );
associateFont( theSaveGC, TEXT1_FONT );

/*
**      theColorWindow;
*/
x += PALETTE_WIDTH;
theColorWindow = openWindow( x, y, width, height,
                            NORMAL_WINDOW, thePaletteTitle,
                            NORMAL_STATE, thePaletteWindow, &theColorGC );

initEvents( theColorWindow, IN_PALETTE );
associateFont( theColorGC, TEXT1_FONT );

/*
**      thePointWindow;
*/
x += PALETTE_WIDTH;
thePointWindow = openWindow( x, y, width, height,
                            NORMAL_WINDOW, thePaletteTitle,
                            NORMAL_STATE, thePaletteWindow, &thePointGC );

initEvents( thePointWindow, IN_PALETTE );
associateFont( thePointGC, TEXT1_FONT );

/*
**      theLineWindow;
*/
x += PALETTE_WIDTH;
theLineWindow = openWindow( x, y, width, height,
                            NORMAL_WINDOW, thePaletteTitle,
                            NORMAL_STATE, thePaletteWindow, &theLineGC );
```

continued...

...from previous page

```
        initEvents( theLineWindow, IN_PALETTE );
        associateFont( theLineGC, TEXT1_FONT );

        /*
        **      theRectWindow;
        */
        x += PALETTE_WIDTH;
        theRectWindow = openWindow( x, y, width, height,
                                NORMAL_WINDOW, thePaletteTitle,
                                NORMAL_STATE, thePaletteWindow, &theRectGC );

        initEvents( theRectWindow, IN_PALETTE );
        associateFont( theRectGC, TEXT1_FONT );

        /*
        **      theFilledRectWindow;
        */
        x += PALETTE_WIDTH;
        theFilledRectWindow = openWindow( x, y, width, height,
                                NORMAL_WINDOW, thePaletteTitle,
                                NORMAL_STATE, thePaletteWindow, &theFilledRectGC );

        initEvents( theFilledRectWindow, IN_PALETTE );
        associateFont( theFilledRectGC, TEXT1_FONT );

        /*
        **      theOvalWindow;
        */
        x += PALETTE_WIDTH;
        theOvalWindow = openWindow( x, y, width, height,
                                NORMAL_WINDOW, thePaletteTitle,
                                NORMAL_STATE, thePaletteWindow, &theOvalGC );

        initEvents( theOvalWindow, IN_PALETTE );
        associateFont( theOvalGC, TEXT1_FONT );

        /*
        **      theFilledOvalWindow;
        */
        x += PALETTE_WIDTH;
        theFilledOvalWindow = openWindow( x, y, width, height,
                                NORMAL_WINDOW, thePaletteTitle,
                                NORMAL_STATE, thePaletteWindow, &theFilledOvalGC );

        initEvents( theFilledOvalWindow, IN_PALETTE );
        associateFont( theFilledOvalGC, TEXT1_FONT );
```

continued...

...from previous page

```
/*
**      theText1Window;
*/
x += PALETTE_WIDTH;
theText1Window = openWindow( x, y, width, height,
                        NORMAL_WINDOW, thePaletteTitle,
                        NORMAL_STATE, thePaletteWindow, &theText1GC );

initEvents( theText1Window, IN_PALETTE );
associateFont( theText1GC, TEXT1_FONT );

/*
**      theText2Window;
*/
x += PALETTE_WIDTH;
theText2Window = openWindow( x, y, width, height,
                        NORMAL_WINDOW, thePaletteTitle,
                        NORMAL_STATE, thePaletteWindow, &theText2GC );

initEvents( theText2Window, IN_PALETTE );
associateFont( theText2GC, TEXT2_FONT );

/*
**      theUndoWindow;
*/
x += PALETTE_WIDTH;
theUndoWindow = openWindow( x, y, width, height,
                        NORMAL_WINDOW, thePaletteTitle,
                        NORMAL_STATE, thePaletteWindow, &theUndoGC );

initEvents( theUndoWindow, IN_PALETTE );
associateFont( theUndoGC, TEXT1_FONT );

/*
**      theFileWindow;
*/
x += PALETTE_WIDTH;
theFileWindow = openWindow( x, y, width, height,
                        NORMAL_WINDOW, thePaletteTitle,
                        NORMAL_STATE, thePaletteWindow, &theFileGC );

initEvents( theFileWindow, IN_PALETTE );
associateFont( theFileGC, TEXT1_FONT );

/*
**      theWipeOutWindow;
*/
x += PALETTE_WIDTH;
theWipeOutWindow = openWindow( x, y, width, height,
                        NORMAL_WINDOW, thePaletteTitle,
                        NORMAL_STATE, thePaletteWindow, &theWipeOutGC );
```

continued...

...from previous page

```
        initEvents( theWipeOutWindow, IN_PALETTE );
        associateFont( theWipeOutGC, TEXT1_FONT );

        /*
        **      theQuitWindow;
        */
        x += PALETTE_WIDTH;
        theQuitWindow = openWindow( x, y, width, height,
                                NORMAL_WINDOW, thePaletteTitle,
                                NORMAL_STATE, thePaletteWindow, &theQuitGC );

        initEvents( theQuitWindow, IN_PALETTE );
        associateFont( theQuitGC, TEXT1_FONT );

        /*
        **      Set up each window's cursors
        */
        associateCursors( DRAW_POINT );

}       /* -- function initWindows */


/*
**      processExpose redraws a given window if it gets an Expose
**      event. This is another example of "lazy" Expose event handling,
**      as this routine redraws the whole window on each Expose event.
**
*/

processExpose( theEvent )

XExposeEvent    *theEvent;

{       /* -- function processExpose */

        if ( theEvent->window == theDrawWindow )
                {
                refreshDrawWindow();
                return;
                }

        if ( theEvent->window == theSaveWindow )
                {
                XDrawString( theDisplay, theSaveWindow, theSaveGC,
                                2, 20, "Save", strlen( "Save" ) );

                XDrawString( theDisplay, theSaveWindow, theSaveGC,
                                2, 45, "@-S", strlen( "@-S" ) );
                return;
                }
```

continued...

...from previous page

```
        if ( theEvent->window == theColorWindow )
                {
                if ( theDrawingColor == BLACK )
                        {
                        XDrawString( theDisplay, theColorWindow, theColorGC,
                                0, 20, "Black", strlen( "Black" ) );
                        }
                else
                        {
                        XDrawString( theDisplay, theColorWindow, theColorGC,
                                0, 20, "White", strlen( "White" ) );
                        }
                return;
                }
        if ( theEvent->window == thePointWindow )
                {
                XDrawPoint( theDisplay, thePointWindow, thePointGC, 5, 5 );
                XDrawPoint( theDisplay, thePointWindow, thePointGC, 15, 8 );
                XDrawPoint( theDisplay, thePointWindow, thePointGC, 3, 15 );
                XDrawPoint( theDisplay, thePointWindow, thePointGC, 25, 25 );
                XDrawPoint( theDisplay, thePointWindow, thePointGC, 5, 21 );
                XDrawPoint( theDisplay, thePointWindow, thePointGC, 7, 25 );
                XDrawPoint( theDisplay, thePointWindow, thePointGC, 25, 21 );
                XDrawPoint( theDisplay, thePointWindow, thePointGC, 5, 13 );
                XDrawPoint( theDisplay, thePointWindow, thePointGC, 17, 15 );

                XDrawString( theDisplay, thePointWindow, thePointGC,
                                2, 45, "@-P", strlen( "@-P" ) );
                return;
                }

        if ( theEvent->window == theLineWindow )
                {
                drawLine( theLineWindow, theLineGC,
                        10, 5, 35, 35 );
                XDrawString( theDisplay, theLineWindow, theLineGC,
                                2, 45, "@-L", strlen( "@-L" ) );
                return;
                }

        if ( theEvent->window == theRectWindow )
                {
                drawRectangle( theRectWindow, theRectGC,
                        5, 5, 24, 24 );
                XDrawString( theDisplay, theRectWindow, theRectGC,
                                2, 45, "@-R", strlen( "@-R" ) );
                return;
                }
```

continued...

...from previous page

```
	if ( theEvent->window == theFilledRectWindow )
		{
		fillRectangle( theFilledRectWindow, theFilledRectGC,
			5, 5, 24, 24 );
		XDrawString( theDisplay, theFilledRectWindow, theFilledRectGC,
				2, 45, "@-F", strlen( "@-F" ) );
		return;
		}

	if ( theEvent->window == theOvalWindow )
		{
		drawOval( theOvalWindow, theOvalGC,
			5, 5, 24, 24 );
		XDrawString( theDisplay, theOvalWindow, theOvalGC,
				2, 45, "@-O", strlen( "@-O" ) );
		return;
		}

	if ( theEvent->window == theFilledOvalWindow )
		{
		fillOval( theFilledOvalWindow, theFilledOvalGC,
			5, 5, 30, 30 );
		return;
		}

	if ( theEvent->window == theText1Window )
		{
		XDrawString( theDisplay, theText1Window, theText1GC,
				5, 20, "A", strlen( "A" ) );
		XDrawString( theDisplay, theText1Window, theText1GC,
				2, 45, "@-T", strlen( "@-T" ) );
		return;
		}

	if ( theEvent->window == theText2Window )
		{
		XDrawString( theDisplay, theText2Window, theText2GC,
				5, 20, "A", strlen( "A" ) );
		return;
		}

	if ( theEvent->window == theUndoWindow )
		{
		XDrawString( theDisplay, theUndoWindow, theUndoGC,
				2, 20, "Undo", strlen( "Undo" ) );
		XDrawString( theDisplay, theUndoWindow, theUndoGC,
				2, 45, "@-U", strlen( "@-U" ) );
		return;
		}
```

continued...

...from previous page

```
        if ( theEvent->window == theFileWindow )
                {
                XDrawString( theDisplay, theFileWindow, theFileGC,
                                2, 20, "File", strlen( "File" ) );
                return;
                }

        if ( theEvent->window == theWipeOutWindow )
                {
                XDrawString( theDisplay, theWipeOutWindow, theWipeOutGC,
                                2, 20, "Wipe", strlen( "Wipe" ) );
                return;
                }

        if ( theEvent->window == theQuitWindow )
                {
                XDrawString( theDisplay, theQuitWindow, theQuitGC,
                                2, 20, "Quit", strlen( "Quit" ) );
                XDrawString( theDisplay, theQuitWindow, theQuitGC,
                                2, 45, "@-Q", strlen( "@-Q" ) );
                return;
                }

}       /* -- function processExpose */

/*
**      highlightChoice highlights a palette window
**      when the user clicks a mouse button in the window.
**      Then, it refreshes the given window.
*/

highlightChoice( theWindow )

Window  theWindow;

{       /* -- function highlightChoice */
        XExposeEvent    theEvent;

        /*
        **      Fill the window to highlight the selection.
        */
        fillRectangle( theWindow, theFilledRectGC,
                0, 0, PALETTE_WIDTH, PALETTE_HEIGHT );

        XFlush( theDisplay );

        /*
        **      Clear the window
        */
        XClearWindow( theDisplay, theWindow );
```

continued...

...from previous page

```
        /*
        **      allow processExpose() to redraw the original
        **      contents of the window.
        */

        theEvent.window = theWindow;
        processExpose( &theEvent );

        XFlush( theDisplay );

}       /* -- function highlightChoice */



/*
**      Releases all window and GC resources used by the DrawApp
**      application.
*/

freeWindowsAndGCs()

{       /* -- function freeWindowsAndGCs */

        /*
        **      Free up all Graphics Contexts
        */
        XFreeGC( theDisplay, theBorderGC );
        XFreeGC( theDisplay, theBlackGC );
        XFreeGC( theDisplay, theWhiteGC );
        XFreeGC( theDisplay, theXorGC );

        XFreeGC( theDisplay, thePaletteGC );

        XFreeGC( theDisplay, theColorGC );
        XFreeGC( theDisplay, theFileGC );
        XFreeGC( theDisplay, theFilledOvalGC );
        XFreeGC( theDisplay, theFilledRectGC );
        XFreeGC( theDisplay, theLineGC );
        XFreeGC( theDisplay, theOvalGC );
        XFreeGC( theDisplay, thePointGC );
        XFreeGC( theDisplay, theQuitGC );
        XFreeGC( theDisplay, theRectGC );
        XFreeGC( theDisplay, theSaveGC );
        XFreeGC( theDisplay, theText1GC );
        XFreeGC( theDisplay, theText2GC );
        XFreeGC( theDisplay, theUndoGC );
        XFreeGC( theDisplay, theWipeOutGC );
```

continued...

...from previous page

```
        /*
        **      Destroy all windows
        */
        XDestroySubwindows( theDisplay,
                thePaletteWindow );
        XDestroyWindow( theDisplay, thePaletteWindow );

        XDestroySubwindows( theDisplay,
                theBorderWindow );
        XDestroyWindow( theDisplay, theBorderWindow );

        XFlush( theDisplay );

}       /* -- function freeWindowsAndGCs */

/*
**      end of file.
*/
```

The contents of the C source file `drawitem.c` are as follows:

```
/*
**      drawitem.c
**
**      Draws items like lines, rectangles and ovals for the
**      DrawApp application.
**
*/

#include   <X11/Xlib.h>
#include   <X11/Xutil.h>

#include   "drawapp.h"

/*
**      External GLOBALS
*/
extern  Display         *theDisplay;

extern  Window          theDrawWindow;
extern  Pixmap          theDrawPixmap;
```

continued...

...from previous page

```
/*
**      Graphic Contexts for theDrawWindow
*/

extern  GC              theWhiteGC;             /* -- Draw White bits */
extern  GC              theBlackGC;             /* -- Draw Black bits */
extern  GC              theXorGC;               /* -- Rubber-band drawing  */
extern  GC              theBlackPixGC;          /* -- Draw Pixmap GC  */
extern  GC              theWhitePixGC;          /* -- Draw Pixmap GC  */

/*
**      drawItem draws a given item
*/

drawItem( theCommand, theColor, x, y, width, height, theText )

int     theCommand;     /* -- what to draw, from drawapp.h */
int     theColor;       /* -- what color to draw in        */
int     x, y;           /* -- where to draw it             */
int     width, height;  /* -- how big to draw it           */
char    theText[];      /* -- text for DRAW_TEXT1, _TEXT2  */

{       /* -- function drawItem */

        switch( theColor )
                {
                case BLACK:
                        drawIt( theDrawWindow, theBlackGC, theCommand,
                                x, y, width, height, theText );
                        drawIt( theDrawPixmap, theBlackPixGC, theCommand,
                                x, y, width, height, theText );
                        break;
                case WHITE:
                        drawIt( theDrawWindow, theWhiteGC, theCommand,
                                x, y, width, height, theText );
                        drawIt( theDrawPixmap, theWhitePixGC, theCommand,
                                x, y, width, height, theText );
                        break;
                case XOR:
                        drawIt( theDrawWindow, theXorGC, theCommand,
                                x, y, width, height, theText );
                        break;
                }

        XFlush( theDisplay );

}       /* -- function drawItem */
```

continued...

...from previous page

```
/*
**      drawIt actually draws the given item, based on the window,
**      GC, ,x, y location and size in width, height.
*/

drawIt( theWindow, theGC, theCommand, x, y, width, height, theText )

Drawable        theWindow;
GC              theGC;
int             theCommand;
int             x, y;
int             width, height;
char            theText[];

{       /* -- function drawIt */

        switch( theCommand )
                {
                case DRAW_TEXT1:
                case DRAW_TEXT2:
                        XDrawString( theDisplay, theWindow, theGC, x, y,
                                theText, strlen( theText ) );
                        break;
                case DRAW_POINT:
                        XDrawPoint( theDisplay, theWindow, theGC, x, y );
                        break;
                case DRAW_LINE:
                        drawLine( theWindow, theGC, x, y,
                                x + width, y + height );
                        break;
                case DRAW_RECT:
                        drawRectangle( theWindow, theGC, x, y,
                                width, height );
                        break;
                case DRAW_FILLED_RECT:
                        fillRectangle( theWindow, theGC, x, y,
                                width, height );
                        break;
                case DRAW_OVAL:
                        drawOval( theWindow, theGC, x, y,
                                width, height );
                        break;
                case DRAW_FILLED_OVAL:
                        fillOval( theWindow, theGC, x, y,
                                width, height );
                        break;
                }

}       /* -- function drawIt */

/*
**      end of file
*/
```

The contents of the C source file `drawx.c` are as follows:

```
/*
**      drawx.c          X11 simple drawing functions
**
*/

#include    <X11/Xlib.h>
#include    <X11/Xutil.h>

/*
**      X11 draws ovals as Arcs, Arcs which start at angle 0
**      and traverse the full circle.  X11 measures angles in
**      terms of 1/64 degrees.  Thus, traversing the full circle
**      means going around an angle 360*64.
**
*/

#define     FULL_CIRCLE      (360*64)
#define     START_CIRCLE     0


/* -- external globals, from initx.c */
extern  Display         *theDisplay;

/*
**      drawLine
**      Draws a line from (x1, y1) to (x2, y2) in the Drawable (window
**      or pixmap) using the graphics context theGC.
**
*/

drawLine( theDrawable, theGC, x1, y1, x2, y2 )

Drawable         theDrawable;               /* -- the Drawable to draw it in */
GC               theGC;                     /* -- Graphics Context           */
int              x1, y1;                    /* -- Starting location          */
int              x2, y2;                    /* -- Ending location            */

{       /* -- function drawLine */

        XDrawLine( theDisplay,
                theDrawable,
                theGC,
                x1, y1,
                x2, y2 );

}       /* -- function drawLine */
```

continued...

...from previous page

```
/*
**      drawRectangle
**      Draws a rectangle (outlines or frames a rectangle) in the
**      given Drawable and with the given graphics context.
**
*/

drawRectangle( theDrawable, theGC, x, y, width, height )

Drawable        theDrawable;            /* -- the Drawable to draw it in */
GC              theGC;                  /* -- Graphics Context           */
int             x, y;                   /* -- upper left corner          */
int             width, height;          /* -- Size of the rectangle      */

{       /* -- function drawRectangle */

        XDrawRectangle( theDisplay,
                theDrawable,
                theGC,
                x, y,
                width, height );

}       /* -- function drawRectangle */



/*
**      fillRectangle
**      Fills a rectangle (outlines or frames a rectangle) in the
**      given Drawable and with the given graphics context.
**
*/

fillRectangle( theDrawable, theGC, x, y, width, height )

Drawable        theDrawable;            /* -- the Drawable to draw it in */
GC              theGC;                  /* -- Graphics Context           */
int             x, y;                   /* -- upper left corner          */
int             width, height;          /* -- Size of the rectangle      */

{       /* -- function fillRectangle */

        XFillRectangle( theDisplay,
                theDrawable,
                theGC,
                x, y,
                width, height );

}       /* -- function fillRectangle */
```

continued...

...from previous page

```
/*
**      drawOval
**      Draws the framed outline of an oval.  This oval is bounded
**      by a rectangle from x, y (upper left corner) of size
**      width, height.
**
*/

drawOval( theDrawable, theGC, x, y, width, height )

Drawable        theDrawable;            /* -- the Drawable to draw it in */
GC              theGC;                  /* -- Graphics Context           */
                                        /* -- For the bounding rectangle:*/
int             x, y;                   /* -- upper left corner          */
int             width, height;          /* -- Size of the rectangle      */

{       /* -- drawOval */

        XDrawArc( theDisplay,
                theDrawable,
                theGC,
                x, y,
                width, height,
                START_CIRCLE,
                FULL_CIRCLE );

}       /* -- drawOval */


/*
**      fillOval
**      Fills the framed outline of an oval.  This oval is bounded
**      by a rectangle from x, y (upper left corner) of size
**      width, height.
**
*/

fillOval( theDrawable, theGC, x, y, width, height )

Drawable        theDrawable;            /* -- the Drawable to draw it in */
GC              theGC;                  /* -- Graphics Context           */
                                        /* -- For the bounding rectangle:*/
int             x, y;                   /* -- upper left corner          */
int             width, height;          /* -- Size of the rectangle      */

{       /* -- fillOval */
```

continued...

...from previous page

```
        XFillArc( theDisplay,
                theDrawable,
                theGC,
                x, y,
                width, height,
                START_CIRCLE,
                FULL_CIRCLE );

}       /* -- fillOval */

/*
**      end of file drawx.c
**
*/
```

The contents of the C source file `errorx.c` are as follows:

```
/*
**      errorx.c
**
**      X Error handlers for the DrawApp application.
**
**      Note: the fatal error handler cannot return.
**
**      These routines would do a lot more if they could,
**      but DrawApp is a very X-oriented program.  Typical
**      error handlers could save files to disk before
**      program termination.
**
**
*/

#include   <stdio.h>
#include   <X11/Xlib.h>
#include   <X11/Xutil.h>
#include   <X11/Xproto.h>

/*
**      setErrorHandlers sets up the program's error handler
**      functions.
**
*/
setErrorHandlers()

{       /* -- function setErrorHandlers */
        int     errorHandler();
        int     fatalErrorHandler();
```

continued...

...from previous page

```
        /*
        **      Set up the normal error handler, for things like
        **      bad window IDs, etc.
        */
        XSetErrorHandler( errorHandler );

        /*
        **      Set up the fatal error handler for a broken connection
        **      with the X server, and other nasties.
        **
        */
        XSetIOErrorHandler( fatalErrorHandler );

}       /* -- function setErrorHandlers */


/*
**      errorHandler handles non-fatal X errors.
**      This routine basically just prints out
**      the error message and returns.  Thus, we
**      can probaly expect many, many errors to be
**      generated, since nothing stops the erroneous
**      condition.  This function mainly exists so
**      that the program does not terminate on a minor
**      error.  No one seems to like unexpected program
**      termination, at least in a production environment.
**
*/

errorHandler( theDisplay, theErrorEvent )

Display         *theDisplay;
XErrorEvent     *theErrorEvent;

{       /* -- function errorHandler */
        int     bufferLength = 120;
        char    theBuffer[ 130 ];

        XGetErrorText( theDisplay,
                theErrorEvent->error_code,
                theBuffer,
                bufferLength );

        fprintf( stderr,
                "X Error: %s\n", theBuffer );

        fprintf( stderr,
                "Serial number of request: %ld Op Code: %d.%d Error Code: %d\n",
                theErrorEvent->serial,
                theErrorEvent->request_code,
                theErrorEvent->minor_code,
                theErrorEvent->error_code );
```

continued...

...from previous page

```
        fprintf( stderr, "Resource ID of failed request: %ld on display %s.\n",
                theErrorEvent->resourceid,
                DisplayString( theDisplay ) );

}       /* -- function errorHandler */


/*
**      fatalErrorHandler takes care of fatal X errors, like a broken
**      connection to the X server.  If this routine does not exit,
**      and returns, the XLib will exit anyway.  Thus, in this function
**      you need to save all important data and get ready for a fatal
**      termination.  Note: Do not call Xlib routines from a
**      fatal X error handler.
**
**      This function is registered with X by use of the XSetIOErrorHandler
**      Xlib function.
**
*/

fatalErrorHandler( theDisplay )

Display         *theDisplay;

{       /* -- function fatalErrorHandler */

        fprintf( stderr, "X Error: Fatal IO error on display %s.\n",
                DisplayString( theDisplay ) );

        fprintf( stderr, "Bailing out near line one.\n" );

        /*
        **      Put any clean -up code here.
        **
        */


        /*
        **      Thus terminates another program
        */

        exit( 1 );

}       /* -- function fatalErrorHandler */
```

The contents of the C source file `eventx.c` are as follows:

```
/*
**      eventx.c
**
**      Contains the event loop (where the major action of most
**      X-based programs occurs).
**
*/

#include   <X11/Xlib.h>
#include   <X11/Xutil.h>

#include   "drawapp.h"

extern  Display         *theDisplay;

/*
**      Under X, a window will never receive an event that it
**      hasn't asked for.  The way to ask for events is to set up
**      a mask indicating those events for which your window is
**      interested in. This mask is then passed to XSelectInput
**      along with a window id and a display pointer.
*/

#define EV_MASK (ButtonPressMask          | \
                KeyPressMask              | \
                ExposureMask              | \
                StructureNotifyMask)

/*
**      eventLoop blocks awaiting an event from X.
**
*/


eventLoop()

{       /* -- function eventLoop */
        XEvent          theEvent;

        /*
        **      Block on input, awaiting an event from X
        */

        XNextEvent( theDisplay, &theEvent );

        /*
        **      Decode the event and call a specific routine to
        **      handle it
        */
```

continued...

...from previous page

```
	switch( theEvent.type )
		{
		/*
		**	Part or all of the Window has been exposed to the
		**	world, or the window is mapped, or its size has
		**	changed.
		*/
		case ConfigureNotify:
		case Expose:
		case MapNotify:
			processExpose( &theEvent );
			break;
		/*
		**	A Mouse button has been pressed.
		*/
		case ButtonPress:
			return( processButton( &theEvent ) );
			break;

		/*
		**	A Mouse button has been pressed, then
		**	released.
		*/
		case ButtonRelease:
			processRelease( &theEvent );
			break;

		case MotionNotify:
			processMotion( &theEvent );
			break;

		/*
		**	A key on the keyboard was hit.
		*/
		case KeyPress:
			return( processKeyPress( &theEvent ) );
			break;
		}

	/*
	**	Return a 0 to quit, a 1 to keep going
	*/
	return( 1 );

}	/* -- function eventLoop */
```

continued...

...from previous page

```
/*
**      initEvents
**      Selects input for the given window, with the default
**      event mask, or if the window is part of the palette,
**      it uses an event mask that does not ask for mouse
**      pointer MotionNotify events.
**
*/

initEvents( theWindow, inPalette )

Window  theWindow;
int     inPalette;

{       /* -- function initEvents */

        if ( inPalette == IN_PALETTE )
                {
                XSelectInput( theDisplay,
                        theWindow,
                        EV_MASK );
                }
        else
                {
                XSelectInput( theDisplay,
                        theWindow,
                        ( EV_MASK | ButtonMotionMask | ButtonReleaseMask ) );
                        /* ( EV_MASK | PointerMotionMask ) ); */
                }

}       /* -- function initEvents */

/*
**      end of file eventx.c
*/
```

The contents of the C source file `filex.c` are as follows:

```
/*
**      filex.c
**
**      DrawApp application file routines.
**
*/

#include   <X11/Xlib.h>
#include   <X11/Xutil.h>
#include   <stdio.h>

#include   "drawapp.h"


/*
**      The Current file name for saving
*/
char    theCurrentFileName[ 120 ];
/*
**      External GLOBALS
*/
extern  char            theDrawName[ MAX_TEXT_LENGTH + 5 ];

extern  Display         *theDisplay;
extern  Window          theRootWindow;
extern  Window          theBorderWindow;
extern  Window          theDrawWindow;
extern  Pixmap          theDrawPixmap;
extern  Pixmap          theUndoPixmap;
extern  GC              theBlackPixGC;
extern  GC              theWhitePixGC;
extern  GC              theUndoPixGC;
extern  in              theDrawWidth, theDrawHeight;
extern  unsigned long   theBlackPixel;   /* -- System black color */
extern  unsigned long   theWhitePixel;   /* -- System White color */
extern  int             theDrawingCommand;


/*
**      loadFile loads in a standard bitmap ASCII file and
**      places the contents, if successful, into the Pixmap
**      theDrawPixmap.
*/

loadFile( theFileName )

char    theFileName[];
```

continued...

...from previous page

```
{       /* -- function loadFile */
        Pixmap  tempPixmap;
        int     status;
        int     width, height;
        int     xHotSpot, yHotSpot;
        char    theName[ MAX_TEXT_LENGTH + 5 ];

        /*
        **      Compile with -DDEBUG while first testing this program.
        */
#ifdef DEBUG
printf( "Reading in file %s\n", theFileName );
#endif

        status = XReadBitmapFile( theDisplay,
                theRootWindow,
                theFileName,
                &width, &height,
                &tempPixmap,
                &xHotSpot, &yHotSpot );

        if ( status == BitmapSuccess )
                {
                /*
                **      Save new name
                */
                strcpy( theName, theDrawName );

                if ( ( strlen( theName ) + strlen ( theFileName ) )
                   < MAX_TEXT_LENGTH )
                        {
                        strcat( theName, ":" );
                        strcat( theName, theFileName );
                        }

                XStoreName( theDisplay,
                        theBorderWindow,
                        theName );

                /*
                **      Destroy old drawing pixmap
                */
                freePixmaps();

                /*
                **      Assign the new pixmap
                */
                theDrawWidth   = width;
                theDrawHeight  = height;
```

continued...

...from previous page

```
		initPixmaps();
		copyPixmap( tempPixmap, theDrawPixmap, theBlackPixGC,
			theDrawWidth, theDrawHeight );

		copyPixmap( tempPixmap, theUndoPixmap, theUndoPixGC,
			theDrawWidth, theDrawHeight );

		/*
		**	Free up temp pixmap storage
		*/
		XFreePixmap( theDisplay, tempPixmap );


		/*
		**	Modify Draw Window
		*/
		XResizeWindow( theDisplay,
			theDrawWindow,
			theDrawWidth,
			theDrawHeight );

		/*
		**	Display the Pixmap in theDrawWindow
		*/
		refreshDrawWindow();
		}
	else
		{
		fprintf( stderr, "ERROR: Could not load file %s.\n",
				theFileName );
		}

	/*
	**	store file name
	*/
	setFileName( theFileName );

}	/* -- function loadFile */


/*
**	saveCurrentFile saves the current file to disk
*/

saveCurrentFile()

{	/* -- function saveCurrentFile */
```

continued...

...from previous page

```
        /*
        **      Set all cursors to the watch cursor,
        **      to reflect the disk operation.
        */
        makeAllBusyCursor();
        XFlush( theDisplay );

        /*
        **      Save the file
        */
        saveFile( theCurrentFileName );

        /*
        **      Restore all cursors
        */
        associateCursors( theDrawingCommand );

}       /* -- function saveCurrentFile */


/*
**      saveFile saves the current pixmap to the given file name
**
*/

saveFile( theFileName )

char    theFileName[];

{       /* -- function saveFile */
        int     status;

        status = XWriteBitmapFile( theDisplay,
                                theFileName,
                                theDrawPixmap,
                                theDrawWidth,
                                theDrawHeight,
                                (-1), (-1) );   /* -- Hot spots for cursors */

        if ( status != BitmapSuccess )
                {
                fprintf( stderr, "ERROR: Could not save file %s.\n",
                                theFileName );
                }

        XFlush( theDisplay );

}       /* -- function saveFile */
```

continued...

...from previous page

```
/*
**      setFileName stores the file name for later saves.
*/

setFileName( theFileName )

char    theFileName[];

{       /* -- function setFileName */

        if ( strlen( theFileName ) < 110 )
                {
                strcpy( theCurrentFileName, theFileName );
                }

}       /* -- function setFileName */

/*
**      end of file
*/
```

The contents of the C source file `initx.c` are as follows:

```
/*
**      initx.c
**
**      Initialization code to talk to the X server
**
*/

#include  <X11/Xlib.h>
#include  <X11/Xutil.h>
#include  <X11/cursorfont.h>

#include  <stdio.h>

/*
**      Program-wide Globals.
**
*/

Display         *theDisplay;     /* -- Which display               */
int             theScreen;       /* -- Which screen on the display */
int             theDepth;        /* -- Number of color planes      */
unsigned long   theBlackPixel;   /* -- System "Black" color        */
unsigned long   theWhitePixel;   /* -- System "White" color        */
Window          theRootWindow;   /* -- System-wide parent window   */
```

continued...

...from previous page

```
/*
**      initX
**      Sets up the connection to the X server and stores information
**      about the environment.
**
*/

initX( theDisplayName )

char    *theDisplayName;

{       /* -- function initX  */

        /*
        **      1) Establish a connection to the X Server.
        **
        */

        theDisplay = XOpenDisplay( theDisplayName );

        /* -- Check if the connection was made */
        if ( theDisplay == NULL )
                {
                fprintf( stderr,
                   "ERROR: Cannot establish a connection to the X Server %s\n",
                   XDisplayName( theDisplayName ) );
                exit( 1 );
                }

        /*
        **      2) Check for the default screen and color plane depth.
        **      If theDepth == 1, then we have a monochrome system.
        **
        */

        theScreen      = DefaultScreen( theDisplay );
        theDepth       = DefaultDepth( theDisplay, theScreen );
        theBlackPixel = BlackPixel( theDisplay, theScreen );
        theWhitePixel = WhitePixel( theDisplay, theScreen );
        theRootWindow = RootWindow( theDisplay, theScreen );

}       /* -- function initX  */

/*
**      end of file initx.c
**
*/
```

The contents of the C source file `keyx.c` are as follows:

```
/*
**      keyx.c
**
**      Handles keyboard events for the example X programs.
**
*/


#include  <X11/Xlib.h>
#include  <X11/Xutil.h>
#include  <X11/keysym.h>
#include  <X11/keysymdef.h>

#include  "drawapp.h"

extern  Display         *theDisplay;
extern  int             theDrawingCommand;
extern  int             theDrawingColor;
extern  int             theDrawingMode;
extern  char            theDrawingText[ MAX_TEXT_LENGTH + 5 ];
extern  int             theDrawX, theDrawY;

extern  GC              theBlackGC;
extern  GC              theWhiteGC;
extern  GC              theBlackPixGC;
extern  GC              theWhitePixGC;
extern  Window          theLineWindow;
extern  Window          theRectWindow;
extern  Window          theFilledRectWindow;
extern  Window          thePointWindow;
extern  Window          theOvalWindow;
extern  Window          theUndoWindow;
extern  Window          theText1Window;

/*
**      processKeyPress handles the keyboard input for the
**      example X programs.
**
**      Note that it is passed a pointer to an XKeyEvent structure,
**      even though the event was originally placed in an XEvent union
**      structure.  X overlays the various structure types into
**      a union of structures.  By using the XKeyEvent, we can access
**      the keyboard elements more easily.
**
*/

processKeyPress( theEvent )

XKeyEvent       *theEvent;
```

continued...

...from previous page

```
{       /* -- function processKeyPress */
        int             length, l;
        int             theKeyBufferMaxLen = 64;
        char            theKeyBuffer[ 65 ];
        KeySym          theKeySym;
        XComposeStatus  theComposeStatus;

        length = XLookupString( theEvent,
                        theKeyBuffer,
                        theKeyBufferMaxLen,
                        &theKeySym,
                        &theComposeStatus );

        /*
        **      Check for META keys.  Many programs use keyboard
        **      shortcuts for menu choices.  DrawApp Meta Keys include:
        **      Meta-F  Fill Rectangles
        **      Meta-L  Draw Lines
        **      Meta-O  Draw Ovals
        **      Meta-P  Draw Points
        **      Meta-Q  Quit
        **      Meta-R  Draw Rectangles
        **      Meta-S  Save
        **      Meta-T  Draw Text in font 1
        **      Meta-U  Undo
        **
        */

        if ( theEvent->state & Mod1Mask )       /* -- META Keys */
                {
                switch( theKeyBuffer[ 0 ] )
                        {
                        case  'F': /* -- Fill rectangles */
                        case  'f': restoreXorItem();
                                highlightChoice( theFilledRectWindow );
                                theDrawingCommand = DRAW_FILLED_RECT;
                                theDrawingMode    = DRAWING_OFF;
                                setCmdCursor( theDrawingCommand, FIRST_POINT );
                                break;
                        case  'L': /* -- Draw Lines       */
                        case  'l': restoreXorItem();
                                highlightChoice( theLineWindow );
                                theDrawingCommand = DRAW_LINE;
                                theDrawingMode    = DRAWING_OFF;
                                setCmdCursor( theDrawingCommand, FIRST_POINT );
                                break;
                        case  'O': /* -- Draw ovals       */
                        case  'o': restoreXorItem();
                                highlightChoice( theOvalWindow );
                                theDrawingCommand = DRAW_OVAL;
```

continued...

...from previous page

```
                    theDrawingMode     = DRAWING_OFF;
                    setCmdCursor( theDrawingCommand, FIRST_POINT );
                    break;
            case  'P': /* -- Draw Points      */
            case  'p': restoreXorItem();
                    highlightChoice( thePointWindow );
                    theDrawingCommand = DRAW_POINT;
                    theDrawingMode     = DRAWING_OFF;
                    setCmdCursor( theDrawingCommand, FIRST_POINT );
                    break;
            case  'Q' :
            case  'q' :
                    return( 0 );
                    break;
            case  'R': /* -- Draw rectangles */
            case  'r': restoreXorItem();
                    highlightChoice( theRectWindow );
                    theDrawingCommand = DRAW_RECT;
                    theDrawingMode     = DRAWING_OFF;
                    setCmdCursor( theDrawingCommand, FIRST_POINT );
                    break;
            case  's': /* -- Save file */
            case  'S': saveCurrentFile();
                    break;
            case  'T': /* -- Draw text in font 1 */
            case  't': restoreXorItem();
                    associateFont( theBlackGC, TEXT1_FONT );
                    associateFont( theWhiteGC, TEXT1_FONT );
                    associateFont( theBlackPixGC, TEXT1_FONT );
                    associateFont( theWhitePixGC, TEXT1_FONT );
                    highlightChoice( theText1Window );
                    theDrawingCommand = DRAW_TEXT1;
                    theDrawingMode     = DRAWING_OFF;
                    setCmdCursor( theDrawingCommand, FIRST_POINT );
                    break;
            }
    return( 1 );
    }

/*
**      Check if theKeySym is within the standard ASCII
**      printable character range.
**
*/
```

continued...

...from previous page

```
        if ( ( theKeySym >= ' ' ) &&      /* -- ASCII 32 is a space  */
           ( theKeySym <= '~' )  &&      /* -- ASCII 126 is a Tilde */
           ( length > 0 ) )              /* -- We have char input   */
                {
                if ( ( theDrawingCommand == DRAW_TEXT1 ) ||
                    ( theDrawingCommand == DRAW_TEXT2 ) )
                        {
                        if ( ( strlen( theDrawingText ) +
                            strlen( theKeyBuffer ) ) < MAX_TEXT_LENGTH )
                                {
                                /*
                                **      save current display for undo
                                */
                                maintainUndo();

                                strncat( theDrawingText,
                                        theKeyBuffer,
                                        length );
                                drawItem( theDrawingCommand, theDrawingColor,
                                        theDrawX, theDrawY,
                                        0, 0, theDrawingText );
                                }
                        }
                }
        else
                {
                /*
                **      Check for special keys on the keyboard.
                **      there are many more definitions in the header
                **      file keysymdef.h (probably in /usr/include/X11).
                **
                */
                switch( theKeySym )
                        {
                        /*
                        **      The BackSpace and the Delete key operate
                        **      the same in this program, and they take
                        **      advantage of the fact that we are using
                        **      XDrawString to draw the text (XDrawImageString
                        **      would work differently).  The method is
                        **      as follows:  first, draw the text string
                        **      over again in the opposite color (wiping
                        **      it out).  Then, redraw the text string
                        **      in the normal color, so that only the
                        **      last character is wiped out.  This can
                        **      still leave some pixel "droppings," but
                        **      works in general.
                        */
```

continued...

...from previous page

```
case XK_BackSpace:
case XK_Delete   :
        /*
        **      save current display for undo
        */
        maintainUndo();

        l = strlen( theDrawingText );

        if ( l >= 1 )
                {
                if ( theDrawingColor == BLACK )
                        {
                        drawItem( theDrawingCommand,
                                  WHITE,
                                  theDrawX, theDrawY,
                                  0, 0,
                                  theDrawingText );
                        }
                else
                        {
                        drawItem( theDrawingCommand,
                                  BLACK,
                                  theDrawX, theDrawY,
                                  0, 0,
                                  theDrawingText );
                        }
                l--;
                theDrawingText[ l ] = '\0';
                drawItem( theDrawingCommand,
                          theDrawingColor,
                          theDrawX, theDrawY,
                          0, 0,
                          theDrawingText );
                XFlush( theDisplay );
                }
        break;
/*
**      Keypad Keys
*/
case XK_KP_Equal :
case XK_KP_Multiply:
case XK_KP_Add    :
case XK_KP_Subtract:
case XK_KP_Decimal:
case XK_KP_Divide:
case XK_KP_0      :
case XK_KP_1      :
case XK_KP_2      :
case XK_KP_3      :
```

continued...

...from previous page

```
                        case XK_KP_4     :
                        case XK_KP_5     :
                        case XK_KP_6     :
                        case XK_KP_7     :
                        case XK_KP_8     :
                        case XK_KP_9     :
                                if ( ( length > 0 ) &&
                                  ( ( theDrawingCommand == DRAW_TEXT1 ) ||
                                  ( theDrawingCommand == DRAW_TEXT2 ) ) )
                                        {
                                        if ( ( strlen( theDrawingText ) +
                                          strlen( theKeyBuffer ) )
                                          < MAX_TEXT_LENGTH )
                                                {
                                                strcat( theDrawingText,
                                                        theKeyBuffer );
                                                drawItem( theDrawingCommand,
                                                        theDrawingColor,
                                                        theDrawX, theDrawY,
                                                        0, 0,
                                                        theDrawingText );
                                                }
                                        }
                                break;
                        default          : ;
                        }
                }

        return( 1 );    /* -- continue processing */

}       /* -- function processKeyPress */


/*
**      end of file keyx.c
**
*/
```

The contents of the C source file `mainx.c` are as follows:

```
/*
**      mainx.c
**      DrawApp application main function.
**
*/

#include   <X11/Xlib.h>
#include   <X11/Xutil.h>

/*
**      external GLOBALS
*/

extern  Display         *theDisplay;

main( argc, argv )

int     argc;
char    *argv[];

{
        int             iconicState;
        int             fileSuccess;
        char            theDisplayName[ 120 ];
        char            theGeometry[ 120 ];
        char            theTitle[ 120 ];
        char            theFont1Name[ 120 ];
        char            theFont2Name[ 120 ];
        char            theFileName[ 120 ];

        /*
        **      1) Parse the command line parameters
        */
        iconicState = getArguments( argc, argv,
                                theDisplayName,
                                theGeometry,
                                theFont1Name,
                                theFont2Name,
                                theTitle,
                                &fileSuccess,
                                theFileName );
        /*
        **      2) Set up our connection to X
        */

        initX( theDisplayName );
```

continued...

...from previous page

```
        /*
        **      3) Initialize application-specific variables
        */
        setErrorHandlers();
        initCursors();
        initFonts( theFont1Name, theFont2Name );
        initPixmaps();
        initIconPixmap();

        /*
        **      4) Open application windows
        */

        initWindows( theGeometry,
                     theTitle,
                     iconicState );

        /*
        **      5) Load up bitmap file and set up pixmaps
        */
        if ( fileSuccess == 1 )
                {
                loadFile( theFileName );
                }
        else
                {
                setFileName( "drawapp.tmp" );
                }

        XFlush( theDisplay );

        /*
        **      6) Handle events
        */

        while( eventLoop() );

        /*
        **      7) Close the connection to the X server.
        */

        quitX();

}


/*
**      end of file.
*/
```

The contents of the C source file `mousex.c` are as follows:

```
/*
**      mousex.c
**
**      Mouse pointer routines for the DrawApp application.
**
*/

#include   <X11/Xlib.h>
#include   <X11/Xutil.h>

/*
**      findMouse gets the current mouse coords in global
**      coordinates.
**
*/

findMouse( displayPtr, x, y )

Display *displayPtr;
int     *x, *y;

{       /* -- function findMouse */
        Window          wRoot, wChild;
        int             wX, wY, rootX, rootY, status;
        unsigned int    wButtons;

        status = XQueryPointer( displayPtr,
                RootWindow( displayPtr, DefaultScreen( displayPtr ) ),
                &wRoot,
                &wChild,
                &rootX, &rootY,
                &wX, &wY,
                &wButtons );

        if ( status == True )
                {
                *x = wX;
                *y = wY;
                }
        else
                {
                *x = 0;
                *y = 0;
                }

}       /* -- function findMouse */
```

The contents of the C source file **pixmapx.c** are as follows:

```
/*
**      pixmapx.c
**
**      Pixmap routines
**
*/

#include  <X11/Xlib.h>
#include  <X11/Xutil.h>

/*
**      The bitmap file "theIcon" is a file made with the DrawApp
**      application (this program).  You can use it, or the X11
**      standard application bitmap to create your own icon, so long
**      as you name the file "theIcon".
**
*/

#include  "theIcon"

/*
**      Program-wide Globals.
**
*/

extern  Display         *theDisplay;     /* -- Which display             */
extern  Window          theRootWindow;   /* -- System-wide parent window  */
extern  Window          theDrawWindow;
extern  GC              theBlackGC;
extern  int             theDrawWidth, theDrawHeight;
extern  unsigned long   theBlackPixel;   /* -- System "Black" color       */
extern  unsigned long   theWhitePixel;   /* -- System "White" color       */
extern  int             theDrawingCommand;


/*
**      Pixmap GLOBALS
*/

Pixmap          theIconPixmap;          /* -- Icon pixmap for windows       */
Pixmap          theDrawPixmap;          /* -- Pixmap for drawing            */
GC              theBlackPixGC;          /* -- GC for drawing into theDrawPix */
GC              theWhitePixGC;          /* -- GC for drawing into theDrawPix */

Pixmap          theUndoPixmap;          /* -- Pixmap for undoing            */
GC              theUndoPixGC;           /* -- GC for undoing                */
```

continued...

...from previous page

```
/*
**      initPixmaps initializes the pixmaps used in the DrawApp
**      application
**
*/

initPixmaps()

{       /* -- function initPixmaps */

        theDrawPixmap = XCreatePixmap( theDisplay,
                                theRootWindow,
                                theDrawWidth,
                                theDrawHeight,
                                1 );

        createGC( theDrawPixmap,
                &theBlackPixGC );
        createGC( theDrawPixmap,
                &theWhitePixGC );
        XSetForeground( theDisplay,
                theWhitePixGC,
                theWhitePixel );

        /*
        **      Undo pixmap
        */
        theUndoPixmap = XCreatePixmap( theDisplay,
                                theRootWindow,
                                theDrawWidth,
                                theDrawHeight,
                                1 );

        createGC( theUndoPixmap,
                &theUndoPixGC );


        XFlush( theDisplay );

}       /* -- function initPixmaps */

/*
**      freePixmaps cleans up all system pixmap
**      resources.
*/

freePixmaps()
```

continued...

...from previous page

```
{       /* -- function freePixmaps */

        XFreePixmap( theDisplay, theUndoPixmap );
        XFreePixmap( theDisplay, theDrawPixmap );
        XFreeGC( theDisplay, theBlackPixGC );
        XFreeGC( theDisplay, theWhitePixGC );
        XFreeGC( theDisplay, theUndoPixGC );

        XFlush( theDisplay );

}       /* -- function freePixmaps */

/*
**      freeIconPixmap frees the iconic pixmap
**
*/


freeIconPixmap()


{       /* -- function freeIconPixmap */

        XFreePixmap( theDisplay, theIconPixmap );

}       /* -- function freeIconPixmap */


/*
**      initIconPixmap initializes the DrawApp's iconic pixmap
**
*/

initIconPixmap()

{       /* -- function initIconPixmap */

        theIconPixmap = XCreateBitmapFromData( theDisplay,
                              theRootWindow,
                              theIcon_bits,
                              theIcon_width,
                              theIcon_height );

}       /* -- function initIconPixmap */



/*
**      refreshDrawWindow refreshes the picture in the draw window.
**
*/
```

continued...

...from previous page

```
refreshDrawWindow()

{       /* -- function refreshDrawWindow */

        XClearWindow( theDisplay, theDrawWindow );

        copyPixmap( theDrawPixmap,
                theDrawWindow,
                theBlackGC,
                theDrawWidth, theDrawHeight );

        XFlush( theDisplay );

}       /* -- function refreshDrawWindow */

/*
**      wipeOutPix clears out the current pixmap and
**      window, to destroy the picture that is being
**      edited.
*/

wipeOutPix()

{       /* -- function wipeOutPix */

        makeAllBusyCursor();
        XFlush( theDisplay );

        fillRectangle( theDrawPixmap,
                theWhitePixGC,
                0, 0,
                theDrawWidth, theDrawHeight );

        XClearWindow( theDisplay,
                theDrawWindow );

        /*
        **      Restore cursors
        */
        associateCursors( theDrawingCommand );

        XFlush( theDisplay );

}       /* -- function wipeOutPix */

/*
**      Copies the contents of one pixmap (or window) into another,
**      used for the undo routines.
**
*/
```

continued...

...from previous page

```
copyPixmap( srcPixmap, destPixmap, destGC, width, height )

Drawable        srcPixmap;
Drawable        destPixmap;
GC              destGC;
unsigned int    width, height;

{       /* -- function copyPixmap */


        /*
        **      XCopyArea would work on a monochrome
        **      system, but not a color system.
        */
        XCopyPlane( theDisplay,
                srcPixmap,
                destPixmap,
                destGC,
                0, 0,           /* -- X, Y */
                width, height,
                0, 0,
                0x01 );         /* -- Plane */

        XFlush( theDisplay );

}       /* -- function copyPixmap */



/*
**      undo undoes the draw display back to the last-saved
**      pixmap (which is maintained by the maintainUndo() function).
**
*/

undo()

{       /* -- function undo */

        copyPixmap( theUndoPixmap, theDrawPixmap, theBlackPixGC,
                        theDrawWidth, theDrawHeight );

        refreshDrawWindow();

}       /* -- function undo */
```

continued...

...from previous page

```
/*
**      maintainUndo saves a copy of the current pixmap so that
**      any drawing operations can be undone.
**
*/

maintainUndo()

{       /* -- function maintainUndo */

        copyPixmap( theDrawPixmap,       /* -- Source */
                    theUndoPixmap,       /* -- Dest   */
                    theUndoPixGC,
                    theDrawWidth,
                    theDrawHeight );

}       /* -- function maintainUndo */


/*
**      end of file
**
*/
```

The contents of the C source file `quitx.c` are as follows:

```
/*
**      quitx.c
**
**      routines to close down X
**
*/

#include  <X11/Xlib.h>

extern  Display         *theDisplay;


/*
**      quitX()
**
**      closes the connection to the X server
**
*/

quitX()
```

continued...

...from previous page

```
{       /* -- function quitX  */

        /*
        **      destroy all GC's and windows
        */
        freeWindowsAndGCs();

        /*
        **      Free all cursors
        */
        freeCursors();

        /*
        **      Free all pixmaps
        */
        freePixmaps();
        freeIconPixmap();

        /*
        **      Free all fonts
        */
        freeFonts();

        XFlush( theDisplay );

        XCloseDisplay( theDisplay );

}       /* -- function quitX  */

/*
**      end of file quitx.c
**
*/
```

The contents of the C source file `textx.c` are as follows:

```
/*
**      textx.c
**
**      Text font routines for the DrawApp application.
**
**      Routines:
**              associateFont   Associates a GC with a font.
**              freeFonts       Frees all DrawApp fonts.
**              initFonts       Initializes the DrawApp fonts
**
**
*/

#include    <X11/Xlib.h>

#include    "drawapp.h"

/*
**      Font GLOBALS
*/

XFontStruct     *theText1Font;
XFontStruct     *theText2Font;

/*
**      GLOBAL display
*/

extern  Display         *theDisplay;


/*
**      associateFont associates (sets) the given GC to use one
**      of the two fonts for the DrawApp applicvation.
**
*/

associateFont( theGC, whichFont )

GC      theGC;
int     whichFont;

{       /* -- function associateFont */

        if ( whichFont == TEXT1_FONT )
                {
                XSetFont( theDisplay,
                        theGC,
                        theText1Font->fid );
                }
        else
                {
```

continued...

...from previous page

```
                XSetFont( theDisplay,
                        theGC,
                        theText2Font->fid );
                }

}       /* -- function associateFont */



/*
**      freeFonts frees up the font resources used by the DrawApp
**      application.
*/

freeFonts()

{       /* -- function freeFonts */

        XFreeFont( theDisplay, theText1Font );
        XFreeFont( theDisplay, theText2Font );

}       /* -- function freeFonts */



/*
**      initFonts()
**
**      Loads in the given fonts into the vars theTExt1Font and
**      theText2Font.
**
*/

initFonts( font1Name, font2Name )

char    font1Name[];
char    font2Name[];

{       /* -- function initFont */

        theText1Font  = XLoadQueryFont( theDisplay, font1Name );
        theText2Font  = XLoadQueryFont( theDisplay, font2Name );

}       /* -- function initFont */


/*
**      textHeight returns the max height of the tallest characters
**      in the given font.
*/
```

continued...

...from previous page

```
textHeight( whichFont )

int     whichFont;

{       /* -- function textHeight */
        int     theHeight;

        if ( whichFont == TEXT1_FONT )
                {
                theHeight = theText1Font->ascent +
                                theText1Font->descent;
                }
        else
                {
                theHeight = theText2Font->ascent +
                                theText2Font->descent;
                }

        return( theHeight );
}       /* -- function textHeight */



/*
**      textWidth returns the width of the given string in the
**      given font.
*/

textWidth( theString, whichFont )

char    theString[];
int     whichFont;

{       /* -- function textWidth */
        int     theLength;

        if ( whichFont == TEXT1_FONT )
                {
                theLength = XTextWidth( theText1Font,
                        theString,
                        strlen( theString ) );
                }
        else
                {
                theLength = XTextWidth( theText2Font,
                        theString,
                        strlen( theString ) );
                }

        return( theLength );
```

continued...

...from previous page

```
}       /* -- function textWidth */



/*
**      end of file textx.c
*/
```

The contents of the C source file `windowx.c` are as follows:

```
/*
**      windowx.c
**
**      Window opening routine
**
*/

#include  <X11/Xlib.h>
#include  <X11/Xutil.h>
#include  <stdio.h>

#include  "drawapp.h"

/*
**      Program-wide Globals.
**
*/

extern  Display         *theDisplay;     /* -- Which display              */
extern  int             theScreen;       /* -- Which screen on the display */
extern  int             theDepth;        /* -- Number of color planes     */
extern  unsigned long   theBlackPixel;   /* -- System "Black" color       */
extern  unsigned long   theWhitePixel;   /* -- System "White" color       */
extern  Pixmap          theIconPixmap;   /* -- Icon pixmap for windows    */


#define         BORDER_WIDTH    2

/*
**      openWindow
**
**      This function takes a x, y pixel location for the upper
**      left corner of the window, as well as a width and height
**      for the size of the window.
**      It opens a window on the X display, and returns the window
**      id. It is also passed a flag that specifies whether the
**      window is to be a pop-up window (such as a menu) or
```

continued...

...from previous page

```
**      not.  This initial version does not implement that feature.
**      The GC theNewGC is a graphics context that is created for the
**      window, and returned to the caller.  The GC is necessary for
**      drawing into the window.
**
**      1) Set up the attributes desired for the window.
**      2) Open a window on the display.
**      3) Send "Hints" to the Window Manager.
**      4) Store the Window, Icon and Class Names with the X Server.
**      5) Now tell the window manager about the size and location.
**      6) Create a graphics context for the window.
**      7) Ask X to place the window visibly on the screen.
**      8) Flush out all the queued up X requests to the X server
**
*/


Window
openWindow( x, y, width, height, flag, theTitle, iconicState, theParent,
theNewGC )


int     x, y;           /* -- Where the window should go        */
int     width, height;  /* -- Size of the window                */
int     flag;           /* -- if > 0 then the window is a pop-up */
char    theTitle[];     /* -- Title for Window                  */
int     iconicState;    /* -- == 1 if start as icon, ==0 if not  */
Window  theParent;      /* -- Parent Window of the new window   */
GC      *theNewGC;      /* -- Returned Graphics Context         */


{       /* -- function openWindow */
        XSetWindowAttributes    theWindowAttributes;
        XSizeHints              theSizeHints;
        unsigned long           theWindowMask;
        Window                  theNewWindow;
        XWMHints                theWMHints;
        XClassHint              theClassHint;

        /*
        **      1) Set up the attributes desired for the window.
        **      Note that window managers may deny us some of
        **      these resources.
        **
        */

        theWindowAttributes.border_pixel      = theBlackPixel;
        theWindowAttributes.background_pixel  = theWhitePixel;
```

continued...

...from previous page

```
	if ( flag == POP_UP_WINDOW )
		{
		theWindowAttributes.override_redirect = True;
		theWindowAttributes.save_under        = True;
		theWindowMask = ( CWBackPixel        |
		                  CWBorderPixel      |
		                  CWSaveUnder        |
		                  CWOverrideRedirect );
		}
	else
		{
		theWindowMask = CWBackPixel   | CWBorderPixel;
		}


	/*
	**	2) Open a window on the display.
	**
	*/

	theNewWindow = XCreateWindow( theDisplay,
				theParent,
				x, y,
				width, height,
				BORDER_WIDTH,
				theDepth,
				InputOutput,
				CopyFromParent,
				theWindowMask,
				&theWindowAttributes );

	/*
	**	3) Send "Hints" to the Window Manager.
	**	Before this window will appear on the display,
	**	an X window manager may intecept the call and
	**	place the window where it wants to.  This next section
	**	tells the window manager "hints" as to where the
	**	window should go.
	**
	*/
	if ( iconicState == NORMAL_STATE )
		{
		theWMHints.initial_state = NormalState;
		}
	else
		{
		/*
```

continued...

...from previous page

```
        **      Not all window managers will support an iconic
        **      initial state -- or even icons at all, but at
        **      least we tried.
        */
        theWMHints.initial_state = IconicState;
        }

theWMHints.icon_pixmap   = theIconPixmap;
theWMHints.flags         = IconPixmapHint | StateHint;

XSetWMHints( theDisplay, theNewWindow, &theWMHints );



/*
**      4) Store the Window, Icon and Class Names with the X Server.
*/

XStoreName( theDisplay, theNewWindow, theTitle );
XSetIconName( theDisplay, theNewWindow, RES_NAME );

theClassHint.res_name  = RES_NAME;
theClassHint.res_class = RES_CLASS;

XSetClassHint( theDisplay, theNewWindow, &theClassHint );

/*
**      5) Now tell the window manager about the size and location.
**      we want for our windows.  USPosition means we are
**      stating the User choose the position, same with the
**      size.  PPosition and PSize would mean that the program
**      choose the size.
**
*/

theSizeHints.flags      = USPosition | USSize;
theSizeHints.x          = x;
theSizeHints.y          = y;
theSizeHints.width      = width;
theSizeHints.height     = height;

XSetNormalHints( theDisplay, theNewWindow, &theSizeHints );


/*
**      6) Create a graphics context for the window.
**
*/
```

continued...

...from previous page

```
        if ( createGC( theNewWindow, theNewGC ) == 0 )
                {
                XDestroyWindow( theDisplay, theNewWindow );
                return( (Window) 0 );
                }


        /*
        **      7) Ask X to place the window visibly on the screen.
        **      Up to now, the window has been created but has not
        **      appeared on the screen. Mapping the window places it
        **      visibly on the screen.
        **
        */

        XMapWindow( theDisplay, theNewWindow );

        /*
        **      8) Flush out all the queued up X requests to the X server
        **
        */

        XFlush( theDisplay );

        /*
        **      9) Return the window ID, which is needed to specify
        **      which window to draw to.
        **
        */

        return( theNewWindow );

}       /* -- function openWindow */



/*
**      createGC creates a graphics context for the given window.
**      A graphics context is necessary to draw into the window.
**
**      Returns 0 if there was an error, 1 if all is A-OK.
**
*/

createGC( theNewWindow, theNewGC )

Drawable        theNewWindow;   /* -- NOTE: Now a Drawable, not a window */
GC              *theNewGC;
```

continued...

...from previous page

```
{       /* -- function createGC */
        XGCValues        theGCValues;

        *theNewGC = XCreateGC( theDisplay,
                        theNewWindow,
                        (unsigned long) 0,
                        &theGCValues );

        if ( *theNewGC == 0 )    /* -- Unable to create a GC */
                {
                return( 0 );     /* -- Error                 */
                }
        else
                {
                /* --  Set Foreground and Background defaults for the new GC */
                XSetForeground( theDisplay,
                                *theNewGC,
                                theBlackPixel );

                XSetBackground( theDisplay,
                                *theNewGC,
                                theWhitePixel );

                return( 1 );     /* -- A-OK                  */
                }

}       /* -- function createGC */

/*
**      end of file windowx.c
**
*/
```

The contents of the C source file `xor.c` are as follows:

```
/*
**      xor.c
**
**      XOR (or rubber-banding) functions.  These functions make a user
**      interface look a lot better for drawing lines and boxes.
**
*/

#include    <X11/Xlib.h>
#include    <X11/Xutil.h>


extern  Display         *theDisplay;

/*
**      xorSetUp
**      Sets up the given window with a Xor Graphics Context
*/

xorSetUp( theWindow, theXorGC )

Window  theWindow;
GC      *theXorGC;

{       /* -- function xorSetUp */

        createGC( theWindow, theXorGC );

        XSetFunction( theDisplay,
                *theXorGC,
                GXxor );


        XFlush( theDisplay );

}       /* -- function xorSetUp */



/*
**      Frees up the Graphics Context storage in the server.
**
*/

xorShutDown( theXorGC )

GC      theXorGC;

{       /* -- function xorShutDown */

        XFreeGC( theDisplay, theXorGC );

}       /* -- function xorShutDown */
```

The contents of the Makefile are as follows:

```
##      X Project Makefile for DrawApp Application
##
EXEC=   drawapp
##
## DEFINES
##
##
##      -g = Debugging info
##      -O = optimize (cannot use -g then)
CFLAGS= -O
##
##
##      Libraries
##      X11     X11 graphics library
##
LIBS=   -lX11
##
##
OBJECTS=        argsx.o         \
                buttonx.o       \
                cursorx.o       \
                dialogx.o       \
                drawapp.o       \
                drawitem.o      \
                drawx.o         \
                errorx.o        \
                eventx.o        \
                filex.o         \
                initx.o         \
                keyx.o          \
                mainx.o         \
                mousex.o        \
                pixmapx. o      \
                quitx.o         \
                textx.o         \
                windowx.o       \
                xor.o
##
##      Command to compile and link objects together
##
$(EXEC):        $(OBJECTS)
                cc -o $(EXEC) $(OBJECTS) $(LIBS)
##
##      Dependencies
##
```

continued...

...from previous page

```
argsx.c:        drawapp.h
buttonx.c:      drawapp.h
cursorx.c:      drawapp.h
drawapp.c:      drawapp.h
drawitem.c:     drawapp.h
textx.c:        drawapp.h
windowx.c:      drawapp.h


##
##
##      end of make file
##
```

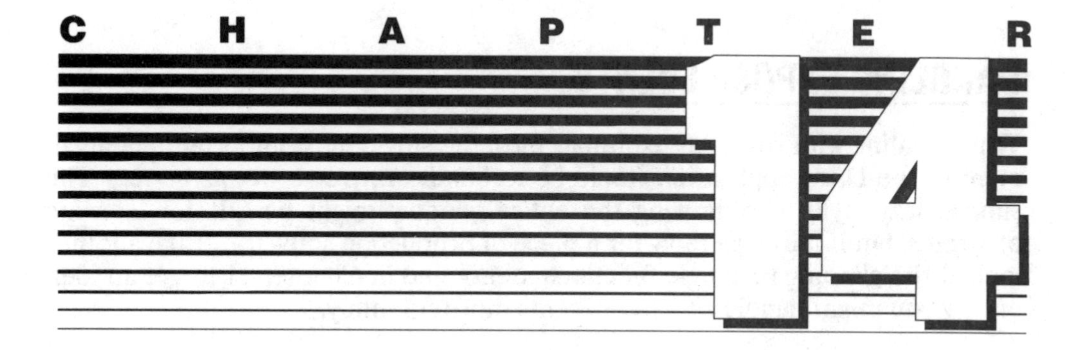

ENHANCING THE DRAW APPLICATION

The Draw application, as presented in Section II of this book, is certainly not the be-all, end-all of X application programming. The Draw application does, however, cover most of the areas of X programming that you will need for creating your own application software.

This short chapter details some enhancements that you might want to make to the Draw application to improve the program and learn more about X. The intention is to provide ideas for both the Draw application and your own software, as well as give you some pointers as to how the ideas could be implemented. This chapter does not provide a step-by-step tutorial on how to make all the enhancements discussed.

HANDLING EXPOSE EVENTS

When dealing with really large bitmap files, the single most important enhancement to the Draw application would be to handle `Expose` events better. The simple, lazy style of redrawing the entire window might be OK for learning programs, but it fails miserably for a piece of production software. Take another look at the clipping rectangle functions mentioned in Chapter 11 to get an idea of how you might handle `Expose` events more smoothly.

ENLARGEMENTS

In comparing the Draw application with the standard X client called `bitmap`, you will notice that the `bitmap` program enlarges the display of the bitmaps it edits.

The Draw application draws everything at real, or normal, size. For small bitmap files, though, editing at real size is next to impossible. (And conversely, the `bitmap` program doesn't work too well on bitmaps greater than 32-by-32 pixels.) Even with a large bitmap, it is nice to enlarge an area (an area of the user's choice) so that you can edit it better (especially for those of us who are not professional graphic designers). For example, there are CAD and electronic-publishing applications in which editing at the bitmap level is essential.

To enlarge an area, you need to know about each pixel in that area, i.e., whether the pixel is on or off. One way to get the pixels in an area is to use the function `XGetImage` to grab an area of the pixmap (remember that the entire contents of the bitmap are stored in a pixmap in the X server). Once the image is captured (into an `XImage` format image), you can use `XGetPixel` to pull out individual pixels and then draw each pixel four or more times larger (depending on how much you want to enlarge the area).

`XGetImage` looks like the following:

```
Display         *theDisplay;
XImage          *theImage;
Drawable        thePixmap;
int             x, y;
unsigned int    width, height;
unsigned long   thePlaneMask;
int             theFormat;

theImage = XGetImage( theDisplay,
                thePixmap,      /* -- could also be a window */
                x, y,
                width, height,
                thePlaneMask,
                theFormat );
```

theFormat can be either **XYPixmap** or **ZPixmap**. Normally, you will want to use **XYPixmap** because it only gets the planes that were asked for (and you are using a one-plane pixmap image). **thePlaneMask** value used here is 0x01 (in the file **pixmapx.c** in the function **copyPixmap**).

Once you have successfully grabbed the full image from the pixmap, you will then want to parse out each pixel in the image and display the pixel enlarged somehow. The enlarging is up to you (try using rectangles to start with), but to get out a single pixel value from an **XImage** structure, use **XGetPixel**:

```
XImage          *theImage;
int             x, y;
unsigned long   thePixel;

thePixel = XGetPixel( theImage, x, y );
```

Note that this is one of the few X routines that does not take a **Display** pointer as a parameter.

thePixel can then be compared with **WhitePixel** (the value returned by the **WhitePixel** macro). The Draw application is monchrome, so if **the-Pixel** does not equal **WhitePixel**, then it is **BlackPixel**.

Now, when the user draws in the enlarged area, you need to also draw those pixels into the main pixmap and window to keep the bitmap up to date.

SCROLLING

How do you edit a bitmap image larger than your available screen real estate? Many programs use some form of scroll bars, i.e., vertical and horizontal bars that allow users to "move" a small image over a large area, much like moving a magnifying glass over a page of text. The `xterm` client program, for example, can be set up with scroll bars that allow you to view text that has scrolled by (and off) the window's display area. Adding scroll bars to the Draw application would certainly improve the program.

CURSOR EDITING

X cursors can be made from bitmaps (see Chapter 8), using `XCreatePixmap-Cursor`. The only missing item in the Draw application is that cursors all need an x, y location specified as a hot spot. The Draw application, however, ignores the hot spots. The function `loadFile` (in the file `filex.c`) calls `XRead-BitmapFile` (which sends back any hot spots identified in a bitmap file) but does not use the returned hot spot in any way. Similarly, the function `saveFile` (also in `filex.c`), calls `XWriteBitmapFile`, but sends `-1` as each hot spot coordinate (for no hot spot). To be able to edit cursor shapes with the Draw application, you would need to add code to save the hot spots read in, write the hot spots back to disk, and allow the user to move and set hot spots in the drawing window.

CUTTING AND PASTING/MOVING AND COPYING AREAS

One of the most useful features of any editor is the ability to cut out areas and paste them back in somewhere else. Most Macintosh programs, for example, allow the user to cut out areas into a clipboard and to paste the clipboard's contents back in at any time to any position. The Macintosh also allows the user to copy an area (as opposed to cutting, or deleting the area out) into the clipboard. As another example, the `bitmap` client program allows the user to move areas of pixels and to copy areas as well. Whatever method you prefer, the ability to cut and paste is a handy feature. In the Draw application, using `XCopyPlane` to copy pixels onto an extra pixmap (and back) would be a start for providing cut and paste functions.

CROPPING

Cropping an image allows you to capture an arbitrary part of the image, leaving out the rest of the picture. With a picture of Godzilla for example, you might want to use cropping to trim out all the picture except for Godzilla's head or foot.

Again, the Xlib function `XCopyPlane` could provide a starting point for a cropping feature.

FLIPPING, REVERSING, AND ROTATING

Other operations that are fun to perform on bitmap images include flipping the image upside down, rotating the image by 90 degrees, 45 degrees, etc., and reversing the image (turning all the white bits black and vice versa, which is available in the `bitmap` program).

SUMMARY

The Draw application is not the great shining path to complete X Window System programming. This chapter offers suggestions on how Draw can be improved—improvements that can be implemented into any X application.

Xlib Functions and Macros Introduced in This Chapter

```
XGetImage
XGetPixel
```

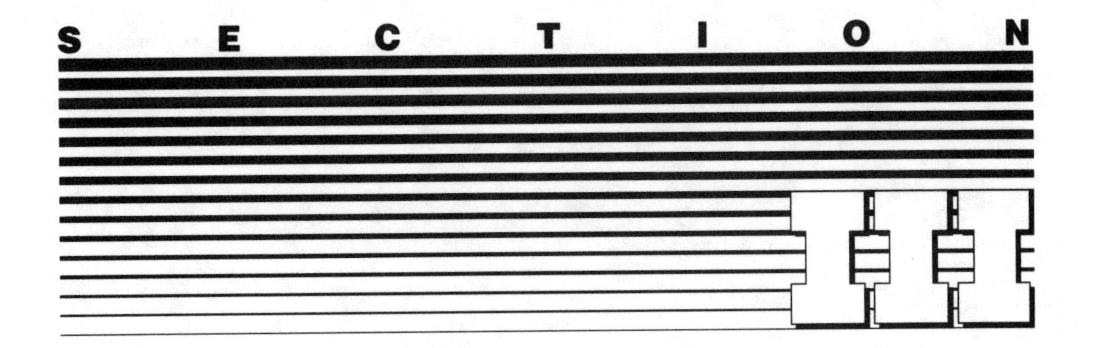

X TOOLKITS

The first two sections of this book discuss programming with low-level Xlib tools. In this next abbreviated section, X Toolkits are examined.

A large part of X's future lies within these toolkits. Essentially, toolkits are prewritten graphics routines that make a programmer's life simpler. By learning how to use X Toolkits well, you can create X applications in less time than in other programming environments.

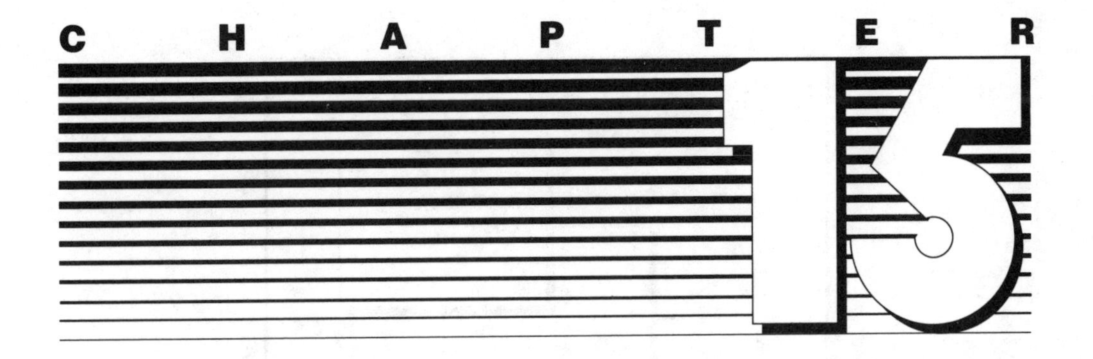

AN INTRODUCTION TO X TOOLKITS

While this book covers Xlib, the X programming library interface, it is a good idea to be aware of the many X Toolkits. If Xlib is a low-level library, the highest level of the X Window System architecture is the X Toolkits.

Toolkits are a recent addition to the X Window System. Essentially, toolkits are preprogrammed graphics routines written in C. The X Toolkit consists of routines for menus, window frames, scroll bars, panels, and other graphical tools that can be assembled into a graphical user interface. The X Toolkit (a standard part of X) sits on top of the Xlib library (see Figure 15.1).

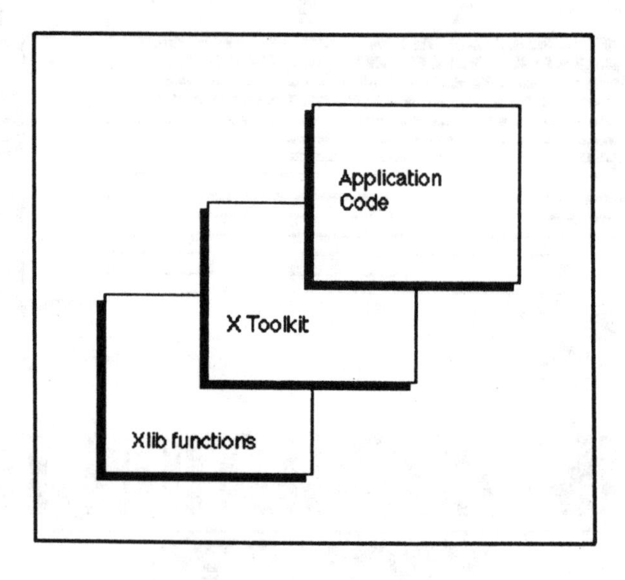

Fig 15.1 *X layers.*

Toolkits provide higher-level access to graphic interface routines than do the Xlib functions described in this book. The X Toolkit, or **Xt**, also provides a means for inheriting aspects of other parts of the toolkit—**widgets**. Each widget is a member of one widget class. The class defines the basic behavior of the widget and what kind of data is stored in the widget. For example, one widget class is the logo class—a widget that provides an X or another logo on your display.

Why toolkits? Two reasons: First, because software portability is a big issue for the X designers, it shouldn't be surprising that they included guidelines for prewritten graphical user interfaces—why should software designers reinvent the wheel? Second, the toolkit is the easiest way to provide consistent user interfaces from system to system and from implementation to implementation.

As mentioned, X Toolkits are prewritten graphics routines. A toolkit is like an Erector set; you can put together different parts to form a program. These parts are basic data types called `widgets` ("objects" in SmallTalk or object-oriented programming parlance). Most X Window System implementations provide either the basic toolkit from MIT (Xt) or the DEC XUI toolkit, or both. If neither of these can fill your needs, you can try the Athena widget set, the Hewlett-Packard widgets, the Sony toolkit, or you can also write your own widgets if you're familiar with C. Because the X designers thought of everything, they also included a style sheet in the Standard Supplement of the X Window System Manual Set.

There's no way to definitively describe all the toolkits because they are constantly undergoing revisions. Much hard-core X development, in fact, is going into widget development.

Though there are several toolkits on the market, it seems that the Digital Equipment Corporation's DECwindows X User Interface (XUI) and the Open Look toolkits are picking up the most steam. Approved by the Open Software Foundation for use in Open Software Foundation/Motif and licensed by Hewlett-Packard and Santa Cruz Operation for SCO Open Desktop, XUI has the backing of vendors aiming for the high-end personal computer market. The Open Look toolkit from AT&T and Sun Microsystems has also generated a lot of interest since its release. Both the OSF/Motif (which is designed to look like the OS/2 Presentation Manager) and the Open Look interfaces have the backing of major UNIX vendors.

THE XT TOOLKIT

The third major toolkit is the only one that is a current X standard toolkit—the X Toolkit, or Xt. Xt is probably more object-oriented than the XUI or Open Look toolkits, which is a two-edged sword. Writing programs using Xt can dramatically cut down on the amount of code you need to write. Writing programs using Xt while trying to figure out the toolkit also dramatically accelerates the process of turning your hair gray.

As an example of using X toolkits, a small Xt program is presented later in this chapter. It is beyond the scope of this book to cover the X toolkits in depth, but a small sample program will give you a flavor of both the good and the bad in the Xt toolkit.

There are five steps in creating a simple widget-based program:

- Choose the right class to base your widget on.
- Initialize the Xt system and create a top-level widget.
- Create your subwidgets.
- Realize the widgets and cause them to be mapped to the screen.
- Handle all widget-related events.

First, you need to choose the right widget class to base your widget on. The X Toolkit is based on an object-oriented design, so all widget classes inherit something from parent classes. All widget classes are child classes of the highest-level `Core` widget class. Underneath the `Core` widget class, there are two other main types of widgets: `Composite` widgets and `Constraint` widgets.

`Composite` widgets are a subclass of the `Core` widgets. Composite widgets are designed to contain more widgets. `Constraint` widgets are subclasses of `Composite` widgets and are designed for holders that need to be constrained, such as limiting a widget to one portion of the screen.

At its base level, a widget is simply a rectangle—a rectangle with a given means for input and output (sounds a lot like these things are based on windows, doesn't it?). In the sample that follows, a simple class of widgets is chosen, the `label` class. `Label` widgets simply place a label in a window on the screen.

The rather short code that follows contains everything that is needed to handle all the events associated with the widget—in one line of code. It also opens a connection to X—automatically—and, in another line of code, takes care of the normally long, drawn-out process of creating a window.

A SAMPLE XT PROGRAM

To begin the source code for a sample Xt program, you need the following include files (which most Xt programs require):

```
#include    <X11/Intrinsic.h>
#include    <X11/StringDefs.h>
```

Also, you will probably need to include a header file for each widget class. Usually this file name is similar to the class name, such as `Label.h` for the `label` widget class:

```
#include  <X11/Label.h>
```

As in most widget class header files, there will also be a file that contains the private parts of the widget class, with a `P` at the end of the name, for example, `LabelP.h`.

Initializing the XT Library

For most Xt-based programs, the next step after choosing a widget class (or writing a widget class on your own) is initializing the Xt system. The Xt library function `XtInitialize` performs a number of functions:

- It sets up a display connection to the X server.
- It automatically handles all command-line parameters (there is a mechanism to include your own special parameters in with the standard X command-line parameters introduced in Chapter 8).
- It creates a top-level widget, which becomes the parent for all your other widgets.

The following code creates `theUberWidget`, the top-level widget in this chapter's sample program.

```
        .
        .
        .
main( argc, argv )

int     argc;
char    *argv[];
{
        Widget                  theUberWidget;
        XrmOptionDescRec        *theOptions;
        Cardinal                numberOfOptions;   /* -- unsigned int */
        Cardinal                cmdLineOptions;
        char                    theShellName[ 100 ];
        char                    theClassName[ 100 ];

        strcpy( theClassName, "Foo" );    /* -- starts with Caps */
        strcpy( theShellName, "foo" );

        cmdLineOptions  = argc;
        numberOfOptions = 0;
        theOptions      = (XrmOptionDescRec *) NULL;

        theUberWidget   = XtInitialize( theShellName,
                                theClassName,
                                theOptions,
                                numberOfOptions,
                                &cmdLineOptions,
                                argv );

        .
        .
        .
```

Note that there is no need for a `Display` pointer here. Also note that `cmdLineOptions` is sent as a pointer to an integer (whose initial value should be that of `argc`). If you wanted to add in some of your own command-line parameters, they would be in the `XrmOptionDescRec` structure, and the number of options passed would be in the variable `numberOfOptions`. In this example, there are none.

Creating Subwidgets

After setting up the Xt library with `XtInitialize`, you can create subwidgets with the `XtCreateWidget` function. As in the previous example, each widget has a unique name, a parent (the top-level widget has a `Core` parent), a class (in this case, the `labelWidgetClass`), and some values (an array of `Arg` structures).

```
Widget                    theWidgetParent;
Widget                    theLabelWidget;
WidgetClass               theWidgetClass;
Cardinal                  numberOfArgs;
char                      theWidgetName[ 100 ];
char                      theArgString[ 100 ];
Arg                       theArgList[ 5 ];   /* -- an arbitrary sizes */

strcpy( theWidgetName, "label1" );

theWidgetClass  = labelWidgetClass;
numberOfArgs    = XtNumber( theArgList );
theLabelWidget  = XtCreateWidget( theWidgetName,
                          theWidgetClass,
                          theWidgetParent,
                          theArgList,
                          numberOfArgs );
```

The macro `XtNumber` should be used to get the number of arguments in the `Args` array.

To fill in the contents of `Arg` structures passed as an array of `Arg` types to `XtCreateWidget`, use the function `XtSetArg`. This function places a value into an `Arg` structure:

```
char            theArgString[ 100 ];
Arg             theArg;

strcpy( theArgString, "This is a test of the emergency X system" );

XtSetArg( &theArg,
        XtNlabel,       /* -- Name of the label widget */
        (XtArgVal) theArgString );
```

The **Arg** structure resembles the following:

```
typdef  long    XtArgVal; typedef char   *String;

typedef struct
        {
        String          name;
        XtArgVal        value;
        }
```

Managing Widgets

The subwidget created earlier needs to be placed under a top-level widget so that **Xt** can manage it, handle events for it, and so on. The function **XtManage-Child** handles this task nicely. Thus, creating a subwidget is essentially a two-step process: First, create the widget with a top-level parent. Then, call **XtManageChild** to place the new widget under the "old" management.

```
Widget                  theLabelWidget;

XtManageChild( theLabelWidget );
```

You can perform both these steps in one function call by using **XtCreate-ManagedWidget**. In this case, the widget parent must be both the parent and the "manager."

```
Widget                  theWidgetParent;
Widget                  theLabelWidget;
WidgetClass             theWidgetClass;
Cardinal                numberOfArgs;
char                    theWidgetName[ 100 ];
Arg                     theArgList[ 5 ];    /* -- an arbitrary sizes */

theLabelWidget  = XtCreateManagedWidget( theWidgetName,
                        theWidgetClass,
                        theWidgetParent,
                        theArgList,
                        numberOfArgs );
```

Realizing Widgets

After a widget is created, it must be "realized." This realization is akin to creating and then mapping windows. `XtRealizeWidget` realizes a widget and maps the widget's windows to the screen.

```
Widget          theUberWidget;

XtRealizeWidget( theUberWidget );
```

Calling `XtRealizeWidget` on the top-level widget will also realize the child widgets.

The Widget Event Loop

In the source code examples in Sections I and II of this book, the main event loop could form a major part of an X program. Using the toolkit, though, you can handle events with one line of code—the function `XtMainLoop`. `XtMainLoop` handles requesting events from X, receiving events, and then dispatching the events to the proper subwidgets for action.

```
XtMainLoop();
```

Sample Widget Program Source Code

In the source code that follows, you will see the most powerful aspect of the X toolkits—the ability to deal with X in a high-level fashion. This program is tiny (about 2K on disk), but the functions it calls are powerful and large. The executable program took up 229K on disk (using X11R2).

This program will create a window on the display with the string "This is a test of the emergency X system" inside the window (see Figure 15.2). The program will handle all events associated with the window, including redrawing exposed areas.

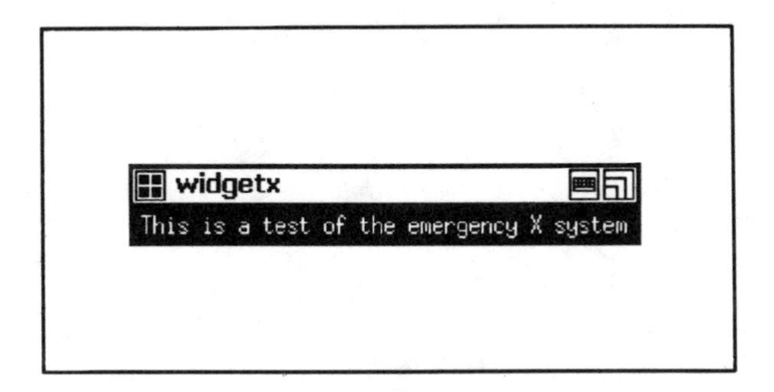

Figure 15.2 Display string inside window.

The contents of `widgetx.c` are as follows:

```
/*
**      Test program shows an example of widgets in action.
**
*/

/*
**      For definition of NULL
*/
#include    <stdio.h>

/*
**      X11 include, needed whenever you write X programs
*/
#include <X11/Xlib.h>
```

continued...

...from previous page

```
/*
**      Needed to use the Xt toolkit, remember to link with -lXaw
**      -lXt and -lX11
*/
#include    <X11/Intrinsic.h>
#include    <X11/StringDefs.h>

/*
**      This program uses the Label widget, so include Label.h
*/
#include    <X11/Label.h>

/*
**      Main function
**
*/

main( argc, argv )

int     argc;
char    *argv[];

{
        Widget                  theUberWidget;
        Widget                  theLabelWidget;
        XrmOptionDescRec        *theOptions;
        Cardinal                numberOfOptions; /* -- unsigned int */
        Cardinal                cmdLineOptions;
        Cardinal                numberOfArgs;
        char                    theShellName[ 100 ];
        char                    theClassName[ 100 ];
        char                    theWidgetName[ 100 ];
        char                    theArgString[ 100 ];
        Arg                     theArgList[ 5 ];
        WidgetClass             theWidgetClass;

        strcpy( theClassName, "Foo" );
        strcpy( theShellName, "foo" );

        cmdLineOptions  = argc;
        numberOfOptions = 0;
        theOptions      = (XrmOptionDescRec *) NULL;

        /*
        **      Set up the master widget, under which any other
        **      widgets will appear. XtInitialize also sets
        **      up the X connection.
        */
```

continued...

...from previous page

```
        theUberWidget   = XtInitialize( theShellName,
                                        theClassName,
                                        theOptions,
                                        numberOfOptions,
                                        &cmdLineOptions,
                                        argv );

        /*
        **      Set up a name for the Label widget to be created below
        */
        strcpy( theArgString, "This is a test of the emergency X system" );

        XtSetArg( theArgList[ 0 ],
                XtNlabel,
                (XtArgVal) theArgString );

        /*
        **      Now, create a label widget, could also use
        **      XtCreateWidget/XtManageChild
        **
        */
        strcpy( theWidgetName, "label1" );

        theWidgetClass  = labelWidgetClass;
        numberOfArgs    = XtNumber( theArgList );
        theLabelWidget  = XtCreateManagedWidget( theWidgetName,
                                        theWidgetClass,
                                        theUberWidget,
                                        theArgList,
                                        numberOfArgs );

        /*
        **      Make my top-level widget "real", as well as all
        **      sub-widgets
        **
        */

        XtRealizeWidget( theUberWidget );

        /*
        **      Handle all events for this simple widget
        */
        XtMainLoop();
}
```

Compiling the XT Program

This chapter's example program fits into one small file, so no Makefile is included here; however, you will need to link in all the proper libraries. Under X11 R3 (the generic MIT release), the following UNIX command compiled and linked the widgetx program:

```
cc -o widgetx widgetx.c -lXaw -lXmu -lXt -lX11
```

This means that the Xaw (Athena), Xmu, Xt, and X11 libraries were all needed. Under X11R2 (on an Apple Macintosh IIx), the Xmu library was not needed (nor was the library found):

```
cc -o widgetx widgetx.c -lXaw -lXt -lX11
```

MORE ABOUT THE X TOOLKITS

Other Xt-based programs include `xclock` and `xlogo`. If you have access to the X source code, check out these programs. Because the documentation on Xt is obscure (to say the least), the best way to learn to write toolkit programs is to examine sample code and then try modifying parts of the code until you understand what the heck is going on.

One of the first places to check for other sources of Xt documentation is in the documentation that came with your version of the X Window System. A document titled *X Toolkit Intrinsics — C Language Interface*, by Joel McCormack, Paul Asente, and Ralph Swick, is distributed with the MIT X Consortium generic X release.

DEC, SCO or the Open Software Foundation are the companies to contact regarding the XUI or Motif interfaces, and AT&T should be contacted for more information on the Open Look interface.

SUMMARY

- Toolkits are prewritten graphics routines written in C that allow programmers to create X applications in less time than in other programming environments. The X Toolkit consists of routines for menus, window frames, scroll bars, panels, and other graphical tools that can be assembled into a graphical user interface. The X Toolkit (a standard part of X) sits on top of the Xlib library. The toolkit is the easiest way to provide consistent user interfaces from system to system and from implementation to implementation.

- Toolkits provide higher-level access to graphic interface routines than the Xlib functions described in this book. The X Toolkit, or Xt, also provides a means for inheriting aspects of other parts of the toolkit—parts called widgets. Each widget is a member of one widget class. The class defines the basic behavior of the widget and what kind of data is stored in the widget. For example, one widget class is the logo class—a widget that provides an X or some other logo on your display.

XT Functions and Macros Introduced in This Chapter

```
XtCreateManagedWidget
XtCreateWidget
XtInitialize
XtMainLoop
XtManageChild
XtNumber
XtRealize
XtSetArg
```

APPENDICES

THE X COLOR DATA BASE

To ensure color consistency across the different hardware platforms running the X Window System, the designers adopted an ASCII-based color name data base, which is listed in this appendix. As described in Chapter 3, this data base can be used to aid portability of your applications.

This list contains 66 distinct colors, although some appear under two different names (gray and grey, for example). Normally, this database can be found in UNIX systems under `/usr/lib/X11/rgb.txt`, although not always.

Some X Window System versions allow you to add to this list. This isn't generally recommended; by expanding the color data base, you're putting more pressure on the processor, which can slow down your system. For most applications, the following list will be more than sufficient.

When using these color names, keep them as one word. If you put spaces into a color name (for example, `Lime Green` instead of `LimeGreen`), X will not be happy. So don't use spaces in X color names.

English word	Green	Blue	Red
Aquamarine	112	219	147
Black	0	0	0
Blue	0	0	255
BlueViolet	159	95	159
Brown	165	42	42
CadetBlue	95	159	159
Coral	255	127	0
CornflowerBlue	66	66	111
Cyan	0	255	255
DarkGreen	47	79	47
DarkOliveGreen	79	79	47
DarkOrchid	153	50	204
DarkSlateBlue	107	35	142
DarkSlateGray	47	79	79
DarkSlateGrey	47	79	79
DarkTurquoise	112	147	219
DimGray	84	84	84
DimGrey	84	84	84
Firebrick	142	35	35
ForestGreen	35	142	35
Gold	204	127	50
Goldenrod	219	219	112
Gray	192	192	192

English word	Green	Blue	Red
Green	0	255	0
GreenYellow	147	219	112
Grey	192	192	192
IndianRed	79	47	47
Khaki	159	159	95
LightBlue	191	216	216
LightGray	168	168	168
LightGrey	168	168	168
LightSteelBlue	143	143	188
LimeGreen	50	204	50
Magenta	255	0	255
Maroon	142	35	107
MediumAquamarine	50	204	153
MediumBlue	50	50	204
MediumForestGreen	107	142	35
MediumGoldenrod	234	234	173
MediumOrchid	147	112	219
MediumSeaGreen	66	111	66
MediumSlateBlue	127	0	255
MediumSpringGreen	127	255	0
MediumTurquoise	112	219	219
MediumVioletRed	219	112	147
MidnightBlue	47	47	79
Navy	35	35	142
NavyBlue	35	35	142
Orange	204	50	50
OrangeRed	255	0	127
Orchid	219	112	219
PaleGreen	143	188	143
Pink	188	143	143
Plum	234	173	234
Red	255	0	0
Salmon	111	66	66
SeaGreen	35	142	107
Sienna	142	107	35
SkyBlue	50	153	204
SlateBlue	0	127	255

English word	Green	Blue	Red
SpringGreen	0	255	127
SteelBlue	35	107	142
Tan	219	147	112
Thistle	216	191	216
Turquoise	173	234	234
Violet	79	47	79
VioletRed	204	50	153
Wheat	216	216	191
White	252	252	252
Yellow	255	255	0
YellowGreen	153	294	50

X EVENT TYPES AND STRUCTURES

Using the information in this appendix, you can decode most any event that comes in. Each type of event is listed with the event types (returned in the XEvent union), the event mask (to ask for in an XSelectInput call), and the event structure. The event types are listed in alphabetical order.

The **XEvent** type returned by the event-checking routines is a union of many structures overlaid on top of one another. When an event is received, the key aspects are 1) determining the event type and 2) pulling out the relevant data from the event structure. Note that the **XEvent** union is defined as

```
typdef union _XEvent {
        int                             type;
        XAnyEvent                       xany;
        XKeyEvent                       xkey;
        XButtonEvent                    xbutton;
        XMotionEvent                    xmotion;
        XCrossingEvent                  xcrossing;
        XFocusChangeEvent               xfocus;
        XExposeEvent                    xexpose;
        XGraphicsExposeEvent            xgraphicsexpose;
        XNoExposeEvent                  xnoexpose;
        XVisibilityEvent                xvisibility;
        XCreateWindowEvent              xcreatewindow;
        XDestroyWindowEvent             xdestroywindow;
        XUnmapEvent                     xunmap;
        XMapEvent                       xmap;
        XMapRequestEvent                xmaprequest;
        XReparentEvent                  xreparent;
        XConfigureEvent                 xconfigure;
        XGravityEvent                   xgravity;
        XResizeRequestEvent             xresizerequest;
        XConfigureRequestEvent          xconfigurerequest;
        XCirculateEvent                 xcirculate;
        XCirculateRequestEvent          xcirculaterequest;
        XPropertyEvent                  xproperty;
        XSelectionClearEvent            xselectionclear;
        XSelectionRequestEvent          xselectionrequest;
        XSelectionEvent                 xselection;
        XColormapEvent                  xcolormap;
        XClientMessageEvent             xclient;
        XMappingEvent                   xmapping;
        XErrorEvent                     xerror;
        XKeymapEvent                    xkeymap;
        long                            pad[24];
} XEvent;
```

First, check the type as

```
int     theType;
XEvent  theEvent;

theType = theEvent.type;
```

Then, if the event is, for example, a `ButtonPress` event, you can access the information associated with the event by using the following:

```
int     x, y;
XEvent  theEvent;

x = theEvent.xbutton.x;
y = theEvent.xbutton.y;
```

ButtonPress, ButtonRelease

Description: These are the pointer button events.

Event Mask: `ButtonPressMask` `ButtonReleaseMask`

Event Structure Name: `XButtonPressedEvent` `XButtonReleasedEvent`

Event Structure:

```
typedef struct {
        int type;                  /* of event */
        unsigned long serial;      /* # of last request processed by server */
        Bool send_event;           /* true if this came from SendEvent request*/
        Display *display;          /* display the event was read from */
        Window window;             /* event window it is reported relative to */
        Window root;               /* root window that the event occurred on */
        Window subwindow;          /* child window */
        Time time;                 /* milliseconds */
        int x, y;                  /* pointer coords relative to receiving window */
        int x_root, y_root;        /* coordinates relative to root */
        unsigned int scale         /* modifier key and button mask */
        unsigned int keycode;      /* server-dependent code for key */
        Bool same_screen           /* same screen flag */
} XKeyEvent;
typedef XButtonEvent XButtonPressedEvent;
typedef XButtonEvent XButtonReleasedEvent;
```

CirculateNotify

Description: `CirculateNotify` events report a call to change the stacking order of a window configuration, including the final order of the window.

Event Mask: `StructureNotifyMask`

Event Structure Name: `XCirculateEvent`

Event Structure:

```
typedef struct {
        int type;
        unsigned long serial;     /* # of last request processed by server */
        Bool send_event;          /* true if this came from SendEvent request */
        Display *display;         /* display the event was read from */
        Window event;
        Window window;
        int place;                /* PlaceOnTop, PlaceOnBottom */
} XCirculateEvent;
```

CirculateRequest

Description: When the stacking order of a window is selected and changed, `CirculateRequest` events report when `XCirculateSubwindows`, `XCirculateSubwindowsUp`, or `XCirculateSubwindowsDown` is called.

Event Mask: `SubstructureRedirectMask`

Event Structure Name: `XCirculateRequestEvent`

Event Structure:

```
typedef struct {
        int type;
        unsigned long serial;    /* # of last request processed by server */
        Bool send_event;         /* true if this came from SendEvent request */
        Display *display;        /* display the event was read from */
        Window event;
        Window window;
        int place;               /* PlaceOnTop, PlaceOnBottom */
} XCirculateRequestEvent;
```

ClientMessage

Description: These events occur when the function `XSendEvent` is called by a client.

Event Mask: Always selected.

Event Structure Name: `XClientMessageEvent`

Event Structure:

```
typedef struct {
        int type;
        unsigned long serial;    /* # of last request processed by server */
        Bool send_event;         /* true if this came from SendEvent request */
        Display *display;        /* display the event was read from */
        Window window;
        Atom message_type;
        int format;
        union {
                char  b[20];
                short s[10];
                int   l[5];
        } data;
} XClientMessageEvent;
```

ColormapNotify

Description: This event charts changes in the colormap attribute or in the attribute itself in a particular window.

Event Mask: `ColormapChangeMask`

Event Structure Name: `XColormapEvent`

Event structure

```
typedef struct {
        int type;
        unsigned long serial;     /* # of last request processed by server */
        Bool send_event;          /* true if this came from SendEvent request */
        Display *display;         /* display the event was read from */
        Window window;
        Colormap colormap;        /* Colormap or None */
        Bool new;
        int state;                /* ColormapInstalled, ColormapUninstalled */
} XColormapEvent;
```

ConfigureNotify

Description: This event highlights changes to a window's configuration.

Event Mask: `StructureNotifyMask`

Event Structure Name: `XConfigureEvent`

Event Structure:

```
typedef struct {
        int type;
        unsigned long serial;     /* # of last request processed by server */
        Bool send_event;          /* true if this came from SendEvent request*/
        Display *display;         /* display the event was read from */
        Window event;
        Window window;
        int x, y;
        int width, height;
        int border_width;
        Window above;
        Bool override_redirect;
} XConfigureEvent;
```

ConfigureRequest

Description: This event reports another client's changes to a window's configuration.

Event Mask: SubstructureRedirectMask

Event Structure Name: XConfigureRequestEvent

Event Structure:

```
typedef struct {
        int type;
        unsigned long serial;    /* # of last request processed by server */
        Bool send_event;         /* true if this came from SendEvent request*/
        Display *display;        /* display the event was read from */
        Window parent;
        Window window;
        int x, y;
        int width, height;
        int border_width;
        Window above;
        int detail;              /* Above, Below, Topif, BottomIf, Opposite */
        unsigned long value_mask;
} XConfigureRequestEvent;
```

CreateNotify

Description: When windows are created, this event is reported to the client by the X server.

Event Mask: SubstructureNotifyMask

Event Structure Name: XCreateWindowEvent

Event Structure:

```
typedef struct {
        int type;
        unsigned long serial;      /* # of last request processed by server */
        Bool send_event;           /* true if this came from SendEvent request*/
        Display *display;          /* display the event was read from */
        Window parent;             /* parent of the window */
        Window window;             /* window ID of window created */
        int x, y;                  /* window location */
        int width, height;         /* size of window */
        int border_width;          /* border width */
        Bool override_redirect;    /* creation should be oveden */
} XCreateWindowEvent;
```

DestroyNotify

Description: As you might expect, `DestroyNotify` events report that a window has been destroyed.

Event Mask: `SubstructureNotifyMask`

Event Structure Name: `XDestroyWindowEvent`

Event Structure:

```
typedef struct {
        int type;
        unsigned long serial;      /* # of last request processed by server */
        Bool send_event;           /* true if this came from SendEvent request*/
        Display *display;          /* display the event was read from */
        Window event;
        Window window;
} XDestroyWindowEvent;
```

EnterNotify, LeaveNotify

Description: These events occur when a pointer enters and leaves a window.

Event Mask: `EnterWindowMask`
`LeaveWindowMask`

Event Structure Name: `XCrossingEvent`

Event Structure:

```
typedef struct {
        int type;                  /* of event */
        unsigned long serial;      /* # of last request processed by server */
        Bool send_event;           /* true if this came from SendEvent request*/
        Display *display;          /* display the event was read from */
        Window window;             /* event window it is reported relative to */
        Window root;               /* root window that the event occurred on */
        Window subwindow;          /* child window */
        Time time;                 /* milliseconds */
        int x, y;                  /* pointer x, y coordinates in receiving window */
        int x_root, y_root;        /* coordinates relative to root */
        int mode;                  /* NotifyNormal, NotifyGrab, NotifyUngrab */
        int detail;                /* NotifyAncestor, NotifyVirtual,
                                    * NotifyInferior, NotifyNonLinear,
                                    * NotifyNonLinearVirtual */
        Bool same_screen;          /* same screen flag */
        Bool focus;                /* Boolean focus */
        unsigned int state;        /* key or button mask */
} XCrossingEvent;
typedef XCrossingEvent XEnterWindowEvent;
typedef XCrossingEvent XLeaveWindowEvent;
```

Expose

Description: These events are generated when a window or a previously covered part of a window becomes visible.

Event Mask: `ExposureMask`

Event Structure Name: `XExposeEvent`

Event Structure:

```
typedef struct {
        int type;
        unsigned long serial;      /* # of last request processed by server */
        Bool send_event;           /* true if this came from SendEvent request*/
        Display *display;          /* display the event was read from */
        Window window;
        int x, y;
        int width, height;
        int count;                 /* if nonzero, at least this many more */
} XExposeEvent;
```

FocusIn, FocusOut

Description: These events are generated when a focus window changes.

Event Mask: `FocusChangeMask`

Event Structure Name: `XFocusChangeEvent`

Event Structure:

```
typedef struct {
        int type;                 /* FocusIn or FocusOut */
        unsigned long serial;     /* # of last request processed by server */
        Bool send_event;          /* true if this came from SendEvent request*/
        Display *display;         /* display the event was read from */
        Window window;            /* window of event        */
        int mode;                 /* NotifyNormal, NotifyGrab, NotifyUngrab */
        int detail;               /* NotifyAncestor, NotifyVirtual,
                                   * NotifyInferior, NotifyNonLinear,
                                   * NotifyNonLinearVirtual, NotifyPointer,
                                   * NotifyPointerRoot, NotifyDetailNone */
} XFocusChangeEvent;
typedef XFocusChangeEvent XFocusInEvent;
typedef XFocusChangeEvent XFocusOutEvent;
```

GraphicsExpose, NoExpose

Description: When `GraphicsExpose` events occur, it means that the source area for an `XCopyPlane` or `XCopyArea` was not available. When `NoExpose` events occur, it means that the source area was completely available.

Event Mask: selected in GC by `graphics_expose` member

Event Structure Name: `XGraphicsExposeEvent`
`NoExposeEvent`

Event Structure:

```
typedef struct {
        int type;
        unsigned long serial;    /* # of last request processed by server */
        Bool send_event;         /* true if this came from SendEvent request*/
        Display *display;        /* display the event was read from */
        Drawable drawable;
        int x, y;
        int width, height;
        int count;               /* if nonzero, at least this many more */
        int major_code;          /* core is CopyArea or CopyPlane */
        int minor_code;          /* not defined in the core       */
} XGraphicsExposeEvent;

typedef struct {
        int type;
        unsigned long serial;    /* # of last request processed by server */
        Bool send_event;         /* true if this came from SendEvent request*/
        Display *display;        /* display the event was read from */
        Drawable drawable;
        int count;               /* if nonzero, at least this many more */
        int major_code;          /* core is CopyArea or CopyPlane */
        int minor_code;          /* not defined in the core       */
} XNoExposeEvent;
```

GravityNotify

Description: When a parent window's size is changed, thus necessitating the movement of a child window, `GravityNotify` events occur.

Event Mask: `StructureNotifyMask`

Event Structure Name: `XGravityEvent`

Event Structure:

```
typedef struct {
        int type;
        unsigned long serial;      /* # of last request processed by server */
        Bool send_event;           /* true if this came from SendEvent request*/
        Display *display;          /* display the event was read from */
        Window event;
        Window window;
        int x, y;
} XGravityEvent;
```

KeymapNotify

Description: An application is awakened through these events when a keyboard or pointer focus enters a window.

Event Mask: `KeymapStateMask`

Event Structure Name: `XKeymapEvent`

Event Structure:

```
typedef struct {
        int type;
        unsigned long serial;      /* # of last request processed by server */
        Bool send_event;           /* true if this came from SendEvent request*/
        Display *display;          /* display the event was read from */
        Window window;
        char key_vector[32];
} XKeymapEvent;
```

KeyPress, KeyRelease

Description: These events are generated for all keys, including those generated through meta-key combinations.

Event Mask: `KeyPressMask` `KeyPressRelease`

Event Structure Name: `XKeyEvent`

Event Structure:

```
typedef struct {
        int type;                /* of event */
        unsigned long serial;    /* # of last request processed by server */
        Bool send_event;         /* true if this came from SendEvent request*/
        Display *display;        /* display the event was read from */
        Window window;           /* event window it is reported relative to */
        Window root;             /* root window that the event occurred on */
        Window subwindow;        /* child window */
        Time time;               /* milliseconds */
        int x, y;                /* pointer x, y coordinates in receiving window */
        int x_root, y_root;      /* coordinates relative to root */
        unsigned int state;      /* modifier key and button mask */
        unsigned int keycode;    /* server-dependent code for key */
        Bool same_screen;        /* same screen flag */
} XKeyEvent;
typedef XKeyEvent XKeyPressedEvent;
typedef XKeyEvent XKeyReleasedEvent;
```

MapNotify, UnmapNotify

Description: When a window changes from mapped to unmapped (or vice versa), these events occur.

Event Mask: `StructureNotifyMask`

Event Structure Name: `XMapEvent` `XUnmapEvent`

Event Structure:

```
typedef struct {
        int type;
        unsigned long serial;     /* # of last request processed by server */
        Bool send_event;          /* true if this came from SendEvent request*/
        Display *display;         /* display the event was read from */
        Window event;
        Window window;
        Bool override_redirect;   /* Boolean, is override set */
} XMapEvent;

typedef struct {
        int type;
        unsigned long serial;     /* # of last request processed by server */
        Bool send_event;          /* true if this came from SendEvent request*/
        Display *display;         /* display the event was read from */
        Window event;
        Window window;
        Bool from_configure;
} XUnmapEvent;
```

MappingNotify

Description: `MappingNotify` events are generated when another client makes changes in mapping functions, such as in the keyboard mapping.

Event Mask: Always selected.

Event Structure Name: `XMappingEvent`

Event Structure:

```
typedef struct {
        int type;
        unsigned long serial;     /* # of last request processed by server */
        Bool send_event;          /* true if this came from SendEvent request*/
        Display *display;         /* display the event was read from */
        Window event;             /* unused */
        int request;              /* one of the MappingModifier,
                                   * MappingKeyboard, MappingPointer */
        int first_keycode;        /* first keycode */
        int count;                /* range of change with first_keyboard */
} XMappingEvent;
```

MapRequest

Definition: These events occur when `XMapWindows` or `XMap-Subwindows` is commanded to map a window.

Event Mask: `SubstructureRedirectMask`

Event Structure Name: `XMapRequestEvent`

Event Structure:

```
typedef struct {
        int type;
        unsigned long serial;     /* # of last request processed by server */
        Bool send_event;          /* true if this came from SendEvent request*/
        Display *display;         /* display the event was read from */
        Window parent;
        Window window;
} XMapRequestEvent;
```

MotionNotify

Description: Any change in a pointer is traced through these events.

Event Mask:
`PointerMotionMask`
`PointerMotionHintMask`
`ButtonMotionMask`
`Button1MotionMask`
`Button2MotionMask`
`Button3MotionMask`
`Button4MotionMask`
`Button5MotionMask`

Event Structure Name: `XPointerMovedEvent`

Event Structure:

```
typedef struct {
        int type;                   /* of event */
        unsigned long serial;       /* # of last request processed by server */
        Bool send_event;            /* true if this came from SendEvent request*/
        Display *display;           /* display the event was read from */
        Window window;              /* event window it is reported relative to */
        Window root;                /* root window that the event occurred on */
        Window subwindow;           /* child window */
        Time time;                  /* milliseconds */
        int x, y;                   /* pointer coords in receiving window */
        int x_root, y_root;         /* coordinates relative to root */
        unsigned int state;         /* button and modifier key mask */
        char is_hint;               /* is this a motion hint */
        Bool same_screen;           /* same screen flag */
} XMotionEvent;
typedef XMotionEvent XPointerMovedEvent;
```

PropertyNotify

Description: When a window's property has changed, these events are generated.

Event Mask: `PropertyChangeMask`

Event Structure Name: `XPropertyEvent`

Event Structure:

```
typedef struct {
        int type;
        unsigned long serial;       /* # of last request processed by server */
        Bool send_event;            /* true if this came from SendEvent request*/
        Display *display;           /* display the event was read from */
        Window window;
        Atom atom;
        Time time;
        int state;                  /* NewValue, Deleted */
} XPropertyEvent;
```

ReparentNotify

Description: Changes in a window's parent are tracked through these events.

Event Mask: StructureNotifyMask
SubstructureNotifyMask

Event Structure Name: XReparentEvent

Event Structure:

```
typedef struct {
        int type;
        unsigned long serial;    /* # of last request processed by server */
        Bool send_event;         /* true if this came from SendEvent request*/
        Display *display;        /* display the event was read from */
        Window event;
        Window window;
        Window parent;
        int x, y;
        Bool override_redirect;
} XReparentEvent;
```

ResizeRequest

Description: These events occur when another client attempts to resize a window.

Event Mask: ResizeRedirectMask

Event Structure Name: XResizeRequestEvent

Event Structure:

```
typedef struct {
        int type;
        unsigned long serial;    /* # of last request processed by server */
        Bool send_event;         /* true if this came from SendEvent request*/
        Display *display;        /* display the event was read from */
        Window window;
        int width, height;
} XReparentEvent;
```

SelectionClear

Description: These events undefine a selection when a new owner is defined.

Event Mask: Always selected

Event Structure Name: `XSelectionClearEvent`

Event Structure:

```
typedef struct {
        int type;
        unsigned long serial;     /* # of last request processed by server */
        Bool send_event;          /* true if this came from SendEvent request*/
        Display *display;         /* display the event was read from */
        Window window;
        Atom selection;
        Time time;
} XSelectionClearEvent;
```

SelectionNotify

Description: A client sends these events to another client that requested a selection, signifying whether or not the selection conversion was made.

Event Mask: Always selected

Event Structure Name: `XSelectionEvent`

Event Structure:

```
typedef struct {
        int type;
        unsigned long serial;     /* # of last request processed by server */
        Bool send_event;          /* true if this came from SendEvent request*/
        Display *display;         /* display the event was read from */
        Window requester;         /* must be next after type */
        Atom selection;
        Atom target;
        Atom property;            /* Atom or none */
        Time time;
} XSelectionEvent;
```

SelectionRequest

Description: These events notify the owner of a selection that the selection is being requested by another client.

Event Mask: Always selected

Event Structure Name: `XSelectionRequestEvent`

Event Structure:

```
typedef struct {
        int type;
        unsigned long serial;    /* # of last request processed by server */
        Bool send_event;         /* true if this came from SendEvent request*/
        Display *display;        /* display the event was read from */
        Window owner;            /* must be next after type */
        Window requester;
        Atom selection;
        Atom target;
        Atom property;
        Time time;
} XSelectionRequestEvent;
```

VisibilityNotify

Description: These events are generated when a window's visibility is changed. This does not include changes in any subwindows.

Event Mask: `VisibilityChangeMask`

Event Structure Name: `XVisibilityEvent`

Event Structure:

```
typedef struct {
        int type;
        unsigned long serial;    /* # of last request processed by server */
        Bool send_event;         /* true if this came from SendEvent request*/
        Display *display;        /* display the event was read from */
        Window window;
        int state;               /* either Obscured or UnObscured */
} XVisibilityEvent;
```

THE GRAPHICS CONTEXT

This appendix includes additional information about the Graphics Context, or GC. The GC contains a host of information about how to draw lines and shapes. Most of this information can be changed by filling in an XGCValues structure and passing that structure to an XChangeGC function call.

The `XGCValues` structure looks like the following:

```
/*
**      From Xlib.h, the data structure used for setting the
**      graphics context.
*/

typedef struct {
        int function;                   /* logical operation */
        unsigned long plane_mask;       /* plane mask */
        unsigned long foreground;       /* foreground pixel */
        unsigned long background;       /* background pixel */
        int line_width;                 /* line width */
        int line_style;                 /* LineSolid, LineOnOffDash, LineDoubleDash */
        int cap_style;                  /* CapNotLast, CapButt,
                                           CapRound, CapProjecting */
        int join_style;                 /* JoinMiter, JoinRound, JoinBevel */
        int fill_style;                 /* FillSolid, FillTiled,
                                        FillStippled, FillOpaeueStippled */
        int fill_rule;                  /* EvenOddRule, WindingRule */
        int arc_mode;                   /* ArcChord, ArcPieSlice */
        Pixmap tile;                    /* tile pixmap for tiling operations */
        Pixmap stipple;                 /* stipple 1 plane pixmap for stipping */
        int ts_x_origin;                /* offset for tile or stipple operations */
        int ts_y_origin;
        Font font;                      /* default text font for text operations */
        int subwindow_mode;             /* ClipByChildren, IncludeInferiors */
        Bool graphics_exposures;        /* boolean, should exposures be generated */
        int clip_x_origin;              /* origin for clipping */
        int clip_y_origin;
        Pixmap clip_mask;               /* bitmap clipping; other calls for rects */
        int dash_offset;                /* patterned/dashed line information */
        char dashes;
} XGCValues;

/*
**      The actual graphics context is contained in a "shadow" variable,
**      so the XGCValues is not the only part of the GC.
**
*/
```

You can use `XChangeGC` to change any of these values stored with a `GC`. `XChangeGC` looks like the following:

```
Display         *theDisplay;
GC              theGC;
unsigned long   theMask;
XGCValues       theGCValues;

XChangeGC( theDisplay,
        theGC,
        theMask,
        &theGCValues );
```

Note that this is one of the X routines where the mask is passed outside of the structure, rather than as a field in the structure. The mask tells X which of the fields in the `XGCValues` structure are actually filled in.

The mask can be created by logically `or`-ing any of the following single field masks (defined in the file `X.h`):

```
GCFunction
GCPlaneMask
GCForeground
GCBackground
GCLineWidth
GCLineStyle
GCCapStyle
GCJoinStyle
GCFillStyle
GCFillRule
GCTile
GCStipple
GCTileStipXOrigin
GCTileStipYOrigin
GCFont
GCSubwindowMode
GCGraphicsExposures
GCClipXOrigin
GCClipYOrigin
```

```
GCClipMask
GCDashOffset
GCDashList
GCArcMode
```

When a GC is created, the default values include the following:

XGCValues Field	Value
arc_mode	ArcPieSlice
background	WhitePixel (1)
cap_style	CapButt
clip_mask	None
clip_x_origin	0
clip_y_origin	0
fill_style	FillSolid
fill_rule	EvenOddRule
foreground	BlackPixel (0)
function	GXcopy
graphics_exposures	True
join_style	JoinMiter
line_width	0 (which means use the hardware accelerators, if there are any)
line_style	LineSolid

XGCValues Field	Value
plane_mask	all planes (all 1s)
subwindow_mode	ClipyChildren

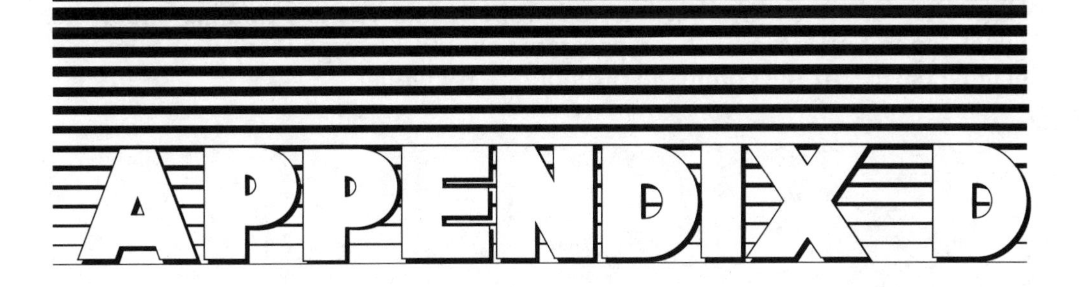

SOME SAMPLE X CLIENT PROGRAMS

The X11 R3 release from the MIT X Consortium comes with literally megabytes of X software. Much of the material was contributed by X users around the world. It's a good idea to take a look at some of these programs, especially if you have the source code. Looking at actual working examples of X code can help improve your code and show you how to avoid some of the traps and pitfalls inherent in X Window programming.

In addition to the contributed code, the base, or core, release of X contains a number of handy X utilities. A few of these X utility programs are introduced in this appendix. Feel free to experiment and play with these programs. The utilities mentioned here have proven to be very helpful to the authors, for programming X and performing tasks such as getting printouts of X window graphics. These are not the most glamorous X programs, but they are among the most useful.

Note: If your system has been set up properly and you are running under the UNIX operating system, these programs should be explained in the on-line manual pages. At the command prompt (`%`), try typing

```
% man bitmap
```

or

```
% man xwd
```

and see if the `man` "pages" are loaded on your system.

bitmap

The `bitmap` editor edits ASCII bitmap files, just as the Draw application introduced in Section II does. `bitmap` enlarges the pictures it edits so that you can better draw the small, detailed parts of small bitmap files.

Figure D.1 shows the enlarged picture of the bitmap picture in part of the `bitmap` editor window. The `bitmap` program is great for creating icons for your applications.

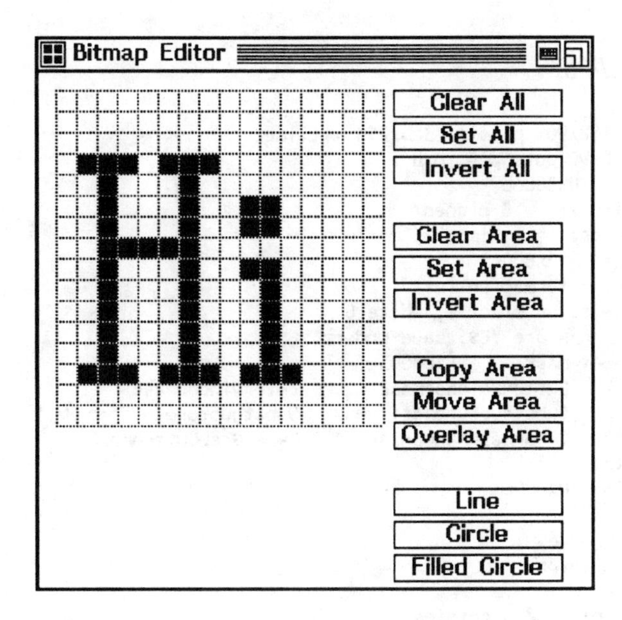

Figure D.1 Part of the bitmap editor.

xdpyinfo

`xdpyinfo` stands for "X Display Information." This program provides information about the display, screen, and X server you are using. `xdpyinfo` can give you information about whether the server supports color, what kind of byte ordering is in use (normally Intel or Motorola ordering, although usually called something else), and so on. Sample output of `xdpyinfo` follows (run on a Sun 386i under X11 R3). `xdpyinfo` displays its output to stdout (or an `xterm` window).

```
name of display:    unix:0.0
version number:    11.0
vendor string:    MIT X Consortium
vendor release number:    3
maximum request size:  16384 longwords (65536 bytes)
motion buffer size:  0
bitmap unit, bit order, padding:    32, LSBFirst, 32
image byte order:    LSBFirst
keycode range:    minimum 8, maximum 129
default screen number:    0
number of screens:    1
```

continued...

...from previous page

```
screen #0:
  dimensions:    1152x900 pixels (325x254 millimeters)
  resolution:    90x90 dots per inch
  root window id:    0x8006b
  depth of root window:    8 planes
  number of colormaps:    minimum 1, maximum 1
  default colormap:    0x80065
  default number of colormap cells:    256
  preallocated pixels:    black 1, white 0
  options:    backing-store YES, save-unders YES
  current input event mask:    0x1b8003c
    ButtonPressMask    ButtonReleaseMask        EnterWindowMask
    LeaveWindowMask    SubstructureNotifyMask   SubstructureRedirectMask
    FocusChangeMask    ColormapChangeMask       OwnerGrabButtonMask
  number of visuals:    1
  default visual id:  0x80064
  visual:
    visual id:    0x80064
    class:    PseudoColor
    depth:    8 planes
    size of colormap:    256 entries
    red, green, blue masks:    0x0, 0x0, 0x0
    significant bits in color specification:    8 bits
```

The following key information can be gleaned from the previous display:

- This server handles eight planes of color (or 256 separate colors).
- The visual class is `PseudoColor` (which is an honest description – just try to display the color called "pink," and you'll see what we mean).
- Backing store and save-unders are supported.
- The screen resolution is 1152-by-900 pixels.
- The server uses Intel byte ordering for image data.

xev

xev is a program that puts a window on the screen (see Figure D.1) and then prints out (to an xterm window, for example) information about each event the window receives from the X server. This program is useful for showing the way events are sent to an application. Try out the program and start typing keys (see if you can find the Help key, for example). xev is a real help when you first start working with events in X.

Figure D.2 The xev event window.

Following is some sample output of xev:

```
Outer window is 0x700001, inner window is 0x700002

PropertyNotify event, serial 4, synthetic NO, window 0x700001,
    atom 0x27 (WM_NAME), time 660526368, state PropertyNewValue

PropertyNotify event, serial 5, synthetic NO, window 0x700001,
    atom 0x22 (WM_COMMAND), time 660526368, state PropertyNewValue

PropertyNotify event, serial 6, synthetic NO, window 0x700001,
    atom 0x28 (WM_NORMAL_HINTS), time 660526368, state PropertyNewValue

CreateNotify event, serial 7, synthetic NO, window 0x700001,
    parent 0x700001, window 0x700002, (10,10), width 50, height 50
    border_width 4, override NO
```

continued...

...from previous page

```
MapNotify event, serial 8, synthetic NO, window 0x700001,
    event 0x700001, window 0x700002, override NO

ConfigureNotify event, serial 9, synthetic NO, window 0x700001,
    event 0x700001, window 0x700001, (102,102), width 178, height 178,
    border_width 0, above 0x300027, override NO

ReparentNotify event, serial 9, synthetic NO, window 0x700001,
    event 0x700001, window 0x700001, parent 0x300075,
    (0,19), override NO

MapNotify event, serial 9, synthetic NO, window 0x700001,
    event 0x700001, window 0x700001, override NO

VisibilityNotify event, serial 9, synthetic NO, window 0x700001,
    state VisibilityUnobscured

EnterNotify event, serial 9, synthetic NO, window 0x700001,
    root 0x8006b, subw 0x0, time 660526368, (0,60), root:(102,162),
    mode NotifyNormal, detail NotifyNonlinear, same_screen YES,
    focus NO, state 0

KeymapNotify event, serial 9, synthetic NO, window 0x0,
    keys:  0   0   0   0   0   0   0   0   0   0   0   0   0   0   0   0
           0   0   0   0   0   0   0   0   0   0   0   0   0   0   0   0

Expose event, serial 9, synthetic NO, window 0x700001,
    (0,0), width 178, height 10, count 3

Expose event, serial 9, synthetic NO, window 0x700001,
    (0,10), width 10, height 58, count 2

Expose event, serial 9, synthetic NO, window 0x700001,
    (68,10), width 110, height 58, count 1

Expose event, serial 9, synthetic NO, window 0x700001,
    (0,68), width 178, height 110, count 0

FocusIn event, serial 10, synthetic NO, window 0x700001,
    mode NotifyNormal, detail NotifyPointer

KeymapNotify event, serial 10, synthetic NO, window 0x0,
    keys:  0   0   0   0   0   0   0   0   0   0   0   0   0   0   0   0
           0   0   0   0   0   0   0   0   0   0   0   0   0   0   0   0

FocusOut event, serial 10, synthetic NO, window 0x700001,
    mode NotifyNormal, detail NotifyPointer

FocusIn event, serial 10, synthetic NO, window 0x700001,
    mode NotifyNormal, detail NotifyAncestor
```

continued...

...from previous page

```
KeymapNotify event, serial 10, synthetic NO, window 0x0,
    keys: 0  0  0  0  0  0  0  0  0  0  0  0  0  0  0  0
          0  0  0  0  0  0  0  0  0  0  0  0  0  0  0  0

MotionNotify event, serial 12, synthetic NO, window 0x700001,
    root 0x8006b, subw 0x0, time 660529456, (0,59), root:(102,161),
    state 0x0, is_hint 1, same_screen YES

LeaveNotify event, serial 12, synthetic NO, window 0x700001,
    root 0x8006b, subw 0x700002, time 660529632, (15,60), root:(117,162),
    mode NotifyNormal, detail NotifyInferior, same_screen YES,
    focus YES, state 0

EnterNotify event, serial 12, synthetic NO, window 0x700001,
    root 0x8006b, subw 0x0, time 660529712, (69,65), root:(171,167),
    mode NotifyNormal, detail NotifyInferior, same_screen YES,
    focus YES, state 0

KeymapNotify event, serial 12, synthetic NO, window 0x0,
    keys: 0  0  0  0  0  0  0  0  0  0  0  0  0  0  0  0
          0  0  0  0  0  0  0  0  0  0  0  0  0  0  0  0

ButtonPress event, serial 12, synthetic NO, window 0x700001,
    root 0x8006b, subw 0x0, time 660530112, (80,67), root:(182,169),
    state 0x0, button 1, same_screen YES

MotionNotify event, serial 12, synthetic NO, window 0x700001,
    root 0x8006b, subw 0x0, time 660530272, (80,67), root:(182,169),
    state 0x100, is_hint 1, same_screen YES

ButtonRelease event, serial 12, synthetic NO, window 0x700001,
    root 0x8006b, subw 0x0, time 660530272, (80,67), root:(182,169),
    state 0x100, button 1, same_screen YES

MotionNotify event, serial 12, synthetic NO, window 0x700001,
    root 0x8006b, subw 0x0, time 660530288, (80,69), root:(182,171),
    state 0x0, is_hint 1, same_screen YES

ButtonPress event, serial 12, synthetic NO, window 0x700001,
    root 0x8006b, subw 0x0, time 660530560, (71,123), root:(173,225),
    state 0x0, button 1, same_screen YES

MotionNotify event, serial 12, synthetic NO, window 0x700001,
    root 0x8006b, subw 0x0, time 660530704, (71,122), root:(173,224),
    state 0x100, is_hint 1, same_screen YES

ButtonRelease event, serial 12, synthetic NO, window 0x700001,
    root 0x8006b, subw 0x0, time 660530720, (69,121), root:(171,223),
    state 0x100, button 1, same_screen YES
```

continued...

...from previous page

```
MotionNotify event, serial 12, synthetic NO, window 0x700001,
    root 0x8006b, subw 0x0, time 660530736, (66,117), root:(168,219),
    state 0x0, is_hint 1, same_screen YES

LeaveNotify event, serial 12, synthetic NO, window 0x700001,
    root 0x8006b, subw 0x700002, time 660530816, (56,63), root:(158,165),
    mode NotifyNormal, detail NotifyInferior, same_screen YES,
    focus YES, state 0

ButtonPress event, serial 12, synthetic NO, window 0x700001,
    root 0x8006b, subw 0x700002, time 660531072, (48,48), root:(150,150),
    state 0x0, button 1, same_screen YES

EnterNotify event, serial 12, synthetic NO, window 0x700001,
    root 0x8006b, subw 0x700002, time 660531072, (48,48), root:(150,150),
    mode NotifyGrab, detail NotifyInferior, same_screen YES,
    focus YES, state 256

KeymapNotify event, serial 12, synthetic NO, window 0x0,
    keys:  0   0   0   0   0   0   0   0   0   0   0   0   0   0   0   0
           0   0   0   0   0   0   0   0   0   0   0   0   0   0   0   0

MotionNotify event, serial 12, synthetic NO, window 0x700001,
    root 0x8006b, subw 0x700002, time 660531216, (48,48), root:(150,150),
    state 0x100, is_hint 1, same_screen YES

ButtonRelease event, serial 12, synthetic NO, window 0x700001,
    root 0x8006b, subw 0x700002, time 660531216, (48,48), root:(150,150),
    state 0x100, button 1, same_screen YES

LeaveNotify event, serial 12, synthetic NO, window 0x700001,
    root 0x8006b, subw 0x700002, time 660531216, (48,48), root:(150,150),
    mode NotifyUngrab, detail NotifyInferior, same_screen YES,
    focus YES, state 0

MotionNotify event, serial 12, synthetic NO, window 0x700001,
    root 0x8006b, subw 0x700002, time 660531248, (48,49), root:(150,151),
    state 0x0, is_hint 1, same_screen YES

VisibilityNotify event, serial 12, synthetic NO, window 0x700001,
    state VisibilityPartiallyObscured

LeaveNotify event, serial 12, synthetic NO, window 0x700001,
    root 0x8006b, subw 0x0, time 660540240, (153,-20), root:(331,269),
    mode NotifyNormal, detail NotifyNonlinear, same_screen YES,
    focus YES, state 0

Expose event, serial 12, synthetic NO, window 0x700001,
    (0,0), width 154, height 10, count 3
```

continued...

...from previous page

```
Expose event, serial 12, synthetic NO, window 0x700001,
    (0,10), width 10, height 58, count 2

Expose event, serial 12, synthetic NO, window 0x700001,
    (68,10), width 86, height 58, count 1

Expose event, serial 12, synthetic NO, window 0x700001,
    (0,68), width 154, height 60, count 0

ConfigureNotify event, serial 12, synthetic NO, window 0x700001,
    event 0x700001, window 0x700001, (0,19), width 154, height 128,
    border_width 0, above 0x300076, override NO

VisibilityNotify event, serial 12, synthetic NO, window 0x700001,
    state VisibilityUnobscured

Expose event, serial 12, synthetic NO, window 0x700001,
    (0,0), width 154, height 10, count 3

Expose event, serial 12, synthetic NO, window 0x700001,
    (0,10), width 10, height 58, count 2

Expose event, serial 12, synthetic NO, window 0x700001,
    (68,10), width 86, height 58, count 1

Expose event, serial 12, synthetic NO, window 0x700001,
    (0,68), width 154, height 60, count 0

ButtonPress event, serial 14, synthetic NO, window 0x700001,
    root 0x8006b, subw 0x0, time 660557872, (91,50), root:(203,355),
    state 0x0, button 2, same_screen YES

ButtonRelease event, serial 14, synthetic NO, window 0x700001,
    root 0x8006b, subw 0x0, time 660558112, (91,50), root:(203,355),
    state 0x200, button 2, same_screen YES

ButtonPress event, serial 14, synthetic NO, window 0x700001,
    root 0x8006b, subw 0x0, time 660560528, (91,50), root:(203,355),
    state 0x0, button 3, same_screen YES

ButtonRelease event, serial 14, synthetic NO, window 0x700001,
    root 0x8006b, subw 0x0, time 660560784, (91,50), root:(203,355),
    state 0x400, button 3, same_screen YES

KeyPress event, serial 14, synthetic NO, window 0x700001,
    root 0x8006b, subw 0x0, time 660562144, (91,50), root:(203,355),
    state 0x200, keycode 63 (keysym 0xffe7, Meta_L), same_screen YES,
    XLookupString gives 0 characters:  ""
```

continued...

...from previous page

```
KeyRelease event, serial 14, synthetic NO, window 0x700001,
    root 0x8006b, subw 0x0, time 660562496, (91,50), root:(203,355),
    state 0x208, keycode 63 (keysym 0xffe7, Meta_L), same_screen YES,
    XLookupString gives 0 characters:  ""

ButtonRelease event, serial 14, synthetic NO, window 0x700001,
    root 0x8006b, subw 0x0, time 660562560, (91,50), root:(203,355),
    state 0x200, button 2, same_screen YES

KeyPress event, serial 14, synthetic NO, window 0x700001,
    root 0x8006b, subw 0x0, time 660567968, (90,49), root:(202,354),
    state 0x1, keycode 8 (keysym 0x41, A), same_screen YES,
    XLookupString gives 1 characters:  "A"

KeyRelease event, serial 14, synthetic NO, window 0x700001,
    root 0x8006b, subw 0x0, time 660568144, (90,49), root:(202,354),
    state 0x1, keycode 8 (keysym 0x41, A), same_screen YES,
    XLookupString gives 1 characters:  "A"

KeyRelease event, serial 14, synthetic NO, window 0x700001,
    root 0x8006b, subw 0x0, time 660568288, (90,49), root:(202,354),
    state 0x1, keycode 64 (keysym 0xffe1, Shift_L), same_screen YES,
    XLookupString gives 0 characters:  ""

KeyPress event, serial 14, synthetic NO, window 0x700001,
    root 0x8006b, subw 0x0, time 660571232, (90,49), root:(202,354),
    state 0x0, keycode 44 (keysym 0xff0d, Return), same_screen YES,
    XLookupString gives 1 characters:  ""

KeyRelease event, serial 14, synthetic NO, window 0x700001,
    root 0x8006b, subw 0x0, time 660571392, (90,49), root:(202,354),
    state 0x0, keycode 44 (keysym 0xff0d, Return), same_screen YES,
    XLookupString gives 1 characters:  ""
```

Note how the `Expose` events come in one at a time and how the count field counts down to zero. Even though this output is edited to reduce space, note also how `KeyPress` events are usually followed by `KeyRelease` events.

xfd

The output of the X Font Display program `xfd` appears in the "Creating Cursors for Windows" section in Chapter 8. `xfd` puts up a window and displays the characters in font, with each character in a box in the `xfd` window. It is normally useful for digging through the font files in your system, especially for deciding what font would look best for an application program to use. The X utility `xlsfonts` ("X List Fonts") will display a list of the font names available to your server.

xwd

`xwd` is the X Window Dumper. It "dumps" the pixels in a window to disk in a special, weird `XImage` format. `xwd` is next to useless by itself, but it comes with a few other programs that also understand the `xwd XImage` format. `xwud`, for example, will redraw the dumped window back onto the screen. This is not always particularly useful, but `xwud` can be used to verify the contents of the file.

`xpr`, though, is much better. `xpr` will print out an `xwd` format file (made by `xwd` dumping the contents of a window to disk). Unfortunately, though, `xpr` only supports a few printer types.

Printing out an image is not the only operation you want to perform with graphic files. In writing this book, for example, we wanted to create graphic files that could be imported into the electronic publishing package used by our publishers, MIS: Press, so we needed the files on disk. In addition, we wanted to be able to edit the screen graphics, such as adding the comments in the file dialog box in Chapter 12. All told, the process was rather painful, more so than it should be. And, because most X software developers will no doubt want to provide pictures of X windows for their documentation, a description of how we managed it might help.

First, we used `xwd` to dump the file to the `xwd` format (really the `XImage` format). Then, we used a software library called the portable bitmap library, or PBM, by Jef Poskanzer. (The version of PBM used came with X11 R3 from MIT.)

PBM comes with a set of programs to convert graphic image files to and from the PBM canonical format. This PBM format is an ASCII format for monochrome bitmap images (thus those with a color screen may have a bit of trouble). An ASCII-based format takes up a lot more disk space than conventional image formats, but ASCII has proved to be the only truly portable format for file exchange between diverse systems (for example, this book was written using UNIX workstations, Macintoshes, and IBM PCs, a diverse group of systems if there ever was one).

The program `xwdtopbm` converts an `xwd` file to a PBM file. Once in the PBM format, we could convert the file to a number of other image formats, including MacPaint files, Sun raster files, and much more. For the images that were OK as is, we converted the files to the MacPaint format (a common format supported by many publishing packages). For those images we wanted to edit, we transfered the PBM file over to an Apple Macintosh and used custom software on the Macintosh to convert the PBM file to a MacPaint file. Once the PBM file was in MacPaint format, we used the program MacPaint to add in text and touch up the images. MIS:Press could then incorporate these MacPaint files into Ventura Publisher.

All in all, this turned out to be a somewhat involved process, but one that worked. Many companies already have set up documentation publishing systems, so a key to presenting X images in that documentation system is the ability to convert `xwd` format files to your company format (or write your own software to capture the images and do the conversion).

xwininfo

`xwininfo` ("X Window Information") provides information about a given window. It is normally run from the command line in an `xterm` window (like `xdpyinfo`). `xwininfo` will change the mouse cursor to a crosshair and then ask you to click a mouse button in any window on the display. `xwininfo` then gives information about the window you selected. Following is the output of `xwininfo` (for an X11 R2 `xwininfo`, note that the R3 version provides more information). Because `xwininfo` provides the coordinate location and size for windows, the program is a handy tool to help you place windows, especially the windows you want to appear when you start up the X server.

```
xwininfo ==> Please select the window about which you
         ==> would like information by clicking the
         ==> mouse in that window.

xwininfo ==> Window id: 0x300041 (has no name)

         ==> Upper left X: 0
         ==> Upper left Y: 337
         ==> Width: 72
         ==> Height: 72
         ==> Depth: 1
         ==> Border width: 2
         ==> Window class: InputOutput
         ==> Window Map State: IsViewable
```

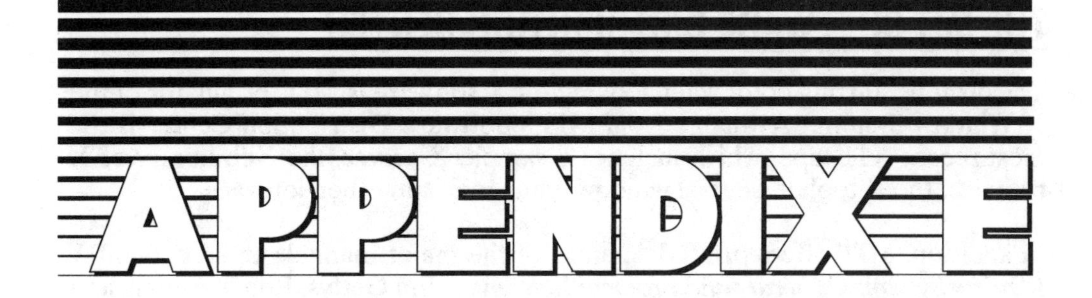

HOW TO ORDER X WINDOW

This appendix tells you how to order X Window from MIT and contains information about The X Consortium and the X User's Group (XUG). Addresses and phone numbers are included.

THE MIT SOFTWARE DISTRIBUTION CENTER

The obvious starting point when looking for X software is MIT, originator of the X Window System. Available from MIT's Software Distribution Center is the most recent X11 tape, which includes a sample X server, the Xlib library of X routines, the X toolkit, several window managers, and other software.

In addition, MIT offers printed versions of the major manuals and a copy of *X Window System: C Library and Protocol Reference* (Jim Gettys, Ron Newman, and Robert Scheifler) for $125. For ordering information, call the "X Ordering Hotline" at 617/258-8330 or the Software Center at 617/253-6966.

MIT Software Distribution Center
MIT E32-300
77 Massachussetts Ave.
Cambridge, MA 02139
617/253-6966

THE X CONSORTIUM

In January 1988, the X Consortium was formed by several large computer vendors and administered by the MIT Laboratory for Computer Science (LCS), with Robert Scheifler as the director of the Consortium. The member organizations do not determine the future of X or oversee its development; MIT is a neutral coordinator for development of standard programming interfaces for X. The member companies get advanced notice of these new X programming interfaces. In addition, the X Consortium regularly releases sample implementations of these interfaces, along with fixes and enhancements to X.

Current members are Apollo Computer, Apple Computer, AT&T, Bull, CalComp, Control Data Corporation, Data General Corporation, Digital Equipment Corporation, Eastman Kodak, Fujitsu, Hewlett-Packard, IBM, NEC, NCR, Prime Computer, Rich, Sequent Computer Systems, Siemens AG, Silicon Graphics, Sony, Sun Microsystems, Tektronix, Texas Instruments, Unisys, Wang Laboratories, and Xerox.

Current affiliates are ACER Counterpoint, Adobe Systems, Ardent Computer, Carnegie Mellon University, CETIA, Evans & Sutherland, GfxBase, INESC (Instituto de Engenharia de Sistemas e Computadores), Integrated Solutions, Interactive Development Environments, Interactive Systems, Integrated Computer Solutions, University of Kent at Canterbury, Locus Computing, Megatek, MIPS Computer Systems, Network Computing Devices, Nova Graphics International, Open Software Foundation, O'Reilly & Associates, PCS Computer Systeme GmbH, SGIP (Societe de Gestion et d'Informatique Publicis), Software Productivity Consortium, Solbourne Computer, Stellar Computer, UNICAD, and Visual Technology.

For more information, write the MIT X Consortium at 545 Technology Square, Room 217, Cambridge, MA 02139.

X USER'S GROUP (XUG)

In addition, there is an X User's Group. For more information, contact XUG via Internet at `xug@expo.lcs.mit.edu`, by calling 617/547-0634, or by writing XUG, c/o Integrated Computer Solutions, 163 Harvard St., Cambridge, MA 02139.

APPENDIX F

FOR MORE INFORMATION ON X WINDOW

This book is an introductory look at the X Window System for people unfamiliar with X, and as such more advanced and in-depth discussions of some of X's capabilities were avoided. After you read this book, the next step is to find a good reference work on X. Because of the relative newness of the X Window System, there aren't many other places to find more information about it. But among the resources that follow, there are a few gems worth picking up, depending on your needs.

Xlib Programming Manual, volume 1. Adrian Nye. O'Reilly and Associates, Inc., 1988.

Xlib Programming Manual, volume 2. O'Reilly and Associates, Inc., 1988.

X Window System User's Guide. Tim O'Reilly, Valerie Quercia, and Linda Lamb. O'Reilly and Associates, Inc., 1988.

These three volumes are based directly on the MIT documentation, and as a result some of the prose is lifted directly from the manuals. Volume 2, a reference for all X calls, is probably the best of the lot. In fact, after reading *X Window Application Programming*, you will most likely want an X reference manual to go with the tutorial here, and volume 2 of the O'Reilly series is a good choice.

X Window System: C Library and Protocol Reference. Jim Gettys, Ron Newman, and Robert Scheifler. DEC Press, 1988.

This book is the definitive reference work regarding the Xlib functions and protocol spec from some of the principal creators of X. This is essentially an enhanced version of the Xlib manual from release 3. You won't find any real introductory information here about X, and some of it is written over most users' heads, but it is useful for advanced X programmers.

Introduction to the X Window System. Oliver Jones. Prentice-Hall, 1989.

This is another introductory book to Xlib programming by a veteran X programmer. After an excellent introduction, Jones jumps in quickly with some complex programs and examples. Like any good X programming instructor, Jones includes a major "Hello World" program as his beginning application.

Suggested magazine articles include the following:

"Network Windowing Using the X Window System," Jim Gettys, *Dr. Dobb's Journal*, March 1989.

This article appeared as part of a series on network windowing.

"The X Window System," Dick Pountain, *Byte*, January 1989.

This introductory look at the X Window System contains some strong examples and some curious examples of applications, most notably from Great Britain.

"Moving X Window to Your Environment," Grant J. Munsey, *UNIX World*, May 1988.

"High-Performance 3-D Graphics in a Window Environment," David R. Nadeau, *Computer Technology Review*, Fall 1988.

This article describes how Megatek (an X Consortium member) integrated its hardware/software systems with X.

"Going for Baroque," David Rosenthal, *UNIX Review*, vol. 6, no. 6.

This includes a version of the "Hello, World" tutorial included in the X Window System documentation.

Also, interested researchers may want to check out proceedings from the last three years of Usenix conferences; these contain several pieces on different aspects of the X Window System.

In addition, your X System installation comes with some select articles; look in the `doc` directory for them. Finally, for further programming tips, check out the `clients` directory and look at sample programs such as `xtm` and `xclock`. Examining other peoples' code will help you out.

INDEX

A

B

C

D

E

F

G

H

I

J

K

L

M

N

O

P

Q

R

S

T

U

V

W

X

Y

Z

ORDER FORM

PROGRAM LISTINGS ON DISKETTE

This diskette contains the complete program listings for all programs and applications contained in this book. By using this diskette, you will eliminate time spent typing in pages of program code.

If you did not buy this book with diskette, use this form to order now:

Only: $29.95

MANAGEMENT INFORMATION SOURCE, INC.
P.O. Box 5277 • Portland, OR 97208-5277
(503) 282-5215

____
NAME(Please print or type)

____
Address

____
CITY STATE ZIP

Call free
1-800-MANUALS

❑ *X Window Applications Programming disk only* ***$29.95***
Please add $2.00 for shipping and handling. (Foreign $6.00)

Check one:

❑ *VISA* ❑ *MasterCard* ❑ *American Express*

❑ *Check enclosed $*__________

____
ACCT.

____
EXP. DATE

____
SIGNATURE

MANAGEMENT INFORMATION SOURCE, INC.